Making Choices, Making Do

Making Choices, Making Do

• •

Survival Strategies of Black and White
Working-Class Women during
the Great Depression

LOIS RITA HELMBOLD

Rutgers University Press
New Brunswick, Camden, and Newark, New Jersey, and London

Library of Congress Cataloging-in-Publication Data

Names: Helmbold, Lois Rita, author.
Title: Making choices, making do : survival strategies of Black and White
    working-class women during the Great Depression / Lois Rita Helmbold.
Description: New Brunswick, New Jersey : Rutgers University Press, [2023] |
    Includes bibliographical references and index.
Identifiers: LCCN 2022007962 | ISBN 9781978826434 (paperback : alk. paper) |
    ISBN 9781978826441 (hardcover ; alk. paper) | ISBN 9781978826458 (epub) |
    ISBN 9781978826472 (pdf)
Subjects: LCSH: Working class women—United States—History—20th century.|
    Discrimination in employment—United States—History—20th century. |
    African American women—Employment—History—20th century. | Women
    immigrants—Employment—United States—History—20th century. | Women,
    White—Employment—United States—History—20th century. | United States—
    Economic conditions—1918-1945.
Classification: LCC HD6095 .H45 2023 | DDC 305.48/230973—dc23/eng/20220224
LC record available at https://lccn.loc.gov/2022007962

A British Cataloging-in-Publication record for this book is available from the British Library.

References to internet websites (URLs) were accurate at the time of writing. Neither the author
nor Rutgers University Press is responsible for URLs that may have expired or changed since
the manuscript was prepared.

⊗ The paper used in this publication meets the requirements of the American National
Standard for Information Sciences—Permanence of Paper for Printed Library Materials,
ANSI Z39.48-1992.

www.rutgersuniversitypress.org

Manufactured in the United States of America

Dedicated to Helen Kuznaik Helmbold, Veronica Christian Kuznaik, Emma Hildebrand Helmbold, and all working-class women of the Great Depression.

Contents

Preface

My History and Positionality

Devoting decades to the lives of working-class women during the Great Depression, reading, writing, reflecting, walking their streets, shivering in bitter cold, wilting in humid heat, and calculating statistics, I have endeavored to bring alive their daily experiences. Scholarly practices of situating ourselves in our intellectual labor are erratic but essential. As a white woman with the chutzpah to write about Black women, I believe the particulars matter.

I learned racism through unique and commonplace experiences. As a child, I played with a Black doll, a gift from white missionaries, whose slideshows of African converts circulated through the five country churches my Pennsylvania Dutch father pastored simultaneously. After my family settled in a working-class neighborhood in West Philadelphia, when a Black family bought a row house two blocks away, I witnessed the remnants of a burnt cross while walking to school. In a subsequent migration to Virginia, taken-for-granted legal segregation and the openness with which white people disparaged "Negroes" exposed me to a reality I knew only from TV news. The photograph of Roxanne Hazzard in my wallet, a "colored" girl who sat next to me or in front of me in eighth, ninth, and tenth grades (Hazzard, Helmbold: it was alphabetical), caused consternation for southern white teenagers. Attending a white southern women's college and working as a waitress in the Midwest, North, and South added to my knowledge of everyday racism.

Teaching at an obscure historically Black college in rural Mississippi in the late 1960s changed my life. A single student had attended an integrated school, during her senior year in high school, more than a dozen years after the U.S. Supreme Court's *Brown v. Board of Education* decision. My students compelled me to make struggle against white supremacy a lifetime commitment. As a teacher and scholar, I taught and studied subjects I wanted to understand that had never been taught to me. Neither gender nor race was addressed in my undergraduate education or first graduate school, although I read Karl Marx and Max Weber. I introduced the course Women, Race, and Class in the early 1970s, grappling with the connections.

Almost my entire academic career happened in public universities in California and Nevada, where students of a panoply of races and ethnicities educated me. African American, Asian American, and Chicanx friends, colleagues, and comrades have challenged me and shared their insights. Unlike many white women intellectuals and activists of my generation, I have been confronted and privileged by being a lone or rare white woman in multiple settings.

Abbreviations Used in Text and Notes

AC	Associated Charities
BC	Bureau of Census, Department of Commerce
BLS	Bureau of Labor Statistics, Department of Labor; *BLSB, Bulletin*
BPW	Bureau of Public Welfare, Chicago
CB	Children's Bureau, Department of Labor; *CBP Publication*
CRA	Chicago Relief Authority
FDR	Franklin Delano Roosevelt
FHLBB	Federal Home Loan Bank Board
FWP	Federal Writers Project, Works Progress Administration
HM	The History Museum (formerly Northern Indiana Historical Society), South Bend
HOLC	Home Owners Loan Corporation
IUSB	Indiana University, South Bend
MLR	*Monthly Labor Review*, Bureau of Labor Statistics, Department of Labor
NACP	National Archives College Park; RG, Record Group
	RG 9, Records of National Recovery Administration
	RG 69, Records of Works Progress Administration
	RG 86, Records of Women's Bureau, Department of Labor
	RG 195, Records of Home Owners Loan Corporation

NIHS	Northern Indiana Historical Society (renamed The History Museum), South Bend
NIRA	National Industrial Recovery Act
NRA	National Recovery Administration
NWA	Negro Welfare Association, Cleveland
PWA	Phillis Wheatley Association, Cleveland
SB	South Bend
SJCPL/LFHS	St. Joseph County Public Library/Local Family & History Services, South Bend
SBW	Service Bureau for Women, Chicago
SBNT	South Bend *News Times*
SBT	South Bend *Tribune*
SNM	Studebaker National Museum, South Bend
WB	Women's Bureau, Department of Labor; *WBB*, *Bulletin*
WPA	Works Progress Administration
WRHS	Western Reserve Historical Society, Cleveland

Making Choices, Making Do

Introduction

• •

Consider how the Great Depression challenged three working-class households living on one block in South Bend, Indiana, in 1932. Leona C, age fifty, Black, single, the designated daughter who remained at home with her elderly parents, supported them as a chambermaid at the Oliver Hotel. She held on to her job, though the hotel cut her wages from $12 to as low as $4 weekly. No South Bend factories employed African American women, but a commercial service job enabled Leona to avoid domestic work. Unlike most Black families, the Cs owned their home, the only dwelling in my sample of 183 South Bend households that lacked electricity.[1]

Across the street, a Hungarian immigrant, Agnes V, forty, could not keep up with the mortgage or gas payments after her husband died in January 1930. Following an argument, a new woman supervisor fired her from Singer, the largest sewing machine cabinet factory in the nation, a major employer of local Hungarians. Agnes searched for work, unsuccessfully, as a cleaner and maid at the University of Notre Dame; she found only occasional day work and home laundry work. She applied for and received the meager relief distributed by local government: grocery orders and coal. In summer 1932, when she received an eviction notice, Agnes and her four school-age children were "eat[ing] plenty of bread to keep from eating other foods."[2]

In the comparatively comfortable A household, five of eight adults remained at least partially employed. Like other daughters of eastern European immigrants, the young women worked assembly jobs at Ball Band Shoes, Studebaker, Wilson Brothers shirts, and smaller factories. One found upward mobility as a dentist's assistant. These young Hungarian Americans—four sisters, two brothers, two husbands, and a baby—cut expenses and altered their habits, even though collectively they earned $232 in four weeks in 1932.[3]

1

The detailed interviews these women gave to agents of the Women's Bureau (WB) of the U.S. Department of Labor are a rich source for employment histories, financial struggles, and household roles. Their microcosm reveals the themes of this book: intersections of class, race, immigration, and gender shaped how the Depression undermined people and how they fashioned strategies for survival. I explore a brief period (ca. 1925–1940) to analyze structure, agency, and white supremacy during an economic crisis. Investigating jobs, reproductive labor, and the work of acquiring relief, I demonstrate that working-class women practiced similar survival strategies but reaped dissimilar results. Structural racism guaranteed that Black women could not be equally successful in efforts to stave off destitution; comparative advantages of whiteness endured. At the same time, white women increasingly adopted survival strategies more frequently practiced by Black women.

A decade of depression upended the presumed prosperity of the 1920s, during which the urban, industrialized North had led the country economically. With a quarter of the labor force unemployed and countless more underemployed, the nation shuddered through harsh times that only ended because of involvement in World War II. The Great Migration of southern African Americans northward, the enduring horrors of the Great War, the antiradical campaigns of the Federal Bureau of Investigation, widespread race riots and the rise of the Ku Klux Klan, and the door slamming shut on almost all immigration from Asia and Europe constitute the background.

Class in the United States: An Analytical Challenge

In the United States the concept of class lacks satisfactory definition. The vast majority of people must sell their labor to those who own the means of production, in return for wages. This classic definition of the working class ignores the history of slavery and the unwaged labor of women that produces, reproduces, and maintains the labor force. Sociologists often define class as socioeconomic status, use the terms *social class* and *economic class* interchangeably, and replace the term *working-class* with *low-income*. Ranking intangibles such as status obscures capitalist exploitation, hierarchical relations among people, and material hardships and privileges. Use of class as a status descriptor obscures it as a potential activator of alliances and coalitions. Class hierarchies are exploitative and oppressive. "Class consciousness is knowing which side of the fence you're on. Class analysis is figuring out who's there with you."[4] I highlight three sets of class relationships: between employers and employees, between social workers / bureaucrats and clients, and between researchers and "subjects." I also consider possibilities for class collaboration across racial barriers.

To identify the 1930s working class I utilized occupation as a tool: so-called unskilled and semiskilled workers employed in mass production and auxiliary occupations. Kitchen personnel, truck drivers, laborers, dime store clerks, receptionists, dayworkers, and watchmen supported the industrial economy. Working-class communities also included housewives, elders no longer in the labor force, and young people who had not begun paid jobs. Class analysis has typically ignored gender and failed to account for women's unwaged reproductive labor. In the U.S., studying class cannot be separated from investigating white supremacy. Institutionalized racism determined people's location in the labor force: job availability, working conditions, and wages. It also regulated where they resided.

Rather than focus on a particular racial, ethnic, marital, or age group, which is a common practice of social historians, I explore and compare the range of urban northern working-class women within a calamitous time frame. I analyze the agency of African Americans, mostly recent migrants from the South; immigrants from eastern and southern Europe; and U.S.-born white women, living in the urban Midwest and North, competing with one another for resources.

Sources and Methodological Contributions

My intention to bring working-class voices to the foreground motivated my excavation and selection of sources. Unwilling to accept the standard advice I was given when I began—that sources from working-class women did not exist—I unearthed unknown interviews conducted by the WB, which documented employment histories and Depression experiences. I sampled thousands of records from Chicago, Cleveland, Philadelphia, and South Bend for clerical, commercial service, and domestic workers. These unambiguously female occupations, the best and worst working-class jobs, exemplified racial coding. I included the entire household of any woman who met the criteria, so industrial and sales workers appeared in my samples of 1,340 women (see appendix A).[5] Observing that women moved from job to job, I realized a singular occupational depiction could be simplistic, and I concluded that it was essential to analyze female working-class jobs in all four sectors.

I also scrutinized approximately eight hundred letters by domestic workers, protesting their exclusion from minimum wage and maximum hour provisions of the National Industrial Recovery Act (NIRA) of 1933. Like virtually all labor legislation, NIRA exempted agricultural and domestic workers, disproportionately denying protection to African Americans.[6] Tens of thousands of household workers composed accounts of hours, wages, tasks, and working conditions as evidence of their need for legislative safeguards. They addressed letters to President Franklin Delano Roosevelt; his secretary of labor, Frances Perkins; "our dear Mother of this country," Eleanor Roosevelt;[7] New Deal officials; and nameless bureaucrats. As unmediated sources for intellectual, political, and emotional responses to the Depression, these letters also require contextualization.

Letter writers initiated the communication, which required English literacy and a two-cent postage stamp. Some had minimal formal education and wrote with dull pencils on lined grammar school foolscap. A few declassed women penned letters on engraved stationary. White women authored most of these epistles; Asian, Black, European immigrant, and Mexican writers sometimes identified their race and ethnicity. I found comparatively few Black-authored letters, mostly from live-in workers. Black women had substantially transitioned domestic jobs to day work by 1929.[8] The National Recovery Administration (NRA) and the WB randomly preserved thousands of letters, filled with common assessments regardless of authors' races, ethnicities, or locations.

Beginning with a comparative framework and unearthing exceptional sources, I have asked questions and drawn conclusions that would otherwise have been impossible. Employment histories illuminate women's decision-making and efforts to balance workplace and home responsibilities, yield significant new insights into millions of lives, and clarify differences between men's and women's experiences. Many white and some Black working-class men labored at a single occupation, even at a single factory, throughout their adult lives.[9] Urban women, both Black and white, entered, left, and reentered the labor force and moved from job to job, occupation to occupation.

The interviewees represent the urban U.S. with the partial exception of western cities and notable omission of southern cities. Two-thirds of principal cities (those with populations of one hundred thousand or more) were located in the Midwest and Northeast in 1930. Western cities had significant immigrant populations, but few had substantial Black communities. Conversely, few immigrants made their homes in southern cities, which were characterized by large African American populations and centuries-long legal patterns of white supremacy.[10] Tiny numbers of Chinese men resided in the four cities I studied. Other women of color shared many employment and housing experiences with Black women, but rarely lived in the urban Midwest and North. Their stories appear peripherally.[11]

Inspired by Black feminist analysis and Marxist feminist challenges to scholarship, I began this project when a single volume of Black women's history, Gerda Lerner's *Black Women in America*, existed.[12] The advantage of wrestling with thorny questions for decades is that other people grapple with related inquiries. Critical race theory, histories of whiteness, and intersectional analysis have left footprints on these pages.[13] I have analyzed mutually constituted aspects of gender, race, and class in actual lives and also compared women across nativity, age, and marital and familial circumstances. American failure to recognize the existence of class and its absence as a legal category means that it is often minimized or missing from important analyses.[14] I attempt to remedy this obstruction.

Putting Sources in Context: Interviewers

Interview records require interpretation. The political goals and research methodologies of the WB, the circumstances of the interviews, and the unacknowledged oceans of race and class distances and assumptions in which social scientists and working-class fish swam: all of these shaped responses. The subjects of this book speak through other women, so the resulting story is more complex than a naive notion of "allowing" them to speak for themselves. The WB determined the questions, and its agents mediated the words of working-class women.

The Bureau reflected Washington, D.C.'s legally mandated segregation and its social scientists' backgrounds in Progressive and suffrage campaigns. Passing labor legislation and educating the public about the necessity that drove married women into paid employment constituted its major goals in the 1930s.[15] Exclusively white, mostly single, mature "Protestant women of privilege," college-educated "statisticians, writers, publicists, economists, union advisors, former teachers, and social workers" designed, implemented, and published research.[16] These archetypal reformers and career women traveled alone or together, lived months in hotels in unfamiliar cities, and led intellectually, politically meaningful, independent lives, frequently obstructed by sexism.[17]

Planning to investigate unemployed "unattached" women (1932), the WB consulted multiple organizations and individuals but did not solicit ideas from African American scholars, social service agencies, or civil rights organizations, even though unemployed women were disproportionately Black.[18] White social investigators' failure to engage with Black peers shaped assumptions behind questions and consequently answers. They did not address residential segregation.

Social work and social investigation had professionalized by developing standardized observation and objective written records, hallmarks of their supposedly scientific basis. Historian Karen Tice characterized case records as "tales of detection" that "buil[t] cases against menacing clients" and "tales of protection" about "promising and worthy clients." Both narratives appear in interview records. Researchers routinely made "normatively determined judgments" about "personality, housekeeping, employability, character, sexual behavior, dress, cuisine, parenting, and leisure."[19] Agents' commitment to working-class women, their class and race distance from that of their subjects, the location and duration of conversations, and research agendas shaped interactions and the quality of data.

Investigators recorded abundant information when they conducted lengthy home interviews in South Bend (1930 and 1932) and Chicago (1937). Imagine the professionally attired woman, writing copious notes on a preprinted form, sitting across the kitchen table from a woman in a faded housedress. South Bend women furnished minute specifics about jobs, hours, and wages, sometimes referring to small notebooks in which they kept accounts. Loquacious when discussing employment, many answered familial financial questions with vague generalities or suddenly became "too busy." Instructions reveal little understanding that working-class women might not want to expose intimate financial details to an upper-middle-class white stranger. The unexpected intrusion discomfited some women, but neither coercion nor reward molded conversations.

In 1937, when an investigator knocked on a Chicago door, most frequently the woman on the other side lived in a single room. The agent possessed considerable data, enabling her to form impressions in advance. Chicago Relief Administration staff copied detailed case records onto questionnaires: occupational and relief histories, health problems, reports from other agencies, involvement in the legal system, and even busybody landladies' tales of tenants' behavior.[20] Interviewers were expected to check veracity, observe living conditions, and assess each client's employability. Handwritten notations on an interview schedule warned agents to "watch carefully" explanations for "seeking relief, health, and support prior to relief."[21] Thoroughly scrutinized and surveilled, women might reasonably doubt that information they volunteered would help them.

Records of brief public interviews in noisy, crowded offices (1932–1933) contain less depth. When women sought jobs at the YWCA in Cleveland, caseworkers ascertained employability. When they applied to Chicago and Philadelphia agencies, workers determined eligibility for make-work, a grocery order, or coal.[22] With a survival stake in conversations, clients stressed that they were looking for work and emphasized their skills, upstanding character, and worthiness. Margaret M, a white widow, fifty-four, an unemployed practical nurse, "wanted to show agent references which employers had given her."[23] Madeline M, a rare Black clerical worker, made her intentions clear. "I'm applying for work, not relief. . . . Now I haven't had anything to eat, but I won't take any help unless they'll let me work for it."[24]

Caseworkers and researchers appraised applicants as being of a "good type" or "very ambitious and wants to be self-supporting"; others were "very vague," "rambling," "evasive"; some were of "poor type" or "odd type" or had a "manner of living questionable on moral basis." In Chicago and Philadelphia hungry, cold, forlorn, "despondent," "discouraged," "highly nervous" women, shamed by their inability to support themselves and by seeking help, and bewildered by the process, "wept throughout interview."

The WB considered interviewees as individuals whose sole frameworks were workplace and family. Historian Ula Taylor's advice, to listen for what is not there, applies.[25] Data are mostly silent on women's embeddedness (or not) in community webs of church or synagogue, neighborhood, and social or ethnic organizations.[26] The category of family did not include relatives left behind in Europe or the South. Schedules omitted European ethnicity, reflecting an ideal of assimilation: ignoring it in the belief that it would disappear into nonethnic white Americanism.[27] Surveys from the fall of 1932 through the spring of 1933 do not mention interviewees' observations on the election or new administration. Despite upheavals in European homelands, records are bereft of comments on encroaching fascism. Evaluations of Black women are fraught with racist assessments. Conversations between unequals, in which researchers determined relevant questions and interviewees self-protectively omitted information, created the written record (see appendix B).

Putting Sources in Context: Working-Class Interviewees, Speaking and Keeping Silent

Not merely passive specimens under a microscope, working-class women also shaped interviews. Faced with the authority of the state in the form of another woman who might appear sympathetic or skeptical, they attempted to maintain their dignity, responded to some queries in detail, averred that they did not know other answers, misunderstood, and became vague and forgetful. Many could not recall particulars that social scientists wanted to know. They mistrusted the government, valued their privacy, were ashamed of being on relief, and/or feared negative repercussions. Some attempted to enlist interviewers in their struggle to find work, acquire assistance, or obtain a higher relief allotment. Occasionally interviewees lectured researchers on topics about which agents were ignorant.

Familial financial inquiries often embarrassed or angered women. In South Bend questions about debt, mortgages, and savings concluded a protracted interview (1932). Women cut off conversation, claimed they were too busy, or responded with generalities: "Land yes, we got to save." Relief applicants and recipients, required to make full disclosures, were "indignant at having to answer so many questions,"[28] "irritated when questioned for dates, wages, etc.,"[29] or "showed no interest in what investigator was doing."[30] Catherine K, sixty and "very nervous at first," said "she had been even more so when at District Office and had not been able to 'remember or think straight' and was fearful lest she be considered untruthful if information did not tally. Memory not very good for dates." This German immigrant widow "regained self-control as the interview developed. Talks intelligently but lack of education apparent. Attitude respectful and polite.... Brought whatever papers she had in order to try to give accurate information."[31] Catherine's deference persuaded the interviewer of her honesty.

Black women concealed aspects of their histories, thoughts, and emotions; they performed subservience, objected to the process or to specific questions, and related elaborate stories. "Acting humble," a calculated tool of survival, had been honed by African Americans for generations. Mary B, thirty, toiled on Virginia farms, as a maid, as a cook in restaurants and private homes, and as a mangle operator in Chicago, Pittsburgh, and Washington, DC. "Quite illiterate," Mary "could not give definite information concerning employment record or even sufficient information as to justify an approximation. [She] says she 'has worked all her life.'"[32]

Racist assumptions by white researchers and Black women's acts of self-preservation ensured that fewer details of Black women's emotional landscapes became visible. Black women refused or failed to answer queries on a broad range of subjects. Elizabeth M, forty-two, a widow, was a skilled seamstress and needle worker with two years training in domestic art at Shorter College in Little Rock, Arkansas, but was unsuccessful in securing work on a Works

Progress Administration (WPA) sewing project. "Sick and tired of begging," she asserted that she only wanted assistance in getting work. The agent characterized her as "very uncommunicative about employment." Elizabeth spoke emphatically. "Caseworkers ask a lot of questions and do nothing for you afterwards."[33]

Relief applicants and recipients risked disqualification by failing to reply fully. Day workers often could not recall wages, dates, names, or addresses of housewife employers. Josephine W, thirty, Black, a chambermaid, was "very afraid of giving [an] answer that might tie her down to anything definite." "I can't always remember," she said, "and if I tell you something, they might find it not just correct and think I lied."[34] She assessed the situation accurately. Similarly to Black women's partial cooperation, some immigrants claimed lack of English facility prevented them from explaining finances after they responded to other inquiries in detail. Sometimes a "little daughter translated." Working-class immigrants rarely allowed children knowledge of family finances, the subjects most frequently left incomplete in South Bend. A Polish family twice branded "shiftless and slovenly" was "reluctant to discuss" finances; likely both interviewers conveyed their judgments, intentionally or unintentionally.[35]

All interviewees had something to lose; they might feel humiliated by a class superior. South Bend women could gain only abstract satisfaction aiding the federal government, distant and unresponsive in the years of the Hoover administration. Work and relief applicants and recipients hoped cooperation would lead to a job, "made work," food, a larger relief budget, or placement on a WPA sewing project. They feared penalties if information was "not quite right" or if they antagonized an interviewer: denial of relief or jobs, reduction of relief, or removal from the rolls. Obtaining and keeping benefits required a sophisticated balancing act.

Interviewees defended themselves with silence and omissions. Relief clients likely concealed sporadic under-the-table work and relatives' or sweethearts' occasional gifts. I found little indication of outright deception, and surprising candor about subjects that interviewers regarded with a jaundiced eye. Autobiographical, fictional, and journalistic accounts confirm reticence and lacunae. In Louise Meriwether's novel *Daddy was a Number Runner*, conversations in a Harlem apartment illustrate attitudes not publicly revealed. The family christened the relief worker "Madame Queen," a reference from the *Amos 'n' Andy* radio show; they nicknamed distasteful free canned meat "Gold Can jive" and broke relief rules by working.[36] Meridel LeSueur's reportage about the Twin Cities—Minneapolis and St. Paul—illuminates destitute white women's efforts to remain invisible.[37]

Language also merits attention. Some agents used quotation marks to convey what interviewees said; others summarized. Colloquialisms, slang, and grammar that characterized domestic workers' letters, WPA interviews in Harlem, and Federal Writers' Project (1936–39) interviews with formerly enslaved elders sometimes appear, but often are absent, as is the broken English of some immigrants.[38] I found no internal WB documents addressing language. Household workers described themselves as "servants," "maids," "employees," working for "private families," or mentioned "the woman I work for." Social scientists and journalists of the 1930s and scholars refer to "mistresses," but domestic workers did not dignify employers with servile language. I have named them "housewife employers."

An Overview of the Book

Chapter 1 situates working-class people in the supposedly prosperous 1920s by analyzing the economics of daily life, the income necessary to survive, and material possibilities to thrive in the context of residential segregation. I delve into South Bend and summarize characteristics of the metropolises. I situate working-class women and men in the labor force, segmented by gender, race, age, and women's marital status.

Chapter 2 utilizes case studies to illustrate job deterioration and unemployment. Industrial collapse swiftly pervaded South Bend. In metropolises, varied levels of unemployment were tied to identities of workers. The disappearance of the least desirable job (domestic work) illuminated the paucity of prospects for Black women. Other forms of discrimination and jobs that were somewhat Depression-proof further clarify liabilities and possibilities in employment. Relative advantages and disadvantages persisted in 1940; the proportion of unemployed African Americans remained far larger than for white people.

Chapter 3 analyzes strategies for finding work: patronizing employment agencies, selling labor in slave markets, peddling door-to-door, geographic mobility, and working in the underground economy. Downward occupational mobility, the most prevalent tactic, advantaged white women and displaced Black women.

I turn to households and families' management of material and financial resources in chapter 4. Women resumed subsistence production to conserve scarce funds for expenses that required cash: rent and mortgages. Running hot water, electricity, and indoor toilets were standard for most urban white women but for fewer Black women, requiring them to undertake far more physical labor. Mothers typically had the lowest standard of living in their households.

Practical decisions reaped emotional consequences. Families nurtured cooperation and conflict tore them apart—the subject of chapter 5. Patriarchal and parental demands challenged wives' and daughters' expectations and dissolved familial and marital bonds. Doubling up was the most common form of cooperation. The number of "unattached" women outside family economies increased; they relied on friendship, not kinship, as is illustrated in chapter 6.

Applying for and acquiring relief, a third set of strategies gendered female, was a gamble. Chapter 7 analyzes means, motherhood, and racial tests of the relief apparatus. As funding changed from private to public, assumptions persisted that work for men would resolve all needs of families and women. Despite society's disdain, women applied for relief in large numbers.

I conclude by examining working-class women's class and race consciousness. How did they make sense of the Depression? Previously unrecognized activism by Black and white women in South Bend illustrates working-class women's leadership in social justice campaigns. Domestic workers' letters exemplify class anger, white supremacy, xenophobia, and anti-Semitism.

In sum, I argue that urban northern working-class women utilized the same survival strategies, but their results differed as a consequence of structural racism. Black working-class men and women suffered the deepest unemployment, immediately and throughout the decade. As a group, white working-class women experienced less harsh consequences. White women sympathized with the losses of the men in their lives; Black women commiserated with and shared the experiences of Black men.

White women's actions became more similar to those of Black women in housework, employment, school attendance, and reliance on friends, not only kin. These commonalities reflect elasticity in gender norms for women. Only when husbands disapproved of wives' paid employment was gender appropriateness a consideration. Downward occupational mobility, taking less desirable jobs (a universal female strategy to remain employed) pushed older Black women out of the labor force. Job segregation by race loosened for white women and hardened for Black women. Notably, employers, private social services, and government bureaucracies less frequently separated women by race than they did men. What are the implications of these previously unnoticed differences?

In each chapter, I evaluate how class, race, immigration, and gender, as well as age and familial and marital status, simultaneously affected women's actions, both individually and collectively. Analyzing women's testimonies reveals new information and clarifies old assumptions. Some questions went unasked and unanswered, especially about interactions with neighbors and communities. Other 1930s sources reflect reliance on communities and not only on kin.

Urban patterns of jobs and housing in the 1930s persisted until late in the twentieth century. My conclusion addresses how Depression lessons about white supremacy and working-class women's agency offer us tools and insights for radical solidarity and class-based organizing.

1

Urban Working-Class
Daily Lives and Work
in the 1920s

● ●

This chapter contextualizes losses and strategies in the Great Depression by sketching the ways working-class people constructed their lives and participated in, or were excluded from, the so-called prosperity of the 1920s. Midwestern and Northern cities were highly industrialized and highly segregated. African Americans typically lived in older, decaying, inner-city neighborhoods, while white workers might live in central areas or outlying districts, in ethnic enclaves and in diverse neighborhoods. Jobs were segregated by gender and race. Most people worked five and a half days, relied on public transportation, worshipped with some regularity, and found sociability and relaxation in families, homes, ethnic communities, employer-sponsored activities, and commercial leisure. They read newspapers and enjoyed rapidly expanding radio programing. Working-class families spent their money on food, shelter, and clothing, in that order. They almost universally paid life insurance premiums but purchased few luxuries. White families who enjoyed comfort usually relied on multiple earners. Black families earned lower wages and paid more for housing. Examples of prosperous, typical, and struggling households illuminate conditions and the efforts required to maintain daily life.

The financial decisions of a young South Bend, Indiana, couple illustrate material prospects and priorities of steadily employed white working-class people. Bonita T had taken a business course and went to work at seventeen as a bank stenographer; in 1930 she earned $19. Her sweetheart, Richard C, made $28–34 a week on the Studebaker automobile assembly line, but it was a less steady job because the company annually laid off assembly workers to set up model changes. While they were still single, Bonita bought furniture and Richard a car—on credit. They married in 1930, set up housekeeping, and planned on an annual income of approximately $2,000 as long as Bonita remained employed.[1] Furniture, a car, their own home: the most affluent young, white working-class couples might expect these promises of plenty. Acquisition of consumer goods depended on the fact that Bonita had not yet traded wage earning for child-rearing and both partners resided with their respective parents. Some women planning weddings purchased a living room or bedroom suite. Regardless of marital status, men prized cars, as practical mobility which signified prosperity.

Black families who migrated north often lived in dismal circumstances. More than half of a hundred families who arrived in Philadelphia during the Great War, studied by economist Sadie Tanner Mossell, did not earn enough to purchase adequate food. They inhabited buildings in "exceedingly poor physical condition" in 1919. Mossell noted "plaster falling in nearly every room. . . . Toilet drainage out of repair. . . . Odor from toilet is vile. . . . So much smoke in the house that I thought it must be on fire." Thirty-seven families lived in two-story brick houses without gas or baths, with toilets in the yard. Fifty-five others rented, often a single room, in comparable buildings. Mossell calculated an adequate annual budget at $1,829.48, possible only with at least two wage earners. More than half the households had incomes lower than $1,670. Half the wives and mothers, and a small number of children, earned wages.[2] Mossell, the second African American woman in history to earn a PhD, conducted research a decade before the stock market crash. Black southerners' ongoing migration and continued relegation to high-priced, decaying, substandard housing and low-paying jobs ensured that little changed by 1929.

Low wages and undependable jobs made prosperity a hope, more than a reality, for white working-class households; for Black working-class families, it was a chimera. The wife of an unemployed white roofer succinctly explained, "When my husband's working steady I can just manage, but when he's out, things go back. First I stop on the damp wash, then on food, and then the rent goes behind."[3] When young adult children held jobs, and when growing numbers of wives—especially Black wives—contributed wages, families could more likely afford necessities and sometimes enjoyed comforts. Not every household included potential supplementary earners, and the employment of wives could be contentious. In households where fathers had died or departed, and in homes of women "adrift," standards of living were lower than in households with an employed man and/or several wage earners. Comfort or privation depended on race and household composition.

Wages were usually the only source of income in working-class households. In 1924 Leila Houghteling found that unskilled and semiskilled white men in Chicago earned median wages of $1,350 annually; Black men's wages were $200 less. Median household income, including the wages of wives and children and payments by boarders and renters, was about $1,400.[4] In Johnstown, Pennsylvania, a medium-size mining and steel city, east central European families considered $1,600 to $1,700 the threshold for a good life. Only one-third earned this much, and probably 40% survived on less than $1,000 annually (1925).[5] By working-class standards, auto workers earned high wages. The Ford Motor Company paid a much vaunted minimum wage of $7 a day to male production workers in 1929, who earned an average annual income of $1,711.87 ($33 weekly).[6] White male industrial workers might earn as much as $40 weekly; urban white women, Black men, and Black women typically earned $10-$20, assuming they had full-time work.

How spartan or comfortable a life women could create reflected racial differentials in housing costs and household size. The American standard of living, an economist calculated in 1927, necessitated $2,000 to $2,400 annually. A family earning $1,500 to $1,800 could afford "subsistence plus," which allowed "health and decency."[7] Annual incomes between $1,000 and $1,700 ($19 to $33 weekly) characterized most urban working-class households. Houghteling concluded that more than two-thirds of households she studied earned less than the yardstick for "dependent" families of the Council of Social Agencies.[8] Frank Stricker found a 1929 income of $1,550 ($29.81 weekly) equivalent to the 1980s poverty level for a family of four; he estimated that 35–40% of non-farm families were poor.[9] One thousand dollars annually bought mere subsistence and more than $1,700 represented high income. For a single white Chicago woman, $20 to $25 in weekly wages ($1,040 to $1,300 annually) was the minimum, depending on whether she lived in a subsidized boarding home or a commercial rooming house.[10]

Most working-class families rented, as did almost all "lone" women, but a substantial minority owned homes in cities where single-family dwellings characterized the housing stock.[11] For immigrants, particularly those from "traditional agricultural areas where status derived from landowning," the goal of homeownership motivated many decisions. Its benefits included status, control, savings, equity, and potential for additional income.[12] In the four cities of my study— Chicago, Cleveland, Philadelphia, and South Bend—European immigrants were most frequently owners. Only Flint, Michigan, and Reading, Pennsylvania, had higher proportions of homeowners than did South Bend in 1930, where three-fourths of immigrant families owned homes.[13] More typically, one-fourth of "ordinary laborers" and one-third of skilled workers owned homes in Johnstown, as did one-third of Detroit's Ford workers.[14] Impeded by residential segregation, restrictive covenants, and banks' unwillingness to consider them for mortgages, to say nothing of low incomes, few Black families owned homes in the urban North. Black homeownership in South Bend (29.0%) was half that of white homeownership (58.7%), but two to three times higher than that of the metropolises.[15]

Buoyed by relatively high wages in the automotive industry, South Bend's white working-class families bought "comfortable modern cottages," wooden-frame bungalows and two-story dwellings of four, five, or six rooms, surrounded by yards and gardens in West Side neighborhoods circling the major plants. South Bend was doubly exceptional for its high rate of homeownership and for construction of new homes owned by immigrants and their children. In 1930, homes were valued at $4,500 to $7,000; mortgages averaged five to ten years, but could call for repayment in as few as three years.[16] The financial commitment to ownership was substantial; families with multiple wage earners more often owned homes. Detroit Ford families typically lived in single-family houses or flats of four or five rooms; owners paid $42.68 monthly, while renters averaged $32.61.[17]

Residential segregation and avaricious landlords ensured that Black families devoted a higher proportion of income and actual cash outlay for housing. In Chicago, 30% of Black families spent more than $30 monthly, contrasting with 3% of white families.[18] Working-class African Americans lived in flats and single rooms in older neighborhoods south of the urban core, in dilapidated, neglected buildings, including overcrowded nineteenth-century mansions carved into multiple units. One-tenth of Black families, one-third of white households, and more than two-fifths of European immigrants owned homes.[19]

Most white working-class homes in the urban North had modern conveniences. Virtually all of the Ford families enjoyed electric lighting (100%) and running water (97%), almost all cooked with gas or electricity (89%), and had indoor toilets (86%), and two-thirds (65%) had hot running water. Electric wiring, indoor plumbing, and gas lines were standard features of new construction. Modern utilities were comparatively cheap; Detroit families spent an average of $8.50 monthly for fuel and light, 6% of their budget. Housewives preserved perishable food in iceboxes.[20] Black working-class families far more frequently carried and heated water, lit with kerosene, and shared toilets, often outdoors. None of the 1919 Black Philadelphia families had electricity.[21] For housewives, the wages of whiteness were energy-saving electricity, indoor toilets, and running hot water.

Ford families spent one-third of their income on food; their conception of a good diet included ample quantities of meat and dairy, which accounted for almost half of their weekly purchases ($4.53 out of $10.69).[22] Meat signified prosperity, and health agencies touted milk as necessary for children's growth.[23] Working-class people improved their diets over previously "nutritionally inadequate and monotonous" dependence on grains.[24] Yet Stricker concluded that "40% of the nonfarm families . . . had insufficient incomes to buy an adequate diet at the end of the decade of prosperity."[25]

Clothing expenditures increased as the socially constructed desire and need for stylishness, the media dissemination of images, and rapid transportation made the latest styles available to and affordable by some working-class women. One study estimated the minimum annual cost to clothe the wife of an urban industrial worker at "a fair American standard" at between $52 and $64.[26]

Employed women could spend considerably more; requirements for clerical and sales jobs mandated stylish clothing, hairdos, and cosmetics. Young white women, attempting to Americanize their appearance or to distinguish themselves from their mothers' generation, were especially receptive to the lures of the fashion industry. Ford families spent $210.67 annually (12.2% of their budgets) for clothing.[27]

Workers' responses to new consumer possibilities evidenced values and priorities. Manufacturers and retailers introduced widespread credit during the 1920s, and some people eagerly purchased goods that had previously been beyond their reach. Half the Ford families bought cars and electric washing machines, and more than one-third owned radios. Fifty-nine percent made installment payments, an average of $10 monthly, on goods that cost an average of $254.02.[28] Autoworkers more frequently owned cars than did other industrial workers. A large majority (79%) of Ford families supported churches and religious organizations, all subscribed to newspapers, and most of their children attended movies. Almost 60% of Black Philadelphia families bought furniture and 83% contributed to churches.[29] Working-class people universally planned for the future with life insurance for funeral expenses; 98% of Black Philadelphia families, 87% of white Ford families, and 95% of South Bend 1932 interview households carried at least one policy. Annual insurance expenditures by Detroit families averaged $60.[30]

Whether they created comfort or struggled for bare existence, urban housewives increasingly purchased goods and services and produced less with their own hands. Women who had previously tended fires, trimmed lamps, boiled and heaved buckets of water, and tilled the soil now reduced their physical exertion. As women's and children's clothing was mass-produced and sold at affordable prices, women bought more garments and sewed less.[31] With the advent of inexpensive home electricity and falling prices of washers, housewives expended less energy in laundry.[32] Almost half of the Detroit families owned electric wringer washing machines, costing, on average, $133.17 each; sent out some laundry, at an average annual cost of $19.23.[33] The consumer economy required new mental skills to manage cash, judge quality, and comparison shop; housewives were responsible for 80–85% of consumer purchases.[34]

The industrialization of the food industry, improvements in distribution, and the growth of chain grocery stores enabled urban housewives to satisfy hunger by purchasing more food.[35] They bought bread (not just flour) and more canned goods; grew and preserved fewer vegetables; and patronized butcher shops rather than slaughtering and curing animals. Their shift to consumption was incomplete, however; some still raised gardens, picked fruit and vegetables in rural areas, and kept chickens. Neighborhood merchants sold traditional ethnic food, extended credit until payday, and offered delivery, telephone ordering, and peddler routes. Instituting "economy stores" that eliminated services and charged lower prices, A&P opened hundreds and even thousands of outlets annually during the 1920s, reaching its peak of 15,700 stores in 1930.[36] Chains made little immediate headway in working-class neighborhoods, partly because minimal savings did not tempt housewives to abandon traditional sources of food, sociability, and credit. In Chicago and South Bend, chains located stores in more affluent neighborhoods.[37]

Families of white, male Studebaker employees were among the most comfortable working-class people, symbolizing the prosperity and security to which white workers' might aspire. Most owned homes, recently constructed, featuring electricity and indoor plumbing. All carried life insurance. Fewer purchased cars than other autoworkers, but they possessed modern living and dining room suites and radios.[38]

Regular employment of an adult man and his wages determined a household's standard of living, but other members of the family economy were hardly incidental. Wives managed money and material resources, consumed necessities and translated them into meals, cleanliness, and well-being. Until they married, working-class children usually lived with parents, who expected young adults to hold jobs. (Some, of course, never married.) Daughters contributed a greater share of earnings to the household than sons, who gratified more of their own desires and only paid board. Increasing numbers of wives, and especially Black wives, held paying jobs. In 1928, men's weekly wages at Studebaker averaged $32 for unskilled and $40 for semiskilled and skilled laborers. Working-class women in South Bend typically earned $10 to $20 weekly, one-fourth to two-thirds the wages of their fathers, brothers, husbands, and sons.[39]

Households without employed men lived at far lower standards. Rarely could working-class families amass adequate savings to support wives and children if men died. If a single mother held a job and her children were old enough to work, they might manage. If her children were younger, or if she did not have paid employment, their prospects were dismal. Older widows and separated women relied upon adult children. Self-supporting women "adrift" typically resided in a furnished room, unless they had risen to the small elite of clerical supervisors and private secretaries who earned higher wages.

Racism determined standards of living, and generalizations hold true only within racial boundaries. Residential segregation relegated African Americans to substandard, overpriced housing. Wages paid to African Americans were so much lower that even if a husband and wife both held jobs, they were unlikely to reach the standard of living of a white working-class family supported by a man's wages alone. Black working-class daily lives, when measured by comfort, physical effort, or access to goods and services, required more labor. Collectively the four cities of my study illustrate multiethnic, biracial, working-class populations. Tracing the history of South Bend (just large enough for inclusion in the census category of "principal cities") and analyzing commonalities and differences among the metropolises illuminates settings in which people coped with the ravages of the Depression.

"Studebaker Rules South Bend"

A hundred miles east of Chicago, surrounded by rich farmland, a wagon works and a plow manufacturer, both homegrown industries, established an industrial city in the nineteenth century. Studebaker converted wagons into automobiles, buses, and trucks, and the plow factory diversified into Oliver Farm Implements. Together with two other nineteenth-century industries, the Singer Sewing Machine Company and Mishawaka Rubber and Woolen Manufacturing, a boot and shoe manufacturer, they employed tens of thousands of men and a much smaller number of women. Wilson Brothers, manufacturer of men's shirts and furnishings (accessories), hired the most women. The Bendix Corporation set up an automotive and airplane parts shop in 1923. Along with numerous small factories, these plants defined South Bend as an industrial center.[40]

Studebaker automobiles and Notre Dame University's football team brought national and international acclaim to South Bend. Proud city boosters envisioned unlimited industrial prosperity, peacefulness, and religiosity and bragged about the city's high rate of homeownership, "the fairness of its business leaders . . . the fine spirit that pervades its working people," and the fact that "labor troubles are unknown."[41] Industrial expansion sparked extraordinary growth in the 1920s as the combined population of Mishawaka and South Bend increased by more than 50% to 132,823.[42]

Most of the workers who built the fortunes of a few industrialists were European immigrants and their children, attracted by tales of good jobs with high pay. Oliver and Studebaker agents recruited peasants, and others crossed the ocean and traveled to South Bend on their own.[43] In 1930, 41.3% of the city's population was first- and second-generation Americans. Hungarians and Poles accounted for half the immigrant population, followed by Germans; Flemish Belgians comprised a tenth of Mishawaka's population.[44] Substantial numbers of Germans and Poles immigrated prior to 1900; peak entries of Belgians, Hungarians, and Poles were 1900–1915 and 1920–1924.[45] African Americans first arrived on the Underground Railroad. The Great Migration expanded the Black community 170% during the 1920s, yet its population of 3,431 remained tiny, only 3.3% of the area's inhabitants.[46]

Industry dominated the male labor force. More than two-thirds of immigrants and more than half of Black and U.S.-born white men held manufacturing and mechanical jobs in 1929.[47] The majority of Hungarians and Poles found employment at Oliver and Studebaker. Singer employed three thousand workers at the peak (1914), when it constructed three-fourths of sewing machine cabinets in the world; in 1929 its labor force was almost two thousand.[48] Bendix also employed eastern Europeans. The majority of Belgians lived on the south side of Mishawaka, within walking distance of Ball Band Shoes (Mishawaka Rubber and Woolen), colloquially known as the "Belgian shoe college." Unlike immigrants recruited for industrial labor, African Americans struggled to find decent jobs. The only industrial employment open to Black men was Studebaker's foundry, a hot, hard, hazardous place to work. In 1929, 267 Black men at Studebaker also accounted for the large majority of the janitorial crew and some watchmen.[49] Among male wage earners in my sample, 58% (157 of 271) were operatives, the largest number at Studebaker. The building trades, railroads, utility companies, services, and miscellaneous occupations employed the rest.

Occupational possibilities were determined by racialized gender. One-fourth of employed women worked in factories, compared to three-fifths of men. Almost two thousand women constructed garments at Wilson, over a thousand manufactured footwear at Ball Band, and close to a thousand worked at Studebaker in peak seasons. Bendix, H. D. Lee (maker of overalls), Singer, and Venus Brassiere Company also employed women.[50] Immigrant women were as likely to work in service as in industrial jobs, and their American-born daughters found employment in all four occupational sectors. Clerical, sales, telephone operator positions, factories, and laundries employed 61% of white women workers; they almost entirely excluded Black women, three-fourths of whom did domestic work.[51]

Religious, social, cultural, athletic, and benevolent organizations, as well as jobs, created communities defined by ethnicity, religion, class, and geography.[52] Hungarians and Poles settled on the West Side of South Bend, within walking distance of men's jobs, and businessmen opened grocery stores, meat markets, a lumberyard, a hardware store, a poolroom, barber shops, a furniture store, a plumbing and heating business, and even banks. In 1929 one-eighth of immigrant men worked in trade.[53] African Americans scattered throughout South Bend rather than being confined to a single neighborhood. Few were able to open businesses that could serve as an alternative to demeaning treatment they received in white-owned stores.[54] A tiny number of professionals served the Black community; otherwise, employment opportunities were found in the white world.[55]

The city fulfilled some American dreams for immigrants, particularly homeownership, as Old World patterns persisted. The contrast between pretentious wealth and modest survival was ever present. In close walking distance to working-class neighborhoods, the nineteenth-century manors of Oliver and Studebaker, constructed of local granite fieldstone, resembled feudal castles, akin to those in whose shadows peasants and tenants had labored for centuries. Surrounded by acres of lawns and gardens, each mansion boasted about forty rooms. The total square footage of most working-class homes would have fit into one of their grand parlors.[56] Besides these ostentatious displays, church spires and factory smokestacks represented towering forces: the spiritual and material powers of God and industry.

Migrants and immigrants created communities especially by establishing religious institutions. African Americans organized their first formal congregation in South Bend, Olivet African Methodist Episcopal (AME) Church, in 1870; Eastern Europeans founded national Roman Catholic churches, starting with the Polish St. Hedwig's Parish (1877) and the Hungarian St. Stephen's Church (1896).[57] By the early 1930s, multiple Catholic parishes, four synagogues, two Orthodox churches, and at least eight Black congregations ministered to local inhabitants.[58] Whether parishioners attended Christian services regularly, or only at Christmas and Easter, churches were centers for social life. Networks of organizations, defined by gender, marital status, and age, connected eastern Europeans to Catholicism, ethnic culture, and one another.[59] African American congregations attempted to fulfill needs Black people could not meet elsewhere, with nurseries, kindergartens, gymnasiums, employment bureaus, welfare agencies, and handicraft clubs. First AME Zion Church sponsored junior and senior choirs, a missionary society, a girls' softball team, a basketball team, the Appomattox Club, Girls Reserves, Well Wishers, and Willing Workers.[60] Life milestones—baptisms, confirmations, marriages, and deaths—endowed churches with familial, generational, spiritual, and sentimental significance far beyond Sunday services.[61]

Secular organizations also sustained communities: a Belgian band, archery club, and three homing pigeon clubs; Hungarian amateur theatricals, choirs, and sports; and Polish Falcon and Polish National Alliance lodges, which combined fraternal, athletic, and insurance functions. By the 1920s ethnic communities owned buildings, permanent locations for meeting and socializing.[62] Black fraternal organizations included Masonic and Odd Fellows lodges and women's auxiliaries. Hering House, a Black settlement house funded by wealthy whites in 1925, affiliated with the YMCA in 1928 and served a multitude of needs on a shoestring budget: recreation for children and youth, racial uplift, and community organizing. The American Legion, the National Association for the Advancement of Colored People, lodges, athletic, dramatic, musical, and social groups utilized its facilities.[63]

In immigrant neighborhoods mother tongues accounted for most daily communication, while American-born children may have been more comfortable with English. The vast majority of immigrants were literate in their native tongue.[64] *Goniec Polski* (*Polish Messenger*), published twice weekly, had a peak circulation of nearly nine thousand households in the 1920s. *Varosi Elet* (*City Life*) stood across the street from *Goniec Polski*, a few blocks from the Oliver and Studebaker mansions.[65] Hering House was in the same vicinity. Hungarian churches first adopted "American" language parallel with Magyar in the 1930s, and Polish priests began to use English in masses later in the decade.[66] Immigrants acquired English skills at uneven rates. Industrial jobs required knowledge of English because foremen, with the power to hire, hailed from northern and western European ancestry.[67] Mothers typically learned English last, especially if they could carry out routine tasks in native tongues. In 1930, 11.5% of immigrant women and 4.3% of immigrant men lacked English language skills.[68]

Poles, Hungarians, Belgians, and African Americans created communities characterized by religious, cultural, social, and benevolent organizations, and, to a lesser degree among African Americans, small businesses. Germans immigrated earlier, were more assimilated, and also maintained traditions.[69] Ashkenazi Jewish, Italian, and Swedish communities also populated South Bend, and scattered members of almost every European ethnic group called St. Joseph County home. Fifty-one Chinese men had arrived mostly in the 1920s; almost all worked in eight Chinese hand laundries.[70]

European immigrants built distinct ethnic communities and interacted with the dominant society, but institutionalized racism excluded African Americans from many possibilities for interchange. Employers practiced strict occupational segregation, yet South Bend's 807 Black families experienced neither the advantages nor disadvantages of residential propinquity. Dispersed across neighborhoods on the West Side and northeast of the St. Joseph River, some lived next to white neighbors. Because of restricted districts, their rapid influx into the city, and a housing shortage, they frequently lived in inadequate, overcrowded dwellings or in undesirable areas, on top of a swamp or next to the dump. They owned homes at a far lower rate than any group except Chinese men.[71] African Americans partook of some advantages of northern urban life but were denied others. At the integrated public schools, Black students participated on sports teams but could not swim in the pool at the same time as white students. Public recreational facilities were off-limits or restricted Black usage to undesirable hours. Stores and restaurants segregated eating facilities, and in dime stores African Americans had to drink out of glasses painted brown. Studebaker promoted racism and eschewed interracial interchange, segregating its shop floor and sports teams. It sponsored Black women's and men's softball teams that competed with white teams. The Studebaker Athletic Association newspaper, the *Accelerator*, printed racist jokes.[72]

If immigrants and African Americans met social, religious, recreational, and some economic needs within their communities, what forces integrated them into the city? "Studebaker rules South Bend," explained a laundry worker,[73] elucidating the city's dependence on its major employer. Small in the national market when compared with the big three auto manufacturers, the leading independent sold over $177 million worth of vehicles in 1928, its peak year. The census acknowledged Studebaker's preeminence when it declined to enumerate the city's manufacturing because more than half of industrial wage earners worked there.[74]

Studebaker consciously promoted its visibility and leadership. In the summer of 1920 it sponsored a parade through the downtown business district, in which six thousand employees marched—men garbed in suits, ties, and straw hats, women attired in good clothing—with some contingents uniform in white dresses. The parade ended at a park, where thirty thousand employees and family members participated in a field day and picnic. The corporation fed the crowd American food (barbecue, peanuts, watermelon, ice cream cones) and entertained it with a Studebaker Band concert, circus and vaudeville acts, carnival rides, dancing to the music of two orchestras, athletic competitions, pie and watermelon eating contests, and a honeymoon race. Frank Toth's family won the competition for largest family with nine children. Frank wore a white shirt, tie, and hat; his wife retained her Hungarian peasant appearance, garbed in a long dark dress, her head covered by a babushka. Their eldest daughters wore stylish white middy blouses, likely a sign that they, too, worked for Studebaker.[75]

Studebaker encouraged assimilation. Unlike many manufacturers, it did not create ethnic work crews, with the exception of African Americans, promoting interethnic cooperation. One man recalled,

When I went to school, I went to a Polish school over here. The neighborhood, everything, was Polish. When we went to Studebaker, the first fellow I worked with was a Hungarian fellow.... He was first generation like me. He spoke Hungarian, I spoke Polish. "How do you say this in Polish?" "How do you say this in Hungarian?" So, we would pick up a few words.... In those days everybody was home-baking or made different sausages or lunch meats they would bring in. During lunch, this one would bring a cake. "Hey, this is German chocolate." This one would bring a Hungarian cookie and you would taste different kinds of food, which you normally didn't have.... So, you made friends.[76]

Studebaker's welfare capitalism included life insurance, vacations, pensions, anniversary bonuses, and stock purchasing rights. Its social and athletic activities vied for time with workers' ethnic social lives: a military band, a men's chorus, and baseball and basketball teams. The *Studebaker Co-operator* attempted to draw employees into the "Studebaker family" and to Americanize them. Published monthly in English and liberally illustrated with photographs, it celebrated employees' marriages, babies, and vacations; mourned deaths; and featured news about sports teams and other company-sponsored activities. Didactic articles about safety on the job and consumer thriftiness addressed workers and their families. Its pages were devoid of references to ethnicity.[77]

Public education, which was a locus of Americanization endeavors, tied children and parents to the larger community. Schooling was nearly universal for fourteen- and fifteen-year-olds; sixteen- and seventeen-year-olds almost doubled their attendance to 54%, necessitating construction of a second public high school. At parochial elementary schools children received instruction in two languages; if they continued, they went to public schools.[78] Native-born white Protestant leadership developed adult English and citizenship classes, church missions, and YMCA foreign festivals to help "make real Americans of all its citizens."[79] Some ethnic leaders encouraged learning English and applying for naturalization. By 1930 almost three-fourths of the European-born had become citizens or had taken out first papers for naturalization.[80] The claim of a Hungarian American doctor, that the second and third generations were becoming completely Americanized and assimilated, was not without foundation.[81]

The resurgence of the Ku Klux Klan and its ideology of white supremacy, anti-Catholicism, anti-Semitism, and xenophobia, reminded African Americans and eastern Europeans that some whites despised them. When the South Bend Klan, which claimed between six hundred and eight hundred members, attempted to impede the construction of a new building by First AME Zion Church in 1924, the minister and members held all-night armed vigils to protect their church.[82] There is no record of white support for the Black church, yet local opposition to a regional Klan parade that same year was formidable. The city was exceptional; the majority of church members were Catholic, and a nationally renowned Catholic university was located there. Laborers from the West Side, aided by students from Notre Dame, disrupted four thousand regional Klan members, removing their robes and hoods; they attempted to remove their cross and hurled eggs, potatoes, and other missiles at them. Both daily newspapers opposed the Klan, and city authorities called off the march.[83]

Less threatening and more pervasive, local popular culture reinforced white supremacy. An amateur blackface minstrel show, performed by Studebaker employees in 1923, merited four large photographs in the *Studebaker Co-operator*.[84] When Wilson factory clubs organized a Stunt Night in 1933, a skit included a male blackface performer, and "Miss Bertha Buckner gave a negro shuffle." On another occasion its Girls' Club sponsored a performance of spirituals by the Eureka Jubilee Singers. Garbed in "traditional picturesque 'cotton pickin' clothes,'" they sang "old and modern folk songs and plantation tunes that everyone knows and loves to hear."[85] At Studebaker summer extravaganzas, Chinese and Japanese acrobatic troupes entertained. Fifteen thousand people, including three thousand children, participated in the 1932 Kiddies Day, where the On Wah Troupe, Chinese Wonders, performed "equilibristic feats peculiar to the Oriental world,"[86] solidifying notions of Asian otherness.

The Chamber of Commerce boasted that South Bend was a good place to live, and many working-class residents would have agreed. The city illustrated defining characteristics of the era: optimism, growth, and economic opportunities (at least for white people) and, at the same time, xenophobia and racism. South Bend exemplified the contradictions of northern Jim Crow.

Midwestern and Northern Metropolises

A resident might become intimately familiar with all of South Bend, especially if she liked to walk, but Cook, Cuyahoga, and Philadelphia Counties, among the nation's five principal industrial counties,[87] could not be measured on the same scale. Besides their immense sizes (with populations between one million and 3.5 million), their economies were more diverse and complex, their immigrant and African American populations proportionally and numerically larger and more disparate.[88] The City of Brotherly Love, a hub of commerce since its Quaker founding in the late seventeenth century, Philadelphia was a manufacturing center and, as a port, second only to New York City.[89] Chicago and Cleveland, like South Bend, developed from nineteenth-century industry. Metropolises awed the newcomer. Skyscrapers, palatial department stores, lush parks, broad thoroughfares, and distinguished cultural landmarks punctuated the landscape. Smokestacks belching fire and smoke, sprawling industrial yards and docks, and tenements were familiar sights to working-class people.

To some minds, almost three-fourths of Chicago and Cleveland residents and more than three-fifths of Philadelphians were outsiders: immigrants, their children, and African Americans.[90] Sizable numbers of Germans and Poles settled in all four cities. Large Irish, Italian, and Russian populations inhabited Chicago and Philadelphia. Cleveland drew immigrants from almost every eastern European country; the largest group was Czechoslovak. Philadelphia had long hosted the largest African American community in the north. All were destinations of the Great Migration. Cleveland's Black community numbered seventy thousand, and almost a quarter of a million African Americans lived in Chicago and nearly that many in Philadelphia.[91]

Metropolitan diversified economies expanded substantially in the early twentieth century and included manufacturing, retail trade, finance, transportation, and port activities. In Chicago, meatpacking, foundry and machine shop products, and printing and publishing each employed roughly twenty-five thousand wage earners.[92] Foundry and machine shops making motor vehicle bodies and parts employed the largest numbers in Cleveland, second only to Detroit in the percentage of workers employed in industry.[93] Knit goods and electrical machinery engaged the largest numbers in Philadelphia, where small- to medium-size family-owned enterprises characterized the economy.[94] Accompanying industrial growth, tens of thousands of new jobs (mostly for women) opened in the clerical, sales, and service sectors.

Reception of eastern and southern Europeans and judgments about their capabilities and assimilability reflected native-born white assumptions and ideologies. Italians, Jews, and Poles (the largest streams in the new immigration), as well as Greeks, Hungarians, northern and southern Slavs, and others, were regarded as races apart ("not yet white," according to some historians), in-between people, superior to African Americans but inferior to old stock whites. Assigned to in-between jobs, men of these ethnicities were neither foremen nor as despised as Black laborers. As James Barrett and David Roediger note, popular entertainment and advertising "cast newcomers as nationally particular and racially inbetween, while teaching the all-important lesson that immigrants were never so white as when they wore blackface before audiences and cameras." Americanization was "never just about nation, but always about race and nation."[95]

Immigrant women, discriminated against for nationality, language, culture, and religion, enjoyed benefits—typically through their relations with "in-between" men—that were denied to African Americans. Better, cheaper housing was a primary advantage, though they usually lived in older inner-city neighborhoods.[96] Mothers' lives revolved around families, homes, and ethnic and religious communities. Their U.S.-educated daughters almost universally entered the labor force and assumed "American" appearances and habits.[97] Their ability to transform themselves in a single generation into what the Women's Bureau called a "dependable American element" was never a possibility for African Americans, who as a group preceded them by a century or more.[98] They learned racist attitudes, behavior, and language to separate themselves from Black people and to solidify their whiteness. Every European ethnic group and its historians claimed the uniqueness of its hardworking members. Linguistic, cultural, historical, and religious specificities shaped daily lives, particularly for the immigrant generation, and discrimination dogged the visibly and audibly old-country members of a community.

The large majority of Black adults in northern cities were Southern born and recent migrants.[99] Beginning with an intense spurt during the war years, more than a million African Americans streamed north between 1916 and 1930. As white men left factories for military service or engaged in strikes, and hostilities cut off the continuous supply of immigrants, northern manufacturers sought a pool of cheap labor in the South. Segregation, racist violence, disenfranchisement, the boll weevil's destruction of cotton, and lack of jobs in the underdeveloped South made conditions fertile for departure. Northern African American populations expanded dramatically yet constituted a small fraction of the total.[100] From 1910 to 1930, Chicago's Black population increased by more than 500% (from 44,103 to 233,903) but accounted for only 6.9% of inhabitants.[101]

It was not only opportunity that greeted African Americans in the North; metropolises responded to what white people perceived as a flood by segregating Black people more strictly. The South Side of Chicago grew increasingly crowded as Black people could find little housing elsewhere. Philadelphia's African Americans were confined to extremely close quarters in old, rundown neighborhoods on its South Side.[102] Cleveland's decaying inner-city neighborhoods, which had housed immigrants, became increasingly Black.[103] Public accommodations and services, such as hotels, restaurants, theaters, taxis, amusement parks, settlement houses, YMCAs and YWCAs, and public beaches, isolated African Americans or refused them service. Hospitals and schools became increasingly segregated.[104] Theaters and large athletic events did not draw the color line, but the sites of participatory amusements, such as roller-skating rinks, bowling alleys, and dance halls, enforced rigid rules.[105] Racial tensions erupted into open violence after the war.[106] In Chicago, imaginary marks divided beaches long after the race riot of 1919. Higbee's, a Cleveland department store, disallowed Black women trying on clothing.[107] Unlike in the South, segregation operated de facto, and individuals and organizations legally challenged denial of access and won some victories.[108]

Eastern and southern European immigrants and their children rapidly learned assumptions of white superiority. The Black riddle, "What's the first word a foreigner learns in the U.S.? N——," encapsulates the process.[109] Immigrant men watched the behavior of native-born bosses who excluded Black men or relegated them to menial, dirty, dangerous labor. Immigrant women and their daughters observed segregation in schools, neighborhoods, and public places. They absorbed "ethnic notions" that saturated material culture, including children's toys and games and household goods such as lamps and salt and pepper shakers.[110] Newspapers, advertising, greeting cards, and movies reinforced white supremacy. Local popular culture, particularly amateur minstrel shows at company-sponsored social events, exemplified how Americanization required learning anti-Black racism.

Radio programing began as a local affair and featured many ethnic programs; advertising and affiliation with national broadcasting organizations helped create a national mass culture.[111] Substantial majorities of American-born households purchased radios by 1930. In Chicago, with its panoply of stations, 54.1% of immigrant and 42.6% of Black households owned radios.[112] Listening was a social event, and those without radios joined neighbors for their favorite programs. The enormously popular *Amos 'n' Andy* show, broadcast nationwide by 1929, conveyed stereotyped notions of the lives of Black migrants.[113]

Chicago—"Hog Butcher for the World, Tool Maker, Stacker of Wheat, Player with Railroads, and the Nation's Freight Handler," "the City of Big Shoulders," and the second largest city in the country—boasted the first skyscrapers, the largest building in the world (the Merchandise Mart), and the notorious rackets of Al Capone. Chicago was South Bend writ large, but while 14,724 first- and second-generation Poles accounted for 11.1% of the population of South Bend and supported five Catholic churches, in Chicago 401,316 Poles and their children, the largest immigrant group, a similar proportion of the population, belonged to fifty-two Polish Catholic parishes and lived in multiple decentralized neighborhoods.[114] Almost a quarter of a million African Americans—more than twice the population of South Bend—resided in a highly segregated area on the South Side.[115] More than five hundred churches, the Black-staffed Provident Hospital, five weekly newspapers, two thousand small businesses, more than five hundred policy stations (the numbers game), and an array of civil rights and racial advancement organizations characterized the second largest Black community in the country.[116]

Jobs and Workers

Need for money prompted working-class women's employment, but it was not their only motivation, nor did it push everyone into the labor force. Social expectations prescribed that raising children and housework should occupy wives and that financial support was the obligation of husbands. The economy did not sustain gender conventions, especially for Black families, and not all women were wives. Adult men expected to work; women's employment patterns reflected race and life stage. Single women twenty and older overwhelmingly held paid jobs, but the majority of wives did not. Black married women were three times more likely to be employed than were white married women, but two-thirds of Black wives were not in the labor force at a given time. Gendered assumptions created separate labor markets, and white supremacy relegated men and women of color to the bottom of both. Understanding social expectations, which women held paid jobs, demands by employers for specific workers, restricted jobs and those without limits, provides the context for women's decisions as the Depression turned lives upside down.

"When the Children Are Grown": Daughters' Employment

Parents and daughters alike anticipated that young single women would become wage earners after leaving or finishing school. A Russian immigrant expected adult offspring to be self-supporting. His comment, "When the children are grown, they can make a piece of bread for themselves," expressed widespread sentiments.[117] In the late 1920s, immigrants and daughters of immigrants left school earlier than did Black and native-born white teenagers.[118] The longer a woman remained single, the more likely she became a wage earner. Employment among single women ages twenty to forty-four, Black and white, hovered around 85% in 1929 in the four cities.[119]

The large majority of daughters remained under their parents' roofs until they married. Bonds of obedience and loyalty ensured that they turned over most or all of their wages, which improved the family standard of living.[120] If fathers died, deserted their families, or became unemployed, daughters' wages staved off destitution. Americanization and consumer pleasures weakened parental authority and daughters' allegiance to Old World demands for respect and compliance.[121] Some daughters yearned for the gratifications of entertainment and dress and insisted on being treated like typical Americans who kept the money they earned. They paid room and board and handed over a greater proportion of their wages than did their brothers. Abraham G, a South Bend junk dealer, and likely an immigrant, did not know his daughter's salary. "She is her own boss." The fact that Rachel G, a stenographer at Studebaker, had earned her way for close to a decade enabled her to assume this prerogative. Not disclosing her income was the hallmark of changing family relations.[122]

Southern Black sharecropper families groomed girls to become domestic workers and taught them that contributing to family coffers was their responsibility. Some girls traveled north to provide childcare and housekeeping for kin who lived in at domestic jobs, then moved into their own jobs and sent home part of their wages.[123] Marie S, born in Birmingham in 1910, started work as a nursemaid at thirteen. A year later her mother brought her to Chicago, where she did domestic work.[124] Adolescents "had mixed feelings of pride and resentment as they turned over hard-earned wages to families who relied on this meager but valuable source of cash, and they chafed under the rule of fathers who wielded an iron hand in enforcing a specific division of labor based on gender and age within the household."[125] Black urban daughters may have been more independent than white daughters in their disposition of wages.[126] Black parents socialized children into self-reliance, a skill necessary for survival.[127]

Concern for daughters' physical, sexual, and emotional safety motivated some Black parents to forego their potential wages.[128] In Chicago and Cleveland, half as many Black girls worked as did European immigrants; more often they remained in school.[129] Sylvia Woods, daughter of a New Orleans roofer and domestic worker, reported, "I came from a family that didn't allow the girls to work because they didn't know who you were going to work with and you couldn't mix and mingle with anybody and everybody."[130] Mothers supplemented the earnings of fathers while daughters assumed responsibility for housework and childcare.

Thirst for adventure and desire to escape strict, unhappy, or dysfunctional families compelled young women to leave home, as did poverty and the promise of jobs. When a parent died and the other parent remarried; when physical, sexual, or emotional abuse oppressed them; or when social conventions about acceptable female behavior, sexual or otherwise, proved too confining, women left home for the city. If they were urban bred, they moved out. Black women searched for a less overtly racist environment. Jobs enabled women to live "adrift" from the moorings of relatives, but they were paid low wages on the assumption that they were subsidized by families. They earned scarcely enough to support themselves; women with live-in positions could contribute cash to their families and help sponsor migration and immigration of kin. Numbers of "unattached" women were not insignificant. Surveys of major cities calculated that at least 14% of the nonservant adult female labor force lived adrift.[131]

Employed Wives: "My Husband's Work Was Never Steady"

In contrast with young, single women's consistent employment, race powerfully affected whether wives held paying jobs. Married Black women were three times more likely to work for wages than were married white women (see table 1). One-third of Black wives held jobs on the eve of the Depression; in Chicago and Philadelphia almost 40% worked. As Jacqueline Jones notes, "Where [Black] men had access to industrial employment—in Pittsburgh and Detroit, for example—fewer wives worked than those in cities where large numbers of men could find little work outside domestic service."[132]

Caught between economic necessity and gender strictures, a married woman might wrestle with the decision to seek paid work. She would evaluate family finances and responsibilities, wages and the local availability of jobs, and personal predilections. The ages at which wives held jobs illustrate distinct racial patterns. White women younger than twenty-five most frequently combined marriage and employment. Their labor force participation declined as their responsibilities as mothers increased. Married Black women, in contrast, were most frequently employed when they were most likely rearing children.[133] Black men's difficulty in finding work, the narrow range of jobs open to them, and their low wages partially explain Black wives' high employment rates,[134] as did the ever-present availability of domestic work and Black women's historic dual roles as laborers and wives/mothers. Black working-class communities did not develop social proscriptions against the employment of wives as fervent as those that white people cherished. Many Black wives held jobs intermittently; others "always worked."

Despite substantial racial differences, paid employment was the exception for married women; two-thirds of Black wives were not in the labor force in 1930. Wives moved in and out of the labor force, responding to husbands' unemployment, opportunities for jobs, changing domestic and child-rearing responsibilities, and individual considerations. Some earned cash accommodating lodgers; caring for children; taking in laundry; pressing hair; or selling their sewing, weaving, chickens, and eggs to neighbors. Home-based activities enabled them to raise children, superintend their households, and earn money simultaneously.

Vera M's history illustrates intermittent employment and marital conflict over a wife's job holding. Born in Hungary in 1895, and now the mother of two children, Vera worked at three jobs and remained out of the labor force only seven months in four years. She washed glassware at the Oliver Hotel in 1926–1927, then quit because she "didn't want to work," according to her "little daughter," who translated. Two months later she took a higher-paying job at Wilson, worked fourteen months, left for the same reason, and stayed home four months. She returned to the hotel in 1929 and worked sixteen months before quitting the following summer. Vera explained that her husband, Stephen, an assembly worker at Oliver, wanted her to stay home if he was working. Vera may have bickered with Stephen over her jobs, convinced him with their mutual goal of home-ownership, or quit work whenever marital tensions threatened to boil over.[135]

The local economy affected married women's job holding far more than it did for single women. White wives' employment varied from 7 to 15% in the four cities; nationally, US-born white wives' employment ranged from 4.9% (Scranton, Pennsylvania) to 23.2% (in Tampa, Florida). Immigrant wives were usually less likely to hold jobs than native-born wives. In the four cities, Black wives' employment clustered around their national rate of 33% (see table 1). Low employment of married women in a particular city did not correlate with low employment of single women.[136]

Men's low wages, irregular work, and unemployment motivated wives to join the labor force. Mabel W "had to get work as [her] husband's work was never steady." This white U.S.-born woman found work as a cook in a high school cafeteria in 1927, and her oldest daughter, age fifteen, likely took over some of the housework.[137] When times were better, wives left jobs. Queen Victoria C, a Black Mississippian, moved to Chicago with her husband in 1923, worked four years in a laundry, and at age forty "quit work to stay at home and take care of the home." Her husband was making a "good wage."[138]

Calamities that beset men—occupational injuries, ill health, "shell shock" from the war, insanity, alcoholism, and imprisonment—impelled wives into employment. When Julius T entered a tuberculosis sanitarium, his twenty-three-year-old wife, Mary, a Hungarian immigrant, took a job at a brass company and later cooked at a Notre Dame dormitory to support their three children.[139] Mabel H, a Black Chicagoan, "states that her husband never had good health so that she always worked to help with finances." By age forty-four, Mabel had cooked in restaurants for twenty-five years and spent another five in daywork and laundries. Her husband worked at a coal yard, and both their children died young.[140] Mary K, a Polish immigrant, "felt it did not matter much whether [her husband] worked or not" because he "spends all his earnings for drink." Employed at Walter's Dry Cleaning since 1915, when she was twenty-four, Mary K declared that her wages paid for their home.[141]

Familial ambitions, particularly daughters' education and homeownership, were aspirations worthy of a wife's employment.[142] As Rose Z, a Polish immigrant, thirty-eight, explained, "I want to send my daughters through high school and my husband could not do it alone." Purchasing a home, the Zs could forgo their daughters' potential wages only if Rose replaced them.[143] Eva A, a Black woman who worked at a policy station (the numbers business) in Chicago, was ashamed of her job, but her $18 weekly wage enabled her to put her child through high school.[144]

Self-esteem, self-expression, and sociability also motivated employment. Mary A, twenty-nine, African American, and the wife of a store porter, cooked in a restaurant. The couple was buying their home, and Mary "was unhappy without a job and her own money."[145] Della H, a Black woman whose husband and son earned good wages, "worked because she wanted to and always banked her money."[146] Anna U, fifty-two, Polish, a widow, spent much of her marriage at Libby, McNeil, and Libby in the stockyards. After twenty-two years on the lard pail machine and in numerous other departments, she proudly claimed she was "able to do any factory work."[147] Economic necessity should not obscure multifaceted motivations and rewards for employment.

"When My Man Pulled Out I Went Out and Got Myself a Job"

If a working-class woman lost her husband, her labor was her most likely source of support. Savings were minimal, pensions rare, and funeral expenses usually consumed insurance. Courts could order men to pay alimony or child support, but working-class women did not necessarily possess the class skills or money required to appeal to the law. The earnings of young adult children maintained some households, but those children departed and formed families of their own. With the exception of infrequent, inadequate mothers' pensions, formerly married women rarely relied on external resources. Those most likely to have motherhood responsibilities, ages twenty to forty-four, held jobs almost as frequently as single women the same ages (see table 1). Black divorcées and widows were more than twice as likely to be in the labor force as their white counterparts.[148] Sarah D, a Black woman, eloped at fifteen after one semester of high school in 1920 and her husband supported her for three years. "When my man pulled out I went out and got myself a job," she said, stuffing sausage links at Armour and Company.[149]

Understanding women's wage-earning patterns requires simultaneous consideration of race, age, and marital status. For young single women in the urban North, expectations of self-support and/or contribution to family economies underlay almost universal employment after they left their teens. Race was decisive in the employment of married and formerly married women. Absence of a husband, rather than responsibility for young children, was most critical for formerly married women. Urban Black women held paid jobs more consistently throughout adult life. They entered the labor market slightly later than white women, particularly immigrants, but more often remained there. More than 40% of Black women between the ages of eighteen and fifty-nine were employed. Race also created white employment patterns. White women held jobs in large numbers between ages eighteen and twenty-four. After twenty-five, single white women were highly likely, and married white women highly unlikely, to be employed.[150] Older single women sustained high levels of employment; half or more worked (see table 1).

These particularities make clear that discussing the employment rate of undifferentiated women (24.8%) utilizes a meaningless abstraction. It describes no actual experience.[151] Women's employment rates varied so much that attention to race and life cycle is critical to analyzing patterns. White wives accounted for more than half of adult women, so their propensity to stay outside the labor market created an average that is a statistical artifact.[152] One-third of Black wives and one-tenth of white wives held jobs. Among older, previously married women, twice the proportion of Black as white women worked for wages.[153] Historians' tendency to frame women's work history through family relations neglects numerous women and impoverishes our understanding of employment. Young single women (some living independently) and wives accounted for three-fifths of the female labor force. But fully two-fifths of employed women were formerly married and older single women.[154] Adult men (more than 90%) and single women (85%, ages twenty to forty-four) consistently worked for wages in the four cities in 1929, regardless of race, ethnicity, or nativity (see table 1).[155]

Jobs and Job Desirability

Patriarchal assumptions created two labor markets, and white supremacy relegated men and women of color to the bottom of both—to the most grueling, most dangerous, least well paid occupations. Manufacturing and mechanical industries employed one-third of all men and one-half of European immigrant men in dozens of skilled, semiskilled, and unskilled industrial occupations. Trade (13%), transportation and communication (9%), and commercial and domestic service (5%) employed the rest and some middle-class men. For men of color, the service sector was a major source of work.[156] Black men disproportionately worked as laborers in every sector. Studebaker placed them in its foundry, the hottest, dirtiest, most dangerous operation in the plant.[157] One of the ways European immigrants confirmed their status as white, according to Roediger, was their avoidance of so-called "n——jobs."[158]

A far narrower array of jobs was designated for women. Domestic service had been the single largest employer of women since at least 1870. Commercial service jobs in restaurants, hotels, laundries, and institutions proliferated. As clerical work continued its long-term expansion, manufacturing slipped from second- to third-largest employer of women.[159] In an industrial economy, clerical and service occupations, not manufacturing, employed the majority of working-class women (see tables 2–3). White women worked in all four sectors, while Black women found clerical and sales positions only in Black businesses. Manufacturing was starting to become racially permeable.

Dana Frank's envisioned platform (see introduction), held up by women of color, describes comparative white advantages.[160] Onerous to the women supporting its weight, and invisible to or taken for granted by those standing on it, a platform captures hierarchy and the cognizance and ignorance of participants. Yet in the 1920s and 1930s considerable racial overlap characterized commercial and domestic service. White women earned higher wages and worked in better conditions, but female "Negro jobs" did not (yet) exist in the urban North.

Working-class women enunciated clear opinions about job desirability; most white women would have ranked jobs in the following order: clerical, sales, manufacturing, commercial service, and domestic service, with some interchangeability between contiguous sectors. Urban Black women, denied entry into clerical and sales positions, usually judged factories and commercial service work preferable to cleaning white women's homes. Each sector displayed substantial variation in conditions and pay: salesclerks in department stores or dime stores, clerical workers in large corporations or small businesses, waitresses or laundry workers, and live-in domestics or day workers (see table 4).

Gender and race were not the only axes of labor market segmentation.[161] Bosses also stratified the female labor force by other personal characteristics: age, marital status, ethnicity and/or religion, and appearance. Qualifications such as training, skills, and experience were not irrelevant, especially for clerical positions, but identity determined a woman's chances and framed her expectations. When employers evaluated working-class men, race and age alone were pertinent.

Appraising potential jobs, women weighed wages, hours, conditions, status, physical and mental labor, and grime and cleanliness within their local context and individual circumstances. They considered practicalities such as distance and the cost of transportation. Mothers assessed how they could accommodate a job to family responsibilities. Some single women valued opportunities to meet unmarried men. Women usually judged as undesirable live-in jobs that limited control over their lives. For some white women, the respectability conferred by clerical and department store sales positions was not only a question of improved finances but mobility from in-between ethnic immigrant to generic white American. Prospects varied significantly. Chicago offered the best opportunities; clerical work engaged a higher proportion of the female labor force, Black and white, and Black women's proportion in factories (16%) was three times the national rate. In Philadelphia and South Bend, manufacturing employed more white women than did clerical work, and immigrants worked in equal proportions in manufacturing and service. In Chicago and Cleveland, immigrants' employment in services outstripped their numbers in factories (see tables 2–3).

Women moved from job to job and occupation to occupation as circumstances changed and opportunities presented themselves. White teenagers might work in a factory or at a service job while attending school, then move to a clerical position. Manufacturing operatives, frequently laid off at the end of the season, especially in the needle trades, sought other work to tide them over or as a permanent change to ensure more steady employment. Some white women alternated between factory and commercial service jobs. They persisted in occupations characterized by high wages, high status, and a well-developed work culture— namely, clerical work, department store sales, and waitressing.

"Girls in Offices Are Much Better Off"

The differing fortunes of three daughters of a Hungarian assembly worker at Studebaker illuminate the desirability of clerical work. Mary T, twenty-eight, earned $22 weekly as an operative at the South Bend Watch Company, where she had worked for five years; shortly after the stock market crash she lost her job. Her younger sister, Bessie, earned $28 weekly at a law firm, and another sister, Emma, made $22 weekly at an investment company. In 1932 Mary, who had no "business training," remained unemployed, despite applying for other factory jobs. Her sisters continued to work, and Bessie earned a raise to $30. Mary concluded, "Girls in offices are much better off."[162]

Working-class women valued the steady work, status, and comparatively high wages of clerical occupations. They judged the work easy: typing, filing, running office machines, answering phones, and completing other office duties, usually in clean surroundings, required little physical labor. Women considered the business world more glamorous than the drudgery of the factory, laundry, or kitchen. Business girls wore fashionable clothing and women's presumed decorative functions were part of the job. Office work promised upward mobility, not in dollars alone. Immigrant daughters altered their identities and rural migrants cast off the label of country hayseed. Female clerical positions had increased 1400% since the turn of the century, while the female labor force doubled.[163] In corporate and government bureaucracies, a new clerical worker usually joined the stenography pool; in 1929, stenographers and typists accounted for two-fifths of female clerical workers.[164] In small offices, a single employee's duties might include bookkeeping, cashiering, typing, stenography, and reception. Wages began at about $12 weekly in small businesses; median wages were approximately $22, and experienced supervisors in large offices earned $35 or more (see table 4).

The desirable office employee, bosses frankly acknowledged, approximated white, male, gentile standards for a sexually desirable woman: she was white, young, single, attractive, native born, and Christian. Three-fourths of clerical workers were single, 70% were younger than thirty, and almost all were white. Older single, married, and formerly married women constituted a noteworthy minority; some were private secretaries or supervisors with top salaries.[165] Most employers refused to hire married or Jewish women. Only Black professionals and Black-owned businesses, such as insurance companies, employed African Americans.[166]

Because they valued the rewards of office jobs, young white women sacrificed free time and potential wages to obtain business training. Often the first in their families to complete high school, they also prepared at business schools. Grace S, a Polish American, began sewing at Lee Overalls at sixteen, without finishing school. After a few years she "wanted to get out of factory work," so she studied at night at business school for two or three years and quit Lee for an office position at higher wages at Bendix.[167]

Sales jobs shared some of the desirable qualities of clerical work and also multiplied.[168] In five-and-ten-cent stores, single white women younger than twenty-five purveyed a vast array of everyday necessities and dime-store dreams.[169] They worked part-time while attending school, or as a short-term strategy that was cast aside when a better-paying job came along. In department stores, white women over thirty, most of them married or formerly married, composed the majority of the sales force. Trying to "match their selling staffs to their desired clientele," department stores "always exclud[ed] Black women and weed[ed] out as much as possible those with too-obvious immigrant or working-class demeanor."[170] Department store saleswomen regarded the job as a career and took pride in their skills. Small neighborhood businesses also hired salesclerks. Part-time jobs were common: a month at Christmas, a week before Easter, occasional one-day sales, and Saturdays. Sales did not exclude married or older women, but the retail sector employed less than one-tenth of job-holding women, and cross-class competition limited opportunities.[171] Nationwide, fewer than 2% of female clerical and sales workers were Black, working almost entirely in Black businesses.

Manufacturing

Most working-class women deemed work in factories preferable to commercial or domestic service, and some Black women aspired to the assembly line to escape service jobs. Primary requirements were stamina and ability to adapt to routine. Some production jobs paid as much as office work, and better than sales, but wages depended on the type of business and opportunities for overtime. Almost any young or middle-aged white woman might find a factory job. Close to half of female operatives were married or formerly married and almost half were twenty-five and older.[172] Proportionally, more immigrants worked in manufacturing; numerically, the large majority was U.S.-born white women (see tables 2–3). Textile, clothing, food, and shoe manufacturing employed more than half of female operatives.[173]

Black women gained access to factories during the Great War, in the dirtiest, most dangerous, most physically demanding, lowest paid jobs.[174] No industry employed more African American women than cigar and tobacco factories.[175] Garment manufacturing, the leading industrial employer of women and the second largest industrial employer of Black women, reserved the job of presser for them. Standing all day and enduring intense heat required more stamina than operating a power machine.[176] Conversely, Beatrice B migrated from Mississippi as a teenager in 1923 and got a job in Armour's fresh sausage department at $15 weekly; she quit the following year because she always got "chilled and cold."[177] Nationally, 5% of employed Black women held operative jobs in 1929 (see tables 2–3).

Industrial advantages included availability, possible overtime, a sense of community, and the fact that English was not always necessary. Some South Bend women earned $27 a week at the Colin B. Kennedy Company, which manufactured radios. Margaret M made "swell money" at Mishawaka Rubber and Woolen: $22.50 weekly, and as much as $29 when overtime kept her at the factory from 6:00 a.m. to 9:00 p.m.[178] Rose S, a Hungarian immigrant who did not speak English, worked at Singer from 1923 to 1930. Singer's workforce was predominantly Hungarian, and her husband, son, and friends worked there. In 1932 Rose said that she would like to go back to work, but not as a factory worker.[179]

Irregular employment; compulsory overtime; layoffs; part-time work in slack periods; strenuous, sometimes dirty, physical labor; an unpleasant and sometimes dangerous environment; long hours; and low wages, particularly on piece rates, constituted disadvantages. In her twenties, Luvara D, a Black woman, made sausages and smoked bacon in a Chicago meatpacking house, earning between $18 and $21 a week. Standing in blood and water all day, her knees and ankles swelled even though she wore rubber boots. After four years she quit.[180] Rose M, a white

Chicagoan, earned between $21 and $25 weekly at a radio and auto parts manufacturer until a thumb injury disabled her from doing detailed work.[181]

For some young white women, the assembly line was temporary. They worked in a factory while attending school or during summers, moved back and forth between manufacturing and service jobs, or occasionally moved into sales. Betty H, a Hungarian American, judged factory work the best. Hired at Wilson in 1929, when she was seventeen, she was laid off after two months because work was "slack." After three months doing domestic work, she left for an opportunity to work at the Kennedy radio company. Laid off a month later, she spent a month looking and found sales work at McCrory, where she remained seven months. Presented with the chance to get back on at Kennedy, she left the dime store, though her hours at Kennedy were so irregular that she earned only a dollar more per week: $12 compared to $11 at McCrory. Betty preferred a factory to working as a salesclerk or cleaning another woman's home.[182] Most of 106 white female industrial workers in the South Bend sample worked in a single factory until marriage, childbirth, or sometimes for many years. In a metropolis a greater range of opportunities presented more choices.

Service Jobs

Virtually all working-class women could find jobs in the service sector, racially indefinite in the urban North, employing the overwhelming majority of Black and the plurality of immigrant women. Fewer American-born white women worked in services; some were disqualified from other jobs by age or inexperience (see tables 2–3). In laundries, food preparation, institutional cleaning, and domestic service, Black and white women sometimes worked side by side, in finely graded racial distinctions, or at the same jobs at different businesses. Exclusionary policies varied. The Oliver Hotel employed both races as chambermaids, but South Bend laundries did not hire Black women. In the urban North no female jobs were labeled "Negro jobs" in the interwar period. Individual white women avoided certain jobs, but female service occupations did not (yet) carry racial designations.

Only a few jobs required qualifications beyond health and physical stamina, though that does not mean employees lacked skills. Pay, status, and conditions varied considerably. Some waitresses and beauticians received high wages and unique benefits. Jobs cleaning hotel rooms, offices, or another woman's home, or laboring in laundries and food preparation, paid poorly, lacked status, strained health, and could impinge on women's freedom; sometimes these jobs were located in harsh (hot or cold) environments.

Some white women preferred service work to factory work, and many African Americans judged commercial services a better alternative than cleaning white women's homes. Sophia P, a divorced twenty-two-year-old white woman, "tried" Wilson a couple of times, but "never could make good on the power machines." She preferred cleaning dormitories at Notre Dame despite summer layoffs.[183] White women who would rather clean institutions or cook in cafeterias may have been unable or unwilling to adapt to the fast pace of the assembly line. Lena J, a Black woman, considered waitressing in a hospital to be her best job. When she left Mississippi for Chicago as a young woman, she found a war job making cores for hand grenades at International Harvester. Subsequently she worked as a housekeeper, day worker, and shaker of wet laundry at a laundry. Because it brought her closer to her dream of becoming a nurse, she "loved" her hospital job, where she had a "nice" room and received meals.[184]

A half million women prepared, served, and cleaned up food at hotels; restaurants; refreshment stands; drugstores; and school, factory, office, and hospital cafeterias. Obtaining food service work did not require education or particular personal qualities. Only in higher-priced establishments that courted a well-heeled clientele did employers demand experienced, trained cooks and youthful, attractive waitresses. Nationally, almost one-third of female hotel and restaurant cooks were Black; more than three-fourths were widowed, divorced, married, and older than twenty-five.[185] Waitresses were overwhelmingly white, native born, from northern European backgrounds, and younger than thirty-five, and half were married or formerly married.[186]

Food service jobs frequently required split shifts, but unique compensations ameliorated this disadvantage. Onda H earned $12 weekly, plus three meals a day, as a salad girl at the Hotel LaSalle for seven-day weeks, on duty from 6:30 a.m. until noon and 5:30 to 8:30 p.m. She quit in the late 1920s because the hours were "too late," a decision that likely pleased her three school-age children and husband.[187] Beyond inconvenient schedules, as many as three split shifts daily, and the discomfort of hot kitchens, food service workers suffered accidents from heavy lifting, rushing, sharp knives, and slick floors.[188] Wages typically ranged between $10 and $20 weekly, depending on size and type of establishment and on whether a woman received tips. Skilled waitresses in expensive restaurants profited from substantial tips. A white career waitress, Lorraine G, earned $40 a month, room, board, and tips as high as $10 to $12 a day during the Christmas season at the Harvey House Restaurant in Santa Fe, New Mexico. She made $225 wages and tips during the resort season in Bermuda.[189]

Many women considered live-in work highly undesirable because it curtailed freedom and limited social life. Unlike Lena J who loved her hospital job, Irene T, a nineteen-year-old white waitress in the nurses' dining room at St. Joseph Hospital, was "tired of being away from home and [tired of] Sunday work." She earned $7 weekly, with room and board, for six-hour days and six-and-a-half-day weeks.[190] Most people worked five and a half days, so weekends were the main opportunities to socialize and to attend religious services.

During the 1920s consumer culture and advertising prescribed a youthful modern look and exhorted women to purchase commercial beauty products and services. Altering their appearance appealed to young women who wanted to set themselves apart from peasant or rural kin. Clerical, sales, and waitress jobs required stylishness and attractiveness.[191] The number of beauticians, a relatively new occupation, rocketed 350% during the decade.[192] Unlike most service jobs, where customers or employers had higher class status, beauticians served both working-class and more affluent clients in racially separate shops. Most businesses were small, and many were owner operated, often located in the owner's home. Department store salons employed as many as ten women. At white shops, haircuts, shampoos, manicures, and finger waves constituted most business; in Black shops it was shampoos and hair pressing. Other services included permanent waves, marcelling, and hair dyeing, but there was little specialization other than by race.[193] Almost two-thirds of beauticians were younger than thirty-five, and 60% were married or formerly married.[194] They learned through apprenticeships or saved or borrowed to pay a few hundred dollars for beauty school training. Urban Black communities especially supported hairdressers; Chicago, Cleveland, and Philadelphia had proportionally twice as many Black hairdressers as white ones in 1929.[195]

Paule Marshall's description of a Black Brooklyn shop evokes the role of the hairdresser in community social relations:

> The talk and laughter spiraled up with the smoke, water gushed in the basins, the electric driers rasped loud—and these sounds along with the smell of singed hair set the rhythm and tone of the shop. . . . Time . . . was measured by the customers filing in and out the booth who, shielded in its semi-privacy, confessed their troubles. Miss Thompson's gaunt face would become almost distorted with compassion as they spoke; she murmured always: "It's the truth, honey . . . ,' 'You telling me . . . ,' and all the while her deft hands wielded the smoking comb, transforming their coarse hair into shiny-black limpness. Time was the fried-fish sandwiches and Pepsi-Colas throughout the day, the number runner sauntering in.[196]

Small- to medium-size operations scattered throughout a city, commercial laundries offered homes and businesses multiple services: wet wash (returned damp), rough dry, and fully finished (ironed). Women worked as sorters and markers; hand washers; shakers of wet laundry; feeders of damp flatwork into irons, folders, and many other types of ironers, such as shirt finishers and mangle operators. In 1929 six commercial laundries employed 328 wage earners in South Bend, and 268 laundries employed 15,524 workers in Chicago.[197] Hotels, universities, hospitals, orphanages, and other institutions ran their own laundries.[198] Small hand laundries, staffed by Chinese men, competed with mechanized plants for patronage.[199] Laundries employed more Black women than any occupation except domestic service in the metropolises; Black women made up half of female laundry workers in 1929.[200] Nationally, one-third of laundry employees were Black, two-thirds were married or formerly married, and two-thirds were older than twenty-five. Sometimes Black and white women worked together, though supervisors often defined tasks racially, assigning Black women to more strenuous and lower-paying jobs. In Chicago and Cleveland the majority were flat-work ironers, press operators, and hand ironers; in each specialty white women earned $3 to $5 more per week than Black women. A substantial number of white women worked as markers and sorters, the highest paid job; few Black women held these positions.[201]

When queried about preference for laundries, women cited better hours and pay compared with domestic service, cleaning hotels, restaurants, or offices. The work was steadier and less difficult than that of some factory jobs, and it lacked the demeaning features of personal service. Common complaints included high temperatures, damp atmosphere, lack of ventilation, poor or nonexistent toilets, washing, and drinking facilities, standing all day, and injuries from unguarded machinery and slippery floors.[202] Laundries ran irregular shifts: long days at the beginning of the week and short days later on. Because managers promised rapid service, the pace of work pushed women beyond their limits. After ironing shirts for eleven years, Florence B, forty-two, a Black woman, was "sure she never wants to go back to a laundry." Standing induced rheumatism, steam rising from wet clothes damaged her eyes, and supervisors who sped up the work strained her mind.[203]

Sylvia Woods got her first job, in a laundry, when she was in her twenties; she took pride in her work, in part because of her difficulty, as an inexperienced Black woman, in getting hired:

I wanted to start shaking sheets because there is an art to shaking sheets. You pick these sheets up and—wham—if you did it right they popped. You made the sheet pop and then you threw it over that pole. This fascinated me. . . . I was going so fast. There were four poles and if we kept those poles full, then I could monkey around.

I'd go over and watch the women feed the sheets into the mangle. One day I said to this white gal (only white feeders—Black shakers and Black folders, the hardest jobs—white table girls), I said, "Will you let me see if I can run this?" She said, "Sure." By the next week I knew how to feed.

So the next week I wanted to fold. I hurried up and filled the poles and they showed me how to fold. I wasn't there three weeks before I knew how to do everything.

Sylvia subsequently proved her skills to the owner and demanded higher wages.[204]

Unique advantages characterized the cleaning of buildings. In the South Bend sample, all fifteen night janitors at the Studebaker headquarters and downtown office buildings were married immigrants (one a widow) with insistent obligations. Lack of job skills or English fluency did not prevent women from contributing financially to family economies, and night work ensured that children would have a parent at home. Cleaning empty buildings was arduous, monotonous, and lonely, yet no other occupation meshed so well with their priorities. Cleaning jobs proliferated with the growth of institutions: in office buildings, hotels, hospitals, college dormitories, country clubs, mental institutions, churches, factories, and stores, as well as railroad cars and taxicabs. Custom and sometimes physical demands determined gender assignments; almost twice as many men worked as cleaners. Employers placed few restrictions on workers; three-fourths were married or formerly married and almost two-thirds were thirty-five or older. Immigrant and Black women dominated female janitorial jobs in northern cities and accounted for more than half of workers nationally.[205] Black and older white women rated janitorial work more positively than did young white women. Beatrice W, a Black woman born in 1886, took pride that she rose to assistant forelady after many years cleaning Pullman railroad cars. She earned the high wage of $5 a day, checking the cleaning and placing head rests on seats before cars returned to service.[206] Cleaners typically earned $10 to $15 weekly. Washing floors on hands and knees and lugging heavy pails of water took its toll. Ethel I, fifty-two, a Polish immigrant wife and mother, "scrubbed nights" at Studebaker for eleven years. "She is old and worn out, and her arms are so weak she can no longer lift them to her head to do her hair."[207]

Office buildings, hotels, and department stores employed women elevator operators; it was a job requiring social skills, an acceptable appearance, and patience, characterized by higher status and sometimes higher wages than other service jobs. In 1929 more than one-third of women elevator tenders nationwide were Black,[208] like Ellabell L, nineteen, who worked at a South Bend office building. Her schedule rotated every three days: a split shift from 6:30 a.m. to 12:30 p.m. and 6:00 to 10:00 p.m., followed by a day working 11:30 a.m. to 5:45 p.m., and a third day, 8:00 a.m. to noon and then 12:30 p.m. to 6:00 p.m. Ellabell earned $16.25 weekly in 1930—thirty-two cents an hour—while an immigrant janitress at the same building earned twenty-four cents hourly.[209] Elevator operators accounted for a tiny number of jobs, but it is notable that a young Black operator could earn more than an older, white, immigrant cleaner.

Lack of personal freedom was the most despised aspect of domestic service, especially for live-in work, causing most women to view it as the worst job possible. According to Rose Bradley of New Bedford, Massachusetts,

> houseworkers work harder than aney girl that works in a factory or store. And they put in double the time that aney of them girls do. As I known for my self. I put in from 95 to 110 hours a week my averige is from 12 to 16 hours a day now that is som days work and that is day in and day out. . . . When you havent any time to yourself and have to do as you are told and then have to stay up half the night after doing a big days work of a million and one things . . . but people dont seem to think that we work harder than factory or store clerks. we have no hours. they have there Sundays evenings and Holladays. we dont have

any . . . before they can get a place they must be of a good carictor and good references which the factory girls dont have to have. Yet and for all they have more rights and liberty than we do.[210]

Hard physical labor and low wages were common; the personalized relationship, because of working in the employer's home, was the most objectionable feature. Almost invariably, employer and employee were women. One-fifth of the female labor force, almost two million women, performed paid housework in 1929.[211] Its major advantage was availability: high turnover meant that finding a job or a better job was an ever-present possibility. Regarded as unskilled, domestic work demanded competence at diverse housekeeping and child-rearing tasks, as well as deference. Whether day workers, live-out workers employed by a single family, practical nurses, or live-in servants, most domestic workers performed a wide variety of tasks. Only wealthy households hired specialized employees.

A worker had to negotiate physical and emotional labor across boundaries of class and often race. Live-in workers lacked specific working hours or privacy and had to cope with employers' attempts to control their lives. Expectations of compliance could be more significant than physical chores. Her boss might constantly hang over her shoulder, supervise each task, and require her participation in servile rituals.[212] Many women took pains to avoid household employment.[213]

With such severe liabilities, domestic work attracted women who did not possess skills or personal attributes desired by other employers. Low-status groups filled the ranks: Black women in the South, Chinese men and Japanese women on the West Coast, European immigrants in the Midwest and Northeast, Mexicans in the Southwest, and poor, native-born white women especially (but not only) in areas lacking low-status racial or ethnic groups.[214] With migration Black women assumed an increasingly larger share of domestic work in northern cities; in Chicago they accounted for 11% of the female labor force and 39% of domestic workers in 1929, and in Philadelphia, 17% of the female labor force and 63% of domestic workers.[215] Nationally, Black women accounted for 52% of domestic workers and 17% of the female labor force.[216] Household labor became increasingly identified with Black women as white women moved into better jobs, yet young and old white women who lacked education or skills also found it their most likely prospect.

Black women took the lead in altering the occupation from live-in positions to live-out ones and daywork during the early twentieth century, gaining a modicum of independence and enabling themselves to hold jobs and meet the responsibilities for their children, home, and husbands. Day workers and live-out workers composed the majority of household employees by 1929.[217] Practical nurses, hired in the short term to care for a new mother and baby or a sick or dying client, usually took charge of housework, as well as nursing. Probably the largest numbers of self-employed working-class women were laundresses, laboring at home, with the advantages of physical distance from customers and the ability to oversee their own households.[218]

In northern cities no female jobs were labeled "Negro jobs" in the interwar period. In laundries, food preparation, and institutional cleaning, Black and white women sometimes worked side by side, sometimes in finely graded racial distinctions, and sometimes competed for jobs. When employers excluded Black women, they created pathways for "in-between" women to improve their status. Consciously or not, when immigrants and their daughters worked in white-only jobs, they were assimilating, moving out of foreign status, and demonstrating their whiteness. Jobs in the clerical and sales sectors and in racially segregated services (especially as beauticians and waitresses), provided such opportunities. Manufacturing jobs might be labeled "for foreigners." Americanization meant becoming white *rather than*—or *in addition to*—Italian or Polish. It could be achieved, in part, by the job a woman held. The female service sector and the male manufacturing sector were the largest employers of working-class people. Women in service occupations were far less racially segregated than men in manufacturing, a significant dissimilarity that requires further attention from historians.[219]

Making Choices

Working-class women made choices, quit jobs that paid poorly or drained them physically or emotionally, and sought alternatives. Young women entering the labor market were often eager to improve their situations. Mary W began work at the age of eighteen at Wilson, quit after three months because she "minded sitting," stayed home a year, then took a chambermaid job at the LaSalle Hotel, which she left after nine months, "sick of Sunday work." She looked for work for two months in 1929, worked at the Kennedy radio company for five months, and was laid off. She waited two months "for a chance to get back to the hotel" despite the fact that she earned half her wages at Kennedy ($13 compared to $27 at Kennedy) and doubtless worked Sundays there.[220] Rose H, eighteen, Hungarian American, quit the Studebaker stenographic pool after a year because there was "too much overtime," but never overtime pay. "They just made machines out of us."[221] Whiteness and youth enhanced choices. After fourteen years as a department store bookkeeper, Mary K, fifty-nine, a white widow, resigned in 1929 because new office machines required her to stand.[222] Black women moved between domestic and commercial service jobs and sometimes factories. Perennial complaints of well-to-do white housewives about the "servant problem" reflected domestics' departure in search of better employers.

Racism was the most salient determinant of female labor market segmentation. In 1929, 61% of white women workers nationwide labored in factories, laundries, stores, or as clerical workers and telephone operators, compared to 6% of Black women.[223] The vast majority of Black women (excluding those working in agriculture) were limited to domestic work (71.9%), while only 10.4% of white women did housework for pay.[224] Ethnicity, nativity, religion, age, marital status, and appearance constructed job limits, but they described more permeable boundaries. The least attractive jobs were available to the greatest number of women. Constrained by structural features of the labor market, women wove together personal, familial, and workplace considerations in making employment decisions. They believed they could make choices, even within narrow limits, and they acted on their options. Then the stock market crashed.

I turn next to thematic discussion of survival strategies, beginning with employment; then to unwaged, reproductive, emotional labor in homes; and, finally, to acquiring benefits/relief, a vastly expanded form of labor primarily gendered female.

2

Job Deterioration
and Unemployment

● ●

"You Just Can't Depend
on a Steady Job at All"

Unemployment and seasonal layoffs had long haunted workers, especially factory operatives, but following the stock market crash of 1929, jobs disappeared abruptly. Joblessness peaked at 24.9% in 1933, and never claimed less than a seventh of the labor force the rest of the decade.[1] Official figures, however, consistently undercounted lived experience by excluding the underemployed, who earned a dollar or two weekly or a thin pay envelope once every six weeks, and the discouraged, who had ceased looking for work. Whether they served meals, shook sheets, sold notions, sewed brassieres, scrubbed toilets, or answered telephones, working-class women recoiled from plummeting wages and deteriorating conditions. Hanging on to jobs depended on the nature of the work, its susceptibility to economic fluctuations, and whether individuals found favor with bosses.

Aggregate figures conceal far more devastating joblessness in specific racial, gender, and occupational groups. The conclusion that sex segregation protected female workers relies on total numbers.[2] I make a more nuanced argument: sex segregation partially shielded some groups, who experienced comparatively less unemployment, and debilitated others, who suffered joblessness higher than 50%. Fewer "office girls" lost jobs than assembly workers; paperwork persisted when production was pared down. Service jobs disappeared as customers redefined commercial services as luxuries and housewife-employers let domestic workers go. Confined to the service sector, Black women were disproportionately plagued by unemployment.

Three case studies illustrate how gender, race, and occupation defined losses. The first case, in South Bend, Indiana, demonstrates how rapidly industrial collapse pervaded a local economy. The second case, of racial differences in female unemployment in three metropolises, illuminates benefits and liabilities of particular occupations as tied to the identities of workers. In the third case, nationwide insecurity in the least desirable female job exemplifies the paucity of possibilities for Black women. Other forms of discrimination, by age and marital status, and relatively Depression-proof jobs further attest to disadvantages and advantages adhering to specific occupations and particular women. Unless analysis incorporates the simultaneity of gender, race, life stage, and occupation, it remains incomplete.

"When Studebaker Doesn't Work, South Bend Is Dead"

The economic collapse of a medium-size industrial city illustrates interweaving of jobs and demography. In South Bend, male operatives reeled from the blows of unemployment immediately after the stock market crash, but the impact on women's jobs was more ambiguous. As Edna B noted, "When Studebaker doesn't work, South Bend is dead."[3] When Studebaker laid off much of its overwhelmingly male production force, white operatives' daughters, sisters, wives, mothers, and sweethearts continued to process paperwork, cook in the cafeteria, and clean offices. Far fewer women held those jobs, but their tasks persisted. Businessmen ate out less frequently and cut back on work and pleasure trips, so commercial services laid off mostly female employees. Housewives let domestic workers go and "stay[ed] home and d[id] their own washing; . . . others were too poor to send out the wash."[4] African American women and men, confined to the worst jobs, suffered severe unemployment.

Within six months of the crash, almost one-fourth of male operatives were out of work, the highest rate of joblessness in the four cities (Chicago, Cleveland, Philadelphia, and South Bend), as were one-seventh of female operatives.[5] As the Women's Bureau (WB) noted, "Short days or weeks, undertime of all descriptions, was more prevalent among the men."[6] By the fall of 1930 Studebaker had laid off 3,310 men, 28.2% of its male operatives, and reduced the workweek from fifty to forty-five, forty, or thirty-six hours.[7] Average wages of remaining semiskilled and skilled men fell from $40.34 to $33.89 weekly.[8] At Oliver Farm Implements in May 1930, "fifty to sixty men in the department [took] turns working, two or three at a time."[9] Ball Band Shoes reduced female and male personnel by one-fifth each, laying off 841 workers. Singer Sewing Machine trimmed more than two-thirds of female but only one-fourth of male employees—629 total. Wilson laid off 663, more than one-third of operatives, reducing the number of workers in every department: shirts, neckwear, hosiery, knit underwear, and nainsook.[10]

Situations changed weekly, if not daily. Catherine S, employed at Ball Band since 1913, judged conditions "the worst ever." A forty-year-old white widow, she earned as much as $26 a week, pulling overtime in the winter of 1930, twelve hours a day. By the fall she was reduced to seven hours daily, making only $13 a week. On a new style of shoe, "the work gets harder every day." Paid a piece rate, Catherine fixed problems herself "instead of taking the shoe downstairs for corrections." In her daughter's department, "The ticket and the price [were] both cut but [she] has to work harder." Helen's winter ticket paid $18 weekly for seven thousand pairs of shoes. In February 1930 her ticket covered five thousand pairs for a total of $10.50. After six years Helen lost her job in 1931. Catherine worked one to three days weekly in 1931 and 1932, until a surge of business in the fall 1932 boosted her wages to $12 weekly.[11]

Fluctuating needs and supervisors' favoritism made layoffs erratic and unpredictable. When one department had little work, another might run at close to full employment. A boss needing hands might hire from outside or arrange transfers within the plant. Bertha W, age fifty-two, kept her job when Wilson dismissed many shirt inspectors, but her responsibilities expanded to many types of shirts. Her wages fell from $20 to $12 weekly, though "shirts were better than most other departments."[12] Singer took Mary K "off piece work because the work was too varied for a piece rate."[13] At Singer "the oldest girls—those who had been there ten years and over—were laid off as soon as those with less service." Helen S and her sisters, Polish Americans who were employed four to seven years packing machines in the warehouse and inspecting cabinets in the woodworking shop, lost their jobs in 1930.[14]

Factories required employees to wait for work without pay and to report at odd hours. "[We were] welcome to stay there but we wait around for hours lots of times,"[15] a Wilson operative reported. At Bendix-Stromberg, "Some days we'd be sent to the dressing room to wait. They'd rather you wait in the dressing room, then it doesn't look so bad, they don't like for a group of us to sit out in the shop waiting."[16] Helen S was, she explained, "called in all hours of the day. I never know what to expect. Sometimes they call me in as late as 1 p.m."[17] At Kennedy Radio, Betty H explained, "Every now and then they get a fit and make us work until 4 p.m. Saturday, then the first thing you know you haven't anything to do." Her days and hours were "so irregular that [she] could not explain fully."[18] Men waited at Studebaker all day to work for fifteen minutes and were paid for fifteen minutes. Their wages plummeted from an average of $.80 to less than $.40 an hour by 1931.[19] A Studebaker bench worker, Irene S, noted, "You never know anything about the hours you will work nor what you will make at Studebaker from one week to another."[20]

In 1933, at its nadir, Studebaker's labor force had collapsed to 6,840, down from 20,365 in 1928.[21] Local manufacturers employed half the workers they had in 1929 and paid less than one-third of their previous wages. Only one-third of sample women who held industrial jobs in 1930 worked in factories two years later; some literally earned a dollar or two weekly. Almost half (sixteen of thirty-six) worked at Wilson, where there was a burst of production in the fall of 1932. Retail employment dropped to a similar degree.[22]

Managers in every sector utilized rotating layoffs. At Oliver, Vincent K, a Polish American, worked six weeks between August 1931 and July 1932, two to four days, five to nine hours daily; in one such week he earned $6.[23] Studebaker laid off office cleaners every seventh week. Julia B, a Polish immigrant wife and mother worked "full" the other weeks: 7:00 p.m. to 3:00 a.m. Monday through Friday and 2:00 p.m. to 2:00 a.m. on Saturdays. Her wages dropped from $13.80 to $11 weekly.[24] Ruth H, a secretary at the county courthouse, was scheduled for a month on, a half month off, in 1931.[25] Leah C, who began working at fourteen at Robertson department store in 1914, sold infants' wear for $20 weekly and had a paid vacation in 1929. In 1930 business was "terrible;" the store eliminated her vacation and cut her wages to $18. In 1932 Robertson tinkered with schedules. In July, Leah worked a three-day week; in August she had a full-time schedule with an unpaid layoff every sixth week; in November, she earned $10 weekly.[26]

The type of work affected managers' strategies. Operatives waited for work; manufacturing, clerical, and sales workers might be assigned more diverse tasks; commercial services sped up when patronage decreased. Leona C (in introduction) earned $12 for seven-day weeks as a chambermaid at the Oliver Hotel in 1930. She was "supposed to have two days [off] a month, but [she] didn't get it." If she took a break, her pay was docked. In 1932, she was "busy until the warm weather," when her days and wages were cut to as little as $4 a week. When football games began, Notre Dame University's Fighting Irish sustained Leona, albeit seasonally, who returned to full-time at $9 to $10 weekly.[27]

Consumer frugality pinched commercial services. A long-term employee at Walter's Dry Cleaning explained, "Several new girls have been laid off. If work gets slacker, the boss told them that old girls would probably be asked to take turns at layoffs."[28] Laundries reduced hours, wages, and then staff. Only four of a dozen or more Chinese hand laundries survived, and several came and went.[29] Julia S, laid off by Singer, found work as a cook in March 1930, for $25 weekly. A month later the restaurant folded, the owner "owed everyone," and she had a hard time collecting her wages. Unemployed three months, this thirty-five-year-old Hungarian immigrant found another job as a cook, at $8 weekly. In 1931, again out of work three months, she secured a third restaurant job, at $7 a week, where her husband frequently ate free meals.[30] Yet cafeteria cooks and steam table servers in factories, public schools, and at Notre Dame continued working. Onda H (in chapter 1) remained full-time at $12 weekly in the County Orphans' Home laundry in 1932.[31] The specific employer, not only the economic sector, affected job trajectory.

Black women, limited to domestic and commercial service (91.4%), were far more vulnerable. In September, 1930 domestic workers had been reduced from four or five days to one or two, and those irregularly. Some attributed joblessness to competition from white women.[32] A skilled, experienced cook, long employed by the city's most popular restaurant, found that race overruled other considerations. Della G, forty-nine, widowed, had earned high wages at the Philadelphia Restaurant, six days a week, twelve hours daily, without vacations, since 1922. Ill, needing to rest, she quit in March 1930. When she looked for a job that summer, she found "private family work hard to get. Whites [were] given preference for cooking." She "answered several ads but [they] did not want a colored person."[33] Loretta V noted that "very few things open [to] colored women and more elevator operators than jobs."[34] Not all service jobs were equally vulnerable, but competition, including from white women, disadvantaged Black women.

Black men worked in more varied jobs, sustained severe unemployment, changed jobs, and departed in search of better fortune. Stewart V waited tables at the Oliver Hotel and subsequently drove a truck for the Star Store, the employer of his (by then former) wife, Loretta. In 1933 he worked as a barber and by 1934 he left the city.[35] Harold H, a porter and receiving clerk at Robertson, was unemployed, worked as a laborer, later directed handicrafts at Hering House as a Works Progress Administration employee, and in 1940 held a custodial job.[36] Among eighteen Black men, six departed and three died during the decade.[37]

The Depression devastated manufacturing and services but did not damage other sectors as severely. Among 1,465 women reinterviewed in 1932, 57% of operatives and 58% of service workers, compared to 67% of clerical workers and 71% of saleswomen, were employed.[38] These numbers understate layoffs because thousands of unemployed workers and their families had departed from the city; employed operatives might work a single shift in alternate weeks.

Layoff policies endorsed patriarchal assumptions and family norms. In 1930, factory managers reported "investigating family responsibility." They retained married men and sought to keep at least one member of a household. Oliver "tr[ied] to give work to the one with most family responsibility"; Bendix Brake and Stromberg Carburetor followed similar guidelines. Venus Brassiere Company's manager noted that 15% of workers were widows, and he "always consider[ed] employees' responsibilities." At Wilson, "the woman was laid off who could get along best without the job," and Ball Band guidelines called for "lay[ing] off married women in preference to single. Married men are given preference over single men."[39] Among all 1932 interviewees, married men and single women were most frequently retained. Compared to 1930 46.6% of married women kept jobs; 73.1% of single women and 61.1% of the formerly married remained employed. Among men, 65.5% of husbands, and 65.1% of husband-fathers kept their jobs in 1932, but only 36.7% sons did so.[40]

Employers might have substituted men for women, but did so infrequently. Julia K understood that at Singer "men were given the jobs of women,"[41] which the assistant general superintendent corroborated. The WB noted, "Women have been laid off in larger numbers than men relatively because men can be used more generally and shifted on different jobs more widely."[42] No other employer crossed gender lines and sex segregation of occupations remained relatively inviolate.

The Depression intensified women's rhythms: moving from job to job, from sector to sector, and in and out of the labor force. Those with the most advantages of race, age, single status, training, and experience—namely, clerical workers—were least vulnerable to the Depression and most likely to find alternative jobs. Employment in the least desirable jobs failed to sustain Black women. Mary A, another unemployed Black restaurant cook, confirmed Della G's experience answering ads: "People in South Bend who have several servants do not want colored help." She found part-time work cleaning the beauty parlor in a department store where her husband was a porter. Both lost their jobs in 1930 and remained unemployed two years later.[43]

Jobless men rarely turned up alternative work. Some returned to the rural hinterland, to the old country, or moved to Chicago. They relied on hopes and promises that they would be "called back in," and sometimes they were. Later in the decade Bendix expanded and hired many former Studebaker workers.[44] In 1940, working-class men's jobs had not completely recovered; 12.2% fewer men were employed than in 1929, while numbers of employed women increased slightly (4.1%).[45] Judging only by total numbers, sex segregation protected women.

Simultaneous comparison by race and gender reveals a more complex story. In 1940 African Americans had recouped far fewer jobs than their white counterparts. Black men suffered the worst unemployment. Only 68.3% had jobs, compared to 92.3% in 1929; among the employed, 32.7% worked on New Deal projects. Without federal intervention, the local economy provided 44.9% as many jobs for Black men. Fewer than one-third as many Black men worked in manufacturing, transportation, and communication.[46] Their continuing joblessness suggests that almost complete unionization of industry and substantial unionization in other blue-collar jobs prompted employers to displace Black men with white men. Unions also practiced racism. Fewer men worked in service jobs, but double the proportion of employed Black men were in service positions. Services typically paid less than operatives or laborers earned, and they often demanded servile behavior. Black men lost work numerically and proportionally; jobs that employed them were less desirable.

Black women recovered more jobs than Black men, but fared worse than white women or men. Their employment rate dropped from 34.7% to 23.5%, a loss of 32.3% of their previous jobs (see table 5). Including public emergency workers, 74.4% as many Black women worked in 1940 as in 1929. Outside New Deal jobs, more than nine-tenths remained in service—overwhelmingly, domestic work—indicating returning white prosperity. Without New Deal jobs, only 65.3% of

Black women would have been employed. For African Americans, the impact of federally funded employment was hard to miss.

Occupation furnished the chief evidence about who suffered the brunt of the crisis. White working-class women—less concentrated in a few workplaces and less identified with a single job or occupation—experienced less unemployment and had better prospects for reemployment than white working-class men. African Americans suffered severe unemployment and had few other options. By 1940, Black women regained more jobs than Black men, primarily because more white people could afford domestic workers. Racial differentials in a city where Black women rarely competed with white women illustrate harsh patterns that will be more evident in metropolises.

Racial Patterns of Unemployment in Northern Metropolises

South Bend's early, deep unemployment foretold nationwide experience. In the metropolises men's industrial unemployment hit 45% in January 1931. Women lost between one-fourth and two-fifths of industrial and service jobs. In Chicago, Cleveland, and Philadelphia, more than 40% of Black men and women were jobless fifteen months after the stock market crash—a rate of unemployment that was much worse than white men or women, immigrant or native born, experienced.[47] Confined to jobs most rapidly eliminated, and employed in more marginal positions, Black workers rapidly lost work.

A metropolis promised multitudinous opportunities, yet where women more frequently competed across race, Black women told stories of white women replacing them. Regardless of whether they worked alongside each other (in the same jobs or in specializations labeled Negro), whether they did similar work in separate locations, or whether they worked in jobs becoming primarily Black, Black women lost work more rapidly. In 1931 the May Company, a Cleveland department store, replaced Black elevator operators with white ones in response to customer pressure.[48] Though it was not a numerically significant source of employment, running an elevator was a rare opportunity for Black women to work in a clean job in the world of business. The May Company validated white assumptions that white women should fill publicly visible positions when jobs were scarce.

Confinement to the service sector provided Black women no security. White employers' and customers' preference for white employees led them to reclassify jobs and displace Black women. In areas not clearly racially delineated, some substitution of white help for Black predated the Depression and intensified as the crisis deepened. Evelyn D, a Texan who moved to Chicago in 1925, worked as head ham slicer at Thompson's, but lost her job in 1928 when the cafeteria hired only white help. "She found it very difficult to secure maid work about this time as north side hotels began to replace colored help with white."[49] Grace K, a young Georgia migrant to Chicago, lost a $10 weekly, job as a rooming house maid which she had held for four years; her employer replaced her with a white couple to whom she paid $7 total per week.[50]

Laundries illuminated the racial differential. Fifteen months after the stock market crash, between 35% and 45% of laundry operatives were out of work in the three metropolises, but almost triple the proportion of Black women workers were unemployed compared to white women in each city. In Chicago 61.8% of Black women laundry workers were jobless, but only 23.5% of white women.[51] Employers laid off black women more rapidly and replaced them with white women. Some workers moved from task to task, but skills such as hand ironing were not unimportant. Always seasonal, laundries' dwindling business is significant because housewives were disinclined to hang laundry outdoors in January's bitterness.

To ensure patronage, businesses sped up workers. Arleathie B, age fifty, a Black woman and a widow, described the strain: "I have been in laundries till 12 o'clock at night. I worked in so many different laundries. I lost my mind. I can't remember them all. I used to come home and put the bacon in the drawers and the knives and forks in the frying pan." She worked as a shirt finisher in 1932 and 1933 at a

"terrible" place. [She] attributes much of her trouble to working here, due to slave driving tactics and to having a team-mate who was very ugly to her and nearly drove her mad. "[My] mind went blank. [I] wouldn't take time to eat. [I] would take lunch to work. No time to eat. Then carry it home again at night and eat that cold lunch because [I was] too tired to fix anything. Not only me. All the rest. We'd stand up and cry! Sometimes. Always saying, 'We got a get this out. The customers want their work.' At night I couldn't raise my right hand."[52]

Independent laundresses who contracted with many customers lost their livelihoods because "people did their own." Elizabeth H, a Black Philadelphia widow, seventy-one, suffered a downward spiral. In 1933 one customer cut her payment from $.50 to $.25 for five pieces of laundry and another paid her $.75 for a washing and ironing every third week. Elizabeth "had to find soap myself." "[I] used to get recommendations from one to another. [I] never had to advertise before."[53]

Factory work was similar. In Chicago in 1931, 54.2% of Black women operatives were unemployed, compared to 35.1% of white women operatives.[54] If they kept jobs, pay and working conditions deteriorated. Sarah P shelled pecans at piece rates, reduced from $.10 to $.06 per pound by 1932. She shelled twelve and a half pounds of good nuts daily, but when the nuts were poor and small her maximum productivity was six pounds. Her weekly pay dropped from $5.50 to as little as $.80.[55] During thirteen years in Chicago, thirty-five-year-old Corrine H, an Alabamian, worked in commercial and domestic services, in a tannery, and at a mattress-making factory. In 1932 she denounced a garment sweatshop: "The place needs investigating over there, that factory. They work the girls so hard they faint. Raw-hide methods. They pay $.24 for six dozen dresses. A girl is lucky if she can make $.48 in a day."[56]

The few Black women in occupations least troubled by unemployment worked in Black businesses. White businesses, including those in Black neighborhoods, rarely hired Black clerical workers, nor did Black women hold clerical jobs in large bureaucracies, with the exception of Black-owned insurance companies.[57] In January 1931 more than half of Black clerical workers and saleswomen were unemployed—two to three times the rates of their white counterparts.[58] Two women holding similar clerical jobs illustrate racial differences and the domino effect of joblessness. Amanda D, a white woman, had managed a group doctors' practice since 1907. In the early 1930s she often did not "receive the full amount [$25 weekly] but would go home with a few dollars." In 1932 the doctors broke up the practice because they "didn't have enough patronage . . . to pay their office rent." Fifty-three-year-old Amanda felt "like [she was] losing a home."[59] Madeline M, an African American, also managed a doctor's office at $25 weekly. Her pay dropped to $18 before she lost her job in 1930. "[I] cut my wages myself," she explained. "[I] knew he couldn't afford to pay me and I thought it was better to take less and hang on a while longer. [I] didn't get my last few weeks' pay until long after I left."[60] White doctors maintained an office employee two years longer than did a Black physician, emblematic of the racial differential in unemployment and illustrative of how rapidly African Americans went into debt for health care or relegated it to the luxury category. Amanda and Madeline thought alike and made the same accommodation.

Commercial services sometimes switched workers across gender lines. When a new firm took over restaurant management of Stevens Hotels in Chicago, "male waiters replaced all except a few girls in the coffee shop."[61] With the repeal of Prohibition in 1933, many restaurants began to serve liquor, increasing profitability and tips. Attempting to gain lucrative positions, waiters argued that it was immoral for women to serve liquor.[62] Arleathie B noted that laundries also substituted men: "Men worked downstairs on shirt finishing on a piece-work basis and earned much more than women; women worked upstairs on the same work at 18 cents an hour. When slack, women were laid off. [She] said that other laundries have men shirt finishers in recent years and mentioned one around 920 on 43rd in which the men can be seen doing this 'from the Cottage Grove street car.'"[63]

In 1931 female unemployment was more than twice as high in manufacturing and service as in clerical jobs in Chicago. When consumers classified services as luxuries, plummeting patronage drove hotels, restaurants, and laundries to cut staff. One-third of Chicago hotel and restaurant cooks and waiters of both sexes were out of work. Management redefined jobs employing Black women as white only. Housewives did their own cleaning or replaced Black domestics with white.

Two-thirds of Black women cooks and servants in restaurants and private homes were out of work, compared to one-fifth of their white counterparts. Black working-class women suffered far deeper unemployment than white women.[64]

Domestic Service

The domestic service stew bubbled with many ingredients. The personal relationship and location in the employer's home did not prevent housewives from practicing the same tactics as business and government. Unlike most jobs, there were no standards. Employers' subjectivity seasoned the stew, long simmered in race and class assumptions. Interviewees and letter writers nationwide told the same stories.

Housewife-employers, managing shrunken budgets, could no longer afford houseworkers, or they saved up all the work for an infrequent employee, whom they paid as little as ten or fifteen cents an hour in 1932–1933. Rosie C, a Black Chicago widow, "about fifty," formerly had "plenty of work" with every day taken, and averaged $15 weekly, plus lunches and carfare. In January 1933, "the last lady," who paid $1.25 and a meal for a half day, "called me up and said she couldn't afford to keep me."[65] "Day work ain't what it used to be," lamented Grace B, a thirty-three year-old, Black Chicagoan. "[You] used to get $4 or $5 a day and wasn't tired at all when you got home. Now you're all worn out. You wash windows, clean, wash, iron all in one day. They save up all the work they can and try to get you to do it all at one time." In 1933 Grace earned $.50 for a half day, one dollar for a full day, plus carfare and a meal.[66] Matilde B worked 8:30 a.m. to 5:30 p.m. for $1.50 and a lunch of bread, butter, jam and coffee. "Then she [the employer] wanted me to stay and do a little ironing that evening, all for $1.50." Expenses consumed one-third of Matilde's wages: $.14 carfare and a $.35 fee to an employment agency.[67] Grace and Matilde described single days of work, not ongoing positions.

Housewife-employers heaped every imaginable task on domestic help, who "stagger[ed] under" increased responsibilities.[68] According to a letter from a Wichita, Kansas, woman, "There is nothing they do not demand in the line of housework—cook, clean, wash, sew, mend, press good clothes, wait table, polish silver, iron, personal maid and valet services, shopping, watering flowers, dogs, and outdoor bird baths, even water the lawn, care of children, daily scrubbing of children's furniture to keep germs away."[69] The duties of a young Slovenian American in Cleveland ranged from "finishing an evening dress to typing manuscripts."[70] Outdoor chores, such as washing cars, cleaning garages, and yard work, had not previously been the responsibility of female domestics.[71] Two Brooklyn sisters "[had] the responsibility of doing the work of a team of horses such as washing walls and ceilings and even want you to keep the furnace going and keep the employers car cleaned."[72] Affluent employers required one woman to accomplish tasks previously carried out by several persons.[73] Most employers were not wealthy or accustomed to specialized services but hired a single worker, reduced wages, and expected the same amount of labor.

"All housework hours are long. Most of the places my day begins at 6:30 a.m. and lasts often till 12:30 or 1 a.m. You know they have parties and they want you to serve. . . . They all have company and they forget the maid,"[74] noted Helen F, a German immigrant and Cleveland divorcée. As a Kittanning, Pennsylvania, letter writer who appended "colored" to her signature, expostulated, "It is something awful the way peoples is working they help an paying such little I an husbon works in private families an we works from 7 a.m. till 2 at night an have to get up at 6:30 next morning an work till 1 at night don't never have time to rest."[75] Live-in workers often put in fourteen to sixteen hours daily, a hundred hours a week, at wages as low as five cents an hour.

Black women's unemployment gushed like a broken pipe, rather than trickled down, from white men to their wives to domestics. Men's financial losses, housewife-employers' penny-pinching, their preference for white domestics when they could be obtained cheaply, and white women's willingness to take jobs they previously might have shunned contributed to severe joblessness of African American women. Mrs. Katherine Rutherford, a Black Baltimorean, described unreasonable demands in 1933:

> These private families work the poor woman to death in these private families they have to work 16 and 17 hours a day when 8 hours are a days work and they put the work of three people on one and pay them less wages and they get no Sundays no holiday days of any kind, They are harder on the colored woman they seem to think that a colored woman have no feeling of tiredness they put 16 and 18 hours work on them and they have to work every inch of their life to get it done and that is all day and best of the night You know the law of health is 8 hours work, 8 hours recreation and 8 hours sleep. but the poor women that works in these private families don't get any recreation they get all work and but very little sleep and if they say they are tired the people they work for will say they are lazy after 16 and 18 hours work in one day that is they work them all day and the best part of the night.[76]

Domestic work remained available, and live-in jobs proliferated. The advantages to the housewife-employer of having a servant on call twenty-four hours a day are obvious. Married women in the Midwest and the North did not usually live in, but unemployed women compromised from necessity. Young women's working reduced the number of mouths their parents had to feed, women on their own saved rent, and single mothers boarded out children to take live-in jobs. Declining wages enabled nouveau middle-class women to hire household help for the first time. Workers did not relish socializing inexperienced housewife-employers who did not know how to treat help and demanded inordinate labor. Some employees identified their status with that of their employer and wanted to work only for "quality" people. Anti-Semitism prompted some workers' disdain for inexperienced employers.

The threat of sexual advances by an employer's husband or sons kept household workers alert. Even in the Depression, women quit jobs to escape sexual harassment if they could not fend off advances without being fired. One eighteen-year-old Clevelander, the daughter of Croatian immigrants, worked at thirty housework jobs between 1930 and 1933: "All of these jobs were given up because job was too hard or salary was cut or husband or sons of employer got 'fresh' with her. [She] could not stand some of the places she had to sleep-cockroaches, dirt, etc. At some places men in family would come before her naked."[77] Another young white Clevelander wrote, "When Mrs. is not around Mr. get fresh[,] and mean when she is around."[78] A Welsh American woman, age fifty, left a job where men in the family were "very coarse and rough."[79] Aware that white women believed they were sexual temptresses of loose morals, Black women did not comment on such provocations to white interviewers. A Black historian who interviewed older Black domestic workers reported, however, that the majority had been sexually harassed by husbands of employers.[80]

"Poor board and shabby rooms," emblems of disrespect, were the norm for live-in workers, according to a Mansfield, Ohio, writer.[81] Sleeping in unheated attics or cellars, on a living room davenport or studio couch, in a child's room, or sharing a bed with a sick, elderly member of the household were not unusual, resulting in lack of sleep and lack of privacy. A Boston widow slept in a room that stored clothing of her employer's husband. "Luckily," she noted, "I did not have many clothes as I had to share it with the man of the house. He also had a large hall closet and had ten suits of beautiful clothes all custom made and a dresser in my room for his linen. All he did not have was his boots under my bed. That I would not stand for and no food to speak of I lived on milk."[82] A Chicago houseworker wrote, "[They] give us their old food they wouldn't eat their-selves."[83] A Pennsylvania woman noted that some employers paid only room and board: "Such board corn meal mush for dinner, half hot dogs. One Who's Who told her maid she did not supply meat or dessert to the maids."[84]

Employers justified low wages because they supplied room and board, which they calculated at far above market rate. An informed woman noted, "Since good table board and lodging can be had in Los Angeles for as low a figure as $5 and $6 per week, it would certainly seem that $5 a week is a fair estimate of the value of the domestic worker's food and room."[85] In Peoria "the housewives that hires girls to work in their homes for them claims that board and room is worth $10.00 a week and from 1.50 to 3.00 salary is enough and I say no," wrote Mrs. Clara Green. "I am at present paying $2 a week room rent and have a $5 meal ticket which is 7 a week for board and room from 10 leaves 3.00 which the girl or woman is cheated out of so the rich can have more."[86] Want ads nationwide offered housework for room and board, and job seekers advertised their willingness to accept such conditions. Elizabeth S, a twenty-one-year-old Hungarian

American, explained a job she held from December through April: "It didn't pay nothing—I just took it to be in off the streets through the winter."[87]

Domestic jobs averaged $3 weekly in the Midwest and the North, whether a woman lived in or lived out. Collecting pay was another matter. Olga U, Polish American, age nineteen, explained, "The pay depends on the people you work for. Some people will pay you and some will not. Some don't care what they pay."[88] Miss J. MacCulloch wrote, "During the banking failure in Detroit my employer would not pay me any wages. He said 'No one is paying their help, because the banks are closed.' He also said he does not intend to pay me back wages."[89] A Philadelphia housewife hired a Lithuanian widow for $5 weekly and tried to pay her with a dress.[90] Caroline Vikartofsky of Ironwood, Michigan, "old enough to work for myself," recounted, "I was to get paid every week, and I had to wait for 9½ weeks before I got a cent. Even then I had to ask for my pay, for which I got a rotten scolding."[91] Catherine B, an Irish-born cook, had earned $125 a month plus room and board in Los Angeles for ten years. After ten months without pay, she quit at age fifty-nine.[92]

Circumstances that elicited housewife-employers' preference for white domestics are unclear, but many hired white women when they could be obtained cheaply. Viola C, thirty-seven, a Black Chicago widow, found a housework job for $15 a week plus room and board—high wages in 1932. Her employer had just moved in, and for three weeks Viola cleaned, set up furniture, and accomplished the backbreaking work required to put a new house in order. Then she was fired: "[She] didn't give me a day's notice. Then she hired a white maid after I had done the heavy work."[93]

Other Discriminatory Practices

Long-standing practices and Depression-inspired tactics harmed older, married, immigrant, Jewish, disabled, less socially attractive, and unconventional women. Male supervisors explicitly acknowledged structural discrimination, which was not illegal. Strident controversy and legislation prohibiting married women's employment cost jobs,[94] but age-discriminatory practices likely caused more unemployment.

Demands for youth and beauty undercut some women and rewarded others. "It's the young people's day," according to Laura G, formerly an assistant hotel housekeeper."[95] When employers discharged women they considered too old or slow, sacrificed their knowledge and capabilities, and favored "the flappers," as an unemployed sixty year-old white stenographer called them,[96] they cut costs and emphasized sexual desirability as a job qualification. A white widow, age fifty-eight, attributed loss of her cashier job at a Chicago North Shore Railroad station concession stand to a new boss who "hired a pretty young blonde with whom he could 'step out.'"[97] The manager at Baumgarth Printing, a seasonal business whose workforce expanded and contracted, articulated preference for youth: "If the girls don't have a lot of sense it doesn't matter as long as they are young and lively. We usually hire with a rush and take what is in line. [We] put on eight yesterday, but if selection had been possible, [I] doubt if one of them would have been hired. They won't last long."[98]

How old was too old? Employers preferred clerical workers and waitresses in their twenties; in other occupations, thirty-five or forty was the typical cutoff. Mary P, seeking work after being widowed, reported that it was "hard for a person past forty to find anything. [She] had friends at Singer's or [she] would not have got in there."[99] In the South Bend sample, no female industrial workers over fifty remained employed in 1932. Edith C, age forty-four, white, formerly a waitress at expensive Chicago restaurants, searched for work in vain. She "was always told her age was against her. At Thompson's she was told that it was useless to apply unless she was under twenty-one. However, she had 'very good' references and felt these might count for something so [she] insisted upon an interview with [the] employment manager. He was very ugly, telling her that the firm positively will not hire over twenty-one and eventually telling her to take her references and get out."[100]

Tillie H, a white woman, traced the loss of her job as a maid and server in "the help's hall" at St. Luke's Hospital in Chicago to a younger boss. When business fell off, with a single day's notice, on Christmas 1930 the hospital "laid off all the older women and kept the young girls." Tillie believed the "new, young housekeeper did not want somebody 'older than herself' working under her." She proudly related that she worked under four previous housekeepers and "pleased them all." Tillie, age forty-nine, answered ads and "walk[ed] and walk[ed] putting my application in everywhere," but "they all say I'm too old." Seven years later, despite her interviewer's opinion that "she does not look to be over forty-five or fifty," the Boston Store announced, "We couldn't have a woman your age" when Tillie answered an ad for kitchen help for a one-day special event.[101]

Domestic workers related similar stories. "If you are past thirty-five years you are too old. . . . They have the high school girls working and the women can't get nothing good," wrote Louise Booth, a "colored maid" from New Rochelle, New York.[102] A Birmingham, Michigan domestic observed, "The homes that used to Employ wemon as day workers will not employ them any more because their employing young girls for a mean nothing."[103] In Rhinelander, Wisconsin, "young girls (kids, high school graduates and what have you?) between the ages of fourteen and thirty, [are] doing heavy housework, and I mean by that, complete charge of the household, working twelve and fourteen hours daily."[104] In Grand Rapids, Michigan, "Many of these workers are not much more than mere children, recruited from orphan homes and other institutions."[105] Even laundresses lost customers more rapidly the older they were. The ubiquity of age discrimination is striking.

Older women indignantly cited their skills, experience, and accomplishments. Julia B, age sixty-four, a Canadian, worked thirty years on cafeteria steam tables but was "too old to get on civil service for regular work." Julia "feels that she is faster and a better worker than many younger than herself."[106] Rebecca C earned $30 weekly as a caterer in 1930. In 1933 the fifty-eight year-old white widow said, "They want young people for cateresses these days. They don't realize how much more capable older people are. I know foods from A to Z."[107] Applicants to Philadelphia's Service Committee for Business and Professional Women were disproportionately unemployed older clerical workers who had commanded high salaries.

Despite the spurious assertion that married women displaced men, the movement to ban their employment won many adherents. National, state, and local legislation and some employers explicitly discriminated against married women.[108] The dispute focused on women in high-paying professional and managerial jobs, less than 3% of the female labor force. The majority of employed wives (55.9%) worked in industry and service, and almost half of Black domestic workers were married.[109] Clerical jobs employed the smallest proportion of wives; large offices usually had "the most definite and drastic policies barring married women" and more firms banned them as the Depression deepened.[110] Wilson and Ball Band explicitly laid off married clerical workers.[111] Manufacturers less frequently discriminated against married operatives, but Ball Band and Singer laid them off. Ostensibly employers let married women go in the interests of fairness, that is, beliefs about the appropriate gender of breadwinners. Alice Kessler-Harris has argued that the working-class concept of providers was not singularly male; employers reinforced their own—not their employees'—values.[112]

Nationwide, managers of clerical workers acknowledged anti-Semitic hiring policies to government investigators with such statements as "very few Jews," "much prefer white Gentiles," and "no one who appears different is hired." The Philadelphia Electric Company answered a question about discrimination, "None as far as the company is concerned, but employees refuse to work with colored people in the clerical field." Jews were hired, but not "too many" Jews could work in any department: "We try to keep a balance."[113]

Employers requiring youthfulness expected a sexually appealing, feminine appearance: white skin, a slender body, a socially defined pretty face, clear complexion, stylish hairdo, makeup, and clothing.[114] A 1935 Women's Trade Union League investigation concluded, "The standards of the daily inspection" at restaurant chains and hotels "are such that home-done manicures and waves will not pass."[115] Josephine S, a white woman, age twenty, found a waitress job after a year and a half of unemployment. "I didn't have anything to wear—no decent pair of stockings, my shoes were all run over. I knew I looked awful but I tried to do my best. [I] thought if I'd work a few days I could get some clothes and look better."[116] Dime store lipsticks cost $.34, beauty shop haircuts ranged from $.25 to $.50, and permanents were $3. Tailored wool suits ran $6.48 to $9.98, shoes appropriate for the office started at $1.49, and winter coats sold for $6.98 and up.[117] A business girl needed stockings, a hat, underwear, and accessories. Few unemployed women could afford these accouterments of femininity. If a woman's body, face, or demeanor did not fit the prescribed mold, purchasing commodities was insufficient. Pimples, deafness, and disability interfered with reemployment of experienced workers.[118] Bertha B earned good wages for three years as a comptometer operator. Asked for a reference, her former employer noted that she was lame. Bertha, twenty-four, white, said her clubfoot did not interfere with her work and was not very noticeable. She was looking for "housework, or anything," "enough to earn a little money to keep up my appearance so I can get an office job."[119] Failure to conform to social standards jeopardized employment, and likely some lesbians suffered joblessness when employers selectively weeded their workforces.[120]

Social demands structured women's employment before, during, and after the Depression. The more desirable the job, the more narrowly employers defined acceptable personal characteristics of workers. Managers and workers alike candidly acknowledged that racism, marital status, ageism, and anti-Semitism affected hiring and dismissal.

Depression-Proof Jobs and Workers Who Quit

No line of work was untouched by crisis, yet expanding occupations sustained growth, and some workers continued to make choices. Recall Bessie (in chapter 1), whose sisters, Mary and Emma, remained employed full-time in 1932 as clerical workers.[121] Anna A (introduction) began work at a dental practice in 1924 at seventeen. Married in 1930, she kept working, and her wages were cut; by 1940 she was promoted to secretary-treasurer of United Dentists.[122] Studebaker honored its chief telephone operator, Vera Ammons, for twenty years of service in 1937.[123] Mary, Emma, Anna, and Vera demonstrate that some clerical positions endured and some white women worked steadily.

The beauty business advertised itself as Depression-proof and beauticians experienced less joblessness than most women. Catherine S, a white woman, earned $22.50 a week at Lady Fair Beauty Salon in 1929; she continued full-time three years later, at $18 weekly.[124] In Chicago in 1931, 12.8% of white beauticians and 26.6% of Black beauticians were out of work, markedly lower rates of unemployment than other service jobs.[125] Considering that many Black women plied the hair trade informally in their kitchens or customers' homes, continuing formal employment testifies to Black women's sacrifice of other needs to maintain appearances.[126]

Comparing joblessness in laundries and beauty shops (commercial establishments primarily serving female patrons) suggests that women more frequently undertook heavier physical labor than they forfeited attractiveness.[127] Beauticians were far less likely to be unemployed than laundry operatives. Especially for younger women, a stylish hairdo was a priority, and commercialization of hair care and beauty products increased.[128] Secular trends affected both businesses.

Cheaper, technically improved, electric wringer washing machines reduced patronage of commercial laundries, and regulation accompanied the growth of beauty culture. State licensing laws undercut beauticians, as illustrated by Gertrude B, a Black woman born in 1892, who migrated to Chicago as a young adult. She paid $225 to a beauty college for a thousand-hour night course, the minimum required for licensing under Illinois law passed in the early 1930s.

> Gertrude was all set to take the exam when the school told her she would have to pay $50 additional for permanent wave course. The man who had written receipt originally had died and since he had not specified on receipt what was to be given in return, she could not prove that she had paid for the permanent wave lessons (which she had received incidentally). Since that time . . . she has never been able to get $50 together to finish. . . . She has renewed apprentice license each year. Now she learns that law is changed so that State now requires eighth grade diploma and she will be unable to renew license ever again. [She] is extremely disappointed because it means that she will 'never' be allowed to do work again.

Gertrude's fourth grade education thwarted her plans to quit working as an apartment hotel maid, although she likely continued to ply her trade informally.[129]

Even during hard times, women quit jobs they considered impossible. Sexual harassment exacted too high a price. Along with production workers, Cecyle J, an office employee at Ball Band, was laid off annually from April through summer and rehired every fall. In 1929 "the boss would not take her because she would not step out with him." Unemployed eleven months, she found factory work at Bendix-Stromberg. Her younger sister, Mary, also a Ball Band office worker, quit the month that Cecyle was hired, as "Mother said too unhealthy." It is unclear if the sisters had the same boss, but apparently their mother timed Mary's departure with Cecyle's hiring to ensure continuous income. Their bricklayer father was out of work.[130] Lucille D answered the telephone at a Cleveland granite company and quit in less than a month because "employer got too familiar, had to leave." Nineteen, and of Bohemian German ancestry, Lucille could not have made this decision lightly, because she and a sister working part-time supported a family of seven.[131] In every line of work women walked out because of sexual harassment. Others likely withstood pressure or capitulated because they could not afford to quit.

The Depression did not always coerce submission to indignities. Blanche L quit Ball Band after nine years of sporadic employment. They were "making nervous wrecks of the women," and she objected to "such low pay and such hard work." Her husband taunted her that soon she would be "paying the company to work like a slave for them." A foreman at a unionized job, he regularly brought home $36 weekly in 1932, one of the highest wages in the sample.[132] Roxy L, a

Black Chicago laundry worker, "quit because her press, which she liked to work on, was given to another girl. She was assigned to a press that didn't operate easily. [She] got mad and quit" in 1930.[133] Retta K, an attendant at the Warrensville Institution, assigned to night duty every third month, left after a year because she "couldn't stand" night hours.[134] Sexual harassment, desire for higher wages, better working conditions, more interesting work, or a job that better fit women's circumstances motivated quitting before and during the Depression. Women also left the labor force because of pregnancy, motherhood, sickness, or the necessity to nurse an ill or dying family member.

"It's Terrible at the Factory, Each One Fighting for More Work."

Almeda R, a Studebaker machinist, assessed intensified workplace competition and added that workers were "so disappointed because they are let out early.[135] The power of bosses was substantial; even businesses which had personnel departments, and many did not, gave authority to supervisors.[136] Undisguised favoritism filtered many bosses' decisions. The head of Studebaker's Cooperative Department explained that company policy was to "spread employment among a few thousand key people for a few days per week whenever possible."[137] Foremen selected key people and penalized and fired workers. One operative judged that they "ruled by partiality as well by as paternalism, and rough indeed was the path of one who dared cross them."[138] Complaints about favoritism were legion.[139] Supervisors had a stock answer: "If you don't like it, there are a hundred men outside the employment office ready to take your job."[140]

Unfettered power fostered workers' vulnerability and rewarded manipulation. Agnes V (introduction) "was told to get her time" (punch her time card out) in 1929 when she disagreed with a new woman supervisor at Singer. She believed her boss wanted to get rid of her so that she could "put her friends on." Agnes appealed to a Polish boss for work on his crew at Bendix, but he turned her down. She attributed this to ethnic loyalties (she was Hungarian) and economic self-interest, because he transported women in his truck for $.25 per day. She made no further efforts at Bendix because "the employment department hires the ones asked for by the boss."[141]

Workers relied on individual, unsanctioned tactics. Studebaker operatives who lived in the country and brought chickens, eggs, or freshly slaughtered meat to a foremen "would get the steadier, easier jobs, because the foreman said, 'I'm not going to bite the hand that feeds me.'"[142] Esther B, a Hungarian immigrant, had worked at Wilson since 1919. Two of her daughters had also worked there, left, and returned. Helen quit in 1929 because she was not making enough money, but she earned less at Baumgarth Printing and Venus Brassiere, so she returned. Martha, laid off in 1930, went to Baumgarth and by 1931 returned to Wilson. In September 1932, in four weeks Helen earned $36 and Martha $58, compared to their mother's $10. Esther's continued employment and the company's rehiring of her daughters, when many workers remained unemployed, suggests that influence helped them, especially considering practices of dismissing married women and keeping a single member per family employed.[143] Neither Oliver, nor Studebaker, nor Wilson stratified workforces ethnically, but supervisors tended to be native born, not coethnics of the other workers.

Insufficient work and bosses' power increased dissension and competition and sparked self-protective evasions and deceptions. Women lied about their marital status and misrepresented how many family members were working. In the anonymity of a metropolis these maneuvers might be successful, but in South Bend coworkers frequently knew each other's situations. Domestic workers shaped tactics to correspond to the personalities of housewife-employers.[144] Workplace insecurity heightened anxieties; increased individual, informal, and manipulative tactics; tested women's stoicism; and motivated collective strategies.

Rarely could workers affect employment policies, but department stores were exceptional. Work culture enabled saleswomen to "[agree] among themselves to ask for and accept furloughs." Two-thirds of forty-six department stores in five states developed policies for spreading out work: rotating layoffs of one or more days per week, extended layoffs, short-time, and abolition of paid vacations. These managerial tactics stemmed partly from workers' collective initiative to "insure the permanency of their own jobs." Saleswomen consciously developed strategies that avoided complete unemployment for some at the cost of cuts for many.[145] Elsewhere, collective strategies to spread out work were infrequent.

Many workers, especially those with a long history at a single factory, "waited to be called back in." Accustomed to fluctuations, they hoped the downturn was temporary. Laid off after six years, Vera V believed that "Singer's would send for her when business picked up."[146] Studebaker and Oliver eventually called back many men, who spent a lifetime in their plants. Expecting to be called back might appear passive, but in South Bend the majority of working-class men labored at a few large factories and rarely found other jobs. High turnover always characterized garment manufacturing because of seasonality, unsatisfactory conditions, and low wages. When Venus Brassiere or Wilson needed help, they called back old workers and hired new ones. Some businesses never reopened. Dorothy M, a young, white, clerical worker laid off by a Chicago insurance company in 1931, reported, "When I started there were 250 of us. When I left there were only forty." In the winter of 1933 she "went back there to see if they needed anybody lately and the building was empty."[147]

Necessity motivated remaining in jobs, regardless of difficulties. "One did not dare give up a job, if fortunate enough to have one, whatever it might be," explained Vera N. Since 1913, when she was twenty-nine, this Hungarian immigrant had labored in the Oliver Hotel kitchen, seven days a week, 7:00 a.m. to 4:00 p.m., with a half day off every other Sunday. Her wages dropped from $15 to $12. In 1931, the hotel hired her nineteen year-old daughter as cafeteria cashier and counter girl. Despite a grueling schedule, Vera benefited from full-time employment, work for her eldest daughter, and meals for both. Family responsibilities dictated her perseverance. Her second husband moved in and out, and she supported their three young children.[148] Betty B, a German American, age thirty-five, operated a mangle at the Lake City Laundry, an unsanitary establishment that regularly cheated employees by stopping the time clock. She contracted a bad case of ringworm there, forcing her off her feet, but she expected to return when she was well. With a fifth grade education and a gap of several years out of the labor force while married, "she has no idea where she could obtain any other work."[149] Waiting to be called back in and not daring to give up a job counter stories of quitting. How many possibilities a woman believed she had determined her actions. Blanche's husband could support them; Vera's disappearing, reappearing husband was unreliable. Fabled stories of unionization have overshadowed informal, individual schemes to maintain employment.

Because the capitalist economy assigned workers to jobs it deemed appropriate for their gender, race, age, and—for women—marital status, institutional racism and sexism determined patterns of joblessness. White women lost jobs least rapidly, least dramatically; some of their jobs were structurally less susceptible to economic crisis. Neither white men nor white women faced the depth of joblessness of Black workers of both genders, concentrated in the most vulnerable occupations. Sex segregation shielded some white women, but not Black women. White women shared the pain of fathers, husbands, brothers, sons, sweethearts, and neighbors whose employment was precarious or vanished. Black women shared the pain and the experience of Black men.

It is difficult to describe white women marking dirty laundry or slinging hash at a dime store lunch counter as privileged. Compared to white male assembly workers, they more frequently remained employed. Nowhere were working-class women concentrated in such large numbers as men were in auto and steel. Because more numerous, more varied workplaces employed women, they more easily moved from job to job, from unemployment to employment. Location of a job, the size of an employer's workforce, seasonal rhythm of hiring and layoffs, and the increasing number and diversity of applicants all affected employment.

African Americans bore a greater brunt of the Depression than did Euro-Americans. At the bottom of both gender-defined labor markets, they suffered the harshest, most widespread, most rapid unemployment and underemployment. In January 1931 at least 40% of Black workers, male and female, were jobless in Chicago, Cleveland, and Philadelphia. In the sectors employing the largest proportion of Black men (manufacturing) and women (service), substantial majorities were out of work.[150] Structural location and racist prejudices and policies targeted Black workers first. White supremacy created common Depression experiences for working-class African Americans, regardless of gender.

Despite loss of employment and the necessity for making do, working-class women continuously attempted to make choices. Chapter 3 illustrates the breadth of employment tactics and highlights common strategies. Because reemployment usually meant backing down the ladder of job desirability, the results of the same ingenuity and perseverance diverged dramatically.

3

Employment Strategies
and Their Consequences

•••••••••••••••••••••

Whether recently unemployed, newly entering the job market, or long out of the labor force, working-class women practiced a seemingly endless array of tactics to find work. With the exception of a single racially specific approach, they followed similar strategies. This chapter analyzes their methods of hunting for work, reemployment tactics, makeshift jobs, and geographic mobility. Similar strategies produced dissimilar results. Backing down the ladder of occupational desirability, women took jobs they would not have previously considered, with worse conditions, wages, and hours. White women took jobs that Black women had previously held, while racism continuously disqualified Black women from so-called white jobs. Pushed down the ladder, women on the bottom rungs lost their foothold, then their grasp, and fell off.

The Search for Employment: "No Money to Pay for a Job"

As the number of job seekers proliferated, they honed job-finding skills and dreamed up new strategies for repeated searches. They scoured newspaper want ads; made the rounds of factories, offices, stores, laundries, hospitals, and other businesses, even if no openings were advertised; called on informal networks; advertised their availability in newspapers and on the street; and patronized employment agencies. Effort, perseverance, and ingenuity sometimes bore fruit, but often they "answered ads and wore out all [their] shoes following clues which led nowhere."[1] Young women checked in with high schools and business schools, which sometimes placed graduates in jobs. Margaret M, a white Philadelphian born in in 1879, typically secured practical nursing positions through newspaper ads. Her high pre-Depression wages ($25 weekly, plus room and board) attested to her skills and the class of clients who hired her. By 1933 Margaret found that laudatory references were not worth the paper on which they were written: "Some days [she] answered six or seven ads without a single reply."[2]

Informal contacts and word of mouth advised women about possible openings. When Helen B, a young white woman, lost her clerical job in 1931, a friend got her a position as a cashier at Wanamaker's, a Philadelphia department store. Their friendship developed at a basketball club that may have been sponsored by the store.[3] In South Bend family members frequently worked for the same corporation, and employees tried to convince bosses to hire relatives and friends. A widow "had friends at Singer's or [she] would not have got in there."[4] Domestics and their employers recommended workers to other housewife-employers, so that a day worker might clean for several women in the same circle.

The Depression limited the efficacy of informal and familial connections. Elizabeth H, a seventy-one-year-old Black Philadelphia laundress, "used to get recommendations from one to another. [I] never had to advertise before."[5] Martha C and Nettie S got jobs at Singer in 1926, where their older sister, Helen S, had worked since 1923. Laid off in 1930, Helen and Nettie found jobs at the Bendix Corporation, where their father had formerly worked, and Singer called back Martha. Neither Elfreda nor Gertrude, younger siblings, found work at either factory.[6] Laura G, a Canadian born in 1877, had worked her way up to assistant housekeeper at Chicago's Congress Hotel, but she was "stumped" and "most disheartened because when she returned to all the large loop hotels in which she worked and in which she knew all the big men, she found them all dead or left, so that she has no one anymore 'who knows me (see chapter 2).'"[7]

As formal applications and informal networks proved fruitless, women patronized the proliferating employment agencies. States, municipalities, and social service organizations sponsored free employment bureaus; profit-making businesses charged fees. Anne S, twenty-eight, single, a Black North Carolinian, went to the Philadelphia state employment office daily in 1933, and Mary S, a forty-year-old Lithuanian immigrant widow, "called again and again."[8] Some women considered free bureaus a waste of time because they overwhelmingly placed women in domestic jobs at low wages. According to an Oakland, California woman, "All they [the Free Employment Agency] have to offer us is 'Cheap Housework' as they call it."[9] A white widow called the State Free Employment Bureau in Dayton, Ohio, to inquire if houseworkers were covered by the National Recovery Administration (NRA) policies. The answer was no. "I said, how much do you ask the Employer to pay household help now and of course, she thought I was an Employer, not a worker and her answer was, 'Oh! anything.'"[10] The white president of the Household Workers Welfare Association of Cleveland wrote, "Our State City Employment and our YWCA that operates a Friendly Service

Bureau supported by our Welfare Federation are sending girls out for $5 per week and telling them if they get three and four to take it."[11]

The Friendly Service Bureau (FSB) primarily placed women in housework, though employers seeking waitresses, clerical workers, sample distributors, and envelope addressers also contacted it. Jobs were supposed to be full-time, but many housewives hired help temporarily to get their houses in order, to assist with holiday entertaining, or found they could not afford the expense. The FSB served young, white, gentile women, often immigrants and daughters of immigrants. It referred Black women to the Negro Welfare Association or the Phillis Wheatley Association (PWA), and it excluded Jewish applicants by requiring a signed pledge professing Christianity.[12]

The YWCA developed a reputation for offering undesirable jobs. Often housewife-employers were newly able to afford help. One wanted to hire a "girl young enough to get along with six children, fourteen months to fifteen years," who would care for her eight-room house, wash and iron, and assist in her husband's dental office for $3 a week plus meals.[13] As Martha E, thirty-two, a widow, and former clerical worker, reported, "None of the housework jobs she was sent on were what they were represented to be. 'They tell the Y one thing and they tell us another. The housework jobs gotten through the Y are the hardest in town. They know the girls there need work, and so impose on them.'" She described eight jobs: "I was all wrong there, I couldn't do enough to please them, more work than I could do . . . Danger of infection there—left, . . . Too dirty; would be afraid of the people. Didn't even take hat off here, left at once." A declassed clerical worker may have been finicky, but experienced houseworkers echoed the same themes.[14] Despite the Y's reputation, one-fifth of those in my Cleveland sample checked in repeatedly; sometimes persistence paid off. Mae M, a French immigrant in her early thirties, visited the FSB fifty-one times in two years, received thirteen referrals, and worked briefly in several homes.[15] More than half the sample received no referrals and a single referral was most common.

YWCA staff scrutinized each applicant's employment record, references, appearance, and personality. Their judgments reflected reigning prejudices. A staff member assessed a thirty-six-year-old who emigrated from Poland in 1917 as "quite foreign, will be hard to place." Judging from Mary S's comments, her English skills were more than adequate. She swallowed her pride and returned to the Y twenty times in six months.[16] Although a previous employer declared eighteen-year-old Mary C "acceptable, well satisfied, well liked, capable, honest," the FSB "refused to send girl on further placements until pimply condition of skin is corrected." Her family relied on her, the second oldest of eight children whose Croatian father died the preceding year, but acne mattered more to the FSB.[17] When placements did not work out, the Y made inquiries. The record of an eighteen-year-old Polish American who quit after one week noted, "Girl says not enough food. Had to sleep in cold attic. Employer says girl contrary, etc."[18]

The Y at least guaranteed employment for its staff with painstaking investigation of applicants.

Hundreds of women swamped Cleveland's Board of Education, City-State Employment Bureau, PWA and YWCA monthly. The Y and PWA recruited young single women to clubs and classes. At the PWA's Unemployed Sewing Club, Black women received instruction, made over old clothes for themselves, and constructed items for the PWA such as dish towels. They sang as they worked and were served a "light lunch" of soup "or the like." It was "a way of keeping their hands and minds occupied—of building up their morale with a little warm food, pleasant society and friendly advice."[19] Morale did not pay rent, facilitate self-support, or aid family finances.

The crush of women thronging through the PWA's doors overwhelmed it. In 1929, one to two hundred women applied monthly, and it placed one-half to two-thirds of them. In January 1932, 692 job seekers showed up; less than one-tenth received placements. Weekly wages declined steadily, from between $5 and $8 in March 1931 to between $2.50 and $4 in the fall of 1932, as did daywork wages. In 1931 a white board member "questioned the wisdom of our employment office charging $.40 an hour for help. . . . If the employer did not agree to pay the $.40 Miss Menifee [a PWA employee] would try to supply them for less." The PWA consulted the City-State Employment Office, whose fee was $.35 an hour plus carfare. By March, 1934, [Miss Menifee] "tries to get $2 per day for day workers, but can do so with only a few; therefore she had to go back to $1.50."[20] The PWA channeled its energies into training, which its Black founder, Jane Edna Hunter, and elite white board members believed would enable women to secure permanent positions as live-in servants.[21] Trustees made it their priority to prepare a few women for standards expected by the wealthy. By the late 1930s, 107 women had received training, while four hundred to seven hundred women applied to the employment office monthly.[22]

When women registered with profit-making agencies, they expected better jobs because they paid for the service. They appreciated that an employer who hired through a private agency "could not judge the woman's finances."[23] They criticized agencies for the same reasons they found free bureaus lacking, as well as for exploitation unique to private business. Helen B, an experienced white clerical worker, reported, "You pay a dollar registration fee and then when they get you a job it costs the first week's salary. They won't even let you pay it in installments the way they used to." Helen secured two months of clerical work at $16 weekly through the Chicago Business Women's Exchange, which charged reasonable fees: $2 registration and $5 per job, regardless of salary.[24] An experienced Cleveland clerical worker got a temporary job in 1933 for $15 weekly, paying 10% of her earnings for three months, which totaled $19.50.[25] Women patronized fee-charging agencies shortly after they lost a job, if other household members remained employed, or if they had savings. Fees were usually payable in advance.

Pettie W, thirty-nine, and a Black Georgian, never found work at free bureaus in Philadelphia. Forty private agencies specialized in Negro help, primarily in female domestic work.[26] In 1932 she "used to go and stand at [the] employment office before 7:30" daily and she got a $6-a-week domestic job for a $2 fee.[27]

Agencies practiced the same discrimination as employers. Betty B, white, thirty-four, a clerical worker, kept in touch with many agencies. She noted, "The younger girl gets first chance at the job. The older girl doesn't get a chance. Even in employment agencies it is impossible to convince the interviewers that an older girl who has worked for $35 or $40 a week won't work for less."[28] Some employers and agencies colluded for maximum benefit. Velma T, thirty, white, a public stenographer and notary public at major Chicago hotels, "gave up" on employment agencies: "[I] paid $2 registration fee at one place and $1 fee at several places. First they want you to pay the fee. After that you don't get any calls. One place sent me to a hotel in the suburbs. . . . They send you out to some impossible place. At least it makes it look as tho they are trying. Later I heard that that agency is working with this hotel and that the manager keeps a girl a couple weeks and then lets her go and then he and the agency split on the fees."[29] Madeline M, a Black clerical worker, "quit going to employment agencies. You can't get a job unless you have cash. [I] had a chance to get a job there yesterday for $35 a month (maid) if I could pay $10. But they only keep you a couple weeks. The employer and the agency work together."[30]

Women also devised other schemes. Unemployed clerical workers attended typing classes and practiced at YWCAs to keep up their speed.[31] Minnie M, sixty-two, an Irish immigrant, wanted to acquire a skill after she was widowed; she paid $27 to learn power machine operation at a Philadelphia factory. It was a scam; the promised job did not materialize.[32] Mary S, a single thirty-four-year-old Bohemian immigrant, had earned $40 weekly as bookkeeper and accountant for a mail order house. She registered with pay agencies, the Illinois Free Employment Bureau, and the Jewish Employment Bureau. She "couldn't pass for a Jew," but they "didn't have any job, so [it] didn't hurt."[33] Some women shunned haughty attitudes of bureaucrats; others resigned themselves to mistreatment; some applied to relief agencies for "made work"; and many continued their daily rounds, even with little success.

Black women advertised their availability for domestic work by standing on street corners in white, middle-class neighborhoods, a racially unique method for obtaining work. In Philadelphia in 1933 a researcher wrote that "numbers of colored women go and stand on the busy corners in a semi-prosperous Jewish section and wait for housewives to come and pick them out and give a few hours of work. These women in most cases used to hire women by the day but now they take them only for a few hours and pay 10 and 15 cents an hour. Sometimes according to one of my women, she has stood all day without an offer and sometimes was offered a quarter for the morning or afternoon. This same woman termed it the worst kind of slavery."[34] In Chicago in 1936, Mary D, age forty-five, "went out along 16th Street near Kedzie and the Jewish women would call her in for half day's work. It was 'ketch as ketch come.' . . . Usually it is washing windows, scrubbing, or heavy cleaning, at which she earns $1.00 or $1.25 a day. She has done ironing for as little as $.50."[35] In the Bronx and Brooklyn, at more than twenty-five street corners near subway stations, "many housewives who had never been able to have help before, considered it an opportunity to get a maid for sometimes as little as ten cents an hour."[36] One woman wrote, "I used to stand around or sit on cracker boxes with other women waiting for someone to come along and offer me a job. Most of the women up there expected you to work for twenty-five cents anyhow. I was even offered ten cents an hour for general housework! And they worked you just like dogs for that money."[37]

New York Black activists excoriated "standing in Jewtown," which they labeled "slave markets," but some job-seeking women preferred to "take to the streets." They endured myriad forms of mistreatment: the selling of their labor reminiscent of the auction blocks of the Old South; low wages; tricks by housewife-employers to pay less than the agreed-upon amount; and sexual exploitation by men. Yet this strategy had advantages. A woman got paid daily, kept all her wages, was not responsible to an agency, and did not have to furnish references or prove experience. She could bargain over terms of work and payment, quit at any time, and work as many jobs as she could accept. Her negotiating skills partly determined her pay and how hard she had to work. Such conditions favored younger, robust women. Workers socialized newcomers not to undercut one another by working for less than $.25 an hour. Not all housewife-employers who hired from the streets were Jewish. Black churches attempted to find jobs for women, Jewish organizations tried to abolish the markets, domestic workers organized unions, and the city briefly experimented with a hiring hall in the Bronx. Only increased employment opportunities during World War II ended the slave markets.[38]

Advertising availability in print failed to bring the hoped-for responses. Gertrude D, white, age forty-nine, took out a newspaper ad: "[I] got only one answer for my $.81, and that was from a man who wanted a sweetheart instead of a maid. [He] said I was too old for his purposes. If my grandmother knew some of the things I've had to take looking for work, she'd crawl out of her grave!"[39] Velma T advertised "in all the papers. [I] didn't get a single answer for a typist. They don't want typists, they want a sweetheart. One answer wanted to know if I would pose in the nude. Several others said they wanted typists who would also be a sweetheart. I often wish I'd answered . . . and led them on and reported them. It's a fright what a girl is up against nowadays." Particularly energetic, Velma typed up small cards announcing her services as a public stenographer and notary public, distributed them in her neighborhood, and launched a campaign. "[She] secured names of all hotels bordering Lake Michigan from 3800 north to loop on south. [She] wrote to each (125 in all), describing her qualifications and asking for work, full or part time. One week later [she] started to make a personal visit to each hotel to which she had written. [She] had no carfare, so [she] visited a few each day. In spite of all [her] efforts, [she] received only one week's work in all."[40]

Looking for work demanded physical, mental, and emotional stamina. Women scrutinized their presentability. Dora M, age sixty-three and "a fine looking, tall, well-built, white-haired Scandinavian woman," was acutely conscious of her deteriorating appearance: "Your clothes get shabby, your shoes are gone, and you get so down and out no one will have you because they get the wrong impression."[41] Sears' cheapest stockings cost $.75 and bargain basement seconds were $.29, but women spent scarce cash to convey a businesslike appearance. Hemlines dropped considerably, necessitating new or remade clothes.[42] When Lucille P applied for work, "she finds it increasingly difficult as her appearance becomes more run-down the longer she is on relief. 'You have to look like a chorus girl to get a waitress job nowadays.' She is unable to keep her hair waved, 'nail polish costs money,' her old uniforms are becoming shabby, and she is 'absolutely' without stockings."[43]

Women weighed shoe leather against carfare (five to seven cents) and clothing against groceries. Helen F, thirty-five, a German immigrant divorcée, checked in with the Y thirty-three times in six months and "tried many places and spent much time and money answering ads and looking for jobs." When her daughter gave her $.50 because she needed stockings, Helen spent $.34 on carfare looking for work.[44] Dora M "saw an ad in the paper by a family who wanted a maid to go to the country with them. This was her type of work so she got up at 4 a.m. and left her place around 3000 North at 5 a.m., walking from there to the Loop [downtown Chicago] because she did not have carfare. She arrived at 9 a.m. and there were already twenty-five ahead of her." Dora lived in cheap places without a telephone. "People would say they liked her appearance and 'would consider her later and would call her' . . . [but] she never could give a telephone number."[45]

Job-seekers lied about their age, padded work histories, and altered their appearance. Married women posed as single; light-skinned Black women passed as white; Jewish women changed names, manner, or appearance to be perceived as gentiles.[46] Olive T, twenty-five, a clerical worker, "did not tell [her] employer she was married as [it was] easier to get work if they do not know."[47] Mary B, born in 1873, an experienced white cook who had earned high wages at resort hotels and in oil camps, disguised her age: "Her top hair is dark—the side grey. She has a long switch of two braids which she winds around her head to cover the grey—but says when applying for work—if asked—[she] does not lie about her age."[48]

Despite emotional depression, hunger, and physical debility, women picked themselves up, persisted in looking for work, and followed every lead. With the significant exception of slave markets, working-class women practiced similar job-finding strategies.[49] Structural racism ensured that white women were far more likely to find jobs; ageism favored younger women. Similar strategies did not assure similar results.

Re-employment Strategies

When a woman lost her job, she had to pick up the pieces, move beyond hurt and anger, and start over. She searched for work in which she had experience, especially if she had invested time, energy, and money in training. If she was unsuccessful or heard about other opportunities, she looked elsewhere. Lower wages, longer hours, harder work, more difficult conditions, part-time work, and worse exploitation typically characterized successive jobs. Replacement jobs often lasted briefly, so changing jobs became a way of life.

The fortunes of Betty B, who "always did bookkeeping and stenography," illustrate difficulties that even skilled white women faced. Betty's $30 weekly salary in 1930 testified to her competence. In 1933 this thirty-four-year-old widow disclosed that she had not "made enough to pay expenses the past two years." She

> "figures" she has had eighteen months since [she was] laid off [her] regular job in which she had no work at all. "[I] keep track of everything. For example, in September and October I made $8. August and July and June I didn't make a penny. May and April I made a few dollars, I don't believe over $8. March nothing. In January and February I had a little job supposed to pay me $15 a week. Some men were trying to organize a travel bureau. I worked the first two weeks for lunch and carfare money. Then two weeks at $15. Then the last ten days I didn't get anything. They couldn't make a go of it."[50]

In every occupation women told stories of intermittent employment and more demanding conditions. Lucille P spent twenty-two years as a waitress, beginning at age fourteen. She earned "good wages plus excellent tips and three of the finest meals ever eaten" at an Evanston, Illinois, tearoom for ten-hour days, six days a week, in 1936. "Believe me, we didn't have time to look sidewise." Waitresses "did everything": cleaned the kitchen, shelves, and birdcages; scrubbed floors; washed window shades and mirrors. When her husband deserted her, she quit, exhausted from working two jobs. Subsequently she found only single-meal, special occasion jobs. "Not fit to move" for two days, she alone served sixty-eight people at a hotel banquet, 5:00 p.m. to 3:00 a.m. for $1.70. "If any tips were left at the office, she did not receive them." An athletic club banquet likewise produced no tips, "not that class."[51]

Piece rates and industrial homework guaranteed low wages. Ruth D, a Black woman, age thirty-nine, plucked chickens in a Chicago poultry house, walking an hour and a half, working 8:00 to 10:00 a.m. daily, "the hours help was required," at a piece rate of $.035 per chicken in 1935. "Since she was new and slow [she] only earned $.50 or so a week. Some were able to pick fifteen to twenty chickens in this time—she could not!"[52] Eva A, a Black woman, sewed full-time at a dress factory, earning $3.50 a week at piece rates in 1932.[53] Amanda D, a former office manager for physicians, took homework in 1933. The work "consisted of hand-stringing steel buckles at home, and she was paid $.30 for two dozen buck-les. It took two days to do the first two dozen working constantly, so [she] refused to take any more."[54] NRA codes outlawed or regulated industrial home-work,[55] yet dozens of young white women hand-addressed envelopes for busi-nesses, a new type of homework at low piece rates.

Some white women sought part-time sales work. Annabelle S, an unemployed clerical worker, got a Christmas rush job at a department store in 1932, along with her roommate, and earned $2.25 daily for long hours at "very hard" work. "[I was] supposed to work until 9:30 but every nite I was there the bell didn't ring till 9:50." After eleven hours of work and a fourteen-hour day, she was "almost too tired to live when I'd get thru."[56] Many stores increased the proportion of temporary sales staff.[57] Such jobs did not offer long-term employment but prom-ised periodic call-backs, even if only for one-day sales.

Unemployed women from every line of work, those previously never employed, and those out of the labor force for years turned to working for private families with "long hours of unending toil."[58] Gender alone qualified women, so intense competition erupted. Women did not discard former standards, but they could not be as picky. An unemployed clerical worker remarked that she would take "housework or anything."[59] Anna T, a fifty-year-old Chicago widow with expe-rience in a hotel linen room and as a domestic, disclosed, "[I] don't hesitate to do anything. [I] would rather wash or scrub or do anything, to have a job. [I] can help with the sick, I don't hesitate. I don't be snobby about the hours. I'd work and give perfect satisfaction if I could get the work."[60] Women who previously spurned jobs with low status, low wages, or difficult conditions, or because of the race of other workers, took those jobs. The Cleveland Y placed women in domestic jobs almost exclusively, yet three-fifths of 1933 applicants had previously worked in other occupations.[61]

Women sometimes quit the worst jobs, kept their ears open, and changed jobs if they heard that another employer was paying slightly higher wages or offering a few more hours. They attempted to make choices, tapped multiple strate-gies, and often felt fortunate to make do with any job. Nydia K, age fifty-seven, operated a candy stand at an amusement park with her husband every summer. During colder months she worked as a domestic and practical nurse. Much older than women targeted by the Y, she checked in at the FSB forty-eight times during winter and spring, 1932 and received three referrals, two of which mate-rialized as housework jobs at which she worked three months each.[62]

Depression Makeshifts

When they could not find jobs or believed other opportunities were more promising, working-class women improvised as independent entrepreneurs, canvassers (door to door saleswomen), with "made work," and in livelihoods in the underground economy. These stopgaps usually supported them briefly and partially, but occasionally enabled a woman to earn a living over a longer period. Women who formerly might have disdained these strategies utilized them during a crisis.

Small-scale entrepreneurial activities, taking in boarders or roomers, and cooking and sewing for cash relied on women's capabilities and material resources, and did not require labor force experience nor subject them to employers' demands. A woman who possessed furniture and housewifely skills could take lodgers, regardless of whether she rented or owned or whether she lived in an apartment or single-family dwelling. In metropolises, sizable populations of unattached individuals created a market, and immigrants and migrants survived by living with people from homelands or home states.[63] Louise C, a Black Chicagoan, kept a rooming house from 1920 to 1935, but as her roomers lost jobs, failed to pay rent, and departed, she moved from a fourteen-room house to a six-room dwelling and sold most of her furniture. Evicted from the second dwelling, her unpaid bills prevented her from getting gas or electric service in a two-room kitchenette.[64] Unemployed tenants impeded success, but after the New Deal created jobs and made cash relief payments, taking in lodgers again became a viable means of support.

In overcrowded, segregated, northern cities, Black women far more frequently took boarders and roomers than white women. The virtual end of immigration, the fact that most immigrants married, and single women's preference to live on their own or with peers (rather than under the sometimes prying eyes of a landlady) contributed to the waning of the practice among white women. In the four cities one-tenth of immigrant households included roomers, compared to one-third of Black households in metropolises.[65] Racially linked rooming and boarding patterns persisted. In 1940, one-third of Black Chicagoans, contrasted with one-tenth of white residents, were lodgers or relatives.[66] Lottie G ran a rooming house from 1912 to 1930, but as unemployment devastated the Black community, she turned to sewing. After she received relief in 1934, this Chicago native rented a five-room flat for $37.50 monthly and charged two roomers $13 each. Despite severe arthritis, she kept the flat "immaculate" and enjoyed a large, "light, airy, quiet" apartment with modern conveniences, rather than a one-room kitchenette, like most African American relief clients had.[67]

Keeping roomers was not an easy way to earn a living. Cora J ran two rooming houses while working as a secretary in a real estate firm, 1925–1932. She suffered a nervous breakdown, was institutionalized for six months, and lost her furniture, unable to keep up storage payments. When she left the hospital, she rented a furnished building from a landlady who evicted prior tenants and kept their furniture. Cora was "afraid to rent at the door" in a "bad neighborhood." The landlady did not maintain the building, and Cora fell on loose steps and broke her arm in 1936. While she was hospitalized, the house collapsed into further disrepair, tenants left, and only relief clients remained. The landlady died, her sister had the gas and electricity shut off the day before Christmas, and Cora lost her livelihood.[68]

Finding solvent tenants was a landlady's most urgent task. If they could not pay, she had to decide whether to evict them and whether to utilize the force of law to do so. Friendship might override financial considerations, but landladies needed cash for rent, mortgage, taxes, and utilities. Frances B, forty-three, a divorced white woman and unemployed factory worker and day worker, borrowed money from her sole roomer to pay property taxes and let the roomer "take it out in rent," temporarily ensuring she kept her home.[69] Women who sold furniture to make daily expenses undermined a future livelihood. Like many schemes, taking lodgers worked for a while but was not continuously reliable.

Early in the decade a few South Bend families opened small grocery stores, hoping self-employment would protect them. Hazel Z and her brother-in-law, Herbert L, both employees at Ball Band Shoes, considered buying a store because "work had been poor." When Hazel was laid off in 1932, she bought stock and set up the business so that Herbert lost no time between quitting Ball Band and opening the store. Hazel, her sister Eva, Herbert, and the couple's child moved into living quarters above the store. They invested their savings, cut expenses to the bone, and "use[d] what we don't sell." After six months, Hazel reported, "[I] don't know earnings. [We] just take out enough for bare existence–all of the other goes back into the store to enlarge the stock." In 1940 the grocery remained in business.[70] A Hungarian couple with the same idea found it "very hard to do a cash business, but they got along better than the last few years working at Studebaker."[71] Anna T, a Black cook and day worker, opened a delicatessen in Chicago with savings and her husband's life insurance; it folded in 1932.[72] Such ventures were more common before bank failures decimated savings and people cashed in insurance policies.

More frequently women produced foodstuffs, sewed garments, and straightened hair. An unemployed, middle-aged factory operative baked ten loaves of bread daily for regular customers, and another South Bend white woman charged $.25 apiece to make housedresses.[73] A Chicago Black woman sewed work caps at $.10 for friends employed at a date factory.[74] A sixty-year-old white former stenographer made and sold hats and "little fancy sewed things."[75] An African American took boarders to pay rent and straightened hair to buy groceries.[76] These endeavors enabled women to meet a few urgent needs but did not support them.

Selling door-to-door attracted more than a hundred women in the samples, via classified ads, the Illinois Employment Service, and the YWCA. Almost any white woman might get work; pay seemed to depend upon initiative, and saleswomen had some control. Companies supplied products—baking powder, coffee, cleanser, toiletries, beauty preparations, washcloths, shoe polish, soap, moth repellant, birds, cards, books, magazine subscriptions, hosiery, and clothing—and determined the commission. Catherine R, a white Clevelander, age thirty-nine, quit after three days soliciting orders for a radio company. She was supposed to receive $.25 for each appointment but she "didn't get a customer. [She] walked from 178th to 105th Street." Out of the labor force ten years, and caring for her invalid mother, Catherine's circumstances explain the popularity of canvassing.[77] Annabelle S, the Christmas saleswoman, sold Chicago World's Fair auto plates, for $.08 commission, during the summer of 1932. Annabelle and her roommate approached motorists at stoplights and in parking lots. It "wasn't a very dignified job for a girl," but working together, "the two of us weren't afraid." On their best evening they sold $5.50 worth of the plates, but other evenings only three or four of them. As cold weather approached, "People wouldn't pay $.25 so we sold them for whatever we could get."[78]

Companies misrepresented jobs. Kate N was supposed to receive $10 weekly, plus a 30% commission, selling beauty creams. After two weeks the company reduced compensation to commission and a streetcar pass, and two weeks later rescinded the pass. For four weeks the company secured appointments; after that she had to find her own. Kate, single, white, thirty-three, a former clerical worker, was among the most successful canvassers; she averaged as much as $3 a day and continued for almost a year.[79] Another woman reported, "[It was] just a racket. [It was] not what they claimed it to be."[80] Even when companies treated canvassers fairly, most women "couldn't make anything." A typical commission was $.04 for a can of cleanser.

Many women lasted less than a day peddling door-to-door; few endured more than a few weeks. "People don't open doors. [They have] no money to buy," explained Ida E, a fifty-two-year-old white woman who sold one corset in three months.[81] Gladys C, a clerical worker, explained: "Try this—try that. Always try to get a cheaper article. Fifty cents looks like $5.00 to people now and they won't buy. Just so you get carfare and meals. That's all you can expect to earn."[82] Some women bought goods wholesale and operated independently. Madeline M, a Black clerical worker, bought dresses from a factory and sold them door-to-door, clearing $.88 on a $2.00 dress: "[I] made good at it but then when winter came people wanted better dresses and I couldn't get enough together to buy them."[83] Women packaged peanuts or candy and cooked and baked and sold their goods on the street. Lulu L, an unemployed clerical worker, sewed dresses for a woman who sold them house-to-house and promised her $10 a week, but she averaged $2.[84] Availability, independence, lack of formal qualifications, and promise that initiative and hard work would pay off attracted women even into their seventies.

Livelihoods in the underground economy—namely, bootlegging, gambling, and prostitution—promised the same benefits as canvassing, plus a higher income, but the risk was potential incarceration. A few women reported this work; interviewers also surmised it from observation, speculation, and neighborhood gossip. Rose B, a Hungarian immigrant, acknowledged that her family produced and sold "home brew." "Everybody around here is doing the same," she explained. "It's the only way they can keep going." Her husband, Steve, was caught and jailed in 1931. The next year their only income was their sixteen-year-old daughter's $3 wages at a domestic job. The interviewer was "impressed by this family's care-free happy attitude.... [Rose], her husband, and two older children were almost hilarious, telling with great glee about being arrested for bootlegging, and husband spending four months in jail.... [They] seemed determined not to be downhearted and to take things as they come.... Though [Rose] and [her] husband denied any bootlegging activities at present, it is possible they are being continued."[85]

The numbers game, a source of recreation, diversion, and hope, created jobs.[86] The Chicago Police Department tried to suppress the long-standing policy business, but a Black-dominated syndicate reorganized it, and by 1938 the numbers game employed over five thousand. More than two thousand walking writers canvassed neighborhoods, wrote up plays for thrice-daily drawings, and earned 20% commissions. Over five hundred policy stations took bets and employed more than two thousand porters, writers, checkers, clerks, and others. Some Black leaders opposed playing policies; others defended gambling because it provided employment. The estimated weekly payroll in 1938 was $26,000.[87] Hope of winning made the policy business virtually Depression-proof, and it was a rare source of employment dependent only on the Black community. One male employee explained, "Sometimes the girls could make $20 a week. There isn't a laundry in the city or a kitchen in Hyde Park where a girl without learning could earn $20 for a week's work."[88] Eva A put a child through high school on her $18 weekly pay between 1925 and 1930. "Ashamed," and often arrested, she noted that "getting bailed out was easy." When police padlocked the policy station, Eva lost her job. She attested she would "do the same again for less money, if chance offered."[89]

Despite the illegality—and, to some minds, immorality—of gambling and selling liquor, women reported these enterprises. None acknowledged prostitution. When they had nothing to sell but their bodies, some destitute women exchanged sex for cash, meals, or material goods. As Meridel LeSueur noted at the time, "Like every commodity now the body is difficult to sell and the girls say you're lucky if you get fifty cents."[90] A Chicago police captain explained, "There are a lot of women here who are trying to make a dollar and will take a chance and 'turn a trick.'... If they could just get a job scrubbing floors you wouldn't see them trying to be whores very long."[91]

Interviewers concluded that several Chicago women were prostitutes judging by appearances ("Client has bleached or dyed blond hair ... eyebrows arched ... nails a bright color"),[92] the gossip of landladies and neighbors, and the presence of men or male clothing in women's rooms. Three pieces of evidence about Edith C, ejected when applying for a restaurant job because she was over twenty-one (chapter 2), convinced her interviewer she was a prostitute: Edith, a white woman, remained in a Black neighborhood after her Black husband deserted her; she was diagnosed with latent syphilis; and she had been arrested as the inmate of a disorderly house and fined $50.[93] According to a Morals Court official, "There are more accidental arrests for persons who are not prostitutes among the colored than would be true in the case of whites. Poor people often have to live around prostitutes because of cheap rent, and when the officers raid a place they usually bring in everybody in the house."[94] Did Edith engage in sex work, or did the interviewer, repulsed by her unconventionality, draw inaccurate conclusions?

The nine-page record of Bessie C twice concluded, "Probable income from prostitution." A white researcher, believing Black women were oversexed and immoral, concluded that two male visitors and a large apartment, where Bessie had been raised and in which she had lived for twenty years, signified prostitution: "Miss C claims to be living alone in the seven room flat. While investigator was there, two negro men entered and greeted Miss C familiarly. It was explained that they were friends. These men waited in the front part of the house. . . . It was investigator's impression that both men were on relief. . . . Miss C mentioned . . . that while her mother lived they had rented rooms and that she had worked."[95] The investigator also demeaned Bessie's work history, religious beliefs, and housekeeping.

Despite legal risks and social censure, gambling, bootlegging, and prostitution facilitated survival. The numbers business thrived, though bootlegging fell off after the repeal of Prohibition. The police captain cited believed that the Depression increased streetwalking, but ended organized prostitution, on Chicago's South Side: "The trade came almost altogether from white laborers around the stockyards district. They were mostly foreigners who were not married and came over here looking for women. Now these laborers have little money or aren't working at all. That's what has knocked out commercial prostitution in the district."[96] Fewer men could pay for sex, but likely more women walked the streets.

Geographic Mobility

Okies driving west and men and women riding the rails were not the only Americans who pinned their hopes on mobility. Between 1935 and 1940 more Black women and men moved to major destinations of the Great Migration than left them, while white departures greatly outnumbered arrivals.[97] African Americans hoped physical movement might be fruitful because little occupational mobility existed at the bottom of job hierarchies.

Metropolises magnetized northern African Americans as well as southern. In 1927 Josephine S, a young Black woman, quit her $40-a-month chambermaid job at a hotel in Niles, Michigan, and left South Bend with her husband. She earned higher wages in Chicago, $16 weekly ($69 monthly), stripping and selecting tobacco at a cigar company. In response to her mother's urging, the couple returned to her parents' home in October 1929. Josephine did not find a job until January 1930, when she got maid work at the Jefferson Hotel at $55 monthly, higher wages than her previous hotel job, but with longer hours and without a free lunch. She quit in March, and for the next six months did daywork "whenever she can get any, but not more than a few days a month." Her husband could not find steady work in a year's time. Although her stepfather was employed and her mother cooked for a private family, Josephine convinced them to relocate to Chicago, where there were "more opportunities for colored people."[98] Three sisters and a brother of Leona C (introduction) moved to Chicago before 1929, but Leona cared for her elderly parents until they died, remained employed at the Oliver Hotel, and lived in the family home in South Bend. Familial obligation, an ongoing job, and homeownership rooted her in Indiana.[99]

Thousands of people disappeared from South Bend between 1930 and 1932, responding to massive unemployment in a city with few other job possibilities for men. Information that researchers elicited from neighbors indicated that families relocated to the rural United States and that older men and couples crossed the Atlantic to homelands. Some unemployed men returned to parents' farms in Illinois, Indiana, and Michigan, leaving wives and small children with their in-laws. Almost half the Black South Bend women interviewed in 1930 had left the city by 1932. Experience in commercial services likely contributed to hopes of employment elsewhere.[100] Five of eight persisters were homeowners; all who left were tenants.[101] Two of three male Studebaker employees died; none of their families remained. Fifteen households is a small sample, but their high propensity to move merits attention.[102]

The Consequences of Downward Occupational Mobility

Comparing employment at both ends of the decade elucidates patterns of occupational growth and decline, the changing composition of the labor force, and shifting demographics of employed women. A smaller proportion of women held jobs in 1940, when official unemployment stood at 14.6%.[103] Increased demands of bureaucracies added more than a quarter of a million female clerical jobs, a growth of 11.2%.[104] Faltering consumption reduced the number of saleswomen by 18.8%.[105] Both positions remained overwhelmingly white. Female operatives increased slightly, 5.2%, while Black women lost 41.4% of their previous manufacturing employment.[106]

Because services employed the largest number and the most varied range of women, they were the last resort of displaced women and best illustrate increased competition and declining prospects. The sector grew by a quarter of a million female jobs nationally. Repeal of Prohibition transformed the hotel and restaurant industry: the number of cooks and waitresses increased, and bartenders—absent in 1930—proliferated. Numbers of white hairdressers increased almost 50% in the metropolises; numbers of Black hairdressers increased only in Philadelphia.[107] The laundry workforce returned to its previous size; Black women's employment dropped.[108] Cleaning jobs proliferated; Black women's share declined. Domestic jobs increased; domestic employment of Black women plummeted, nationally and in the four cities.[109] Chicago maintained a stable number of elevator operators; Black women's proportion in this position plunged from 43 to 15% as white women soared from 57 to 85%.[110]

Nationwide, Black women's employment dropped sharply, 22.6%, compared to white women's slight decline (see table 5); the racial composition of the service sector changed significantly.[111] In the four cities, Black women's employment fell farther than nationally, 32.3% in South Bend and 42.3% in Chicago (see table 5). Chicago had offered Black women the most diverse work opportunities. They lost twelve thousand service jobs, while white women gained four thousand (see table 6). Total service jobs declined in the metropolises, 9.0% to 17.8%, although they increased nationally.[112]

Although stigmatized, domestic service witnessed intense competition. Housewives, previously unable to afford domestic workers, could hire help at low wages and "took advantage" of the desperation of the unemployed. A white Denver woman wrote that they preferred to hire women from "other lines of work" because they "could get them for a lot less pay than the experienced houseworkers."[113] Household employees at the Des Moines YWCA argued that the "inexperienced girl, teachers, business girls, young girls, working for $2 and $3 a week" lowered wages of long-term domestic workers.[114] Downward mobility dislodged women with the fewest advantages in labor market competition. Black women fared poorly because employers hired white women when they could and white women took jobs previously held by Black women. A woman on the bottom rung had no job to which she could descend, so she fell off the ladder. Disproportionately, destitute women were older, Black, domestic workers who were disadvantaged by dishonored age, stigmatized race, and work experience restricted to the bottom of the ladder.

The marital status, age, and race of employed women shifted significantly.[115] Married women increased their share of job holding 22.2%, while single and formerly married women lost (see table 7). Women ages twenty-five to forty-four, most likely to be married, gained jobs. This cohort, women who had been in their teens to early thirties at the onset of the Depression, had continued working or resumed employment despite marriage and children. Adolescents entering the labor market in the late 1930s were less successful than teenagers a decade earlier (see table 8). These transformations reflected crisis and long-term developments and characterized every working-class sector and the entire female labor force.[116] Despite explicit discrimination, the share of married women in clerical and sales jobs expanded, from 23.7% to 32.1%; young single women held a smaller proportion of jobs.[117] The same phenomena characterized manufacturing: married women gained, single women lost, and women ages twenty-five to forty-four gained most.[118] Black women lost jobs they had held in the clerical, sales, and manufacturing sectors, which remained almost entirely white.

National, regional, and local factors contributed to Black losses and white gains in employment. Julia Kirk Blackwelder demonstrates that some groups' employment could grow while others' declined because "virtually six separate labor markets functioned" in San Antonio, Texas. White women did not "trespass" into jobs formerly held by Black or Mexican women.[119] In cities in the Midwest and Northeast, white women did take jobs formerly held by Black women. In San Antonio, Black female employment fell 15.7%.[120] In a major biracial southern city, Atlanta, where the largest proportion of Black women had worked for wages, they lost 24.4% of their previous jobs.[121] Nationally, increased job holding by the twenty-five to forty-four cohort and by married women illustrates changes in white women's decisions and suggests that "in-between" women, the daughters of immigrants, were a significant component of this change.[122]

Dana Frank's formulation of white working-class women standing on a platform held up by women of color captures the cognizance and lack of awareness of participants.[123] Onerous to the women supporting its weight, the platform is invisible to or taken for granted by those standing on it. Utilizing the metaphor of an occupational ladder adds depth to the analysis. Women looked up as they climbed. When high winds sway a ladder planted on the ground or extended from a fire truck, occupants of the top rungs travel in the largest arcs, making their hold the most precarious. The job ladder, however, was not rooted to solid ground but bolted inside a well, suspending workers above a gaping chasm. Its bottom steps were the most dangerous. When forced to descend, women may or may not have glimpsed over their shoulders those below them. Women at the bottom, without footing, and whose fingers were being stomped on, lost their handholds and fell into the abyss.[124]

Even as the economy began to gear up for war, male manufacturing employment had not returned to 1929 levels.[125] In South Bend, white men's manufacturing jobs dropped 15.5%; Black men's fell 55.7%. Only 68.3% as many Black men held any job, including New Deal employment.[126] To quote Langston Hughes,

I am the worker sold to the machine.
I am the Negro, servant to you all.
. . . .
I am the man who never got ahead,
The poorest worker bartered through the years.[127]

Without state intervention, African American unemployment would have been even more severe. In 1940 a far larger proportion of Black women and men worked on New Deal projects than white, inaugurating a trend that continues to characterize Black women's job holding. In the four cities, 9–19% of employed Black women were public emergency workers, compared to 2% of employed white women (4% in Cleveland).[128] Since the 1930s, proliferation of public-sector and nonprofit or third-sector employment has extended this pattern. In 1979 almost one-third of employed Black women worked for the state, compared to less than one-fifth of white women.[129] In 1990, 46% of Black women worked in government and nonprofit jobs, compared to 37% of white women.[130]

Working-class women pursued the same strategies to overcome joblessness; structural racism distinguished their results. Relation to the labor market was primarily individual, but most people lived in families. Women practiced similar household strategies, but specific tasks were determined by residential segregation, as chapter 4 will demonstrate.

4

The Family Economy

●●●●●●●●●●●●●●●●●●●●●●●

Daily Survival and
Management of Resources

"Use it up, wear it out, make do, or do without." This aphorism exemplifies how people managed in the Great Depression despite insufficient income. Material and monetary needs, family hierarchies, and emotions intertwine intimately, yet a brief artificial separation can promote clarity. This chapter focuses on material, subsistence, and financial strategies; chapter 5 addresses intensified demands for loyalty and increased conflicts. Chapter 6 examines strategies of women "adrift." I have reframed the typical comparison, between so-called complete and broken families, to contrast women whose tasks facilitated family survival (with or without husbands) with those who struggled alone. I will demonstrate that urban working-class women practiced similar subsistence and financial strategies. Institutionalized racism, and structural disparities in availability, cost, and conditions of housing, dictated boundaries within which they created and refined the wherewithal of daily existence.

Working-class people who had achieved the American dream of homeownership were loath to jeopardize their foremost financial investment. In a modest dwelling in Mishawaka, Indiana, Calina V explained, "We've taken food out of our mouths to save for taxes and [house] payments." Calina and Rene, Belgian immigrants, worked many years at Ball Band Shoes; in 1930 his work was "slack" and the factory cut her hours and wages, so they gave up luxuries such as their teenage daughter's music lessons to "keep up payments." By 1932 Calina had lost her job as a janitress in the women's washrooms; their daughter was looking for work, without success; and Rene's pay envelope contained only $11.50. They "just d[id] anything to get along": they raised a garden, ate less, bought cheaper coal, depleted savings, canceled a life insurance policy to save ninety-three cents monthly, and relied on Calina to make over and patch old clothes. Declining to specify housing expenses, Calina informed a researcher from the Women's Bureau that they had not fallen behind on the mortgage or taxes, nor taken out loans, nor incurred debts.[1] Subordinating other needs to ensure the security of their home sounded a common refrain.

Across town, Alice H, a long-term Black South Bend resident and a widow, owned the home that she shared with two sons, a daughter, a son-in-law, and two grandchildren. There were three wage earners in the household, and Alice looked after the children. Loretta V, her daughter, ran a department store elevator and Loretta's husband, Stewart, waited tables at the Oliver Hotel. Alice's older son married and moved out. Hotel business deteriorated, Stewart's wages fell, and eventually he was laid off; he found work as a driver for the Star Store, where Loretta worked. In 1932 he left his marriage and moved out. The store reduced Loretta's wages by one-third, to $8 weekly, for a job that required working twelve hours on Saturdays. At twenty-eight, she became the sole support of her children, mother, and teenage brother Wilbert.

Loss of two male breadwinners and reduction of Loretta's wages meant they could not afford milk for the children, and there were "lots of days with nothing but bread and not a penny in the house." Alice's married son had bought them a load of coal the previous winter, and the women used their furniture as security for a $40 loan to pay property taxes. Because they were homeowners, local government turned down their application for assistance. It referred them to a charity that gave them groceries for two weeks, then disqualified them for the same reason. The WB interviewer described a "poor house, badly in need of repair."

Alice was irate: "I have lived here twenty-six years and paid taxes and when I wanted help I couldn't get it." In September 1932 Wilbert could not return to high school because he needed clothing, glasses, and health care. As Alice explained, "My son and I both need medical attention. There are many days when I am too sick to get out of bed. Then my son takes care of the children. We can't afford to go to a Dr. but I can't live much longer if I don't. What I have come to and what I have had!" Relying on Loretta's wages, assistance from a married son, child care by a teenager, and Alice's housework and management, they managed to remain in their home in 1940.[2]

These households are emblematic of deprivation and determination. Working-class homeowners continuously invented strategies dedicated to paying mortgages and taxes. Tenants made rent a priority, but displayed greater flexibility in keeping a roof over their heads, because they could, and did, move.

Working-class people typically sustained themselves solely with weekly wages, which shrank rapidly. In the fall of 1930 no one had a steady job in 45%

of 2,852 South Bend households interviewed, even though the large majority included multiple wage earners.[3] Two years later, only one-third of 1,120 homes revisited contained a steady worker; more than one-tenth lacked a wage earner. Male operatives' work had almost disappeared. In households with earnings, median income for four weeks was $45.45. If that period was representative, median annual earnings of the employed dropped to $590.85. Other sources of income were uncommon; less than one-fifth of households received cash from rental property, roomers, or life insurance. Sickness insurance, workmen's compensation, and pensions for war disabilities replaced, rather than supplemented, wages.[4]

Understanding family economies and management of resources is synonymous with attending to the gendered division of labor. Hard physical labor constituted daily routines, burdens that women relieved primarily by passing tasks on to daughters. White northern urban women regularly benefited from electricity, gas stoves, indoor flush toilets, and hot running water. Black women more often lit their homes with gas lamps, cooked on coal stoves, heated water, and used outdoor toilets.[5] Access to modern utilities lightened the load, but persistent, pervasive tasks, such as emptying cold water from iceboxes; washing, wringing, and hanging out heavy loads of laundry; securing and storing groceries; and scrubbing floors, kitchen appliances, and bathroom fixtures required strength and elbow grease. The quest for cleanliness compelled constant vigilance. Most working-class men and some women tracked job grime home on shoes and clothing, and industrial soot showered the landscape. Black workers more frequently labored in dirty environments.

Subsistence Labor and Self-Sacrifice

When they could not rely on workers' earnings, housewives substituted their labor for purchasing goods and services. Roxie H moved from rural Indiana to South Bend after her husband died and found work as a marker at the White Swan Laundry to support her two school-age children. She earned as much as $18 weekly in 1930, but as housewives cut back on sending out laundry, her hours and wages shrank to $6 weekly in the fall of 1932. Roxie found an opportunity to get "free" rent as the janitress of a tabernacle, so they moved to Mishawaka. They altered habits to conserve cash, doing without heat on November mornings and cooking with kerosene. "We don't try to dress fancy," Roxie noted. Her fifteen-year-old daughter Ruth got working papers and found a job doing housework and childcare, for which she received meals and the use of her employer's electric washer to do her own family's laundry. Every day that summer Roxie and her children walked a mile and a half each way to a garden lot, growing enough produce to can for the coming winter. "It was a terrible job," Roxie explained; "the children helped all they could." The agent described Roxie with a single adjective: "lame." Roxie said, "We could get along all right on $10 or $12 a week." Lacking that possibility, she and her daughter worked harder to provide necessities.[6]

Across town, Marie and Frank W and their four young children moved into her parents' home because they could not afford rent and the joint cost of housekeeping was less. Studebaker laid off Marie's father, John M, and her brother, and in 1931 Marie lost her job as an ironer at Superior Laundry. Frank drove a truck for a lumber company, though irregularly. The 1932 four-week income for a household of ten was $15. The Ms had made no mortgage payments for a year, the real estate company threatened foreclosure, and a brother-in-law bought the house "at a bargain" and rented it to them. They had paid no rent in eight months, and taxes and street assessment charges were a year or two overdue. Electricity had been disconnected three months earlier, they had not paid the water rent, and they owed a butcher and several grocers. On the rare occasions John M was called into work, his wages were garnished by grocers. They could not afford milk for the baby; John needed shoes; Tillie, Marie's mother, a diabetic, was unable to buy medicine and wore only bedroom slippers. She reported, "[I am] almost distracted with worry. [I] have never felt this way in the forty years that I have had a home." The Ms allowed part of their insurance to lapse, ate less protein, and grew a garden. They relied on relatives, borrowing, and food and coal from the county. When a workman came to shut off the gas, Marie begged him to wait a week so she could bake bread "ahead." They had a coal range, but could not afford an oven. "[I] don't know what we are going to do, because we can't afford bakery goods," Marie noted. Marie and Tillie borrowed flatirons to keep up appearances; as Marie explained, "[It's] awfully hard to get along without an electric iron. [I] do not know what the family will do for coal and extras this winter. [You] have to have cash for coal."[7] For Roxie and Ruth, labor secured housing, meals, use of an electric washing machine, and garden produce. They did without heat and clothing. Marie and Tillie managed without electricity or gas.

Women consistently, indefinitely, replaced cash consumption with subsistence production. In almost every household in the South Bend sample, they constructed and repaired clothing (94.5%). Large majorities scrimped on food (82.9%) and utilities (64.8%) and cultivated gardens (71.3%). More than three-fourths (77.3%) of households used three, or all four, of these tactics. Labor-intensive, self-sacrificing strategies were housewives' immediate responses to hard times and their most protracted methods for survival. They invested physical, mental, and emotional effort to conserve scarce cash as they resumed the routines of earlier generations, habits still practiced in rural areas and by the poorest urban women. New patterns of consumption were not irreversible, nor had subsistence skills vanished from collective memory. Women shivered through cold winters in poorly heated dwellings; built wood fires; lugged and heated water to clean garments, bodies, and homes; wore layer upon layer of threadbare clothing; and went hungry. Physical labor was an apparently infinitely renewable resource as long as a woman possessed bodily strength, psychic energy, and/or other people whose labor she could direct.

Compensating for missing wages with subsistence labor was a gendered strategy of housewives, who managed the program of economizing, though they might delegate tasks. Families lacking mothers drafted the oldest daughter, a grandmother, or an aunt to serve as housewife. In households without men, women and children accomplished traditionally "male," as well as "female," tasks. The single subsistence activity considered appropriate for men was cutting and hauling wood. Most men and boys lacked the inclination or skill to do housework, though some pitched in on chores.[8]

Gardening—the most labor-intensive and time-consuming, yet money-saving, activity—could be gender neutral. The location of a plot, in the backyard or at the edge of town, determined the participation of women, men, and children. Municipal government and local corporations made vacant land available.[9] A garden demanded regular attention for four or five months; entailed hot, dirty, muscle-as well as back-straining work; and was subject to the vagaries of nature. Rain, hailstorms, tornados, birds, insects, blight, dogs, or chickens might destroy a garden. Some people took pleasure in the creativity of growth; others considered it an onerous chore. One young mother explained, "We've just lived off our garden."[10] More than two-fifths of gardens cultivated by sample households produced surplus for storage, and gardeners and nongardeners alike "cann[ed] everything we can get our hands on."[11] An unemployed middle-aged white woman and her mother "picked all the fruit we've eaten this summer on shares; some of it we've canned—berries, peaches, and today we picked grapes."[12] The hot, heavy job of cleaning, preparing, and cooking fruits and vegetables and sterilizing, filling, and processing canning jars was condensed into the brief period of the harvest. Nationwide, sale of canned goods declined, and in 1931 purchases of glass jars surpassed purchases of each of the preceding eleven years.[13]

Housewives cut food costs by half or more, reducing or eliminating milk and meat. A young mother explained that her family "couldn't have any variety—just beans and potatoes."[14] Hazel L, a marginally employed white widow, eliminated luxuries like pie, replaced butter with oleo, bought no milk, and tended a garden patch. Her three children had consumed a quart of milk and a meal featuring meat daily, but in 1932, "We do well if we have [meat] once a week."[15] Beans, potatoes, and bread were less satisfying than meat, milk, desserts, and side dishes. Baking with "cheap flour" saved only pennies, if the cost of other ingredients and utilities was calculated, but pennies counted when a loaf of bread cost seven to nine cents. In 1929, Ford Motor Company families in Detroit had bought twelve pounds of bread weekly and spent close to half their grocery budgets on meat and dairy products.[16]

Financially strapped housewives weighed the advantages of credit or cheaper prices and altered their shopping habits. Their indebtedness to grocers and butchers attests that they traded at neighborhood stores as long as merchants kept them on the books. One woman noted, "You don't get credit for groceries like you used to, if you don't pay they won't give you any."[17] Another reported, "It's hard to get along because stores will not trust colored people."[18] If grocers required cash, customers' loyalty might vanish. As a Polish immigrant widow with nine children explained, "We look around and buy where it's a penny cheaper."[19] A young woman echoed, "Mother buys at the A & P now. We used to buy from the store on our way home."[20] Switching to chain stores avoided the embarrassment of facing a grocer to whom a family was indebted. Relatively few South Bend working-class families owned cars, and most A&P stores were located in middle-class neighborhoods, so housewives took the bus, used children's wagons, and carried heavy loads to conserve cash.[21]

Women limited clothing purchases. The Ford families spent $210.67 annually on clothing, and South Bend families had spent as much as $300-$400. Most bought next to nothing in 1932. An unemployed laundry worker, age twenty-eight, purchased two housedresses at $.87 each and eight pairs of hose for $.50 to $.70 apiece in a year's time. Her brother, working irregularly at Studebaker, spent $3 for shoes, and their widowed mother, a Polish immigrant, bought nothing.[22] "I wouldn't know how to wear a new dress," exclaimed a young Polish woman; another remarked, "Why I've forgotten how to go into a store."[23] As Nellie G, a fifty-two-year-old white divorcée, confided, "My underclothes are falling off. [I] have worn house slippers to work." She walked to and from her job at Clark Laundry, thirty blocks each way. Operating old kick presses on a concrete floor was "very hard on her shoes. For several days she wore house slippers and finally bought a pair of shoes for $1.98. These are almost worn out again."[24]

Women prided themselves on being "good at sewing and remodeling."[25] Marvin Arnett, a Black woman, while recalling her childhood in Detroit described her mother's skill at dressing her for attending a theater performance. Constructing a red dress, "she used the material from a velvet bathrobe she bought at the Goodwill Store for a nickel. Trimmed with a white lace collar, it was the equal of any of the expensive children's frocks." White women, impressed by her outfit, hired her mother for several months' worth of seamstress work.[26]

Utilities cost relatively little, but almost two-thirds of South Bend families trimmed expenses, reducing the temperature in winter. Pre-Depression expenditures for coal in cities in the Midwest and Northeast ranged from $45 to over $100 annually.[27] Sample families estimated savings of up to $32 in 1931–1932, compared to the preceding year. Few households could scrape together a large sum in spring or summer when prices were lowest, so they bought cheaper grades of coal, later on, in smaller amounts and at higher prices. Some shut down furnaces and built a single fire in a kitchen coal stove: "We live in the kitchen, we will only heat that this winter."[28] In late October 1932 one household burned leaves "to take the chill off the house,"[29] and another burned rubber beads and tires, which were quite smoky.[30] Men and boys foraged for downed trees and branches from woods outside town, and Hazel L heated with wood her children gathered.[31]

Wood was cumbersome, did not burn as long as coal, and required more atten-tion. Many women stocked the woodbox or coal scuttle, tended fires, and shov-eled ashes: physically demanding, ever-present tasks.[32]

When households needed to conserve cash, when utility companies shut off service, and when families moved into poor quality housing, women increased their physical labor. Lack of heat, electricity, gas, hot running water, or indoor plumbing required more lifting and carrying and more elbow grease to create and sustain a clean, comfortable environment. A dozen households in the South Bend sample substituted kerosene, oil, wood, or coal for cooking to save money, though gas had been disconnected in only five homes. Four households lost electric ser-vice; many others, months behind on bills, were "wondering when they'll shut it off."[33] One woman reported, "We only use our radio when there's something very important to listen to—so we can save on the electricity."[34] A single family lost running water, but many were indebted for water rent, and fewer had hot running water, making laundry, bathing, scrubbing floors, cleaning kitchens, and sanitizing bathrooms arduous. In 1929 electricity and gas bills averaged approx-imately $2 each in the Detroit Ford homes.[35]

With extra cash, laundry was the first task women farmed out.[36] A young Hungarian mother exclaimed, "[I] can't even give the wash out, I don't make enough."[37] Commercial laundries rapidly lost customers. Some families had pur-chased electric wringer washers on credit for $60 to $200, but most working-class women used washboards, tubs, boilers, and hand wringers. Without electricity, laundry required lugging water, "rubbing, wringing, and lifting water-laden clothes and linens," and hand cranking wringers. Without hot running water, women heated vessels on stoves. Without gas, they hauled coal or wood to burn, and then lugged the ashes away.[38]

Lack of modern conveniences worked hardships disproportionate to the cash involved. The small number of South Bend households that lost access to mod-ern utilities exemplifies a significant benefit of whiteness for urban women. At the nadir of the Depression, far more white women could count on electricity and running water than could Black women. Scholars of white privilege have given no attention to the advantages of whiteness in the home, a workplace for virtually all women.

Cutting expenses required physical stamina and ingenuity; reclassifying rec-reation, home repairs, and health care as unaffordable luxuries demanded emo-tional resourcefulness. Adults and children did without dental and medical care and eyeglasses. Handy husbands tackled home repairs, but some wives emptied pails of water, avoided rotten spots on porch floors, stepped cautiously on tilt-ing steps, or were depressed when gazing at peeling paint. Encouraging her children to take pleasure in free activities called forth a mother's patience when they wanted to attend movies and play with new toys. Forfeiting children's music lessons saddened parents. A twenty-year-old broke into tears: "We used to go to a movie, but now we can't go to church. We have no money for the collection."[39]

Years of doing without fostered physical deprivation and shame. Malnutrition increased susceptibility to colds, flu, and serious illnesses like tuberculosis. Hazel L's children were often hungry.[40] Mothers worried about depriving children of nutrition necessary for growth, and authorities added their weight. In 1932 Fannie H, unemployed, thirty-nine, divorced, and white, scraped together a meager living for her six children, with $5 weekly relief grocery orders, occasional daywork, and her oldest daughter's $5 weekly wage. Fannie bought, at most, a quart of milk daily, and the school nurse sent a note recommending that she give her children more milk.[41] Shame over inability to provide adequately and chastisement from an authority figure were among the costs of doing without.

Institutional racism ensured that Black women endeavored to keep body and soul together with fewer modern conveniences than their white counterparts. Bureau of Labor Statistics (BLS) studies for 1934–1936 dramatically demonstrated racial differences. Significant numbers of Black urban families lacked basic amenities that most white urban families took for granted. Almost two-fifths (38.8%) of Pittsburgh Black renter households, and one third 32.1% of their Philadelphia counterparts did not possess all the basic necessities: an inside flush toilet, hot and cold running water, electric lights, and gas or electricity for cooking. In Pittsburgh, 27.1% did without hot and cold running water; in Philadelphia, 22.6% lacked modern cooking facilities.[42] Comparable proportions in Cincinnati, 33%, and Indianapolis, 28%, lacked all the basic amenities; two-thirds of Black renters lacked running hot water and central heating.[43] The average annual income of Black families was $1,203 in Philadelphia, $1,071 in Pittsburgh, $1,110 in Cincinnati, and $990 in Indianapolis—roughly double the wages the South Bend (89% white) sample families earned in 1932 (estimated at $591).[44] Black housewives undertook far more physical labor, even when their families earned far higher wages. Few South Bend households did without electricity, gas, or hot running water, emphasizing newer housing and the advantages of whiteness. Notably, BLS study households were much smaller than the large, often Catholic, families of South Bend.

Americans have mythologized Depression gardens, canning, and old clothes made over, but the mental acuity these plans required, not only bodily labor, requires attention. Working-class women, stigmatized as ignorant, unthinking drudges, planned and calculated as they managed material and financial resources. Family account books and kitchen wall calendars recording daily details rarely survive to document mental labor, but interviews enable us to comprehend intellectual as well as corporeal requirements. Subsistence labor and self-sacrifice were the tools at hand with which women compensated for absent wages.

Financial Strategies

Three years after the Crash of 1929, many South Bend families held on to some or most of their financial assets and had not acquired new debts. Working-class people reluctantly drew upon material and monetary assets or went into debt, because most financial strategies were one-shot tactics: depleting a savings account, cashing insurance policies, or selling or forfeiting possessions. Few owners lost their homes, and few households liquidated savings; many lost reserves in bank closures.[45] As the crisis lengthened, some had no recourse other than to deplete financial resources and convert material goods to cash.

Housewives' unanimous subsistence practices sharply contrasted with families' infrequent, and much more varied, utilization of financial assets. No single monetary strategy was preferred, and fewer than half the households practiced any of eight tactics conceptualized by the WB. Most often they slid on the slippery ice of bills that "got away from them." More households (43.3%) were indebted for regular living expenses—grocers', butchers', and utility bills—than practiced any other financial tactic. Over one-third (37.6%) owed rent or mortgage payments and 37.4% lost or cashed in insurance. A fifth (20.6%) fell into arrears on property taxes. The WB's interview questions did not distinguish between active, reluctant choices and default. Deliberate financial initiatives were less widespread. Almost one-third (34.4%) of households negotiated a lower house payment, and 32.6% borrowed money. Relying on credit from employers (16.5%) or spending savings (15.1%) were less common. Families' comparatively limited practice of financial strategies, unintentional or deliberate, contrasts with housewives' purposeful, pervasive, conscious, and continuous increased labor.

Financial strategies cut to the heart of working-class goals, self-worth, and integrity. Indebtedness occurred by default more often than it was consciously undertaken. Negotiating a lower house payment was an active tactic, without negative repercussions, unlike most financial maneuvers. Decisions to spend savings and to cash in or forfeit insurance were not made lightly. Recovering those resources would be difficult, if not impossible.

Diminished earnings framed decisions. An annual income of $1,200 is a convenient figure for comparison: higher than pre-Depression estimates of $1,000 for bare subsistence, and lower than the $1,600 threshold for comfort. Even at reduced prices, a monthly income of around a hundred dollars ($92.31 for four weeks) was inadequate to secure "health and decency." In four weeks before the 1932 interviews, sample households earned $49 median wages. Almost four-fifths earned less than $100, and one-tenth had no wages.[46] If those weeks were typical, half of the households earned $637 or less annually.[47] In 1935 the Works Progress Administration estimated a maintenance budget for a manual worker's family of four at $1,210 in fifty-three cities.[48] Most working-class households comprised more than four people, and in the 1932 sample they ranged as high as fourteen.[49] The large majority of working-class households could not afford bare subsistence.

Housewives ingeniously manipulated monetary assets. Bertha C, a Jewish mother of six, had managed her household on the wages of her oldest children since 1917, when her husband died. In 1932 her son Lewis lost his job at

Studebaker, a drug store laid off her son Samuel (a soda jerk), and the county eliminated her daughter Florence's clerical position at the courthouse. Only her daughter Leah, a saleswoman at Robertson's Department Store (chapter 3), remained employed. Florence found part-time work as a Saturday clerk at Kresge, a dime store. In four weeks preceding their interview, the sisters earned $54, higher wages than usual because Florence worked three and a half extra days before Halloween, and Leah's required layoff every sixth week did not take place. Bertha owned their home outright, made sure the family saved, always "[bought] for cash," and had "no bills." She watched for sales and by early November purchased the winter's coal supply. She raised a large garden, cut back on necessities, dropped an insurance policy on Leah, drew on their postal savings account for regular expenses, and postponed paying three two-year-old doctors' bills totaling $140 and a $15 bill for glasses. She imaginatively transferred $100 in a closed bank to the dairy man, who applied it to his debt to the bank and gave her credit for milk and butter. Bertha explained, "We have to use every scheme we can think of to get along."[50]

Financial schemes were not always successful. Leona C (introduction), who supported her widowed mother, reported, "If we sell the [bank] book, [we] cannot get anything for it"; the interviewer added, "i.e., no good as credit." Whether Bertha's success and Leona's failure at parlaying savings in closed banks reflected racism or practices of particular banks is unclear. What is noteworthy is their mental acuity. Both called upon financial and familial strategies. When Leona's father died in 1931, his life insurance, and the occasional $5 and $10 bills her sisters sent their mother from Chicago extended Leona's declining wages. The C family economy stretched across state borders.[51]

Close to half of the households resurveyed in 1932 had had savings, and almost half lost them when banks closed.[52] Small ethnic financial institutions as well as big downtown banks swallowed young women's Christmas Club accounts, schoolchildren's skimpy nest eggs, and families' life savings—as much as $800. Hazel L said that when a bank failure wiped out $1.60 in her son's school bank account, he was as upset "as if it had been $1,600."[53]

Life insurance policies, a universal form of working-class savings, proved more reliable. Families often carried insurance on every member; the father's policy had the highest cash value and longest duration. The Ms, a prosperous Polish American family comprising Casimir, Catherine, four children, and an eighty-four-year-old grandfather, owned their seven-room home clear, insured all members, accumulated savings, and enjoyed luxuries. Casimir, at Studebaker, and his daughter, Elizabeth, at Davis Laundry, might have earned $45 to $55 weekly between them in the late 1920s. Feeling flush, they borrowed $400 against their home to buy a player piano in 1930. Two years later Casimir worked so irregularly and Elizabeth's wages dropped so low that their four-week income was $37. Their bank closed, consuming unspecified savings. Predictably, they cut down on food and clothing, raised a garden, and delayed house painting, porch repairs, glasses for Casimir and Catherine, and dental care for everyone. Unable to make $3 biweekly mortgage payments in 1931, they renegotiated with the loan company for a $200 mortgage requiring a monthly payment of $2.40. In October, 1932, they missed a payment for the first time. They owed $120 to a grocer, $16 for coal for the upcoming winter, and $50 to a relative for the previous winter's coal.

Their substantial investment in life insurance helped and hindered the Ms. They cashed in several policies and fell behind on others. From an outlay of $175 on the children over the preceding seven years, they received $15 when they liquidated policies. They had paid over $900 into a twenty-seven-year-old $1,000 policy on Casimir and a twenty-five-year-old $500 policy on Catherine; the monthly fees were $2.15 and $.87. When they made no payments for four months, the adults' policies and two small, recent policies on the youngest children lapsed. They owed $14.18 and possibly penalties. Catherine hoped to reinstate these policies but was not sure their lodge would allow this.

Estimating the minimum cash required for daily life clarifies why the Ms were on the verge of losing an investment of almost three decades' duration, because they could not scrape up $3 monthly. By the 1929 standards of Ford families, the Ms needed $90.70 monthly for groceries alone, yet their 1932 income was less than half this amount. Taking into account falling prices, their garden, and economies on meat and dairy, the Ms could barely feed themselves, much less pay bills.[54] The fact that they owed little on their mortgage, had few debts, and did not deny themselves a warm house suggest that potential loss of insurance was a passive forfeiture, not an actively chosen strategy.

Most families endeavored to maintain the longest-running policies, sacrificed newer ones, and realized a small return, or none, if they cashed in or forfeited insurance. Policies usually lapsed after three months without payments. Terminating insurance reduced expenditures, but proceeds, if any, were a brief stopgap in the protracted struggle for survival. When another family liquidated a policy on an adult son, $30 "bought him shoes to go to Chicago to look for work."[55] His mother spoke metaphorically, for sturdy men's work shoes cost about $5. Once insurance and savings disappeared, their provisions for the future might never be recouped. Loath to lose this protection or to jeopardize burying family members, one-third of sample households lost or cashed in insurance by the fall of 1932. Establishing eligibility for relief subsequently forced many more to do so.[56]

Decisions to dispose of material goods depended upon their gendered significance. A minority of South Bend working-class families owned cars, the province of men, which they were unlikely to sacrifice. Some reduced usage, dropped car insurance, or quit driving because they could not afford licenses and gas, but no interviewee mentioned selling or forfeiting a car. Men may have judged the price used automobiles commanded too low; some earned small amounts transporting people and goods. They held on to cars primarily because they valued them and they expected to make such decisions with impunity. Hard-pressed women sold furniture and their most common luxury, jewelry. Mabel H supported her "crippled" son by keeping boarders and provided a home for her unemployed daughter and grandchild. She cashed in two long-running insurance policies to pay property taxes, fell a year behind on her mortgage, and "[could] hardly buy food, much less clothes." Mabel "sold everything she [could] sell except two diamond rings" but noted, "[I] will probably sell my rings this winter for coal."[57]

Working-class participation in the consumer economy was ambivalent; availability of easy credit had not enticed everyone. Bonita and Richard C, who purchased furniture and a car (chapter 1), found themselves less well-off than anticipated. Unemployed five months, Bonita found a clerical position at a doctor's office for $12 weekly, compared to her $19 wages at a bank. Richard's days and hours at Studebaker were so irregular that in four weeks he earned $18. Installment payments on the $500 they owed "obliged them to give up their own home;" they moved in with Bonita's parents.[58] The Cs chose their car and furniture; others forfeited goods purchased on credit; some households had none. A Hungarian-American daughter reported, "[We] have never had anything except what we could pay for, [we] have no car, nor radio." Her family owned their home clear.[59] The A sisters (introduction) lost furniture because the firm went bankrupt and the receivers demanded the total balance due, but the business could not comply. The As "had never missed a payment." At the auction, "You never saw such a stock of furniture—dozens of beds, chairs, cribs, etc. Some were dirty and all broken—just as they had come from the houses they took them out of."[60] Values and circumstances dictated a range of attitudes about and possession of material goods.[61]

South Bend working-class families attempted to avoid losing or jeopardizing tangible and financial resources or going into debt during the first three years of the Depression. Almost half (44.5%) of the sample households practiced only one or two financial tactics; only 37.6% used four or more of eight financial tactics that WB agents identified. Yet 77.3% relied on three or all four subsistence methods, explicitly testifying to reluctance to lose assets and to expectations that women would increase their labor. The high propensity for white working-class households to practice every subsistence strategy, compared to disinclination to rely on financial methods, reflected attitudes about gender, the value of women's unpaid labor, and the meanings of the fruits of paid jobs.

Black and white households, matched for income levels, did not make drastically different financial decisions.[62] Mid-decade BLS studies found that Black families, compared with white families at the same income levels, spent more for housing and less for food, contributed more to relatives, and saved more because of their "almost universal practice of paying insurance premiums." Only families comparatively unscathed by unemployment met criteria for inclusion. In New York, Philadelphia, and Pittsburgh, relief excluded 52%, 61.5%, and 72.5% of African American households, respectively. The BLS acknowledged that those surveyed represented "the higher stratum of Negro wage earners and clerical workers." Most white South Bend sample households would have been excluded if their incomes had not increased substantially. African Americans conserved financial resources for the same reasons as white households: to pay bills that necessitated cash—namely, housing, which cost them more.

The Centrality of Shelter

Photographic and written chronicles from the 1930s emphasize homelessness. Evictions, Hoovervilles, and migrants grip our imaginations. Less dramatically, and more commonly, most working-class people maintained homes, often at the cost of great sacrifice and discomfort. Rent, mortgage, and property taxes required cash. In South Bend, more than one-third of sample households successfully negotiated lower payments with financial institutions and landlords. The S family, German immigrants, enjoyed relative prosperity as their children entered adulthood and took jobs. Studebaker employed four of five family members, who together earned $80-$100 weekly in the late 1920s. The parents were production workers, their son an office errand boy, and their daughter Mary a stenographer. In 1930 Mary worked regularly, her father's work was "not steady," and her mother and brother were laid off. Formerly paying $150 semiannually on their house contract, they renegotiated to $10 monthly. Despite a 60% reduction, they fell six months behind. Two years later, they only paid interest and took out a $75 loan for property taxes. Mary's $14.50 weekly wages and her father's occasional weeks at $5 or $6 gave them an income greater than two-thirds of sample households, but they could not keep up with house payments.[63] They benefited from the fact that local financial institutions reduced mortgages and renegotiated contracts rather than foreclose and have empty houses on their hands.

Negotiating lower rent was likely more successful in a medium-size city with few apartment buildings. Tenant and owner might have a personal relationship; a landlord might be a working-class neighbor trying to ensure financial security by purchasing and renting a second property. Theresa and Canzio B, middle-aged Italian immigrants with three children, could not afford $30 monthly rent when Ball Band reduced them to irregular hours in their jobs as cafeteria cook and shoe worker. Their landlord told them to pay as much as they could and said that $10 or $15 would suffice, because they were burdened with medical bills when their oldest child was sick for seven months. After Theresa lost her job in April 1931, and Canzio worked as irregularly as one day weekly, they could not pay rent. Eighteen months in arrears, the Bs owed the grocer for a year and had no coal. Their relationship with their generous landlord, who may have been a friend from the old country, provided stable housing.[64] Another landlord told unemployed tenants that "he would settle at a lower rate because rents have come down all over." His tenant noted, "[We] have not paid for so long, [the] new rate has never been mentioned."[65] In a city dominated by a few hard-hit industries, owners understood that evictions would leave them with empty properties. In a metropolis studded with apartment buildings, tenant-landlord relations were impersonal, strictly business propositions.

South Bend residents fared better with housing than people elsewhere. The proportion of owner-occupied homes declined only 10% over the decade, and in the worst years (1933 and 1935) only 4% of homes were foreclosed. Partial recovery in manufacturing jobs mid-decade aided housing stability, as did dramatic decline in rent and in the value of owned homes.[66] Families allocated an ever larger share of resources to housing. Economists advised that working-class families should spend 15–20% of their budgets for housing.[67] In 1932, 49.7% of the sample households spent more than 20% for rent or a mortgage, excluding utilities and taxes, even at lower rates. The fact that only 37.6% fell into arrears illustrates the priority working-class people assigned to shelter.[68] Homeowners attempted not to endanger their most valuable asset.

People moved regularly. Evictions and foreclosures forced some out, and others purposefully sought cheaper rent, doubled up, or relocated. Hazel L and her three school-age children lived in three homes between 1930 and 1932. Hazel earned as much as $.55 an hour as a bench girl at Studebaker, perhaps $25 weekly, in the late 1920s. Sick for four months in 1930, when she returned to work she was "put in as [a] matron" at $11 a week. She moved that year and again the following year, from a house with three rooms and a cellar to a building a few doors down, which a neighbor referred to as "that garage house," two rooms without a basement, reducing her rent from $16 to $4 monthly. In 1932 Hazel earned $15 in four weeks, and despite unusually low rent, she fell four months behind. Three years later her family remained in this substandard dwelling.[69]

Rarely could families find housing outside the cash nexus or circle of kin. Roxie H, the tabernacle janitress, was exceptional. Men occasionally worked out rent with carpentry, plumbing, and maintenance, but that strategy could not last long unless the landlord owned multiple buildings. Retta K, fifty-four, widowed, absent from the labor force almost thirty years, broke up her family to work as an attendant at the Warrensville Institution, receiving room, board, and $60 monthly wages. She later managed a Cleveland fraternity house, which provided two rooms and board for herself and a daughter and $40 monthly salary.[70] Living-in jobs at institutions typically housed a single person. Bartering labor for rent was rarely practicable for families.

Moving became increasingly common. More than one-third of South Bend households interviewed in 1930, over six hundred families, had moved by 1932. Close to half of those whom investigators were able to trace settled nearby, usually in rural areas where housing was cheaper. They moved in with relatives, returned to places of origin, left the city for a farm, or struck out for California. Their destinations indicate that job opportunities had drawn people to South Bend from across the Midwest and South.[71] Older couples, widows, and widowers returned to Belgium, Germany, Hungary, Italy, and Portugal, while their adult children remained in the United States.[72] Not anchored to a dwelling, renters more easily pulled up stakes; two-thirds (30/46) had moved during the preceding two years. Dozens of owner households doubled up.

Later, New Deal housing initiatives benefited owners more than renters and harmed African Americans. The Home Owners Loan Corporation (HOLC) purchased more than a million defaulted mortgages from banks and building and loan associations and refinanced them for fifteen-year terms. To determine loan policies it hired local real estate agents to rate neighborhoods; they drew red lines excluding the "riskiest" neighborhoods, which they appraised in explicitly racist and xenophobic language. The HOLC favored middle-class over working-class homeowners and restricted clients to "sound moral risks."[73] The Federal Housing Administration (FHA) insured mortgages for new homes and lengthened the amortization period to twenty years. Areas with Black families were redlined, and few could meet FHA qualifications. Housing projects, the primary assistance to renters, rejected the lowest income groups. In Cleveland they maintained residential segregation and spread slum conditions by dispossessing tenants to construct developments.[74]

Structural racism, including residential segregation, high rents, overcrowding, and deteriorating buildings, restricted Black people's possibilities for shelter. White working-class people more often owned homes, a resource and a burden that anchored them in their cities. Housing strategies illustrate creativity, ingenuity, and external limits on resourcefulness. Gendered assumptions about the needs of women and men also constricted plans, but those boundaries were often internalized.

The Gender Significance of Strategies and Priorities

Family economies relied on disparate, complimentary contributions from members for the benefit of all. This assumption, underlying scholarship on white family economies, ignores hierarchy and power. Members did not make decisions collectively nor benefit equally. Housewives often fared worst, whether measured by consumption of food, clothing, or pleasure, or by physical and emotional exhaustion. Young adult daughters were expected to dedicate loyalty, obedience, and wages to parents. Their goals were buried by the family's need for their self-sacrifice. Interviews convincingly display the inadequacies of white family economy analyses.[75]

How can we interpret white working-class households' virtually unanimous practice of subsistence strategies but much less frequent reliance on financial strategies? How can we account for decisions they made, as well as possibilities they rejected or never considered? As housewives balanced needs, decided how to allocate financial and human resources, and attempted to maintain their standard of living, they put men first, acknowledging them as wage earners and deferring to patriarchal norms. Children required good nutrition for growth, and shoes and winter coats for school, but the needs and desires of adult men could not be defined so simply. Eating more and better food, holding on to their cars, or being assured of small pleasures were perquisites that men commanded, even in impoverished households. In an anonymous letter, a "seventeen year old American born girl of Slovak parentage" explained that her parents ordered her and her sister to quit school to support the family. Working as much as fourteen hours daily at domestic jobs in Cleveland, their weekly wages of $4 and $5 paid for rent, groceries, and their father's creature comforts: "My father [works] very little, yet he must have his tobacco and beer."[76]

Fathers, husbands, sons, and brothers expected and accepted preferential treatment as their due. Amy C and her mother Emma B lavished care on Amy's young adult sons. Emma owned their older Mishawaka home, and Amy, a white widow, age fifty-three, cooked seven days a week at a restaurant. Her older son Lawrence worked as a bellhop at the Mishawaka Hotel and her younger son Ervin attended high school. In 1930 Amy lost her job and could not find another. Two years later Lawrence earned $6.25 weekly at the hotel, plus meals and tips, and Ervin drove a route for Sunshine Cleaners, earning $5 in commissions in four weeks. Amy and Emma took in a roomer. The young men benefited from numerous sacrifices made by the women. They "have to have clothes," Amy explained, so the women sewed to keep them "fit to go to work." For themselves they "made one dress out of two old ones." Amy, Emma, and Ervin lived on the dangerously low sum of $6 a month for groceries, without a garden. The women did without food to pay property taxes and to "let [Ervin] have a little meat." They heated with a single fire that they often allowed to die during the day. Lawrence contributed his wages to the household, but kept his tips and did not tell his mother how much spending money he had. Ervin earned "very little over the upkeep of his car." In sum, the young men enjoyed a higher standard of living than their mother or grandmother, including better food and clothing, a car, and pocket money.[77]

Housewives deprived themselves of necessities and often endured the least comfort in their households. The concept of a family standard assumes equitable distribution of resources, but families did not apportion food, clothing, recreation, and luxuries evenly nor expect members to assume equal shares of chores. Gender, age, role, employment, public presence, or days passed at home determined how much each person lived in ease or tolerated privation. Working-class pride demanded a presentable appearance in public. "The children must have clothes for school, so they get them," explained Katherine W. Shoes and winter coats were the most expensive items in a wardrobe. Katherine stretched her husband's irregular wages from Studebaker but bought no clothing for herself in two years.[78] Anna and John F scraped by on her $7.50 weekly wages as a janitor at a downtown office building, where she cleaned from 5:00 to 11:30 p.m., six evenings a week. After Studebaker laid off John, Anna washed, cooked, and canned on a woodstove in the garage to save on gas. One of their children had ear trouble, bad tonsils, and decaying teeth, but they would consult a doctor only when such problems became severe. Anna likely spent sleepless nights comforting her child. Among their many economies were "seldom" using their car, which they apparently considered a necessity, despite the fact that they lived within walking distance of John's (former) job.[79] Attuned to emotional nuances, wives negotiated husbands' despair with delicate awareness of their feelings and learned to use a "casual conversational tone" to discuss serious matters of survival.[80]

Black working-class men, also primary breadwinners, shared prerogatives and assumptions with white men. Adam and Henrietta are a fictionalized version of Louise Meriwether's parents in her novel *Daddy Was a Number Runner,* which takes place in Harlem in 1934. Their neighbors Robert and Elizabeth and their children double up with his Robert's mother-in-law, about whom he regularly complains. Robert is not working, but Elizabeth is "breaking her back in that laundry." Adam and Henrietta discuss the hardships:

> "It's a shame how Elizabeth never used to have milk for her kids but Robert kept gas in that car so he could ride around Harlem like a big shot."
>
> "A man's got to have something like that car," Daddy said, "so he knows he's a man."[81]

Working-class men took pride in their provision of homes and life insurance, and their families valued the tangible fruits of their labor. Unemployment struck a harsh blow to men's self-esteem, and discussions about disposing of assets undermined their pride. Financial strategies drew attention to men's inadequate contributions, so families reserved the material rewards of men's labor as a final resort. Decisions to expand housework were decisions not to sacrifice or jeopardize financial resources. Strategies that increased women's labor compensated for men's hopelessness. Historians have formulated unemployment as emasculating men.[82] The Depression might be better conceptualized as causing men to despair. Increasing housework to counteract men's unemployment and to minimize bleakness is not conceived as defeminizing women, even though it entailed arduous physical labor. Women could not expect silk stockings, a pretty hat, a permanent, or other female equivalents of tobacco, beer, or cars, much less to play decorative rather than utilitarian roles.

Financial strategies might undermine men's self-esteem and dignity, so unemployed Johns and Roberts needed to keep cars to know they were men. Gender conventions encouraged subsistence production because housework is always infinitely expandable. Women's increased labor did not violate notions about appropriate roles. Men might grumble about cold living rooms, patched clothing, or having to eat beans and potatoes, but their wives' self-sacrifice did not disrupt expectations. Interviewees readily discussed subsistence strategies in detail, but often disguised monetary matters in generalities. Their relative reticence about finances is additional evidence that they regarded women's labor differently from tangible resources. Women took pride in hard work, both physical and managerial. To admit financial details of impoverishment reflected failure, nothing worthy of pride.

If structural unemployment is interpreted as emasculating men, can it be claimed to hyperfeminize or to masculinize women? Femininity was associated with beauty, exemption from paid labor, and childbearing. When women assumed more responsibilities in the labor force, were they masculinized? Why are the results of capitalist failures interpreted as gender disruption? Did any Depression consequences increase or decrease gender attributes?

Across racial lines, housewives engaged in the same strategies and justifications; fewer assets limited Black families' exercise of financial tactics. Whether Black wives' much more frequent employment made their marriages more equitable than white marriages is a provocative question. Interviews and other 1930s sources illustrate similar strategies, both Black and white.

It is tempting to conceptualize financial strategies as male and subsistence strategies as female, but this risks oversimplification. The financial domain involved husbands and wives, though most men maintained distance from the domestic realm. Men were primary wage earners and women primary managers, juggling bills and the provision of clothing, food, and comfort. They took pride in the fact that their skills and ingenuity enabled their families to outlast the Depression. Husbands and wives talked over and fought over some plans, but the emotional labor and managerial adeptness to initiate and implement decisions belonged primarily to women.

Women's reproductive labor underlies and subsidizes capitalism, which survived its 1930s contradictions partly because the working class relied heavily on unwaged labor when paid jobs disappeared. In the language of the factory, subsistence labor was speed-up. Women rarely challenged increased workloads, for the love of their families, to spare husbands, for self-preservation, and because they saw no other choice. Labor historians celebrate workplace resistance but take for granted the reproductive and maintenance labor of unwaged female workers. Resistance—a general strike of housewives, for example—would undermine daily life and directly harm the people women loved. This essential difference between waged and unwaged labor continues to confound us if we do not directly address it.

Administration of the family economy was isolated and private. Demonstrations, strikes, and other public challenges to the prevailing order rested upon women's invisible labor. South Bend interviews include abundant evidence of assistance within extended families, but little in neighborhoods or communities. Some scholars have argued that communal responsibility underlay white working-class survival, but interviews indicate little support for that argument.[83] More evidence illustrates Black community contributions.

Housewives ensured survival by substituting their labor for consumption; they fulfilled social expectations and gender norms of wifely and motherly self-sacrifice. The flexibility and resourcefulness with which women sustained their families reflect resistance and consent. Increased labor, characterized by racial discrepancies in available tools, meant that more white women's daily activities paralleled those of Black women. When a flush postwar economy made it possible, consumption of goods and services replaced subsistence labor. Permanent expectations of flexibility, however, continue to require women to undertake whatever labor is necessary for household survival.

FIGURE 1. Clerical workers, Dictaphone Sales Corporation, 1931. (Courtesy of WB, RG 86, NACP.)

FIGURE 2. Studebaker Hourly Time Department, 1937. (Courtesy of Studebaker National Museum, South Bend, Indiana.)

FIGURE 3. Philadelphia Restaurant, South Bend, Indiana, 1940. (Courtesy of The History Museum, South Bend, Indiana.)

FIGURE 4. Assembly line, Wilson Brothers, South Bend, Indiana. (Courtesy of The History Museum, South Bend, Indiana.)

FIGURE 5. Assembly line, Wilson Brothers, South Bend, Indiana. (Courtesy of The History Museum, South Bend, Indiana.)

FIGURE 6. Waitresses, Smith's Cafeteria, South Bend, Indiana, 1935. (Courtesy of The History Museum, South Bend, Indiana.)

FIGURE 7. Industrial kitchen, Chesapeake and Potomac Telephone Company, Cleveland, 1927. (Courtesy of WB, RG 86, NACP.)

FIGURE 8. Aerial view, Pilgrim Laundry (city unknown), 1927. (Courtesy of WB, RG 86, NACP.)

FIGURE 9. Hand ironing in a commercial laundry (city unknown), 1928. (Courtesy of WB, RG 86, NACP.)

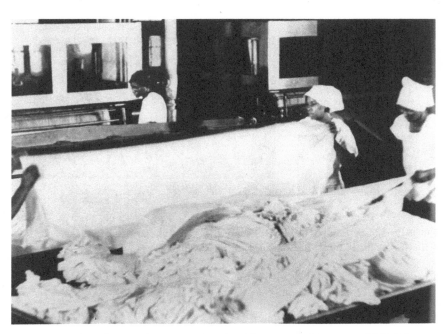

FIGURE 10. Shaking sheets, Palmer House laundry, Chicago, 1931. (Courtesy of WB, RG 86, NACP.)

Vol. 1 — October, 1933 — No. 1

BY AND FOR THE WILSON FACTORY FAMILY - - NAMED BY BETTY TORZEWSKI

Betty Torzewski Names Our Paper

Wins first prize for suggesting most suitable name, "Sew and Sew."

Second and Third Prize Winners

Walter Sweitzer, second, suggesting "Loose Threads."

Donald Hess, third, suggesting "Findings."

• • •

Several hundred names were suggested in the contest for a name for our magazine, all of which, appeared on our ballots. The vote was so scattered that no one name was elected, and Mr. Crawford, with the help of the Girls' Club Presidents, made the final selection of the three winners from the ten names receiving the highest number of votes. And here are the three prize winning names, with the persons who suggested them.

Walter Sweitzer   Donald Hess

APPRECIATION

We all have the Girls' Club to thank for this first issue of Sew and Sew. Months and Months ago, in talking with several members of the Girls' Club, some one of them told me of how much pleasure they would get out of some sort of a bulletin that would contain all the news and goings on of the Wilson family of Workers. Quite by chance, in talking to one of the boys in our printing plant several weeks ago, I was told about the possibilities of printing the bulletin in our own printing plant.

You cannot realize what pleasure I have had in the enthusiasm on the part of every one in getting it up. I surely appreciate the honor in being asked by the President of the Girls' Club, Virginia Bolf, and the other officers of the Club, to have my photograph taken, presenting the first issue of Sew and Sew to the President of the Girls' Club and its officers.

It is my understanding that Sew and Sew is ever to be a bulletin of happiness, fun, good cheer, filled with happy, homey news of what is going on. With all our trials and tribulations of life, we must never, never lose our sense of humor and our ability to smile; ever looking on the bright side of everything, with the fullest possible confidence in our own future, confident that right will ever come through; taking every possible advantage of every opportunity to say a kind word, to do a kind deed, helping each other, confident in so doing we will find greater happiness ourselves.

I would like to suggest to the Girls' Club that this ever be the creed of Sew and Sew.

So, here is to Sew and Sew, the homey bulletin of good cheer.

L. H. Crawford

Mr. Crawford Presents "Sew and Sew" to President of Girls' Club.

Center Mr. L. H. Crawford, President of Wilson Brothers and Virginia Bolf, president of the Wilson Brothers' Girls' Clubs. *Seated* Left to right are the presidents of the department clubs: Marie Coleman—Box Mfg., Bertha Pietrzyska—Hosiery, Phyllis Goralska—Assembling Room, Mary Farkas—Laundry, *Standing* Emma Vasel—Shirt Sewing, Clara Splitt—Shirt Sewing, Thelma Powell—Offices, Elizabeth Egyhazi—Samples, Mary Zrolkowska—Neckwear, Glenna Land—Knitting Mill, Gertrude VanDusick, Nainsook Department.

FIGURE 11. Wilson Brothers newsletter, *Sew and Sew* 1, no. 1, South Bend, Indiana, 1933. (Courtesy of The History Museum, South Bend, Indiana.)

WILD NELL. Presented by Sample Dept.
Directed by Mildred Jena

Lady Vere de Vere........Helen Pawlowska
Handsome Harry...........Myrna Newman
Wild Nell................Bernice Strakowska
Sitting Bull.............Josephine Skoving
Hula Hula...............Mary Kopczynska
Bull Durham.............Elizabeth Egyhazi

The reader, Helen Desits, and the pianist, Jolan Borbely, are not shown in the picture.

BACK TO PROSPERITY
Presented by Neckwear Dept.
Directed by Theresa Paszli

Madame Z................Regina Bonkowski
Mary Ann Waybury........Florence Kryzewski
Madame Rose Waybury....Helen Skubiszewski
George Waybury..........Anne Korlowicz
Joan Waybury............Regina Weisel
A Friend................Mary Wolaczyk
Madame X................Mary Molnar

Jarvis..................Jack Craig
Lord Roberts Packam.....Maxwell Goff
The Woman...............Henrietta Kahler

CURSES! WHAT A NIGHT!
Presented by Hosiery Dept.

Gondelena...............Anna Weiger
Dominot.................Mary Weiger
Sheriff.................Bertha Pietrzycki
Animosity...............Helen Baumgartner
Arsenic.................Bertha Buckner
Directed by Bertha Pietrzycki

THE GOLLY HOPPERS
Winner of Girl's Club First Prize
Directed by Glenna Land

Standing, left to right: Virginia Superczynska, Ruth Kline, Helen Palicki, Edith Rodgers, Henrietta Superczynska, Viola Banning, director of orchestra, Emiline Simmons Bernice Tschida, waltzers.
Seated: Sophie Walorski, Florence Houser.

Josephine Harmacinski, Gertrude Frederickson, Dorothy Torzewska, and Violet Horvath-tap dancer. Pianist, Evelyn Hay.

Stella Markiewicz, who took the individual prize for excellent performance, was not present when the picture was made.

Standing, left to right:

Martha.................Agnes Henning
Minnie.................Irene Wozniak
Mrs. Hanks.............Rita Grace
Lena...................Edna McEndarfer
Frank..................Ronald Bradley
Pianist................Lottie Nowicki
Director...............Katherine Seeley
Sarah..................Henrietta VanVlasselaer
Mandy..................Effie Knappen
Babs...................Evelyn Kaczmarek
Larry..................Wayne Brown
Emaline................Martha Earnes (on bicycle)
Oscar..................Mary Balough
Balson.................Leo Webster
Spitz..................James Heintzelman

SEWING CIRCLE

Mrs. Smith.............Marie Coleman
Flora Smith............Ina Jones
Mrs. Gray..............Clementine Szymczak
Mrs. White.............Jane Noble
Mrs. Green.............Betty Ekamp
Mrs. Brown.............Ethel Karacson
Miss Jones.............Josephine Klodzinsak

STUNT NIGHT BIG SUCCESS!

Eleven Clubs Present Stunts

The stunt night held by the Wilson Bros. Clubs on Thursday, Nov. 23rd, at the Washington School was one of the most successful events in recent years.

A capacity audience was present to enjoy the entertainment, and many more were disappointed that they were unable to obtain tickets.

Among those in the audience were Mr. and Mrs. L. H. Crawford, Mr. Little, Mr. and Mrs. Carol Alton, and Mrs. M. K. Wilson. Mr. Crawford, Mr. Little, Mr. Alton and Mrs. Wilson acted as judges and awarded first prize from the Girls' Club to the "Golly Hoppers" from the Knitting Mill, and the second prize to "School Days" put on by the Advance Guards.

In addition to these prizes which had been previously announced, Mr. Crawford presented four prizes to individuals. The judges awarded first prizes of $10 each to Stella Markiewicz, comedian with the "Golly Hoppers," and to Wayne Brown, the storekeeper in "The Cross Roads Store." Second prizes of $5.00 each were awarded to Lenore Goslin, with the Minstrels, and to Phloye Mitchell, who took the part of the minister in "Rosebud's Wedding."

In addition to the program of stunts, orchestra music between the acts entertained the audience. Miss Bertha Buckner gave a negro shuffle, and John Mulders brought down the house with his fan dance number. A vocal solo was also presented by Miss Virginia Goebel.

Because of the excellence of all the stunts the judges had difficulty in arriving at their decisions.

"The Cross Roads Store" was most effective. The background had been well worked out, and the costuming was particularly good. Splendid comedy bits were played by Henrietta Van Vlasselaer, Martha Earnes and Leo Webster.

"And the Lamp Went Out," was a clever bit of pantomime, put on by the Assembling Department. All the parts were well taken, and much favorable comment was heard on this act.

FIGURE 12. Wilson Brothers newsletter, *Sew and Sew* 1, no. 3, South Bend, Indiana, 1933. (Courtesy of The History Museum, South Bend, Indiana.)

FIGURE 13. Lucille Normand, Works Progress Administration Sewing Project, Chicago, 1940. A lengthy WPA publicity series featured Lucille Normand, a widow supporting her children and parents. (Courtesy of WPA, RG 69, NACP.)

FIGURE 14. Lucille Normand, WPA, Chicago, 1940. (Courtesy of WPA, RG 69, NACP.)

FIGURE 15. Lucille Normand, WPA, Chicago, 1940. (Courtesy of WPA, RG 69, NACP.)

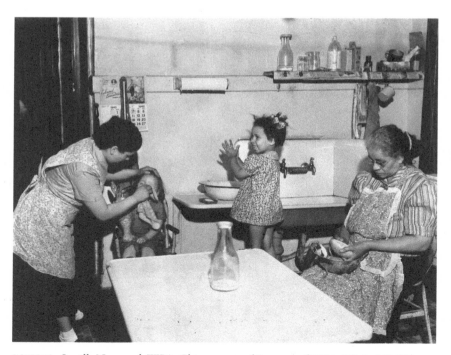

FIGURE 16. Lucille Normand, WPA, Chicago, 1940. (Courtesy of WPA, RG 69, NACP.)

FIGURE 17. Lucille Normand, WPA, Chicago, 1940. (Courtesy of WPA, RG 69, NACP.)

FIGURE 18. WPA mattress-making project, Topeka, Kansas. (Courtesy of WPA, RG 69, NACP.)

FIGURE 19. Works Progress Administration Household Training Project, Cleveland. (Courtesy of WPA, RG 69, NACP.)

FIGURE 20. WPA Household Training Project, WPA, Michigan. (Courtesy of WPA, RG 69, NACP.)

FIGURE 21. WPA academic and home arts classes, Philadelphia. (Courtesy of WPA, RG 69, NACP.)

FIGURE 22. WPA brush-up and preemployment training classes, Chicago. (Courtesy of WPA, RG 69, NACP.)

FIGURE 23. WPA adult elementary class, location unknown. (Courtesy of WPA, RG 69, NACP.)

FIGURE 24. WPA literacy and citizenship class, St. Adalbert's School, Philadelphia. (Courtesy of WPA, RG 69, NACP.)

FIGURE 25. WPA literacy class for Hungarians, Cleveland. (Courtesy of WPA, RG 69, NACP.)

FIGURE 26. WPA English and citizenship class, Donora, Pennsylvania. (Courtesy of WPA, RG 69, NACP.)

FIGURE 27. Wilson Brothers employees party, country club, South Bend, Indiana, 1935. (Courtesy of The History Museum, South Bend, Indiana.)

FIGURE 28. Guardettes basketball team, South Bend, Indiana, 1933. (Courtesy of The History Museum, South Bend, Indiana.)

FIGURE 29. Zion African Methodist Episcopal Church members, South Bend, Indiana, 1925. (Courtesy of The History Museum, South Bend, Indiana.)

FIGURE 30. Zion African Methodist Episcopal Church Senior Choir, South Bend, Indiana, 1925. (Courtesy of The History Museum, South Bend, Indiana.)

FIGURE 31. Bendix Corporation sit-down strike, South Bend, Indiana, 1936. (Courtesy of The History Museum, South Bend, Indiana.)

FIGURE 32. Bendix sit-down strike with lynched dummy of the company union, 1936. (Courtesy of The History Museum, South Bend, Indiana.)

FIGURE 33. WPA Negro Recreation Project trio, broadcasting on WSBT and WFAM, South Bend, Indiana. (Courtesy of WPA, RG 69, NACP.)

5

Interrupted Expectations

● ●

Loyalty and Conflict
in the Family Economy

During the Great Depression, daily survival in the absence of adequate wages depended upon a family's ability to command the allegiance and deploy the labor of the entire household. Collective survival was the goal, not the means. Parents asserted authority over children, and men exercised masculine prerogatives. Obligation and coercion generated additional income. Grudging cooperation joined hands with resentment and discord when parents and/or men wielded power. Acquiescence and even commitment to prevailing gender, age, and familial hierarchies did not ensure that children and wives complied with parental or patriarchal plans.

Strategies to sustain faltering family economies required girls and women to reconsider, postpone, or abandon assumptions about education, jobs, marriage, children, and reliance upon parents, spouses, siblings, and offspring. Compelled to make do while they struggled to make choices, women adjusted expectations to survive years of uncertainty. Predictability persisted as wives' responsibilities for producing, reproducing, and maintaining the labor force never abated. Stymied in their ability to fulfill breadwinning roles, men despaired, but little evidence suggests that they assumed tasks and roles that were coded as female.[1] Adolescent and young adult daughters quit school and took jobs; most eventually married and moved out of their parents' homes. Responsibilities of and expectations for married women cut across race and ethnicity and underlay common tactics and common strains.

When fathers, husbands, and sons were out of work or underemployed, families turned to daughters and wives to bring cash into the household. As increasing numbers of women entered the labor force, or remained despite planning to leave, their wages accounted for a greater share of household income. Parents expected daughters to turn over their paychecks, not just to pay room and board, reversing their slowly won right to retain more of their wages. Families made few adjustments in employed wives' reproductive labor to compensate for their double day. Other female members of the household, if any, shouldered housework and supervision of children while mothers were on the job. Because the Depression disrupted expectations, relationships, and life passages and challenged assumptions about appropriate behavior, it also demanded more emotional maintenance work from wives and mothers. No evidence of racially unique home and family tactics appears in the sources I have consulted. The constraints of institutionalized racism predicted women's success in using particular strategies rather than the nature of the strategy.[2]

The Need for Wage Earners

When working-class men lost jobs, women not in the labor force volunteered for, or were drafted into, breadwinning obligations. Parental demands and filial loyalty inspired or required daughters to cut short their education. Helen M, the daughter of Polish immigrants, began doing housework after school and on Saturdays at age fourteen in 1930. At fifteen she quit domestic work to take a "regular" job, and by sixteen she left school to work full-time. In 1933 Helen supported a sick mother, a father unemployed for two years, and four younger siblings. Earning $5 weekly for sixteen-hour days at housework, this young Clevelander boasted, "I'm just about keeping the family."[3] Young white women who came of working age early in the Depression quit school and entered the labor force in large numbers. Almost one-third of job seekers at the Cleveland YWCA in 1932–1933 were teenagers.[4]

Crisis transformed slightly older daughters from supplementary to primary earners. Rose H, a Hungarian American, went to work as a stenographer at age seventeen in 1928; a year later she moved to a better job at higher wages. In 1930, when Oliver Farm Implements laid off her machinist father, Frank, for eight weeks, and her brother, Frank Jr., worked two days weekly at Studebaker, Rose explained, "I am just about the support of the family." Family finances continued to deteriorate. Frank Sr. was laid off for more than half of the 1931–1932 year and worked two to four days when he was called in. Frank Jr. worked irregularly and was laid off in June 1932. Rose changed jobs, was unemployed for five months, and began her fourth clerical job in March 1932, at $15 weekly, her lowest pay. Her pre-Depression wages likely accounted for less than a quarter of household earnings; in August 1932 she earned 60% of the income. A grandmother moved in, requiring Rose's mother to stretch money further.[5]

Urban Black families historically attempted to protect daughters by keeping them out of the labor force, and the refusal of industry to hire African Americans also contributed to their remaining in school. The jurist Constance Baker Motley noted that in New Haven, Connecticut, "Black students usually did not drop out of high school, like the Italians, for example, to get a factory job, even though such income would have aided our families."[6] In 1929, single Black women younger than twenty-five had lower labor force participation rates than single white women, native-born or foreign-born, in the four cities (see table 1).

A sign of prosperity was the ability of wives to work only at home because husbands earned wages adequate to support the household. Evelyn D, a Black woman, worked in service and industrial jobs in Texas and, after 1925, in Chicago. Widowed as a teenager, she remarried; her second husband, James, a store porter, supported them. Evelyn kept house, even after James lost his primary job. He still had "a piece of a job," which covered rent, and every Saturday he cleaned the windows of a meat market in exchange for a few days' worth of groceries. Subsequently he found more reliable income via the Works Progress Administration (WPA). Evelyn considered James a "swell husband—good in every way. . . . [He] took care of me."[7]

Many wives preferred one job, not two, and public controversy underscored that women's place was in the home. Yet married women, Black and white, entered, reentered, and remained in the labor force. Brides and women planning weddings kept working even if they had anticipated quitting. As Anna A (whose family story appeared in the introduction), a dentist's assistant for six years, commented a month before her wedding in 1930, "Times are too uncertain to give up a job." In 1940 she remained employed at the same dental practice. Her husband's jobs were far less stable.[8]

Mothers of small children were less likely candidates for employment. Genevieve L, a Polish American woman, quit Oliver's assembly line in 1929 when she married. After the company laid off her husband, Steve, in 1930, they moved into her parents' home. In the fall of 1932, two of seven adults in the household of fourteen were working. Genevieve, who had borne three children, was looking for a job. Two years elapsed between Steve's layoff and Genevieve's job search, which likely reflected her desire to begin a family and her reluctance to leave her toddlers and infants. Yet living with extended family facilitated sharing domestic tasks and furnished built-in childcare.[9]

Middle-aged wives sought employment for the same reasons. A forty-four-year-old white woman, Edna H had not earned wages in more than twenty years of marriage. Her husband, Leland, a printer at Ball Band Shoes, worked three days every other week. Their daughter, Ruth, a clerical worker in the county recorder's office, earned two-thirds of her former pay after the county cut her hours. Their son Robert attended high school, and a grandmother, who lost everything in a bank failure, planned to move in. Edna explained, "We were having such a hard time getting along on the little the others could make, I thought

I'd try to help some too." Robert remained in school; Edna found a job at the South Bend Bait Company. She worked about half the time and was laid off the other half. The following year Leland injured his hand in a roller, and although he expected to collect workmen's compensation, payments would be small since irregular hours had reduced his wages drastically. Three years later, Edna worked for the same company.[10]

Wives of all ages and maternal circumstances explained their entry or reentry into the labor force in the same economic terms used by job-holding wives in the late 1920s. They did not necessarily assume paid employment cheerfully. Emma D, a Belgian immigrant and Studebaker assembler, worked because her husband's hours were so irregular. Buying a home, they "[had] to scrape to live." Only a son in high school still lived with them, but Emma regarded breadwinning as her husband's responsibility: "[I] wish he could work more so I could stay home and tend my business."[11] A white wife in her twenties echoed, "I would not go to work if he was getting steady work."[12]

Just as daughters' wages converted from supplementary to primary income, so did the earnings of wives. Sophie E, a Polish woman born in 1897, gave birth to her first child in 1914 in the old country and had three more children after her family immigrated. While they were young, she cleaned Studebaker offices at night. Sophie and her husband, Walter, a Studebaker assembly worker, purchased a home in 1922, less than a decade after their arrival in South Bend. In May 1930 Studebaker laid off Walter and reduced Sophie's wages from $16.75 to $15 weekly. That fall, Sophie was ill and Walter, "very much worried," told the interviewer that he would "gladly take her job if he could." He appreciated her contribution: "What [my] wife earns just keeps us going, otherwise we would be stuck right now." Two years later, Walter remained unemployed and Sophie continued to clean, for $11 weekly. They lost the contract for their house, but remained as renters. In the 1920s Sophie's wages had helped to purchase a home; during the 1930s her job put food on the table and paid utility bills.[13]

Some married women had mixed feelings about holding jobs, and some husbands felt threatened that their wives had work when they did not.[14] Men rarely alleviated women's double day by taking on housework. Although Walter would have taken Sophie's job, employers rarely replaced women with men. Men subverted the Depression by cutting wood to heat their homes, bartering labor with landlords, or doing odd jobs, such as peddling watermelons or washing cars,[15] none of which violated masculine norms. A single husband in the samples suggested that he do the housework. Doris L, his wife, came to Cleveland at eighteen in 1926, worked three years as a waitress, married, had a child, and quit working. After her husband lost his job, Doris applied to the YWCA, which referred her to a good-paying waitress position that never materialized. The YWCA noted, "Husband will stay with child and keep home, husband is so discouraged, has tried everywhere for work."[16] Did some husbands don aprons, literally or metaphorically, yet hide that fact, because they were shamed by joblessness and doing "women's work"? Susan Porter Benson argues that there was continuity in roles during the interwar period and that men participated in household chores. My sources, specific to the Depression, suggest that men's joblessness altered women's behavior, but show no evidence of men's participation in housework.[17]

Economic pressures on daughters and wives increased, but the significance of their employment differed. Daughters' employment promoted familial stability, while wives' job holding might have the opposite effect. Daughters had consistently worked and, especially in white homes, turned over part of their pay to their mothers. Their employment expanded, and the share of their wages that parents expected increased, but neither practice was out of the ordinary. What was new was the increased importance of their wages to the family economy. Wives' job holding, on the other hand, potentially threatened marital power balances and undermined stability. African American families were far more accustomed to wage-earning wives, and Black wives' pay historically accounted for a larger share of family income because of Black men's low wages. Wives' employment and husbands' joblessness doubly threatened some men, regardless of race, when they could not fulfill gendered mandates. Some interpreted wives' jobs as implicit criticism. Others juggled mixed feelings: they appreciated the money, but missed the emotional and material comforts their wives had less time to provide, and sometimes felt compromised. Because women still did housework despite a paid job, the demands of a double day might exacerbate dissatisfaction with husbands and their health might suffer. Wives' employment brought needed cash into homes, challenged gender roles and power relations, exhausted women, and disrupted some marriages.

Despite obstacles to their employment, married women's job holding increased 22.2% between 1929 and 1940 (table 7). If job-seekers are included, the growth was even greater.[18] White wives accounted for most of this growth; Black women remained unemployed in large numbers.[19] Black wives, overwhelmingly employed in domestic service, characterized by high turnover, moved in and out of employment. Census data understated employment of married women because snapshots camouflaged entrances and exits and many wives worked intermittently.

White wives acted more like Black wives as they increased job holding. Formerly supplementing husbands' thicker pay envelopes, their jobs became essential to survival. The growth of married women's employment actually predated World War II, though at a slower rate. It came, Winifred Wandersee has argued, not only from the striving of "middle income" women to "protect" the values of family life, security, and material comfort. Putting food on the table, preventing utility companies from turning off lights or water, and paying rent or mortgage were necessities.[20]

Virtually every comparison possible of employment and wages of women and men, among all South Bend households interviewed twice and among those in my sample, illustrates the increased importance of women's wages. When

Studebaker men once earned $40 weekly, and more with overtime, daughters' and wives' wages constituted a small fraction of the total. When men took home meager wages or none, women's proportion of family income leaped. In 1932, women's median earnings were slightly higher than men's: $31 compared to $29.50. Twice as many households had full-time female workers (40.4%) as had full-time male workers (20.2%).[21] In my sample, 54.4% of the men worked in 1932. Women were more likely to remain employed, at 63.3%, and more likely to work full-time. Women alone supported one-third of sample households, whether or not men were present. Wives earned higher wages and a slightly larger share of household income (68%) than daughters (64%), but many households included multiple employed daughters.

Little evidence suggests that new divisions of household labor sustained women's increased responsibilities. Whether employed women were relieved of demands of the double day depended primarily upon the existence of daughters outside the labor force onto whose shoulders the burdens of household chores could be shifted.

Interrupted Expectations

From the perspective of family economies, women's unplanned, longer-term, or new wage earning flowed logically from men's unemployment. From the vantage point of individuals, the Depression interrupted life passages and interfered with plans for education, independence, marriage, and children. Unable to count on the future they anticipated, women responded with flexibility, resourcefulness, and resentment.

Adolescent daughters were torn between loyalty and obligation to families and their own desires. A Cleveland-born immigrant daughter quit school at fifteen because no one in her family of seven was employed. "I was next on the program to try to get work."[22] Ruth K set aside her dream of attending college, a rare prize for a working-class daughter, declining a scholarship to Wittenberg College in 1931 because her family needed her wages. Her father, a Bohemian immigrant fur finisher, had little work, and her younger brother could not find employment when he graduated from high school. Ruth held two jobs and almost single-handedly supported six people. She earned $55 monthly as a doctor's secretary and assistant, and another $10 doing clerical work three nights a week. Unable to "take advantage of" the scholarship, but long on perseverance, Ruth took a chemistry class at night school on her free evenings.[23] Her self-sacrifice typifies the cohort who came of working age early in the decade. Their younger sisters fared differently, finding it increasingly difficult to secure jobs. New Deal work programs penalized fathers for children's wages. Consequently, daughters remained in school because families could gain little if they quit. Between 1930 and 1940, school attendance of sixteen- and seventeen-year-old girls, Black and white, increased dramatically, from one half to three-fourths of young women in the four cities.[24]

Economic crisis undermined heterosexual expectations for marriage, homes, and children. Marriage rates mirrored employment rates; both took nosedives. In 1932, three-fourths as many couples married as during the late 1920s. The pre-Depression rate was equaled in 1937, a year of hoped-for recovery, and then fell again.[25] Some young adults believed they had to "stay by their families," and some parents opposed marriages. Sophia P explained that her brother, Andy S, "[couldn't] get married for having to help us." Mr. P, a Polish American, and five of his seven children once held jobs. By 1932 he and two sons were unemployed and Sophia and her sister each earned $14 in four weeks. Andy, a carpet layer for a department store, no longer paid board, but he turned over his $25 weekly wages to his mother and postponed marriage to "keep us from losing our home."[26] Interviews more often recounted that young women sacrificed plans to support their families, and Andy may have been exceptional.

The birth rate also plummeted, from ninety-eight births per thousand women of child-bearing age in the late 1920s to lows of seventy-six per thousand in 1933 and 1936.[27] Popular opinion judged women's attempts to regulate births as "selfishness and convenience," and a strong moral stance condemned them.[28] Women postponed marriage, abstained from sex, used birth control, and obtained illegal abortions, despite practical, legal, and ideological impediments. Dispensing birth control information or devices through the mail remained illegal until 1938. The most common methods were back fence contraception, techniques learned informally from family, friends, and acquaintances: folk methods, withdrawal, condoms, and douches. Increasing numbers of working-class women, Black and white, patronized birth control clinics that opened in many cities during the 1920s and 1930s, and manufacturers of condoms and douches did a booming business.[29] In desperation and determination not to have children whom they could not feed, women risked their health to terminate pregnancies with illegal and self-induced abortions. Abortions have been estimated at a half million to two million annually during the 1930s. There may have been almost as many abortions as births, and at least one abortion for every 2.5 births in urban areas.[30]

A white agricultural worker in Bakersfield, California, approached Lorena Hickok, a field investigator for the Federal Emergency Relief Administration:

> Falteringly, terribly ill at ease at first, she told me she wanted to talk to me about something that had nearly driven her crazy when she and her husband were on relief and that she knew was one of the worst problems of women whose husbands were out of work.
>
> "It's this thing of having babies," she said. "You've got no protection at all. And here you are, surrounded by young ones you can't support and never knowing when there's going to be another.

"You don't have any money, you see, to buy anything at the drugstore. . . . Maybe you could tell your case worker, but lots of women don't like to talk about those things to outsiders.

"I suppose you can say the easiest way would be not to do it. But it wouldn't be. You don't know what it's like when your husband's out of work. He's gloomy and unhappy all the time. Life is terrible. You must try all the time to keep him from going crazy. And many times—that's the only way."[31]

If married women found it difficult to satisfy their partners' and/or their own sexual desires and to limit the birth of children, heterosexually active unmarried women suffered severe sanctions. Anna P, a Polish American woman who left school at fourteen to work, bore an illegitimate child at twenty-one in 1931. The child was taken from her and placed in an orphanage. Two years later, she found herself "that way" again, and her sexual partner threatened her life if she divulged his name. Six months pregnant, she purchased abortifacient pills for $7, that "nearly killed her." She ended up in Cook County Hospital, where she was sterilized. When she applied for relief a few months later, the psychiatrist evaluated her as a "high grade defective, committable" based on her school record, violent family history, and "sexual delinquency." He "[felt] that institutionalization would be urgent were it not for the fact that she has been sterilized."[32]

Agents did not inquire nor did interviewees volunteer information about birth control or sexual habits, but numbers testify that women successfully limited births. Even in South Bend, where a large proportion of the working-class population was Catholic, the birth rate dropped significantly.[33] In urban areas, abortionists were available.[34] Working-class women suffered extreme consequences for their sexual and reproductive decisions. Loss of children, involuntary sterilization, ill health, and death were the prices exacted.

Providing for children they already had posed wrenching quandaries for mothers, who doubled up, broke families apart, placed children in orphanages, or gave them to sympathetic strangers. Sagas of the reunification of adult siblings, separated as children during the 1930s, were a human interest feature in popular media in the later twentieth century. Often mothers had died, and adult children reconstructed stories from fragments of memory. Dorothy C desperately contemplated giving her children away. She bore her third child in 1930 while her husband battled tuberculosis. She left Bendix for two months for childbirth, was taken back on a lower-paying job, and laid off three months later in July. Her husband died in August, things were "going from bad to worse," and by October Dorothy offered her two youngest babies for adoption. According to the record, "She says she cannot see them starve and she hasn't been able to get work." A few weeks later Dorothy received small payments from Associated Charities. In 1932 she had all three children with her, but her economic situation had not appreciably improved. Her mother was dead, and apparently she could not call upon female relatives to help care for her children.[35]

Single mothers entrusted children to family or friends when they migrated to cities in search of jobs. Beginning with the Great War, Black southern women traveled north; some brought children along, only to send them back. Maya Angelou recalled, "The United States [was] crossed thousands of times by frightened Black children traveling alone to their newly affluent parents in Northern cities, or back to grandmothers in Southern towns when the urban North reneged on its economic promises."[36] White mothers, caught between the demands of child-rearing and wage earning, practiced similar strategies. After she was widowed, Matilda C, a Finnish immigrant, moved to Cleveland to search for work, leaving her three children with her mother in a nearby city.[37] Christine B kept her family together for eight years after her husband died. In the winter of 1932–1933, this Scots immigrant could no longer support and raise her children, ages ten and sixteen, so she sent them out of Chicago to live with her sister.[38] Maternal grandmothers often raised children, and mothers boarded offspring with any adult women they could trust: sisters, aunts, grandmothers, and friends, neighbors, and landladies whom they treated as kin.

Families dispersed if no relatives possessed the resources or will to take in an entire household. Beatrice T once earned $150 a month in a clerical position, but was reduced to around-the-clock housework for $8 a week in 1933. Her Irish immigrant parents lost their home and furniture and her family scattered across Cleveland to the homes of relatives.[39] Women shuttled between rural families and hoped-for urban job prospects. Retta K, who lived in at an institution and managed a fraternity house (see chapter 2), lived with a married daughter on a farm when she was out of work. Another daughter, Doris, an intermittently employed clerical worker, lived with Retta at the fraternity, then with a married sister in Cleveland, then with a friend of her sister, and in 1933 took a room at the YWCA. Retta's son, a high school student, also lived in Cleveland, likely with relatives. Optimistically, Doris planned, "When the Depression is over we'll all get back together again."[40]

Marriages fractured when unemployed men left town in search of work. Young, white, jobless men from rural Illinois, Indiana, and Michigan, once seduced by Studebaker's promise of high wages and steady work, returned to family farms where they could contribute their labor and incur few expenses. Many left city-bred wives and children behind, usually with the wife's parents. Black urban men returned to southern homes. Beatrice B married and moved to Chicago in 1923, and her husband supported her "pretty well." "Discontented and unhappy over his inability to find work and support for them," he left in 1936, planning to "hobo his way to [his] old home in Mississippi to see if [there was] work there." Nine months later Beatrice had not heard a word.[41] After more than two years without steady employment, John V, a fiftyish immigrant carpenter, sailed to Belgium in 1931 expecting to find work. He was stranded without sufficient money to return to the United States, where his wife and four children remained.[42] Some traveling men returned home, especially in winter. Some found work and sent for families. Other marriages dissolved permanently.

Family economies collapsed when husbands died, separated from, or abandoned wives and children. If women did not have, or could not count on, adult children for support, men's departure jeopardized their well-being. When skilled, experienced women could not find jobs, those outside the labor force were ill equipped because they lacked recognizable skills. Age discrimination further lessened their chances. Old women's opportunities were extremely limited; old Black women held jobs most frequently.[43] At any age, women's life progressions, hopes, and plans were waylaid or forfeited because of the Depression.

Doubling Up

When Antoinette K's husband died in December 1929, she had eight children at home and a large mortgage. She considered selling the house, but could not find a buyer. In 1932 only her daughter Gertrude and son Anthony were working, at a laundry and a meat market; between them they earned $50 in four weeks. Two sons were unemployed, and four younger children had not yet entered the labor market. Antoinette's married daughter, Genevieve L, her husband, a core maker at Oliver, and three young children moved in after he lost his job. The Ls contributed their relief, $4.50 weekly grocery orders, and a half ton of coal. The bank raised the interest rate on the mortgage from 8 to 9%, increasing the semiannual payment from $70 to $78. In October 1932, payment was six months overdue. The bank failed and attempted to make the Ks pay off the mortgage, though it was not due for another five years. Gertrude, age twenty-one, queried the interviewer, "How can they do that when it isn't in our contract?" Indebted to the grocer, the butcher, and the doctor, and with the gas shut off, the Ks took out two loans and cashed in thirteen insurance policies. Doubling up, fourteen people shared hardship and resources; in 1940 Antoinette and some of her children remained in their home.[44]

Sixty-four of 183 South Bend sample households doubled up during the first three years of the Depression. Before the crisis, complex households usually included unattached women: single sisters, widowed mothers, or separated or divorced daughters. In 1932 almost three-fourths of doubled-up households were two-, three-, or occasionally four-generation extended families. Like Genevieve, young adults who married and went to housekeeping returned with spouses and often children, as did women whose husbands died or were absent. Some adults married and added spouses to the household. Married or formerly married daughters were more than twice as likely to double up with parents as were sons.[45] Children remained with mothers, and the younger generation almost always moved in with the older.

Both adult generations contributed to and benefited from extended households. The Ms, Hungarian homeowners, were accustomed to an income of over $200 monthly in the late 1920s, from Vincent's work as a molder at Oliver and his daughter Mary's well-paid clerical job. Mary married in 1930, her husband moved in, and in 1931 she quit work to care for their baby. Vincent was laid off, and his younger daughter, Virginia, found her first job, as a stenographer at a law firm, for $8 weekly. Mary's husband, who made $17.50 weekly at a filling station, earned two-thirds of the household total income and the entire family used his Ford. Mary, her husband, and baby would have struggled to survive on his wages alone, and the Ms could have bought only groceries on $8 weekly. Doubling up, they shared a home, a car, and wages from two poorly paid jobs.[46] Women usually cited economics to explain doubling up: sharing resources cut costs. Parents with a modicum of financial security might house children and grandchildren rent free. Adult children might contribute half or all the cash income. Doubling up increased the number of potential earners and unwaged household workers and supplied built-in childcare.

Three-generation households with daughters' families typified doubling up in South Bend, but siblings, aunts, uncles, and cousins also joined or stayed together. Edna and Leland H planned to move in a grandmother. Their daughter explained, "[We] will have to provide home and clothes for her, she has nothing of her own now, [she] lost [her] savings in a bank failure."[47] Parents of middle-aged working-class adults often resided in the old country. Doubling up arrangements reflected location, space, and habits of migration and immigration.

The adult siblings whose story introduced this book illustrated peer cooperation. Elizabeth A, a Hungarian widow with six children, lingered through a long illness and died in the late 1920s. Her oldest daughter, Betty, quit work for a year to nurse her mother and replace her as housewife. In 1930 four sisters, eighteen through twenty-seven, all worked and supported their brothers. Joseph, laid off by Bendix in 1928, remained out of work, and Peter attended high school. Two sisters married and purchased furniture on installment payment plans, planning to start their own homes. Anna and Ira M moved out but returned when Ira was laid off. George K moved in when he married Mary; they subsequently had a child; and Mary quit work. In the fall of 1932 Betty, Anna, and Cecilia earned half of the household income, and Ira and George earned the other half. Their four-week income, $232, ranked in the 98th percentile in the sample. Considering that this sum supported seven adults, a teenager, and a baby, it was hardly luxurious, and the family sacrificed to carry on daily life.[48]

The Great Migration and the increasingly overcrowded South Side determined the ways Black Chicagoans doubled up, just as immigration and local housing formed the South Bend context. Largely recent migrants, African Americans did not necessarily have relatives nearby. They took friends, members of their churches, and even strangers into their homes, sharing resources within the community. Charity D came north after separating from her husband in 1929 and did housework and waitressed until the restaurant folded in 1932. She moved in with friends, the Hs, who gave her a room in return for housework. A year later she returned to her former employer, where she worked for room and board. Declining health incapacitated her, and in 1936 she moved back in with the Hs, a couple and their two nieces, and applied for relief. The Hs' six-room apartment was well furnished, well ventilated, and possessed modern conveniences. One niece worked in a beauty parlor and the other attended the University of Chicago. Charity, age fifty-four, did light housework to compensate for the low rent she paid. She rarely went out because her heart condition made climbing stairs difficult. The interviewer noted that the "advantages of living with the Hs outweigh the disadvantages of living on the second floor."[49]

A younger woman, Marie S, twenty-six, single, and an Alabama migrant, lost jobs at housework and in a laundry and applied for and received relief in 1936. She paid $8 a month to live with the K family, which included a father, two adult daughters, a son-in-law, and a teenage son. Mr. K had a job, and his son-in-law worked on the WPA. Marie shared a bed with the single daughter. She bought food until she exhausted her grocery budget, then continued to eat with the family. She helped the sisters with the housework, but "as they are two already, they don't need her help, and she considers they keep her from kindness."[50] The distinction between doubling up and tenants could be hazy, but the principle of sharing resources was clear. Combining assets—an apartment, furniture, a job, or relief—provided survival for a group when individuals could not make it on their own.

Customs of sharing hardships within southern Black communities continued in the urban North as households extended across kin and friendship lines. White families in South Bend doubled up with kin. African Americans often lacked multigenerational families in northern cities; non-kin more often shared households. "Unattached," unrelated women of both races joined together in ways more evocative of Black community practices than white, as chapter 6 will illustrate.

Cooperation and Conflict

Depression survival is not only a tale of harmonious cooperation but a chronicle of intense conflict, brutal assertions of power, and coerced capitulation. Working-class families relied on women's resourcefulness and self-sacrifice, but relationships were often jagged. Parents asserted authority over adult children, and spouses fought. Cramped quarters abetted tensions in doubled-up homes. Parents, husbands, siblings, and adult children expected female self-sacrifice. Sometimes they abandoned daughters, wives, sisters, and mothers who did not comply or whose labor was no longer necessary. I found little evidence for community cooperation and softening borders in white working-class gender roles.[51] Family economies ostensibly served the common good. They also ran roughshod over dissenters and expected female self-sacrifice without recompense.

Whether parental command or personal responsibility determined Ruth K's forfeiture of a college scholarship is uncertain, but parents expected to exert control over their daughters' behavior and disposition of their wages as long as they lived under their roof. Josephine B "had to take" her daughter, Irene, out of high school in 1931 because she "needed her wages." Neither Josephine nor her husband, Constanti, Polish immigrants raising four children and paying off a mortgage, worked regularly after 1929. Their son apparently continued to attend high school, while Irene worked "off and on" as a domestic. The following year, at eighteen, she married and moved out, thwarting a mother's plan to utilize a daughter's potential earnings.[52] Generational conflict over young women's behavior did not require an economic crisis, but parents demanded allegiance and clamped down because daughters' wages had become critical to survival.

Dutiful daughters cut short their education to take paid employment or to assume chores and childcare while mothers, sisters, and sisters-in-law earned wages. Some regretted how little cash they could contribute. Eleanor K, an honor student and a leader highly regarded by the Cleveland YWCA staff, earned $12 weekly at a clerical job after she graduated from high school in 1931. Laid off, she subsequently found housework at $3 a week, which cost $1.25 for carfare. She was "very much discouraged because she has only $1.75 to give to her family."[53] Young women living independently also helped families. Irene N, a twenty year-old Hungarian-American, and her roommate both paid for younger sisters' clothes and schooling.[54] Grace K, a Black woman who migrated to Chicago at eighteen, continued to send money to her mother in Georgia a decade later.[55]

Daughters took pride in their financial contributions, yet parental dictates that they leave school and turn over "every cent" also elicited indignation. The seventeen-year-old who resented her father's consumption of tobacco and beer (see chapter 4) described herself and her sister: "There are hundreds of girls just like herself and me. Neither of us could finish our high school education, we had to go to work." She chafed under this responsibility, which thwarted her plans. "Many girls of my age have a well started hope chest. I haven't. How can I start a hope chest, help eliminate the family debt contracted during the depression years and still support myself on $3.30 a week?" Her signature, "One of the Hundreds," underlined that many young women felt torn between familial obligation and their own desires.[56]

When stepmothers and stepdaughters failed to get along, fathers sacrificed daughters. Margaret T, a young Clevelander, reported that her father had been unemployed for a year; her "stepmother won't let girl stay at home." When she was out of a domestic job, Margaret stayed with friends.[57] Nellie E, age twenty-three, an unemployed clerical worker, "ran away from home and refused to return." Home consisted of a father and stepmother.[58] "Difficulties with family in Philadelphia and didn't want to return home," the interviewer's summary of Helen B's situation, could have covered a multitude of conflicts.[59]

Quarrels sometimes accompanied decisions about wives' jobs, as Louise Meriwether's portrayal of a Harlem family in the novel *Daddy Was a Number Runner* illustrates. Adam Coffin, a fictionalized version of her father,[60] is an unemployed house painter who reinvests most of his income as a numbers runner into playing the numbers himself. He forbids his wife, Henrietta, to look for domestic work in the slave markets or to apply for relief. Their daughter narrates their argument:

> She was asking Daddy one more time if she could go up in the Bronx and get some day's work.
> "Why don't you stop nagging me, woman," Daddy said. "You know I don't want you doing housework."
> "It's not what we want anymore," Mother said. "It's what we need. The children needs shoes and school clothes. We're all in rags."
> "They also need you to be home when they get out from school."[61]

Expecting to earn $30 one weekend playing piano for three rent parties, Adam comes home with only $9.30, and Henrietta renews the struggle:

> Mother was so mad she was trembling. "I can't sit around here and watch these children go hungry," she said. "Either you let me go up in the Bronx and find some day's work or we'll have to go on relief. There ain't no other way."
> Mother kept at it until finally Daddy hollered that a man couldn't have any peace in his own home and yes, goddammit, go on up in the Bronx and find some work if she wanted to.[62]

Marital discord resulting from wives' taking jobs appears in sources far more frequently than evidence of husbands' assuming housework. Henrietta hides her trips to the slave markets because of her husband's vehement opposition. Adam does not expect to welcome his children home from school. Some wives wanted to take paying jobs and some husbands forbade them.

Marriages foundered on the shoals of the Depression. Men's unemployment and sense of failure, unemployment of both partners, women's job holding in the absence of men's employment, and wives' anger multiplied separations and desertions. Divorces declined sharply because of the expense, but by 1935 they surpassed the 1929 peak.[63] Countless marriages ended without legal sanction. Mollie and Philip S, a white couple, married in 1927. Philip worked intermittently after 1931, and they separated and reconciled several times during the next six years. "Mrs. S thought Mr. S was lazy and did not want to work." The interviewer also attributed "marital discord" to "religious differences, Mrs. S being a Catholic and Mr. S a Seventh Day Adventist." The Court of Domestic Relations ordered Philip to support Mollie, but she received only $50 in five years' time. The court wanted to jail Philip for nonsupport, but Mollie "thinks it is no use." In 1937

Philip tried to locate Mollie, but she refused to see him because he was "cruel."[64] It is not possible to disentangle their knotted skein of anger, but the Depression was a clear catalyst for their pain.

A Black couple came to Chicago from Savannah in 1908. Elizabeth H worked only during the "dull seasons" for her husband, Alfred, a plasterer, taking in boarders to tide them over until Alfred's work picked up. They split up in 1931 because of her "husband's unemployment and resentment re losing their home." Elizabeth once considered Alfred a "good provider," but after they lost their home he "got the big head" and "dropped" her.[65] The Depression shredded the fabric of some relationships, but most survived, and some grew stronger.

A wife's unemployment could precipitate marital disintegration, particularly if her earnings maintained the household. An interviewer described Mary B, a Black woman, as "quite depressed and entirely through with men." Married at fifteen, Mary usually supported her husband, but hard physical labor broke her health. Her "cruel" husband "mistreated" her and went off with another woman after thirty-one years of marriage. Mary "looked through her life and decided that she was too easy, that she was a fool." When questioned about a possible future marriage, she responded, "No next time for me—never no more for me."[66] A white woman wept when recounting a similar story. Gertrude W said her husband "forced" her to work and at times refused to work to "preserve his own health." Laundry jobs exhausted her so that she could "hardly drag along." After nineteen years of marriage, he deserted her, which she attributed to the fact that he "drank and told lies."[67]

Alcoholism, physical abuse, in-law conflicts, and the allure of other women had long marred some marriages, but the Depression made them unbearable. A thirty-five-year-old white woman divorced her husband because he started running around with other women after the repeal of Prohibition.[68] A Black woman of the same age felt "compelled" to leave because of her husband's drinking and her mother-in-law's nagging.[69] A young Black woman, Alberta C, married in 1934. After her husband, Joseph, got a WPA job, he deserted her when he received his first paycheck, returned drunk and beat her up, then departed while she was hospitalized with injuries. Alberta appealed to the Court of Domestic Relations, which ordered Joseph to support her. He left town.[70] Domestic violence assuredly increased, but interviewees rarely revealed it explicitly. Desertion shocked women, and some suffered nervous breakdowns. Others were relieved, like the white widow who concluded, "Married life was hell."[71]

The Depression nurtured the best and the worst of family relations. Doubling up was the most visible form of cooperation, though not necessarily the most prevalent. Kin loaned cash and made gifts of money, garden produce, bags of groceries, and old clothes. They cared for children and ill parents. When Irene and Raymond G lost their jobs, Raymond's mother regularly gave them food. Irene, who had a baby, reported, "It's a blessing we've got her to help us."[72] Vera N held on to her seven-day-a-week hotel kitchen job and supported her three youngest children by her second husband, who moved in and out of their home. She gave cash and "everything else we could" to her unemployed son, his wife, and three children.[73] Fannie C, an ailing, elderly Black woman whose daughter's story began this book, divided her time after her husband, William, died in 1931. She spent six months with children in Chicago and six months in South Bend with her daughter Leona.[74]

Doubling up shared meager resources and created tensions. Eighteen couples in the South Bend sample married between 1930 and 1932, and six formed complex households with in-laws. Numerous other couples who had earlier gone to housekeeping doubled up, usually with the wife's parents. Loyalties to both her families might compete in a woman's heart, but necessity drove her, her husband, and children back to her parents' home. Some parents attempted to exert authority over adult children or judged unemployed sons and sons-in-law harshly. Some couples resented abandoning independence. When two generations of adults, each accustomed to authority in their households, shared cramped quarters, they might disagree about finances, child-rearing, and daily practicalities. Betty G, her husband, and their two young children moved in with her parents and four siblings after her husband lost his job in 1930. He subsequently moved to his parents' home in Illinois. Betty explained, "[My] mother couldn't afford to support him any longer. [She has a] large family of her own." The household was comparatively solvent; her father was unemployed, but Betty and two siblings worked steadily. Her account masked tensions between the generations and within her marriage.[75]

Overcrowded, doubled-up homes, noisy children, and inadequate space strained relations. The Bs, a family of six, lived in a four-room flat and "boarded" relatives for several months "until they could get on their feet." A daughter explained, "We had to sleep on the floors to do it. There were eleven of us living here at one time."[76] Walter and Helen D married, lived with Helen's parents rent free, and paid half the utility bills. After her sister returned home in 1931, seven people shared the two-bedroom house, which Helen judged too crowded. Despite the fact that she was unemployed and Walter worked quite irregularly, they moved out the next summer.[77] When Mary T's husband entered a tuberculosis sanitarium, she moved into her in-laws' home with their three children. They moved out two years later because the children were "too lively" for their grandmother, who was ill, and made her "nervous."[78]

Finding her son reading, one mother asked: "You're not throwing away money buying those magazines, are you?" Richard Wright was barely supporting his mother, aunt, and younger brother. Neither woman could understand his reading. On one occasion when he was without work, their living arrangements quickly deteriorated. "In Aunt Maggie's eyes I was a plainly marked failure and she feared that perhaps she would have to feed me. The emotional atmosphere in the cramped quarters became tense, ugly, petty, bickering. Fault was found with my reading and writing; it was claimed that I was swelling the electric bill." Wright arranged for his mother, brother, and himself to move in with another aunt.[79]

By definition, the Depression interrupted expectations. Economic survival overshadowed hopes, plans, and dreams. Working-class women made do emotionally, as well as materially, endeavoring to make choices, making an art of the possible. Nothing could be taken for granted. Only expectations of women's flexibility and resourcefulness never faltered. As familial relations deteriorated, more women joined the significant numbers who lived unattached to kin and exercised their ingenuity and capabilities on their own.

6

Outside the Family Economy

● ●

"Most Times I'd Go to a Friend"

Some women chose independence and circumstances propelled others into self-sufficiency. Familial relations did not constitute the daily worlds of all women. Young single women left home in search of autonomy; women whose marriages ended, and unmarried women of all ages, lived on their own. Economic crisis increased the number of "unattached" women by exacerbating tensions and deepening rifts within marriages and families. The newly unattached struggled with economic and emotional losses, while others had long practiced living without a male wage earner's income. Socially stereotyped or made invisible, as much as 15–20% of adult women in Chicago and Philadelphia lived alone or as lodgers. Black and white, immigrant and native born, women "adrift" congregated in metropolises.[1]

Unattached women bore sole responsibility for securing income and sustaining daily life. Instead of exchanging reproductive labor for financial support, turning over wages to parents, or contributing income and housework to a family economy, they did not and usually could not rely on kin. Like women in family economies, they expertly managed meager resources to ensure a modicum of shelter, food, clothing, and comfort. Structural racism, particularly segregated housing, constructed the context for and affected the success of their strategies. Unlike women in families, they relied on friends rather than kin.

Complicated casts of characters populated their stories: friends, neighbors, and members of their churches; landlords and landladies; relief officials; acquaintances; and sometimes parents, husbands, children, or siblings from whom they were estranged. Some painted themselves as plucky and capable, surviving against the odds, without mentioning relatives. Others revealed dramas of marital or familial betrayal. They told tales of malicious, judgmental landladies and grasping property owners who had no compunctions about evicting them. Unattached women sought out relations of reciprocity. A few were isolated from human contacts. All trusted their wits and physical labor.

Creativity and resourcefulness knew no boundaries, but age limited the strategies women could practice successfully. Energy, optimism, and health, to say nothing of the social value accorded to young women, opened opportunities to find work, a husband, or alternative methods of survival, even in the Depression. Among single female relief recipients in Chicago in 1937, only one-sixth were younger than forty, testimony to younger women's successful strategies.[2] Gray hair and wrinkles, declining physical and mental health, years of hard labor, and oppressive marriages made older women increasingly unlikely to find jobs or husbands, but experience endowed them with mental and emotional resources and wisdom.

Unreliable Relations: "[She] Bursts into Tears When Questioned about Relatives"

Deeply rooted expectations of familial fidelity proved unreliable for structural and individual reasons.[3] The Great War had killed and injured men, depriving women of income and exhausting their energies with necessary care. Depression-induced insecurities undermined marriages and families. Husbands walked out; families exploited and then rejected dutiful daughters; and older women could not count on adult children. When resentment accompanied support, it often foretold its termination. Stung by desertion, death, or being disowned, newly unattached women shouldered betrayal and the unexpected task of surviving on their own.

One relatively affluent white woman's story illustrates losses, despair, and adaptation. Lucille P, a forty-one-year-old waitress (chapter 3), and her husband, Guy, a salesman, once earned "good salaries." In the early 1930s Guy lost his job and fell ill, and Lucille nursed and supported him for four years. By the summer of 1936 they were "so up against it" that Lucille worked ten-hour days at an Evanston, Illinois, tearoom, six days a week, as well as all-night Saturday shifts at a roadhouse, after which she had to report to the tearoom on Sunday mornings. After thirteen years of marriage, Guy walked out. Devastated because she "still loved him" and "so nervous [she] could not carry a cup of coffee to the table," Lucille quit both jobs. She sold her furniture, best dresses, and good shoes, pawned her watch, allowed insurance to lapse, and lost a piece of property she was buying. She gave up their apartment and moved three times, from friend to friend. In November she applied to the Chicago Relief Administration (CRA); its cash assistance enabled her to rent a furnished room with cooking facilities and running water. Her interviewer described a "neat, light, outside room in well kept up old apartment building" in a white, middle-class, North Side neighborhood several blocks from Lake Michigan. The monthly rent, $17.33, consumed the $12 housing allotment and more than half the food allowance. As Lucille explained, "You can't get anything fit to live in for $12 a month."[4] As soon as she obtained regular income, she reestablished a home and sacrificed pressing needs, especially food, to live in a neighborhood that met her standards.

A less privileged Chicago white woman, Catherine T, left school at fourteen and worked in garment, drapery, shoe, and electrical parts factories. Laid off in 1930, she supported her invalid mother with sporadic short-term seasonal jobs in factories and concession stands. When her dwindling earnings no longer covered their bills, they moved in with one of Catherine's married sisters. Catherine paid room and board, and her siblings took over their mother's expenses. Her mother's health worsened in December 1934, so Catherine quit work and nursed her full-time until she died the following April. Because Catherine had borrowed to keep up her mother's insurance, her mother had made her the sole beneficiary of its payout of $390. Her sister demanded $150 for assistance she claimed she had provided Catherine, a paying boarder.

Catherine moved out and attempted to find a full-time job, but around-the-clock nursing, an inadequate diet, worry, and grief had taken their toll. Completely run-down, Catherine could not stand the stress and noise of the sewing factory or the thirteen-hour days and seven-day weeks at the concession stand. For a year and a half she lived on insurance money, sporadic short-term jobs, occasional assistance from friends, and by gathering rags and papers and selling them to junk dealers. The interviewer "commented that it was hard to visualize a woman like herself rummaging about in alleys." Catherine responded, "If you're hungry you'll do anything." In September 1936, at age thirty-four, she applied for relief and rented a room without running water, after living in five places in the preceding year. The CRA contacted her siblings; still jealous of her inheritance, they refused help. For this dutiful daughter, virtue went unrewarded.[5]

Mothers could not necessarily rely on adult offspring. Mary P, a middle-aged Black woman, turned to her sons when she lost her last daywork job in 1932. The youngest son, single and living in Chattanooga, Tennessee, never contributed to her support. She described another son, William, as a "good boy" and his wife as "a lovely girl. I love her like my own." William and his wife usually gave Mary twenty-five or fifty cents each payday over several years. They had no furniture, and always roomed in other people's homes, so she could not live with them. She moved in with Ossie, her third son, and his wife Maud, a "good girl," but her affection for her daughter-in-law could not sustain the relationship. Mary and Ossie did not get along; after three months she left in despair. For five years Mary survived on irregular relief and occasional work, but scarcely any help from Ossie. Maud died, and Ossie moved in with another woman and her three children. His failure to marry his new partner may have contributed to his mother's displeasure, but even a marriage she approved of had not sustained their relationship. "He's no good, that boy, I'd sooner see him dead. He curses me out." Raising children did not entitle a mother to help or even respect.[6]

The abandoned wife, the adult daughter who cared for a dying parent and was put out by a surviving parent or siblings, and the mother denied help by children because she did not get along with them or their spouses were stock characters in the Depression drama. Devoted women's sacrifices went unappreciated. More important, they did not entitle them to a share of a family economy. Lucille, Catherine, and Mary are emblematic of the strains, disruptions, and acrimonious family relations that wreaked hardship on women. Institutions and history, as well as money and emotions, must frame analysis of familial cohesion or lack thereof. Migration and immigration patterns determined the range of kin in proximity. Membership in a particular racial or ethnic group neither protected nor harmed familial relations. Assuming or searching for racial and cultural differences is not a useful analytic strategy, though it has long been a popular explanation for poverty.[7] Nonfamily women found more possibilities for self-support in metropolises. In medium-size cities, they usually moved in with kin or left town.

Avoiding Homelessness

The need for a place to lay their heads, their vulnerability to assault and rape, and norms of female respectability required lone women to find a home. They improvised repertoires of methods to keep a roof over their heads because no single strategy sufficed. They moved more frequently than families, from apartment to apartment, room to room, friend to friend. In contrast to armies of homeless men, women turned to the streets rarely, and only temporarily. Shelters housed and fed hundreds of thousands, if not millions, of men, but scarcely existed for women. Black women, vulnerable to rape because of racist and sexist assumptions, had fewer material resources than white women to meet their need for housing.[8] A French Canadian widow on relief, once comparatively comfortable, summarized her situation. "I'd starve with a roof over my head and pay my rent rather than starve outside."[9]

Like Hazel L, living in the "garage house" (see chapter 4), unattached women moved into less satisfactory dwellings as resources dwindled. Less space and objectionable environs were the usual consequences. A white Cleveland clerical worker and her sister "complained that no landlord (from whom they cared to rent) would allow them to move in when he learned they were unemployed," noting, "Finally we had to move into an undesirable neighborhood just to get a place."[10] White women might relocate to a poorer area, but African Americans were confined within a small circumference of segregated neighborhoods. In Chicago the worst housing disintegrated and was demolished throughout the 1930s. Landlords reconfigured apartment buildings into single-room kitchenettes, substantially increasing profits.[11] Black women relocated more frequently than white women, reflecting worse unemployment, paucity of material resources, and discriminatory real estate practices.

The necessity to move, often repeatedly, was practically guaranteed. Almost two-thirds of 1,654 unemployed Philadelphia women moved at least once between 1931 and 1933.[12] Two-thirds of Chicago women in the 1937 sample had moved in the preceding year—usually once or twice, and as frequently as eight times—to secure cheaper rent, share housing, or live in a relief district rumored to have sympathetic caseworkers.[13] Landlords threw their belongings into the street or confiscated property when they locked tenants out. With each move, women might lose more of their possessions.

When the CRA failed to pay rent allotments in September 1936, two women illustrate emergency decisions and their consequences. Gertrude B fell $9 behind on rent, and the owner insisted on payment. She appealed at the district relief station, applied twice at United Charities, and tried every strategy she could think of to get work or assistance, without success. She told her landlady, an older white woman, that she would leave the following day and went to the grocery store to collect cartons for packing. When she returned, she received a phone call, and while she was in the hall talking, the landlady locked her out. She had only a hat, summer coat, and purse, "not even a comb." A bad back and other health problems had driven Gertrude, age forty-four, Black, out of chambermaid work and onto relief the previous year.

Needing a place to stay and the means to retrieve her possessions, Gertrude pondered and planned in a booth at an all-night drugstore. The next day she appealed to the police, the CRA, and friends. The police, from whom she sought assistance to retrieve her belongings, referred her to court; the CRA told her it had no legal jurisdiction; friends took her in. When rent payments resumed, the CRA mailed her check to her old address and her ex-landlady confiscated it. Gertrude contacted the post office, which took two weeks to retrieve the check. Meanwhile, her thin coat was inadequate for the autumn wind and when she washed her only outfit, it did not dry overnight. She described herself as a "nervous wreck."

Gertrude decided to take her former landlady to court to obtain her belongings. When the police tried to serve the summons, the woman feigned illness and refused to leave her bed. According to the notes, "The police were going to arrest client at first because they thought she was annoying [landlady] and contributing to the latter's illness, so clever was the old lady in turning the tables." Gertrude said that the police in another district "caught on," and after fifteen days the summons was served. The landlady appeared in court; the judge gave Gertrude an order for her belongings, but could not furnish a bailiff; she feared her efforts were in vain. Two months later, on the advice of friends, she consulted an undertaker with political connections. She subsequently secured her possessions, though her barbering and manicure tools were lost. The unscrupulous landlady evicted another woman and rented out the rooms, equipped with the former tenant's furniture.[14] Gertrude relied on friends, persevered in efforts to hold the landlady accountable, and eventually recovered most of her possessions. Her informal networks—friends who housed her and advised her about a businessman with political connections, and the undertaker who pulled the right strings—met her needs more reliably than did the authorities.

Most women stayed with friends when they were evicted. Dora M did not want to "sponge" or regarded homelessness as temporary when she was dispossessed. Sixty-three and single, Dora had emigrated from Sweden as a young woman and worked as a live-in domestic for well-to-do families. She spent three nights in Lincoln Park. The first night, five women and some men sleeping nearby were coughing. Frightened that she might contract pneumonia, Dora took a streetcar to Howard Street and back for $.14. "[You] couldn't get a room for that," she explained. The following night, she joined people lying on the steps of the Museum of Natural History. The concrete was cold and hard, so she sat on a bench and talked with other women until daylight.[15]

Unattached women consistently made housing their first priority. Mindful of their vulnerability to assault, Black women may have been less likely to sleep outside. Gertrude and Dora ensured their safety by staying awake all night in public places. When Dora tried to sleep outside, she sought the protection of numbers with other women. Maud J, a middle-aged white woman, lost her job as forelady in a bindery and slept eight nights in a chair on the pier.[16] Pearl M, a middle-aged Black woman, cleaned a church in return for living quarters and subsequently slept in a shed, without the owner's knowledge, in Morgan Park, a middle-class Black neighborhood.[17] This location provided anonymity and a greater modicum of safety than a public park, the usual destination of homeless white women. Some young women took to the rails in search of work elsewhere.[18]

More than two-thirds (68.9%) of the 1937 Chicago sample lived in furnished rooms, usually in older, often deteriorating, overcrowded buildings. They had lost their furniture or never owned any. Black women typically resided in single-room kitchenettes and enjoyed more space only if they shared apartments; white women lived in single rooms, apartments, and small houses. When the CRA inaugurated cash rent payments, property owners set rates they could be assured of getting, but almost one-third of sample women paid more than the $12 allotment. Three white women, two of them widowed during the Depression, remained in modest bungalows they owned.[19] The third, separated from her bootlegger husband, attempted to stay in her home through the winter, though it had been foreclosed by the Home Owners Loan Corporation.[20]

The inconveniences of kitchenette apartments required substantial labor. Mamie G lived in a "huge" five-story building in Woodlawn, a boys' home converted into one- and two-room kitchenettes housing three hundred relief families. Fourteen families on her floor shared bathroom facilities, which repulsed the investigator. The men's room had two dirty toilets and "a trough from which women secure water for cooking." Women went in and out frequently, and the swinging doors to the toilet rooms were open. The women's room contained the sole bathtub, used by everyone, three washbowls, and "filthy" plumbing; one of two toilets was boarded up.

Mamie, age fifty-one, Black, and a widow, conducted daily life in a small room crowded with a stove, bed, dresser, and table. She "lugged" water from the men's room and heated it on a gas plate. She bathed in a tiny galvanized tub and used two large and two small kettles to heat water for dishes and laundry. With a single set of bed linen, Mamie rose early on wash days, dried the sheets on the radiator, and explained, "Every little while I turns em." She dried clothes on a line over the bed. The interviewer noted, "All of this in a room in which there is not enough room left to turn around!" Lacking an ironing board, Mamie begged for newspapers, padded her kitchen table, and heated a broken electric iron on the gas plate as though it were a flatiron. Mamie engaged in constant physical labor, but her circumstances were far from the worst. Her building had central heating, so she did not have to purchase and carry coal, build fires, haul ashes, or shiver in the cold. Hot running water, a working toilet, and a bathtub were located on her floor, though modesty prescribed that she care for personal cleanliness in her room. Mamie enjoyed good health, "never" saw a doctor, and was able to lift and carry water, which exceeded the physical capacity of some women.[21]

Black and immigrant women less frequently lived in buildings equipped with modern conveniences than did U.S.-born white women. They worked harder, had fewer comforts, or both. More than two-thirds of the 1937 sample presumably had central heating, but malfunctioning furnaces, stingy landlords, poor insulation, or location often made rooms uncomfortable. Immigrant (44.7%) and Black (36.7%) women tended a single wood- or coal-burning stove for heating, cooking, and boiling water far more frequently than native-born white women (16.7%). Relief checks could not cover more than a few sacks or baskets of coal, and women paid dearly when purchasing small quantities. Tillie H, fifty-five, and white (chapter 2), fell and cracked her ribs while toting a basket of coal in an effort to save the $.75 carry-up charge. The stairs leading to her attic "hovel" were "crooked, slanting, and loose-in-some places." Tillie never removed her coat and stuffed newspapers and rags in cracks to keep out the wind.[22] Inadequate plumbing was especially burdensome. Large kitchenette buildings had few toilets, so tenants climbed stairs and heaved buckets of water to flush if landlords did not keep the plumbing in repair. Bathtubs were far from universal. Women took sponge baths, visited friends to bathe, or went to the park for showers. Lena J, a Black woman, forty, lived in a dark room "just large enough for a cot and one chair," with a gas plate in the closet and a wardrobe trunk, in which she stored her food, in the bathroom. Lena enjoyed the unusual circumstance of having a "private bathroom, which she loves. She proudly showed it to the investigator, saying that she liked it much better than the room in which her bed is located. She says she really lives in the bathroom."[23]

Even modern buildings lacked facilities for food preparation and storage. Women used a landlady's kitchen; cooked on hot plates; ran hot water over canned goods to warm them; prepared coffee, tea, and cocoa on radiators; and preserved food on window ledges in winter. In summer, the lack of iceboxes or the expense of ice dominated meal planning. The large majority of buildings had electricity, but more immigrant (15.8%) and Black (16.5%) women relied on oil, kerosene lamps, or candles than native-born white women (5.6%). Some landlords refused to turn on electricity or gas for tenants on relief.

Poorly functioning plumbing, unlit or dimly lit hallways and staircases, erratic heat, and infestations of bedbugs and rats typified landlords' neglect. Despite paying $14 rent, Alvina K "washed and sprayed" the wooden frame of her studio couch daily in hot weather to ward off bugs. An unemployed practical nurse, white, age fifty-nine, Alvina was afflicted with numerous health problems, including "hands and feet badly deformed with arthritis."[24]

A few women remained settled for years, living illegally in condemned and abandoned buildings, purchasing autonomy with hard labor and discomfort. Bessie E, a thirty-four-year-old Black woman, rented for four years, then remained in her four-room flat another two years after her building, next to the elevated tracks, was condemned. The place was dirty, musty, and dark, the walls were pockmarked by chipped plaster, and steps to her second-floor apartment were missing. Water and electricity had been disconnected, so Bessie heated with a coal stove, used kerosene lamps, and "got water where [she could]." Living rent free enabled Bessie to take in friends, a couple with two babies; to remain in one location for six years; and to avoid relief until 1936.[25] Julia L, age forty-five and a Polish immigrant, was an unemployed cook who was once widowed and once divorced; she lived rent-free for two and a half years in a "dilapidated" house facing railroad freight tracks. She carried buckets of water from neighbors, used an outside toilet, and burned wood from sheds she dismantled nearby. The dismal environment had not destroyed her self-respect or diligence: in mid-April Julia was spading the backyard to plant flowers and vegetables.[26]

Enduring stories and photographs of masses of unemployed men who haunted soup lines and slept in shelters in the 1930s are not matched by similar accounts or images of women. Meridel LeSueur maintained that women on their own colluded to keep themselves invisible.[27] Multitudes moved from room to room, friend to friend, protecting themselves and maintaining respectability. Any type of housing enabled them to remain hidden. As they moved into worsening accommodations, the amount and type of necessary housework increased, especially during frigid winters. Black women's daily routines were more onerous than those of white women.

Management of Resources: "She 'Never' Wants to See Another Bean"

Women alone manifested the same ingenuity in managing dwindling assets as did housewives superintending households, piecing together survival from numerous, often temporary strategies. They managed every resource to ensure housing. Reliance on physical exertion, self-sacrifice, and labor-intensive strategies persisted. Five years after white families in South Bend had been reluctant to go into debt or to lose or jeopardize tangible and financial resources, unattached Chicago women managed small, unreliable relief payments, a maximum of $23.05 monthly. Their spending decisions revealed their priorities and values.

Dora M possessed none of the assets that marriage might confer, but forty years as a live-in housekeeper for well-to-do families enabled her to amass a small cache of worldly goods. In 1929 she quit a well-paid position because she was "'too lonesome' in a large house all day in winter and in the suburbs," a decision she subsequently "greatly regret[ted]." Unable to find a regular job for the next six years, she did daywork; canvassed door-to-door; drew on savings; sold her silverware, draperies, and lamps; and pawned and lost rings and a brooch "which were dear to her." Having exhausted all reserves in 1935, Dora applied for relief.[28]

As the Depression lengthened, unemployed, unattached women resorted to strategies they had been loath to consider. They cashed in insurance, sold or pawned possessions, and moved repeatedly. Wage disparities ensured that Black women possessed few material assets—furniture and insurance policies were most common—and their more rapid unemployment caused them to exhaust resources sooner than white women. If women stored possessions when they took live-in jobs or moved in with others, and could not pay storage charges, they lost them inadvertently. Furniture, pianos, and wedding rings disappeared. Loss of typewriters undercut their ability to capitalize on a useful skill.

Some married white women once enjoyed comfortable circumstances, owning homes, savings, stock, and/or real estate.[29] Celia B stretched her husband's insurance, their savings and possessions, occasional housework positions, and help from friends and relatives for five years after she was widowed. Forty-seven years old when her husband, Clarence, died in 1931, Celia spent $500 of the $900 insurance benefit on the funeral. She rented out rooms, decided she was not making enough money, sold her furniture at auction, and moved. Although their bank failed, it paid three small dividends on their $2,000 savings, the largest of which was $100.84. Celia pawned two diamond rings but could not redeem them. She secured occasional short-term jobs as a maid and housekeeper. In 1936 she spent five months on relief, worked as a maid three months, cashed in insurance, bought clothing, paid $42 in back rent, and lived another three months before reapplying for relief.[30]

Multiple assets sustained Celia for five years after Clarence's death, unlike Black women who applied for relief while their husbands were alive. Amanda T requested aid with her husband, Esau, in 1932. Both were unemployed and had exhausted their savings. For two years direct relief and work relief supplied a meager livelihood. When Esau died in 1934, Amanda received $275 from his insurance and spent $250 for the funeral. Removed from relief rolls because of this income, she spent it in a month and reapplied for assistance.[31] The differential between these widows is stark.

Lone women were not equally bereft of possessions because relief policies continuously changed. To be certified eligible for assistance in Chicago early in the Depression, unattached women had to forfeit virtually all belongings. Women applying for assistance mid-decade might own furniture and even homes. The CRA required applicants to sign a pauper's oath affirming that they had no savings and that legally responsible relatives could not contribute to their support. It did not require a lien on property, a common practice in other localities.[32] Thus, three white women who owned homes kept their most important possessions. Conversely, Black women typically retained little more than clothing and kitchen utensils.

Cash payments afforded relief clients flexibility in managing meager financial resources. The maximum grant to a Chicago woman, $23.05 monthly ($12 rent, $9.25 for groceries, and $1.80 for clothing) was inadequate; the majority received less.[33] Women compromised health and nutrition by reallocating food budgets, the most elastic portion of their income, to pay higher rent, evidence of the importance they attached to housing. They spent cash on carfare to look for work, repaid rent debts, visited doctors, purchased medicine, and fed cats and dogs. Laura G once earned a high salary as an assistant housekeeper and room inspector at major hotels, but she had lost or sold everything from her "better days." When she received relief, this fifty-nine-year-old Canadian took $.25 weekly "out of eats money" to keep up her insurance policy.[34] At the margins of survival, women defined their priorities and redeployed meager incomes.

Feeding themselves required ingenuity, and clients and the Women's Bureau (WB) alike judged $9.25 inadequate.[35] Gertrude B reported, "Food is high." She ate "starch, starch, starch!," rice, potatoes, and macaroni, and had so many beans, in all colors and all sizes, that "she 'never' wants to see another bean."[36] Catherine T spent grocery money on carfare to look for work and lived on "spaghetti and more spaghetti," although she felt she should have a "more varied diet" with milk and vegetables. Almost three-fourths of Chicago women received food from the Federal Surplus Commodities Corporation: typically, six grapefruit, a sack of walnuts, two pounds of prunes, and a can of meat. "Grateful" for surplus food, Catherine didn't care for the boiled beef, which was "all water and very salty."[37] Housing conditions often made food preparation and storage difficult. Shopping and cooking carefully and supplementing grocery allowances with meals given by friends or exchanged in return for services, women nevertheless felt "hungry all the time."[38]

Insufficient clothing imprisoned women indoors in harsh weather, exposed them to illness, prevented them from securing jobs, and damaged self-esteem. Many women displayed inadequate wardrobes to interviewers. They borrowed coats, shoes, and galoshes during inclement weather. Dora M filled her days sewing, mending, and "going around to see where she can find cheap clothes" to maintain a presentable appearance. She frequented Goodwill and Salvation Army stores and was pleased when she acquired a "dandy" pair of shoes for $.26 and rubbers for $.10; she usually dismantled old shoes she found on rubbish heaps to sew new ones. She wished she had a sewing machine. A friend gave her a secondhand winter coat, and another with a sewing machine altered it for free. Dora needed a "nice" hat; she had "been making my own, they look terrible."[39] Occasionally relief clients obtained clothing and linens from Works Progress Administration (WPA) projects or the Red Cross, but it was difficult to get the correct size, and even new garments were out of style.[40] Nellie B, forty-eight, an Irish immigrant, received two aprons, two housedresses, two pairs of shorts, and two cotton slips. She was "quite amused at the shorts—amused and regretful, because she needs winter underwear. She has always worn knit bloomers and in summer cotton bloomers. Those given her are cut exactly like men's shorts—with wide leg openings—making them quite 'immodest.' She has tried to put rubber in the legs, but [they] are cut too high for this, so will give them to the landlady's husband.... 'He says, "God, I could wear those." 'I says, "Honest to God, you're right, you are."'"[41]

Unattached Chicago women did without more necessities and often undertook heavier physical labor than did South Bend women, but engaged in less subsistence production. Densely populated neighborhoods afforded no space for gardens, though rural and small-town migrants had previously relied on vegetable plots. Most women lacked facilities for canning, and given their propensity for moving, a stock of heavy jars would be a liability. Those living in single family homes or small apartment buildings with yards did garden and can. They invested hours shopping, sewing, and trading services with friends to clothe themselves in a respectable manner.

No longer useful or valued as mothers, wives, or workers, older unattached women bore sole responsibility for reproducing themselves as they carried coal up rickety stairs, lugged water, and improvised meals. They did not organize their days around the needs of children and husbands, though most had once done so. Women adrift did not defer to patriarchal norms, nor could they count on family to accomplish tasks beyond their strength or skill. Gender appropriateness of their labor was rarely a concern.

Worn down by unemployment, malnutrition, impoverishment, and physical ailments, women might not possess the stamina to wage constant battle for more than survival. For some, emotional depression undercut will to care for themselves. The WB judged two-fifths of Chicago relief clients interviewed in 1937 to be permanently unemployable due to ill health. This estimate seriously underestimated physical hardships, because the WB excluded almost four thousand women ages sixty-five and older, one-third of unattached female relief clients.[42] As health declined, women may have lowered their standards and endured even more deteriorating conditions.

The most significant differences among unattached women were age and race. Younger women far more frequently survived by combining jobs, assistance from friends, and makeshift strategies, especially if they were white. Among women interviewed in 1937, those in their twenties and thirties were 61.8% Black, testifying to a broader range of possibilities open to young white women.[43] Structural racism prevented Black women from accumulating material or financial assets and required that they invest more money and elbow grease for less desirable living quarters. Disproportionately, they were forced to seek help early in the Depression.

The changing requirements of relief systems had a racial differential in effect, if not intent. Early in the decade, exhausting savings, life insurance, and even selling furniture to establish eligibility decimated the assets of applicants. When New Deal policies allowed retention of possessions and homes, some previously comfortable white women kept material underpinnings of former lives and received relief. Imagination and persistence were the primary assets of any working-class woman. The urban context and the material resources she could call upon structured the plans she devised and her likelihood of implementing them successfully. Some women literally starved to death, but most turned to a reliable resource, their network of friends.

"Get[ting] by on Her Friends"

Youth and white skin opened the most doors for single women. Recall Annabelle S (in chapter 3), who sold World's Fair license plates and took Christmas rush sales positions with her roommate. Devising plans, sharing practical strategies, altering habits, and encouraging each other, friendship enabled them to transgress gender norms and ensured their survival. When Annabelle applied to the Service Bureau for Women in January 1933, the agency granted her food tickets and unspecified work relief.[44] After the written record ended, she might have continued to piece together a living, sharing strategies and hardships with her roommate. She might have found a steady job, married and created a new family economy, or returned to her family. Annabelle and her roommate each might have followed any of these paths, or a misunderstanding might have ended their friendship. The small number of women younger than forty on relief rolls four years later and their shorter duration on relief than older women testify to successful strategies of younger white women. Annabelle's story may be read as the narrative of a spunky young single girl, out on a lark, but as crisis deepened and resources diminished, friendships grew more critical.

Women adrift counted on friends for material assistance and emotional support. They shared sociability and information: leads about jobs and tips about applying for relief. Friends made gifts and loans of cash, groceries, coal, clothes, meals, and discarded newspapers and magazines; they paid insurance and utility bills. Hungry women showed up at friends' homes at mealtime or visited when they needed a tub to bathe in, a kitchen to prepare food, a warm spot to wash and dry laundry, or a place to spend winter days when they had used up their coal.

In 1933, Black and white unemployed women in Chicago and Philadelphia mentioned assistance from friends, neighbors, and landladies far more frequently than they mentioned relatives.[45] Four years later, three-fifths of Chicago women reported help from friends but less than one-fifth from families. Kin might be geographically distant, financially unable, or estranged. Almost none of the 1937 interviewees mentioned the possibility of marriage. Occasionally men treated them to shows or other recreation, but assistance from sweethearts was minimal or unreported. Younger women more likely received meals and gifts from boyfriends.

Friends not only offered aid but also gave lie to the assumption that women's lives are confined to families. They doubled up, though this language was rarely applied to them. When an unemployed woman moved in with a still-employed friend, she assumed housewifely tasks. Committed attachment and nongendered division of labor made survival possible. If the employed partner lost her job, they might separate, each needing to link up with an employed friend. Lone women bartered labor for a place to live when they exhausted other possibilities. In acute crises, especially evictions and husbands' deaths and desertions, women took one another into their homes. Far less frequently, an unattached woman moved in with a couple or family and earned her keep caring for children, walking the dog, running errands, and sharing housework. This arrangement ended if the man lost his job.

When unrelated women doubled up, they engaged in practices more characteristic of Black communities than white ones. In 1930, one-third of Black homes in the four cities had lodgers, while in immigrant or native-born white homes, only one-tenth did so. A larger proportion of Black women lodged with nonrelatives in 1930 and 1940.[46] One-fourth of women in the 1937 sample lived with friends or strangers, and many more had shared housing, especially before cash relief was inaugurated. Often friends came from hometowns and home states. The sense of community reflected Black women's southern pasts.

Penniless women's pride and sense of responsibility required them to contribute their only asset, their labor, to avoid sponging and to acknowledge kindness. Anna M, a fifty-four-year-old Black woman, an unemployed chambermaid and household worker, had "been able to get by on her friends" but eventually "wore out her welcome." When lack of coal forced her out of her room during a cold spell, Anna turned to "the last friend I knew I had left." She stayed with that friend day after day. "[I] was afraid they'd get tired of me, so I tried to lay low and not be in the way," she recounted. "Every day I planned something to do the next day for them—mended hose, cleaned, made 'em a quilt, but yesterday I couldn't think of anything else to do and they got bored with me, so I had to come to the relief."[47] Women who exchanged labor with friends subsequently contributed cash to the household coffers and paid part of the rent when they received relief. If they lived with friends when they applied to the CRA, it granted only grocery and clothing allotments, assuming rent was free. When the CRA failed to make rent payments, some relief clients "worked out" their rent.[48]

For young women, loss of employment threatened independence and required reconsideration of the future. Some entertained thoughts of moving home, a strategy encouraged by social service and relief agencies. Some parents were unwilling to support young adults, and some stepmothers made clear that their husbands' daughters were not welcome.[49] Others resisted accepting parental supervision and relinquishing autonomy. Helen B, twenty-five, single, and white, lived with a friend. When she was laid off from her clerical job in 1931, a friend from her basketball club helped her get a sales job at Wanamaker's, a Philadelphia department store. Out of work again a year later, Helen searched for work unsuccessfully for two months, fell nine weeks behind on rent, and applied to the Bureau of Unemployment Relief. When the interviewer suggested she return home, Helen replied that home "difficulties" made it impossible.[50] For Black migrants, returning home typically entailed a costly train journey rather than a trip across town or to the regional hinterland. Mandolyn B migrated to Chicago in 1928 at age twenty-three. Nine years later, when unemployment drove her to the CRA, the interviewer inquired whether her family might support her if she returned to Missouri. Mandolyn would not consider returning; she "felt hindered a great deal socially in a small town."[51]

Women who failed to conform to conventional behavior were unlikely to count on kin. Lesbians used the same tactics as heterosexual women, but their lack of respect for sexual norms diminished the strategies they could practice successfully. Some survived adrift by dint of resourcefulness. Others returned home and may have been forced to hide or terminate relationships with lovers. Some participated in a family economy, others were denied assistance by families, and still others married for economic survival. No interviewees revealed lesbian identity, but stories suggest the possibility. Middle-aged women who shared a home and described themselves as cousins, a young woman who found social life through a basketball team, and another who refused a job because it conflicted with her basketball games may or may not have been lesbians. Interviewers noted two Chicago women in their early thirties: a Jewish woman who "dresses queerly" and a deaf Croatian American swimming instructor, "boyish looking with severely cut hair."[52] These actions and descriptions mirror the behavior of "lady-lovers" in the 1930s.[53]

Whole communities, not only individual friends, contributed to women's victories, as illustrated by Gertrude B's reclamation of her possessions. Evelyn D, Black and a widow at age thirty-nine, asked her landlord for a grace period when relief failed to make rent payments in September 1936. He refused. Evelyn made arrangements to stay with a friend temporarily, packed her trunk, and went down to the street where she hailed two men to carry it from the third floor. From a neighbor she borrowed a child's wagon to move the trunk, and neighbors and members of her church sent children to assist her. Each carried a bundle—a radio, clothing, a piece of bric-a-brac—and formed a procession that Evelyn thought "looked like a circus parade." The lesson she drew was to pay her rent first: "Some days I don't have no bread but I have got a comfortable place to stay."

Evelyn persevered through a fourteen-month bureaucratic runaround with material and emotional sustenance of friends, neighbors, and church members after her husband died in 1935. Her husband, James, was owed $27.50, half a month's pay, on his WPA job. Evelyn spent nine days trying to get his check so she could bury him. Church members gave her carfare, telephone money, and food, as she made the rounds of CRA, WPA, and city officials, unsuccessfully. Finally the congregation taxed themselves to pay for the funeral, and church trustees signed a note to pay the balance on the installment plan. Friends lent her a black dress, a hat, and gloves. Evelyn "could not buy a job." The CRA deemed her ineligible. "Why Mrs. D, you are going to receive your husband's check for $27.50. We can't put you back on relief." Evelyn "tried here and there. . . . I'm telling you now honey, a friend would give me a quarter or fifty cents. Most times I'd go to a friend. [I] like to went crazy." The story of her efforts to obtain her husband's final pay, extending to local, state, and federal bureaucracies and reaching Washington, DC, filled six typewritten pages appended to interview notes. Evelyn persisted for more than a year, relying on friends for survival. She received $27.50 in January 1937.[54]

Offering and accepting help elicited shame and dependency as well as loving sharing. Belief that joblessness signified personal failure ran deep, and it was difficult for women to accept assistance. Self-respect required an exchange, so they bartered their labor. Despite the reciprocity of work exchanged for room and board, the shame of sponging off others injured women's pride. A middle-aged Black woman explained, "When you have got a dollar of your own it's all right, but when you have got to depend on someone else for food and shelter, it's awful, it's awful."[55] Another unemployed Black domestic worker, receiving rent and food from her landlady, felt "ashamed," and her landlady "would make remarks about 'charity.'"[56] Friends "had troubles of their own." They wanted to help and resented women who needed help.

Generous friends came from all racial, ethnic, nativity, and age groups, but were mostly middle-aged and older women. Luck and good health kept some women one step above destitution, able to aid less fortunate friends. Many relief applicants and recipients previously or currently assisted others. A few

Black-and-white interracial friendships appeared in the samples. A widowed Hungarian immigrant, Gertrude A, age sixty-one, took a Mexican couple with a baby into her two-room apartment.[57] Women made friends within class boundaries and among neighbors, landladies, tenants, coworkers, and members of religious, ethnic, and social groups. Acquaintances from relief offices blossomed into friends, and strangers showed compassion. Former employers, including housewives for whom women had cleaned for years, rarely helped.

When Bessie W, at age forty-one, a widowed Black woman, lost her live-in job as a children's nursemaid, she had $2 to her name and no place to go. Walking up and down the street crying, she was approached by a woman who inquired about her distress and took her home. Seven months later she still lived in this woman's two-room flat, sharing a bed "because of the scarcity of bed clothing." Although her benefactor was on relief, she fed and housed Bessie for over a month and helped her fill out a relief application. When Bessie collected relief, she received only a grocery allowance because her friend's relief paid the rent.[58]

Landladies ran the gamut from friends to adversaries. This imprecise term described absentee, middle-class, and well-to-do investors in real estate, as well as working-class women who rented rooms in their apartments. The intimacy of sharing a room or an apartment both nurtured sympathy and bred tensions. Some landladies were friends created by circumstances. Numerous Chicago and Philadelphia women "ran up a rent bill," as much as hundreds of dollars, when they lost jobs. They benefited from relationships with sympathetic landladies, often working-class women whose circumstances had not deteriorated. Some landladies evicted renters, and others moved penniless lodgers into their own rooms and beds so that they could rent vacated rooms for cash, or let them stay without paying. The difference between "lenient landladies" and women who doubled up is often semantic.

Gossipy, malicious, jealous, backbiting busybodies were also landladies. One reported to the district relief office that Mary C, age thirty-seven and a white divorcee, "could not be very moral account of irregular hours. Company after 10 p.m. (men and women). Client usually left and did not return until a.m. Sleeps all day."[59] Relief clients were vulnerable to landladies who refused to rent to "charity cases" or mistreated them. One landlady rented to relief recipients so she could insist that they clean the building. She demanded that Sarah G, a sixty-eight-year-old African American, scrub the halls despite her ill health and despite the fact that relief paid her rent.[60]

Society placed few expectations upon female friendships, yet they proved to be the most reliable resources for unattached women. Marriage and kinship were well defined, but husbands and relatives failed to meet obligations. We lack language to describe the solidarity among women who joined forces, strategized survival, and divided work with pragmatism and friendship and not on the basis of gender roles. Internalized values about self-reliance, accepting gifts, and begging clouded relationships, but sympathy, solicitude, and practicality enabled women to carry on. Women benefited from reliable friendships, including those with women whom they had not known previously. Friendships fell apart from economic pressure, just as marriages and families did. Women who might have extended camaraderie scorned and mistreated other women. What is remarkable is the consistency and importance of bonds among women and the invisibility of these attachments.

Women understood other women's vulnerability. Christian ethics and the need for propriety—to appear worthy and deserving to the world, including relief workers—also motivated women's aid to one another. They housed impoverished friends and acquaintances to protect them from assault and rape and to enable them to maintain self-respect. Experts on racialized and sexualized assumptions about them, Black women understood each other's susceptibility to attack. They experienced and/or knew stories of sexual assault in both the North and South. Darlene Clark Hine has theorized a "culture of dissimulation," and Kali N. Gross reminds us that "Black women closeted their emotions, sensuality, and pain in an effort to minimize their vulnerability."[61] They were unlikely to discuss fear of rape with white interviewers, but that dread could not have been far from their hearts.

White women's actions became more like those of Black women, practicing community assistance. When estranged from or lacking families, they turned to friends for a cup of hot tea, a place to sleep, a meal, a warm spot on a bitter winter day, or a loan of appropriate clothing or footwear. Sharing homes and lives, including one-room kitchenettes, illustrates the persistence of Black southern community responsibility and concern.[62] We need to recognize that white women adopted habits that were much more common among Black women.

Unattached women exemplify a vast stratum whose lives were, for the most part, unseen and unacknowledged. The difference between attached and unattached lay in women's ability or inability to rely on the labor and income of others. Those adrift from the moorings of families lacked the respectability accorded to wives, mothers, and daughters, yet the necessary resourcefulness was no different. Unattached women patched together multiple strategies to sustain themselves. Waged jobs, the informal economy, relief, careful management of resources, onerous physical labor, and reliance on friends lacked racial or ethnic specificities. As they aged, decreasing possibilities for employment meant that older women increasingly relied on informal methods of survival, their ingenuity, creativity, perseverance, and friends.

7

Relief

• • • • • • • • • • • • • • • • • • • •

"I Never Thought I Would Come to This. I Am So Willing and Anxious to Work"

Taking charity was a last resort. When employment and family failed, when women exhausted material and human resources, hunger drove them to relief offices, where applications peaked in the coldest months. Understanding the mindsets of women who exposed their destitution and asked outsiders for help, and of those who did not entertain such thoughts, or did not act on them, requires knowledge of the relief system and the opprobrium attached to it. The shame that assistance incurred, to say nothing of the scarcity and inadequacy of relief, circled through women's minds as they mulled over applying for aid. The infrequency with which they utilized relief is one of its most significant, if underappreciated, characteristics. This chapter analyzes working-class women's actions regarding relief in the context of its constantly changing parameters.

The stigma of relief etched harsh imprints on working-class minds, yet it enabled survival. Insufficiency, fluctuating requirements and benefits, gendered assumptions, racial disparities, and segregation characterized provisions in the era of President Herbert Hoover. Lauded for inaugurating federal responsibility for poverty and for assisting millions, New Deal innovations in direct cash relief and work programs remained structurally sexist and racist. Unlike playing the numbers, a ritual of hope and recreation, acquiring benefits lacked dream books or guidelines. Betting that investing time and energy and proving worthiness would pay off in goods, services, or cash was never guaranteed. Information about acquisition of food or clothing one week was inapplicable the next.

There is little evidence of differences between Black and white women's agency, attitudes, and actions regarding relief. African Americans became impoverished more rapidly, so they applied for relief sooner, in larger proportions than their white counterparts. Assumptions of laziness discredited them and racial differentials in eligibility standards and in types and amounts of relief grated on them. They adapted to bureaucratic constraints out of necessity.

Relief before the Depression

Poverty has always been a disgrace. As Josephine Chapin Brown notes, "To be 'on the town' or 'on the county' was the lowest state outside prison to which a member of the community could descend." Assistance was the responsibility of local governments, which, assuming poor people would waste cash or spend unwisely, lodged them at the poorhouse (indoor relief) or gave them groceries, fuel, or used clothing (outdoor relief). States financed mothers' pensions and institutions for "dependents": orphans, blind, deaf, and mute persons. The federal government acknowledged responsibility only for veterans: health, vocational rehabilitation, institutionalization, and pensions. Policy makers believed that "relief should be made so disagreeable to the recipient that he would be persuaded or forced to devise some means of self-support in order to get off the list as swiftly as possible."[1]

Private charities, the settlement house movement, and public agencies professionalized and rationalized programs in the early twentieth century. They associated in citywide federations, established social service exchanges to centralize information and avoid duplication, and organized joint community chest appeals for financial support.[2] Typically linked to religious denominations, private charities assisted specific ethnic, racial, and/or religious groups. Some municipal governments founded departments of public welfare that administered outdoor relief. The Cleveland Welfare Federation included casework societies (Associated Charities, the Jewish Social Welfare Bureau, and the Salvation Army); agencies aiding children (nurseries, orphanages, homes for unwed mothers); group work organizations (the Negro Welfare Association, the Phillis Wheatley Association in Cleveland, the YMCA, the YWCA, and settlement houses); hospitals and health care providers; and homes for the elderly.[3] Fourteen organizations comprising South Bend's Community Fund focused on health: home nursing care for poor and disabled children, free milk for babies, and a day nursery for children of working mothers. Municipal government operated a tuberculosis sanitarium, and the St. Joseph County Poor Asylum lodged the "ill and indigent poor."[4]

Gendered, racialized, and classist ideologies molded assistance. The only meritorious adults—disabled persons—were impoverished through no fault of their own. Unemployed, able-bodied men could work, but apparently would not, so were undeserving. Social workers condescendingly sought to guide clients to better adjustment to society, disregarding cyclical, structural unemployment. The work ethic they sought to inculcate was accompanied by a family ethic, the assumption that wife and mother was the only appropriate role for a woman. White social workers assumed that African Americans were lazy and immoral, therefore undeserving.[5]

Mothers' pensions, a Progressive reform enacted by most states in the 1910s, presumably enabled women without husbands to care for children full-time by remaining outside the labor force. Pensions barely supported families and many recipients supplemented them with laundry or domestic work.[6] In 1930, one-half of counties nationwide sponsored mothers' aid. Average monthly grants ranged from $4.33 (in Arkansas) to $69.31 (in Massachusetts).[7] Recipients were almost exclusively white widows who kept "proper" homes; Black women were ineligible, and neither unmarried mothers nor divorcees were "deserving." Despite severe limitations, women raising children without husbands' support were the single group meriting aid because of poverty. The contrast with workmen's compensation, also enacted during the 1910s, set a gendered pattern for public assistance. Workmen's compensation represented a return for risk. Mothers' pensions, granted for ongoing service, relied upon casework to determine individual worthiness, setting a precedent that endures.[8] Casework relied on "surveillance practices, including investigation, registration, observation, and classification."[9] In 1929, monthly payments averaged $40.17 to $52.88 in the four cities.[10] In Chicago, where pensions were highest, a woman could provide a better standard of living if she earned $12 weekly, less than most industrial and service jobs paid. Far more single mothers chose employment.

Economics was not women's sole consideration. Public opprobrium, minute scrutiny by presumed class superiors, and working-class aversion to charity played a part in decisions. In Chicago, a Juvenile Court probation officer questioned an applicant about her husband, finances, citizenship, religion, and relatives and double-checked through the social service exchange. Officers conducted home visits and consulted doctors, clergy, and children's schools; court physicians examined the children before a formal court hearing. A grantee was obliged to keep a two-week itemized account of expenses and submit to home visits at least monthly.[11] Community gossip, if not derision, followed. An intrusive, anxiety-producing process conducted by judicial authorities helps to explain women's reluctance to apply.

Independence, pride, the insufficiency of pensions, and racial exclusions motivated women heading families to take jobs, move in with relatives, and/or rely on wages of adolescent and young adult children. In 1930, forty-three families received mothers' pensions in South Bend, where 2,762 widows and divorcees headed households and one-third of formerly married women were employed.[12] Working-class people availed themselves of social services when other strategies proved inadequate. Clients paid the cost of receiving assistance in shame and self-esteem.[13]

Few resources were available to destitute African Americans. In their southern pasts, they relied on family, neighbors, friends, and Black institutions (primarily churches, lodges, and mutual aid societies). In Chicago, middle-class women's clubs helped fund the Home for Aged and Infirm, the Phyllis Wheatley Home for Working Girls, Provident Hospital, and programs to protect girls.[14] Cleveland's Negro Welfare Association (NWA) and Phillis Wheatley Association (PWA) fulfilled numerous community functions. None were relief agencies.[15] White reformers, even when sympathetic, rarely served Black people. Sometimes county poor relief assisted them.

Stigma, insufficiency, infrequency, and racial exclusion characterized assistance. Poverty, an individual failure, warranted mitigation only for "deserving" single white mothers, required to expose their lives to strangers of a higher class. Working-class lodges and religious institutions assisted the worthy: widows and orphans. Relief was local, yet common assumptions underlay it nationwide.

Public and Private Relief during the Hoover Administration (1929–1933)

As layoffs mounted, local institutions were neither prepared for nor capable of meeting the needs of the unemployed. Desperation and the inadequacy of relief were legendary. Tax-funded agencies rapidly exhausted assets. Private charities, supported by the wealthy and community chest drives, were overwhelmed, despite increased fundraising. Gendered, racialized, and classed assumptions characterized distribution of aid. Policy makers assumed that work and shelter for men or material aid to households would address all hardships because women belonged to families. Women's need for employment was rarely considered, and relief typically ignored women outside families. Most assistance was racially segregated and little was directed to African Americans, despite deeper unemployment.

If they grew so distressed that they sought help, working-class people looked to local ethnic and class institutions. Churches, synagogues, and social, fraternal, and benevolent associations struggled to maintain viability and could do little to assuage unemployment. In South Bend, St. Stanislaus Catholic Church's *Grona Dobroczynnych Parafianek* (Society of Charitable Parish Women) helped widows and orphans, parishes held annual pre-Lenten bazaars, and the Polish Lady Falcons held one-cent bazaars.[16] When parish and fraternal groups organized soup kitchens and used clothing giveaways, the women who cooked, collected, sorted, and distributed goods remained invisible.[17] The American Legion, which had substantial immigrant membership, sponsored a "man-a-block" program to give men work. The Friendly Workshop of What Would Jesus Do?

engaged five hundred men to make sixty different articles as a form of self-help.[18] Hering House, financed by the city's Committee of 100 (elite white business-men) served 44,524 meals to homeless Black men and lodged them for 12,147 nights. Other assistance was modest: acquisition and distribution of 245 articles of clothing, forty-five pairs of shoes, 252 quarts of milk, four stoves, and medical aid for 187 persons. Its new Social Service Department referred needy families to appropriate agencies.[19]

Working-class and cross-class ethnic and religious institutions could not meet needs. In South Bend, immigrant and Black communities lacked business and professional elites who could sustain welfare institutions. Cleveland's NWA and PWA, the former an affiliate of the Urban League, played numerous politi-cal, civil rights, and social roles, but neither was a relief organization and both were beholden to white philanthropy and the Community Fund.[20] Chicago Black women's clubs initiated a family relief station and health clinic, a few drops in the vast bucket of needs.[21] Increasing numbers of urbanized Black people charged that the church—and, specifically, established denominations—was a "racket."[22] As Lottie G, age forty-seven and a widow, expostulated, "Church people are always calling up money but they ain't giving out any."[23]

Indiana law mandated county responsibility for poor relief, and Portage Township (South Bend) overdrew its relief fund by December 1930. St. Joseph County subsequently passed poor bills, sold bonds, increased the tax rate, and borrowed from the Reconstruction Finance Corporation to fund outdoor relief. Eligibility was limited to "paupers" without property or funds. Homeownership rendered most households ineligible, until the county lifted this restriction in August 1931.[24] During the harsh winter of 1932–1933, relief applications constantly increased and recipients peaked at 6,463 families, one-fourth of all households, in April 1933.[25] Minimal income disqualified applicants; eligibility ended when workers were occasionally called back temporarily.

Family size determined the amount of grocery orders, redeemable at neigh-borhood grocers, not at lower-priced supermarkets. Men's labor was required in exchange. Steve B, a Hungarian immigrant, worked sixteen hours weekly for a $6 grocery order for his family of eight,[26] which translates to $.375 hourly, a lower rate than Studebaker paid men at its nadir. Women-headed households without working-age sons apparently received grocery orders without exchanging labor. Mary P, thirty-seven, a Hungarian widow with five children, lost her job as a veg-etable cook at the Oliver Hotel. She received coal and $3 weekly grocery orders for three months in 1930, six months in 1931, and two weeks in 1932. When her nineteen year-old son earned $9 or $10 weekly as a hotel bellhop, the township removed them from relief.[27] Mary and John A, a Black couple in their thirties, both lost jobs. Mary negotiated with county authorities for a year of grocery orders and coal in exchange for their savings account when their bank failed. No white family had to trade a savings account for public assistance.[28] St. Joseph County failed to sell its bonds, so some grocers stopped filling food orders in

April 1932.[29] One-sixth of sample households were "on the dole line" between 1930 and 1932.

Cleveland's well-organized welfare and health agencies garnered national attention for rapid recognition of and coordinated responses to escalating unemployment and homelessness. The city passed $950,000 in bond issues in 1930, funding unemployed men to work 144,000 days on parks, streets, and other public property.[30] The Community Fund had "spectacular success" in its November 1930 annual drive, raising the largest sum "ever subscribed up to that time by any city for current local social welfare and relief purposes." Private and public agencies cooperatively opened a Bureau for the Homeless and increased the capacity of the Wayfarers' Lodge; both served men.[31] Associated Charities (AC), the largest source of direct relief, sustained families with assistance worth $809,129 in 1930, primarily food orders and fuel, almost triple its 1929 disbursements.[32] Homeowners were excluded, so many white working-class families had nowhere to turn.[33] It did assist Black clients with outdoor relief.[34] Unusual in fundraising, Cleveland proved predictable, aiding unemployed men, heads of families, and homeless transient men. Women could claim no entitlement to aid. In 1932, AC accounted for almost three-fourths of $6,459,092 expenditures—primarily in-kind assistance to families. Mothers' pensions, soldiers' and sailors' relief, and the Jewish Social Service Bureau (JSSB) comprised 9%, 8%, and 7% of relief outlays, respectively.[35]

South Bend's private charities possessed meager resources. AC assisted 287 continuing cases, twenty old cases, and thirty-two new cases, primarily with advice and referrals (5,430 home visits and 1,569 office interviews), but minimal concrete aid: 255 articles of clothing, sixty-three pairs of shoes repaired, and eleven jobs obtained in 1932.[36] Dorothy C, who considered giving up her youngest children for adoption (in chapter 5), received $4 weekly grocery orders for two months; then AC transferred her to the county.[37] The Red Cross gave $3 rent one month to Louise P, a fifty-three-year-old white divorcee laid off by two laundries.[38]

Despite the obvious inadequacy of poor relief and private charity in addressing unmistakable distress, South Bend's elite acted slowly, hesitantly, and disjointedly. Not until September 1931 did the Chamber of Commerce, fearing a recurrence of the previous winter's unemployment, organize the Committee of 100. It purchased peaches and tomatoes and arranged for public school domestic science classes to can them for distribution. It asked corporations to pledge $2 per employee, hoping to collect $50,000, and appealed to children to bring discarded clothing to schools for distribution by parent-teacher associations.[39] The Committee funded lodging and meals for single, unemployed men, segregated at Hering House and the City Rescue Mission.[40] Other organizations provided goods and services piecemeal: an ice fund, community gardens, bulk gardens, canned goods, clothes, and school aid (clothing, shoes, and books). City-sponsored clinics furnished dental work for children and adults, and regular

checkups and medicine for newborns, and occasionally funded adult hospitalization and operations. Schools placed some children in fresh air rooms and gave
them milk. Measures constantly changed, as one agency took over work formerly
carried on by another, implemented new methods for delivering aid, and modi-
fied eligibility requirements.[41]

Besides urging employees to contribute to the Committee of 100 campaign,
corporations instituted inexpensive measures to mitigate unemployment as they
abandoned costly welfare capitalist pension plans, health care, and recreation.
Oliver Farm Implements and Studebaker made land available for gardens, and
Studebaker "allowed" its underemployed male workforce to clear undesirable
wood from its proving grounds.[42] One-sixth of sample households received grocery or coal credit, interest-free loans deducted from paychecks when employees
were called back to work. When credit applications exceeded the amount Studebaker was willing to extend, it limited eligibility according to a man's marital
status. Edward S received grocery credit briefly, but then it was abruptly with-
drawn because he was single. His household of eight adults and two children had
$24 income in four weeks.[43]

The contrast between Cleveland's well-organized private philanthropy and
South Bend's primarily public assistance exemplified local variation and universal inability to cope with unemployment. Regardless of funding, outdoor relief
remained the most widespread aid in the Hoover years. Housing fell outside the
scope of provisions, though private agencies might pay a month's rent to fore-
stall eviction or to install a family in a new dwelling. Most people received no
assistance. In the South Bend sample, fewer than half the households (eight of
seventeen) without income during four weeks in 1932 received relief. An average
of 2,130 households citywide received public assistance worth $21.92 monthly,
and private agencies aided 693 households with $3.29 monthly; together they
helped one-tenth of households.[44] South Bend's total relief expenditure per cap-
ita ($6.08) compared favorably with Cleveland's ($5.57) and Philadelphia's
($5.16), but poorly with Chicago's ($10.11).[45]

Agencies nationwide aided two groups deemed worthy: families and homeless men. The needs of women, presumed to be part of families, would be met by
male employment and family outdoor relief. Transient men received employment
and shelter and earned the appellation "forgotten." Unattached women were
invisible, despite long histories in their cities. Jobs for unemployed women and
assistance for unattached women fell almost entirely outside the conceptual
framework.[46]

Cleveland singularly addressed women's unemployment with segregated,
free employment agencies. The YWCA gave a few of the most "deserving"
women—unemployed, orphaned, young white clerical workers—room and
board, and a few received carfare, cafeteria meals, and even cash.[47] The PWA
reduced room rent to the prewar rate of $2.75 weekly.[48] Ann Brown, a white
woman who quit a "good job in a factory" to keep house when she married,

subsequently "lost a baby." Her husband, laid off from his job as a "movie picture operator," began running around with other women. Unable to work after a "nerves brake-down," Ann appealed to AC, which gave her $1.60 for groceries. Her husband gave her $3 weekly for rent; when he stopped, she was evicted. She returned to AC, which "sent me to the Police Women's Bureau, where I was put in with Colored people crooks and What not. Not being to well I was afraid of letting my nerves go to pieces. After putting up quite a fuss I was released."[49]

Chicago and Philadelphia assisted women years after they implemented relief for homeless men and families. In October 1931 the Illinois Emergency Relief Commission established a Service Bureau for Women to serve "unattached resident women." Philadelphia's Committee for Unemployment Relief made grants to private agencies and left specifics to them. In 1932 Pennsylvania funded counties, and the Philadelphia County Relief Board began direct relief to "lone" women.[50] Agencies granted successful applicants grocery orders, $1.50 weekly in Philadelphia and $1.75 in Chicago (increased to $2 in March 1933).[51] A small number of Philadelphia clients received clothing or coal. None addressed penniless women's most pressing need, a place to live. Fewer than 2% of applicants got lodging at the YWCA, and a few received occasional rent payments from a private agency or housing at a private shelter.

Perplexed by the needs of unemployed women adrift, policy makers believed women were incapable of managing their affairs and needed institutional housing.[52] The Illinois Emergency Relief Commission operated three shelters for women, segregated by race and age, from the fall of 1931 to the summer of 1933. Cathedral Shelter housed white women over the age of twenty-five "who need the association of other women and institutionalized housing... until they would become reconciled to the plight that had befallen them and the necessity to accept public relief." The Department of Public Health maintained a fourth site, the Municipal Home for Women, for those women who "because of health and mental condition" were "unemployed and in need of rest, occupational therapy, and general medical supervision."[53] Neither Cleveland nor Philadelphia funded shelters for women. Seven percent of women (seventy of 956) studied at the Service Bureau for Women (SBW) received lodging between 1931 and 1933.[54] Private charities restricted accommodations. The New York Mercy Shelter of the Home Missionary Society admitted only morally acceptable Protestants, "positively no one with social diseases," and refused "drunks or prostitutes."[55]

Gendered, racialized, and classed assumptions guided social work practices, which created work relief for men but assumed unattached women would benefit from institutional living. A few agencies recognized women's need for employment and developed "made work." Philadelphia's Service Committee for Business and Professional Women secured eight or ten weeks of low-wage work at social service agencies, hospitals, educational institutions, and other nonprofit organizations for a small number of unemployed white clerical workers who earned a few dollars and hoped it might turn into a permanent job. The SBW awarded a small number of clients two days of work relief: clerical and steno-graphic assignments at $3 daily or sewing and laundry at $2.50. One-seventh of clients studied by the WB received work relief and grocery orders in alternate weeks. White clerical workers most often received work assignments, com-pared to industrial workers, who were favored over service workers.[56] Inade-quate, part-time, poorly paid, limited in duration, and preferentially awarded by race and class, women's work relief was in no sense comparable to the inade-quate work relief created for men.

Applications for mothers' pensions increased. Anna K, a South Bend Polish immigrant, took a job as a bank janitor upon her husband's death. Laid off in 1930, she remortgaged her home and applied for mothers' aid. In 1932 she received $.30 a day for each child younger than sixteen, $63 monthly.[57] Anna E, thirty-seven, a white Cleveland widow, earned comparatively high income as a night shift head waitress and short order cook. She lost her job in 1932 and secured short-term housework through the Y, such as a Christmas Day job for $1. In April 1933 her application for a pension was accepted.[58] Appropriations for mothers' pensions fell and benefits dropped in all four cities. Numbers of families receiv-ing pensions increased slightly in Cleveland and Philadelphia, declined slightly in Chicago, and increased fourfold in South Bend.[59]

The insufficiency of relief during the Hoover years is common knowledge, but little attention has been paid to the lack of assistance available to women, gen-dered conventions that placed women in families, and racist assumptions that limited relief for African Americans.

The New Deal: "Aren't There WPA Factories Where I Can Sew and Be Paid for My Work?"

New Deal innovations have been celebrated for creating jobs and benefits for mil-lions and for pioneering reliance on federal funds, yet gendered and racialized policies continued to characterize fluctuating programs and to determine types, amounts, and conditions of assistance. Congress appropriated funds and required private organizations to transfer caseloads to public agencies.[60] Federal policy mandated that relief be implemented without racial discrimination, which northern and Midwestern cities partially honored.[61] Policy makers continued to act as though women and men had different needs and to assume the ubiquity of white heteronormative families supported by men. Policy presumed women's family status and disregarded their employment status. Because Black wives had been three times more likely to work for wages and were far more likely to be unemployed, gendered assumptions had racial implications. Women outside the family model were rendered invisible, though fissures cracked the edifice. Some employment programs hired women, and a rare relief program directly aided unattached women.

Work programs employed men only or in disproportionate numbers.[62] The Civilian Conservation Corps hired 2.5 million unemployed, single, male citizens—ages eighteen to twenty-five and Black, Mexican, and white—to work on reforestation and soil conservation. Earning $30 monthly plus room and board, they were required to allot a minimum of $22 to their families. "Just a bunch of ambitious jobless girls" from New Jersey wrote to Secretary of Labor Frances Perkins, "Why can't us jobless girls have a camp just like the boys, we are sure every girl is willing to work, and most girls can out work boys. We will do any kind of work from chopping trees, fixing roads and a lot of other jobs; just give every girl a chance."[63] With Eleanor Roosevelt's support, the government established "she-she-she" camps, which employed 8,500 young women at $.50 a week plus room and board. Budget cuts curtailed this minuscule effort in 1937; the CCC persisted until US entry into World War II.[64]

Some work programs hired women in sex-stereotyped jobs, never in proportion to their share of the labor force or of unemployment. Among four million employees of the Civil Works Administration, 7.5% were women, as were 12% of Federal Emergency Relief Administration (FERA) workers and 13–19% of Works Progress Administration (WPA) employees.[65] An official acknowledged, "For unskilled men we have the shovel. For unskilled women we have only the needle."[66] FERA and WPA women's projects preserved fruits and vegetables, repaired old garments, constructed new ones from surplus materials, sewed linens, and manufactured mattresses for relief families, hospitals, and public institutions. Sewing employed 56% of female WPA workers. Housekeeping aides cared for families of sick women and of single fathers, and household training projects prepared women for domestic work.[67]

Numerous Black women expressed avid interest in sewing projects because they could learn to operate power machines, a skill that they hoped would move them out of white women's kitchens permanently. Alberta C, twenty-two, did factory work and housework in Chicago and New Orleans and completed a six-week session at a WPA Household Training School. Alberta did not aspire to domestic work; she wanted to sew and sing.[68] Sewing appealed to older Black women, worn by a lifetime of hard physical labor and demeaning treatment in white homes. Frances B said, "I'm tired of housework. Aren't there WPA factories where I can sew and be paid for my work?" She "believes she could do sewing in a factory if she were taught how." The interviewer considered that her age (fifty-eight) and eyesight "prohibited" factory employment and judged her "fit to do housework cooking or laundry work."[69] Gender stereotypes had race and class content. Work perceived as undesirable by some white women was prized by Black women who had been excluded from it.

The WPA was not a reliable solution to women's need for employment. It limited jobs to so-called economic heads of families and to a single worker per family, making unemployed daughters and wives ineligible. Employment of mothers of dependent children was prohibited. Nonfamily women met criteria, but workers with dependents were given preference.[70] Black women constituted 2.1% of WPA workers and white women 11%, proportions inconsistent with their shares of unemployment.[71] Women made numerous unsuccessful attempts to obtain WPA certification; if pronounced eligible, they had to find a project. The WPA had more difficulty creating jobs for women than for men, and consciously limited the proportion of women to enforce family norms and to ward off criticism that it employed too many women. Although federal policy forbade racial discrimination, Black women were not considered suitable for most projects because most lacked experience outside agricultural and domestic work. Local communities devised methods to keep them available for domestic service.[72]

To ensure that the WPA did not become more desirable than market employment, the government regulated wages. Fifty-five dollars monthly was the low end of pay for white working-class female jobs. For Black women, WPA wages often made possible a higher standard of living than previous employment.[73] For anyone, $55 was a dramatic improvement over relief. When WPA projects ended, there was no recourse but public assistance. A dozen women in the 1937 Chicago sample held WPA jobs and subsequently received relief; others, certified eligible, were unable to find work.[74]

Direct relief to women was rare. Chicago, home of national female leaders in reform and social welfare education, may have been unique in incorporating unemployed, unattached women in direct relief. The Chicago Relief Administration (CRA) made payments to 12,529 unattached women in November 1936, roughly the same number as for male single-person cases.[75] Women received a maximum of $23.05 monthly: $9.25 for food, $12 for rent, and $1.80 for clothing.[76] Only women deemed unemployable received rent allowances; some employable women received small amounts for utilities. Some clients secured health care, carfare to hospitals or clinics, and surplus food and clothing, and a few received extra cash for a special diet prescribed by a doctor. When funding failed, the CRA withdrew rent allowances, resulting in evictions. Cecile Hillyer, coauthor of the WB study, summarized conditions in September 1937:

> As to stability of Chicago relief, the less said the better. While it is quite true that January 1937, the month of the study, was a relatively stable period, it was so only in comparison to the budget cut of March 1936, the closing of the [relief] stations in the summer of 1936, and the recent crisis. At the present time no rents are being paid (rents for employable cases were stopped in the early summer), fuel allowances are not issued, evictions are numerous and shelter care is increasing. It seems to me that nothing kind can be said about the CRA.[77]

Chicago's female nonfamily relief clients were typically older than forty and formerly housewives and/or employed in low-paying service occupations.

Black women accounted for 44.8% of clients but 7.1% of the female population.[78] Among women sampled by the WB, 62% in their twenties and thirties were Black, testifying to more possibilities available to young white women.[79] Duration on relief rolls was surprisingly brief: a median of seventeen months. A few women received assistance as early as 1931, but more than half applied in 1935 or later.

The promises of the Social Security Act of 1935 benefited few white women and almost no Black women. It institutionalized mothers' pensions as Aid to Dependent Children (ADC) and required statewide implementation, but four years later, ten states had not complied. Triple the number receiving mothers' pensions a decade earlier collected ADC: 298,000 families. Benefits remained inadequate (from $8.14 monthly in Arkansas to $56.96 in Massachusetts), despite partial federal reimbursement.[80] Concern for "suitable" homes and "fit" parents persisted. Orphans and children of white widows continued to predominate. Sixty-one percent of ADC mothers were widows; 25% were deserted, divorced, or separated; Black mothers and children were underrepresented.[81] Old Age Insurance benefited retired workers, and Old Age Assistance helped the elderly poor. Both explicitly omitted domestic and agricultural workers, disproportionately excluding African Americans.[82] Benefits were linked to wages, so qualified women received minimal pensions. Congress extended coverage to dependents of retired or deceased workers in 1939.[83]

New Deal funding assisted private organizations with job creation. Activities at Dunbar Center expanded substantially when National Youth Administration and WPA funds increased staff from two to nineteen (1936). Paid and volunteer workers conducted a nursery school, organized recreation for children and adolescents, and taught adult education.[84]

Midwestern and northern cities presumably administered New Deal programs without racial discrimination, as unattached Black women's disproportionate numbers on relief in Chicago testified. Treatment remained unequal. Caseworkers, overwhelmingly white, sympathized more with white clients. Eligibility policies had racial results, if not intent. The ubiquitous requirement of liquidating insurance harmed all applicants, but life insurance was more likely to be the single form of savings in Black households. In Chicago, unattached women could receive relief without forfeiting owned homes, a policy that benefited white women.

New Deal projects limited funding and duration, so acquisition of a job or direct relief solved the need for income only temporarily. Women were underrepresented in publicly funded jobs compared to their proportion in the labor force and among the unemployed. Because urban Black women had been largely confined to the service sector, New Deal jobs were likely to be domestic work. The WPA was notorious for placing Black women in domestic training projects, which most Black women did not want.

The Work of Getting Relief: "It Almost Gives Me Nervous Prostration to Have to Ask for Relief"

Itemizing forms of assistance, eligibility qualifications, means and motherhood tests, and program changes describes relief from the vantage points of hindsight and scholarship. Destitute women rarely knew this much. Stark physical distress—hunger and cold—compelled them. Obtaining information, applying, becoming certified eligible, and actually acquiring aid were invisible labor, usually sex typed as female. Women had to learn new skills to negotiate with the relief system to satisfy bureaucratic imperatives rather than husbands.[85] Black women faced demeaning treatment by white caseworkers who had imbibed racist assumptions.

A woman considering relief needed information, though she might apply before, during, or after gathering it. Which agencies should she approach? What aid did they offer? Where was she most likely to be successful? She relied on informal networks of relatives, neighbors, landladies, friends, women's groups at church or synagogue. She solicited information and eavesdropped, reluctant to let others know her plans. Acquiring accurate information was difficult, and hearsay about a neighbor's experience might not apply the following week. For three years agencies appeared, disappeared, changed names, moved, defined clients more narrowly, disbursed different goods and services, tightened eligibility requirements, and depleted resources. In January 1932, on the verge of exhausting $12 million that it expected to last through the winter, Chicago mandated that prospective clients liquidate all assets. SBW staff informed Elizabeth K that owning furniture made her ineligible.[86] Previously, only savings accounts and insurance disqualified women.

Proliferation of agencies required applicants to engage in multiple bureaucratic negotiations. Applying for relief was most women's first experience with social service agencies. Young women likely were familiar with the PWA or YWCA, but relief applicants were disproportionately middle-aged and older. Three-fourths of 1933 Chicago sample women made at least two forays into social services. Sizable numbers applied to the Unemployment Relief Service (URS) and fewer to the Bureau of Public Welfare (BPW) and United Charities (UC). These large agencies, as well as Hull House, the Catholic Central Charities Bureau, the JSSB, the Women's Church Federation Protectorate, pastors, ward committeemen, and aldermen directed them to the SBW. Those who applied there directly were disproportionately white clerical workers fluent in English. Newspapers reported inauguration of public agencies and sometimes noted policy changes, but not all impoverished women had regular access to newspapers.

Perseverance, repeated applications, and development of new skills were essential. Sarah H migrated to Chicago from Louisiana, was widowed, and then laid off from her laundry job. In December 1930 she applied to the BPW, which turned her down. In February 1931 on a subsequent visit, it referred her to UC, which assisted her until October 1932, then referred her to the URS, which sent her to the SBW in January 1933, where she obtained grocery orders, coal, and health care at a free clinic.[87] Marital and familial changes necessitated new applications. The URS aided couples with unemployed husbands; if husbands died, it cut off women because it did not assist widows.[88] Women applied, spent days waiting, and often were directed elsewhere—indications of agencies' changing policies, women's lack of information, and the necessity for persistence.

Acquiring help was not one-stop shopping, especially during the Hoover years. Desperate women kept their ears to the ground to learn which agency was giving out clothing, bedding, or Christmas baskets. Alice M, a widowed sixty-six-year-old Black unemployed domestic worker, received grocery orders and fuel from the Philadelphia Joint Application Bureau and two dresses, a sweater, underwear, and hosiery from the Red Cross.[89] Even in a medium-size city, women invested hours applying to the plethora of groups distributing goods and services piecemeal: ice, canned goods, garden plots, milk, health care, clothing, grocery orders, and coal. Multiple applications increased possibilities but might disqualify applicants. In Cleveland, fourteen clerks at the Social Service Clearing House answered 176,848 inquiries from 150 agencies in 1930.[90] A woman with a history at many agencies risked being categorized as a chronic client and thus undeserving. The record of a twenty-four-year-old white Philadelphian stated, "Whole family has long record with social agencies; low type. . . . Not truthful."[91] Philadelphia's centralized record-keeping system monitored applicants by itemizing agencies contacted, often for health care, as far back as twenty-five years.

Pride and self-respect suffered in applying for relief. Some women asserted that their purpose was to obtain work and refused other assistance. All had to convince caseworkers of their eligibility and worthiness by exposing their destitution and shame. Amelia B voiced a common sentiment: "It almost gives me nervous prostration to have to ask for relief." Amelia supported herself as a barber after her husband's death in 1917. She lost the barber shop in 1931, exhausted her savings, and borrowed money until she could no longer rely on friends, who "[had] troubles of their own." This fifty-six-year-old white woman confided, "I never thought I would come to this. I am so willing and anxious to work."[92]

At relief bureaus, women fainted from anxiety, exhaustion, and empty stomachs. Many wept. They borrowed money for carfare or walked miles to agencies, often located downtown. In the winter of 1931 Philadelphia opened five branch offices for male applicants for work relief, "strategically located close to the centers of unemployment and work," but maintained a single office for women.[93] Applications peaked annually during the coldest months, especially the weeks before Christmas. Women borrowed shoes, boots, and coats, or braved the elements ill prepared and risked illness. Nervous applicants invariably waited in long lines, bewildered by a cacophony of sights and sounds, including activists recruiting for their organizations. Nor was the experience a one-time ordeal.

Catherine B, age sixty-one, a single Irish immigrant in ill health, applied to the CRA on November 16, 1936. She returned four days later for a formal intake interview after completing an affidavit attesting to her destitution. The following day she was certified eligible, but assistance did not begin until December 3, following a home visit.[94] Some women felt too demeaned or disheartened to complete the process.

Class, age, and racial gulfs separated the working-class applicant and the middle-class social worker. In 1932 at Chicago's four largest agencies (the BPW, the JSSB, UC, and the URS), caseworkers were overwhelmingly young, white, inexperienced, college-educated women. Public agencies hired hundreds of case-work aides; 83% had less than a year's experience in social work, more than two-fifths were younger than twenty-five, and less than one-fifth had taken a single course in social work. Aides were not supposed to assume full responsibility, but the press of applicants enlarged the scope of their jobs. Caseworkers, slightly older, possessed a median of two years' experience; two-thirds had some social work training, and only one-fourth were twenty-five or younger. Chicago caseworkers held more formal qualifications than those in smaller cities.[95]

A woman entered an agency as a supplicant, ashamed of her poverty, and strove to make the right impression on a woman of a higher class who held the key to immediate survival. Mattie M, a "perfect relief client," impressed her interviewer as "energetic, resourceful, anxious to take care of herself and appreciative of help, but with self-respect and without self-pity."[96] Mattie was rare. At their best, caseworkers sympathized with clients, and at their worst, they indulged in demeaning stereotypes and wielded power accordingly. Ever-increasing workloads and high turnover underlay clients' complaints that they did not see or hear from caseworkers for lengthy periods and that workers changed constantly. Sustained contact with destitution numbed caseworkers. Some succumbed to "the superficial popular judgment that [clients'] situation is due to laziness, immorality, or other personal fault."[97] An SBW official described clients who criticized the paucity of grocery orders as "everlasting kickers."[98]

Relief administrators assumed that clients were not humans, like themselves, who had simply lost jobs, but a species apart. The SBW believed in the rehabilitative value of work relief and "alternated [it] with direct relief in part because of a limited budget, but also as a disciplinary measure. The high psychological value of work relief was demonstrated, and in some cases proved exceedingly important as a means of rehabilitation of clients. The joy that spread over the countenance and the buoyancy that reacted in the walk of most of those who gained a work relief ticket reflected the depth of a change in feeling when they were allowed to earn the assistance they needed in place of accepting it as a last resort of subsistence."[99] Most women preferred work. The supposition that they needed discipline and rehabilitation speaks volumes about the insults they endured and the emotional work they undertook to maintain self-respect.

Clients' mental state was a professional concern, particularly as psychiatric social work gained popularity. The SBW employed David Rotman, a psychiatrist, to evaluate unemployability due to mental illness. His patently sexist assessments affected relief granted and referrals to mental health services. The SBW assumed that Black women did not suffer from mental illness, or that their mental health did not affect their ability to work, and rarely referred them to Dr. Rotman.[100] The Philadelphia study noted a "sharp contrast" between Black women, rated as definitely employable or definitely unemployable, and white women, who "predominate in the doubtful and limited employability classifications." Its author concluded, "This appears to be due in part to mental handicaps among the whites which appear to be almost non-existent among the colored, and in part perhaps to better analysis of the whites by the field workers."[101]

Contrasting with dismissive assessments of Black women, caseworkers described declassed white women in psychological detail and aided them generously. Marion N, age sixty-one and a widow, "appears to be refined and cultured" and had an "air of having known better days." St. Luke's Clinic characterized her as "discouraged," "extremely sensitive about being so helpless and dependent upon public relief," and concluded that she needed "encouragement and friendship almost as much as medical treatment." Her caseworker wrote: "Seems decidedly inadequate and lacking in her psychological orientation. She has developed a compensatory mechanism for her physical illness and regards this as a manifestation of her refined breeding and former status." Dr. Rotman evaluated her as "psychoneurotic and inadequate, and therefore unemployable." Refinement earned Marion a psychological diagnosis rather than a dismissal as lazy, and direct relief continuously from March 1932 through at least January 1937, with the exception of five months of work relief. The CRA awarded her maximum benefits, an additional $1.75 monthly for a special diet, and numerous visits to St. Luke's Clinic.[102]

If an applicant passed internal and external tests of stamina and worthiness, once certified eligible she engaged in further work. To acquire commodities and services, a woman walked or took the streetcar to warehouses and free clinics, waited, and sometimes endured demeaning treatment. Rescuing used, out-of-style clothing required an imaginative seamstress, and producing palatable meals from an unappealing assortment of staples demanded creativity. To avail herself of health care at Provident Hospital, Mattie N, a Black fifty-seven-year-old widow with heart trouble and other ailments, "has to walk to the district office to get two tokens to ride to the hospital. They will give her only two at a time."[103]

Women declined free health care, suffered ill health, saved to pay a private doctor, or relied on home remedies rather than endure humiliations to which discourteous interns and residents subjected them at free clinics. Annie G, forty-seven, a Black woman with "Indian blood," refused to return to the charity dentist; he was "too rough and she wants to wait until she has money to secure her own dentist."[104] Edith C, the waitress thrown out of Thompson's because she was too old (see chapter 2), needed to have teeth extracted. The agent wrote, "Client would like to know 'what in h——' she will eat with as Relief does not furnish replacements."[105] After treatment at Northwestern University Medical School Clinic and Cook County Hospital, Mary C refused to return because she did not "want to be experimented on as white mice."[106]

Enduring indignities was part of the emotional work of acquiring relief. Poverty was a disgrace and being "on the county" a sign of moral degeneracy. A woman not only lost pride in her self-sufficiency but was shamed by appealing for charity. She needed emotional stamina to endure internal judgments and external affronts, including insulting treatment from caseworkers and condemnation by neighbors, relatives, friends, merchants, and landlords.

Women bore the emotional costs of accomplishing relief-related tasks, despite the much-vaunted blows to men's self-esteem from unemployment. Applying for and acquiring relief was gendered. Investigating possibilities, applying, waiting, negotiating, and dealing with bureaucracies were not (and are not) perceived as work. Before the Depression, Minneapolis wives were twice as likely as husbands to approach AC; sometimes daughters made the pleas.[107] If assistance required an exchange of labor, men fulfilled that role. Despite insults such as "we poke along" directed at WPA workers, shoveling dirt for a paycheck commanded more respect than receiving direct assistance. The paucity of work opportunities for women limited their ability to earn integrity or dignity. Even when policy mandated equitable distribution, convincing caseworkers of their eligibility and worthiness was more difficult for Black women.

Attitudes toward Relief: "A Person Would Rather Have Work Than Go through This"

Despite severe deprivation, many working-class women adamantly refused "charity." Justine K, a twenty-two-year-old Slovak immigrant, could not feed her three-month-old baby "properly," but her husband was "proud" and would not apply to AC.[108] Although John M needed shoes and his wife, Tillie, had only bedroom slippers, he was "too proud to go to the county."[109] Publicly acknowledging need would further damage his class and male pride, which was already crushed by his inability to put food on the table. Mary K, thirty-nine, a Hungarian immigrant wife, "would rather die than ask" for aid.[110] Bessie W, Black and recently widowed at age thirty-three and unable to find work, exclaimed, "It's terrible isn't it. A person would rather have work than go through this."[111] Julia T, an unemployed waitress, thirty-five, a single Hungarian immigrant, "never asked aid of any association. There are many who need it worse than I do."[112] A self-described "young girl" worked to "help both mother and father from asking for charity so their pride would not be injured."[113]

When seeking assistance, women maintained personal ethical codes and held on to vestiges of pride. The YWCA noted on one record, "Family choice about work they accept. Mother resented being offered used clothing."[114] Some women contacted agencies, then balked at the next step. An unemployed clerical worker visited the Service Committee for Business and Professional Women, but declined to apply for a grocery order, even though she did "not know where to turn."[115] Others refused to give their address, to be interviewed, to accept "made work," to take psychological tests, or to be placed in Household Workers Training Schools or on housekeeping aid projects.[116] Mary M reported, "Three days last week I hadn't any fire but still I wouldn't give up and come down here. [I] nearly froze to death." Forty-seven, Black, this widow took in washing and roomers, but neither endeavor proved adequate.[117] Lillian C, a Greek immigrant and unemployed waitress, age thirty-one, searched "all over Chicago" for work. She lived with her brother, who was sentenced to the penitentiary. After exhausting savings, she resigned herself: "All I can do is come here and take what they can give me."[118] Applicants were typically in debt, evicted, cold, hungry, poorly clothed, ill shod, and/or disabled by illness or injury.

Determined to preserve autonomy, dozens of women in the samples explicitly rejected shelter lodging, tantamount to the poorhouse, even if it was the only assistance offered. Clara R, an unemployed domestic worker, was referred from the URS to the SBW to Sunshine Haven, a shelter for Black women. Described as "quite crippled," Clara "never showed up."[119] Desperate women took pains to avoid this disgrace and "made [their] own plans," as scribbled notes on interview forms recorded. The hard-pressed women staying in shelters objected to overcrowding, dirt, offensive roommates, prisonlike practices, staff coercion, institutional environment, and rigid rules. The Chicago Municipal Home required employable women to accept live-in housework for room and board alone. It threatened recalcitrant residents with psychiatric evaluation, hospitalization, and being barred from shelter facilities.[120] After three months at Sunshine Haven, Sarah B, forty-eight, taking care not to burn bridges, explained that the staff had been "very nice" but she "feels she'd have better opportunity to look for work if she was in room of her own."[121] Lorraine G, age thirty-five, single, white, and a waitress at resort hotels (see chapter 1), was disciplined for her inability to perform on a sewing project by being sent to Cathedral Shelter, where nine women were crowded into a single room and the air was bad.[122] Boxcar Bertha Thompson, a bohemian, hobo adventurer, sporadic shelter client, and occasional shelter administrator, claimed that many residents at the Manhattan Municipal Lodging House were alcoholics. She described shelters as intermittent resources: "Most of them came periodically. When they got a job they would leave, and when it failed they came back."[123]

Applying for assistance challenged women's conceptions of themselves as competent and self-reliant. Public exposure of their destitution and caseworkers' sometimes disparaging treatment humiliated them. Newspapers referred to them as "indigents" and "on the dole line." Women engaged in subterfuge and curtailed activities to keep their relief status secret. Millie M, age sixty, white, who had been employed for thirty years as a stenographer, "ask[ed] that her relief should not be sent in the mail because other people will know she is getting help and will point at her on the street." She "[made] elaborate plans for the landlord to bring in her mail so no one else can see letters from the relief station."[124] Mary B, a sixty-two-year-old white widow and unemployed restaurant cook, seldom attended church because she felt that "people [were] not so cordial to her when they find out she is on relief."[125] Everyone in South Bend knew that Studebaker was in dire trouble, yet local residents complained about welfare "chiselers" and demanded an end to relief "extravagance."

Declassed women most successfully claimed maximum resources. Madge R, the daughter of a music professor who trained opera singers, married an advertising man who left her "well provided for." She had never "known the meaning of money" and "never thought she would come to such a position, she who had wintered in Miami." After this sixty-year-old white widow lost furniture and could no longer rent rooms in her large apartment, her class skills enabled her to manipulate the system. The CRA classified Madge as unemployable, entitling her to maximum benefits. Her private doctor diagnosed gall bladder trouble, leakage of the heart, high blood pressure, and anemia and prescribed port wine. Madge stressed her "weakness," caused by "lack of proper food and nervous strain." When she was evicted, a bailiff dropped a piece of furniture on her toe, and she said that sometimes the pain incapacitated her from standing. She "says she is 'mentally ill' and mentioned that one tenant in the building had committed suicide by walking through an open window and implied that she might sometime do the same thing." She spent "a great deal of time crying" but had "no apparent mental abnormality."

Madge narrated her story with "very definite dramatic mannerisms." Her lawyer described her as "an excellent actress" who could "assume the manners of a grande dame or 'a park bum.'" The agent wrote, "She is a sweet, pleasant person, has a good sense of humor, laughed at times about her situation and then went suddenly into tears about it, not with bitterness, but utter sadness and shame at her being placed so low." Madge dressed in a "worn black velvet robe and slippers" and made "an attempt to keep an appearance. . . . She has always been found in attractive flowing housecoats and negligees, with her face made up and her hair in curlers." Madge's class skills sustained her. She sued for $100,000 for her injured toe and kept most of her expensive furniture in storage and in her lawyer's garage.[126]

Working-class women usually considered relief a final recourse. Linda Gordon describes an "opportunistic and resourceful approach" toward child protection organizations. Clients "denounced the 'intervention' of outside social control agencies . . . and they eagerly used and asked such agencies for help."[127] Lizabeth Cohen argues that working-class people came to feel entitled to relief, to believe their tax dollars should carry them through economic crisis. Women's anger about shabby treatment and inadequate relief substantiates this analysis. Yet there is far more evidence of their shame. Madge carefully calculated her relief strategy, but most working-class women suffered deep humiliation. Opportunism, resourcefulness, and entitlement tell a part of the story. Disgrace, degradation, and humiliation also framed women's responses to relief.

The most trusting, cooperative women, perhaps the least humiliated and not the most desperate, received more of the meager resources available. Their ability to convince caseworkers of their worthiness determined whether they ate, kept warm, obtained health care, or had roofs over their heads. Relief, like jobs, was unreliable. The state assumed the role of husband, furnished minimal support, and set conditions for the relationship. Women expressed autonomy by refusing aid they considered undesirable: "made work," grocery orders, shelter housing, free health care, and housework jobs for room and board. They "made [their] own plan." Destitute women still had standards.

Black and white women alike refused charity and emphasized their autonomy, pride, and shame in applying for and accepting relief. The evidence does not support a supposition of racial differences in attitudes. It is more useful to reemphasize that Black women endured far worse unemployment, had fewer material resources, faced greater difficulties in establishing eligibility, and more frequently swallowed their pride out of lack of other possibilities. Black women accounted for disproportionate shares of nonfamily relief applicants and recipients in Chicago and Philadelphia, 45% in three studies (1933 and 1937). Philadelphia Black applicants were significantly younger and more likely to have received help from relatives than were white applicants.[128] Anomalously, Black Chicago relief clients in 1937 had applied more recently than white women.[129] Racist and xenophobic attitudes toward relief clients circulated publicly and privately, while clients emphasized their autonomy, pride, and shame about applying for or receiving relief.

Gendered, racialized hierarchies in administration of relief demand attention. During the Hoover administration, Black and white men, searching for relief or shelter, infrequently encountered one another. Philadelphia opened five local offices for unemployed men, serving the majority of Black men at a single office. Provisions for women, when they existed, were inaugurated years later and were not segregated. Chicago and Philadelphia each opened a single relief office for women. CRA clients experienced separation through neighborhood offices, and a few white women lived in predominantly Black neighborhoods. Just as no exclusively "Negro jobs" existed for women (in sharp contrast to men's occupations), Black and white women encountered each other in search of relief. Women more frequently mixed in public spaces.

The tale does not end with women's humiliating descent into, or resourceful manipulation of, the relief system. In the conclusion I will elucidate women's class and race consciousness and actions.

Conclusion

● ●

Working-Class Women's Class and Race Consciousness

Focusing on working-class strategies to survive material losses during the Great Depression, I have concluded that women practiced common strategies across race, but experienced dissimilar results because of structural racism. How did working-class women theorize their daily lives and the big picture? Prudence, distrust of government, and classist and racist impediments to communication tempered conversations, but some interviewees aired opinions about business, unemployment, government, and relief. Letter writers, in contrast, penned angry accusations and excoriated housewife-employers, revealing themselves as full human beings, not mere beasts of burden or cogs in the machine.

"If somebody doesn't do something for the working people—My God what is going to happen?" questioned Arleathie B, a Black laundry worker (see chapter 2).[1] Working people did something for themselves. The Bonus Army; communal thwarting of evictions; housewives' bread and meat "riots"; Black women's mobilizations in Don't Buy Where You Can't Work campaigns; the Congress of Industrial Organizations (CIO) union organizing in mass-production industries; thousands of demonstrations by the unemployed in Chicago alone, often led by the Communist or Socialist Parties; support for the Scottsboro Boys; and successes of the Brotherhood of Sleeping Car Porters were among working-class challenges to capitalism, government, and white supremacy.[2] Depression activists, journalists, novelists, and historians have chronicled these stories. I address unfamiliar examples. Working-class women in South Bend, Indiana, led CIO, Communist Party, National Negro Congress, and Unemployed Council activism. Nationwide, letter writers professed race and class consciousness, as well as xenophobic, racist, and anti-Semitic attitudes as they entreated government to act. The record, and the potential for solidarity, is contradictory.

Challenges to Business and Government: Theory and Practice in South Bend

Working-class people identified with major employers, whose welfare capitalist programs encouraged such bonds. Ball Band Shoes, Studebaker, and Wilson Brothers created community and instilled loyalty with bands, clubs, sports teams, newsletters, entertainment, and summer picnics. Yet when Studebaker announced that it would retain only married men, so some young men wed their sweethearts but were laid off anyway, they felt that Studebaker had violated their trust.[3] The corporation justified dismissing Alice K, a file clerk, a month after her wedding, on grounds that her husband "was employed on a good job at Studebaker." Alice explained that he was "out of work practically four months out of the five since that time."[4] According to Lizabeth Cohen, when corporations betrayed employees' expectations, workers criticized their failure to adhere to a moral capitalism.[5]

Layoffs that workers perceived as unjust or as undercutting familial needs incurred their indignation. Bessie B considered it "very unfair" that the lathe works laid off "family men and those buying homes."[6] Julia K criticized Singer for giving men "women's jobs;"[7] Helen S, a cabinet worker, bristled that the "oldest girls—those who had been there ten years and over" were laid off as soon as newer hires.[8] Leah C, a Robertson's Department Store saleswoman for eighteen years (see chapter 2), told a cautionary tale of a successful worker who lost her job. When the store switched from wages to commissions as a cost-cutting measure, one clerk earned $40 in a single week. Robertson's refused to pay; the clerk sued, won her case, and was fired.[9]

Studebaker urged employees to donate 1% of their income to the Community Fund,[10] but Casimir M's compulsory contributions yielded no returns to his family of seven (see chapter 4). Believing taxpayers were entitled to relief and services, he was disgruntled that his wife and children were denied free dental work, disqualified by his marginal wages. In October 1932 Casimir said his taxpayer meetings (which the interviewer parenthetically questioned, "Unemployed Council?") unanimously endorsed these ideas.[11]

Working-class anger erupted in January 1933 in massive demonstrations organized by the Unemployed Council. St. Joseph County, heavily indebted, and unable to sell bonds, ceased issuing grocery orders, which allowed people to select goods and stores, and switched to the "standard order plan." Between two thousand and twenty-five hundred marchers converged on the courthouse demanding abolition of the "basket system." Banners rallied, "Don't Starve—Fight!"[12] A week later, police stymied a larger demonstration, blocked the courthouse steps, and charged the crowd (estimated at four or five thousand by newspapers and at eight thousand by the Unemployed Council). They arrested twenty-four participants from multiple ethnic and racial backgrounds, including six women, and raided the organization's office and five homes.

Twenty-four-year-old Stella Machulias, leader of the Unemployed Council, leaped onto the roof of a parked car to speak when police blocked the courthouse steps. Stella shared the history of many young, white, working-class women. Daughter of a Studebaker operative, a Polish and Lithuanian immigrant, she had left school after eighth grade, entered a factory, and joined the YWCA industrial girls club. Recognizing her leadership potential, staff arranged her participation in a University of Wisconsin workers' education program in 1931. She studied at the Vineyard Shore School in West Park, New York eight additional months, joined the Communist Party, and returned home. Stella's snappy responses at the trial and pride in her communist affiliation gained her the sobriquet "girl agitator," and the headline "Stella Backs Red Theories in City Court."[13]

One couple in the sample, Mary and Julius Takacs, Hungarian immigrants, consistently pursued justice. When Julius was hospitalized with tuberculosis in 1930, Mary, who worked in a Notre Dame University kitchen, held Studebaker responsible: "When she applied at the employment office, they paid no attention to her and did not make any effort to place her. After trying to get work repeatedly, [she] told them . . . if they did not get her something to do she would take her problem to court, they gave [her] her present job." The redoubtable Mary, who moved their three children in with her in-laws when Julius was hospitalized (see chapter 5), won third prize in the ladies' nail driving contest at Studebaker's Kiddies Day in 1931. Studebaker laid off Julius in April 1932, and in October, Mary earned $2. They energetically solicited bread, farm produce, and clothing for Unemployed Council members.[14] Julius was arrested at the 1933 demonstration and their home was among five raided by police. He served two months at the penal farm and joined the Communist Party.[15]

Interracial cooperation characterized the Communist Party and the Unemployed Council. International Labor Defense and the National Unemployed Council called a "mass protest meeting" four days after the thwarted demonstration, arrests, and raids. A leaflet exhorted, "Fellow workers, negro and white regardless of your political or religious views, organize and protest against the starvation program of the township trustee and county government. Continue the fight against the basket system: fight for unemployment insurance at the expence of the bosses and their government: demand the unconditional release of all arrested workers. . . . HUNGER KNOWS NO MASTER."[16] In 1934 the party ran a biracial slate for local offices, featuring Julius Takacs for sheriff; Lawrence Kanouse, a young white man for mayor; and Sam Jones Bay and Thomas Payne, Black migrants, for city council. All were Unemployed Council activists, and three had been arrested.[17] None of their candidacies were successful. Bay and Payne left the city, as did Stella when she married.[18]

Beginning with a campaign at Studebaker in summer 1933, CIO unions organized every major plant: Ball Band, Bendix, Oliver, Singer, Studebaker, and
Wilson. At the auto industry's first plant-wide sit-down strike in November 1936,
a thousand workers remained inside Bendix, women and men together, unlike
the sit-down at General Motors in Flint, Michigan, a few months later. Women
foiled gossip that strikers engaged in sexual relations by setting aside designated
sleeping areas for women, thus also mollifying uneasy wives. They supported a
grievance committee to undercut supervisors' sexual harassment.[19] In 1937
United Auto Workers (UAW) Local 5, at Studebaker, prided itself on attaining
a contract, a union-negotiated wage structure, and 100% membership, without
a strike, several years before other UAW locals.[20]

Wilson employees, almost entirely female, expressed avid interest in a union.
At Wilson's Stunt Night (November 1933) neckwear department workers staged
a politically pointed skit about the National Recovery Administration (NRA).[21]
To defuse critical sentiments, the company inaugurated an Employees' Council
and launched a newsletter, Sew and Sew, that castigated unions in issue after issue.
In 1937, Wilson employees received a charter from the Amalgamated Clothing
Workers, which also established locals at laundries and smaller garment manufacturers, and United Retail, Wholesale, and Department Store Employees
founded a clerk's local.[22] Astonishingly, local unions quadrupled, to seventy-four,
in a half decade.[23]

With a broader focus than the workplace alone, the Dunbar Community
Center connected radical politics and Christianity.[24] Its expanded staff, courtesy
of the National Youth Administration, organized community activities such as
National Negro Health Week and Negro Achievement Day and hosted annual
regional youth conferences. Nine African Methodist Episcopal, Baptist, and Seventh Day Adventist churches cosponsored the 1935 conference. Black churches
had long promoted social, political, and educational development of young
people, but this level of interdenominational cooperation was unusual. The
planning committee, primarily women, included an elevator operator, a maid, a
Dunbar employee, and a janitor. Small businesses, such as lunchrooms, barbers,
beauty shops, and tailors, supported conferences with program ads.

At the 1937 Midwest Youth Conference Black youth debated national
and international issues and passed resolutions favoring equal opportunity in
education and employment, world peace, and a consumers' cooperative movement. They condemned lynching, mob violence, and racial discrimination
in craft unions. Cecilia Williams, a member of National Negro Congress
National Council, listed in the South Bend City Directory as a maid, led the
youth convention. The NNC, an umbrella for over five hundred organizations,
exemplifying the Communist Party's Popular Front strategy, had held its first
convention in Chicago in 1936.[25] At the Youth Conference, 350 participants
chose the name Northern Negro Youth Movement and elected Williams its
president.[26]

Radical campaigns persisted. Louise Thompson, an African American intellectual and Communist Party activist, spoke about the antifascist struggle in Spain, where she had traveled, to a mixed-race audience of twenty-two hundred autoworkers that fall.[27] In 1938 William Patterson, a leading Black communist, addressed the state Communist Party's convention in South Bend.[28] Robin D. G. Kelley links political engagement and Christianity in Black Alabama communities in the 1930s, and a northern industrial city repeated the same connection.[29]

Local research provides evidence of class solidarity and demonstrates working-class women's groundbreaking leadership: Stella Machulias, Cecilia Williams, four women who served jail time for Unemployed Council demonstrations,[30] union advocates at Wilson, and sit-down strikers at Bendix. In a medium-size city, the CIO, Communist Party, Unemployed Council, and Black leftist activists won radical and union victories.

Race, Class, and Ethnic Suspicion and Separation

In interviews and letters, working-class women articulated working-class conceptions of class, race, and gender in regard to jobs and relief. At the same time, prey to assumptions that created separations rather than alliances, some interviewees and letter writers misplaced responsibility for economic crisis onto immigrants, African Americans, or Jews. Anti-Semitism framed some domestic workers' anger toward exploitative housewife-employers. Xenophobia and homegrown support for Nazi Germany and fascist Italy also fanned flames of bigotry.[31]

Disgruntled, native-born white women believed African Americans and "foreigners" benefited more from relief than they did. Fifty-year-old Harriet G, an "expert tambourinist," the wife of a Salvation Army preacher, and a former WPA housekeeping aide, cared for the eight-person family of a Polish worker whose wife suffered a breakdown. She "'never could understand' why clients sitting in relief office had always told her that 'the Negroes, Poles, and Italians got what they want because the relief workers are afraid of them' but now she is ready to believe this as there was 'never a day' but what this Polish man did not receive something from the Relief."[32] Another Harriet, a declassed white widow, age sixty-two, sent numerous letters to the Chicago Relief Administration containing "amazing vindictiveness about foreigners who get more relief than she." Formerly a clerical and political worker at the Cook County Recorder's Office, Harriet B once spied on "the Reds" for the Republican Party. She "resents fact that 'foreigners' (foreign birth or parentage) are being helped by charity in this country when 'our own people' (citizens of long standing through many generations) are starving." Her "bitterness towards foreigners seems pathologically strong. . . . All foreigners are 'gangsters' or 'chiselers' to her." Harriet received relief far longer than average, from November 1931 until at least 1937, and "put in complaints about relief through a radical group."[33] Another white interviewee attempted to hide materials from the National Union for Social Justice, an anti-Semitic organization founded by Father Charles Coughlin, a popular radio priest.[34]

"I told her she had better get a foreigner, she didn't want an American," expostulated Vera F when the YWCA sent her to a domestic job. Twenty-six, white, and divorced, Vera had worked eight years in a clerical position.[35] Declassed women and long-term domestic workers both argued that housewife-employers' requirements were so demanding that only immigrants could accomplish them. A self-described white, Protestant, forty-three-year-old Jersey City, New Jersey, widow, "once in good circumstances," wrote to President Roosevelt, "Why does our country allow all these foreigners come over here and spoil it for us American women, we do not object to work as domestics, but we cannot work like the foreign element, as they are like horses. . . . We are of the finer type."[36] A San Franciscan justified, "There are too many foreigners in our country, the American people born here from many generations are not given a chance in their own country. Foreigners comes here and will work so cheap an American hasn't much chance to get ahead."[37] Writers appealed to New Dealers to remember "their own people."

Eastern and Midwestern white women typically disparaged generic "foreigners" (eastern and southern Europeans), while their western counterparts often specified the ethnicity of presumed unfair competitors. A Los Angeles woman contended, "The trouble with California is that they hire too many Mexicans, Japs, and Phillipa instead of our American people [illegible] and more reliable and spend there money in our country where it is earned."[38] A Portland, Oregon, woman asked, "Is it fare that we should have to work with colored or phillipna boys?"[39] A San Francisco "trained children's nurse" wrote, "Surely American women ought to give American women a square deal, since you can't ask a Chinaman to care for a baby."[40] Josephine Morales, secretary of the Domestic Workers Association of El Paso, requested the NRA to "[stop] comuters from Juarez Mexico coming to our city and taking our rightful work at a much lower wage than we can possibly accept. . . . The standards of living in Mexico are not what our standards are therefore enabling commuters to work for $2.50 to $3.00 per week."[41]

Similarly, white interviewees occasionally claimed unfair competition from Black women. Caroline M, age sixty-three and a Hungarian immigrant, concluded, "Colored people will take anything and do everything just to get the work."[42] Bridget M, a middle-aged Irish American domestic worker, reported, "The wet wash and the colored people have taken all my places."[43] Such indictments countered stereotypes of Black laziness, but this contradiction was lost to white women.

Indignant houseworkers specified the ethnicity of exploitative housewife-employers only if they were Jewish. A Black Chicagoan wrote, "The Jewish people are Rich and they are the wourst one to work for they drive you all day like a slave."[44] A Brockton, Massachusetts, woman attributed the drop in wages to Jews, who are "out to ruin our people I have worked for them and I know what

I am talking about."[45] According to a Dayton, Ohio, houseworker, "One Jewess tells the other what she pays her maid and if the other one thinks she is paying more than the other then the wage-cutting begins. . . . Jews seem to have a maid if nothing else but pay so little."[46] A Brooklyn woman summarized, "A different type of people keep help today mostly the New Rich one generation removed from the old countries, too much money. and not much refinement."[47] Needless to say, housewife-employers collaborated on cutting wages at restricted country clubs as well as at "sisterhood meetings."

Class Anger: "Would It Not Be Much More Appropriate to Have a Little Bit of Social Justice?"

Houseworkers powerfully justified their rights as workers, but they did not use explicit class language. The single writer who named her employer a "boss" cleaned for a priest. Instead, they cataloged behavior of housewife-employers that they believed inappropriate. Because the employers who mistreated them were women, and women bosses were an oxymoron, their class claims to fair treatment as workers were entangled with their gendered expectations for privileged women. Women who went out in the evenings, ignored their children, and spent lavishly on liquor, clothing, cigarettes, cosmetics, entertainment, cars, and vacations while pleading poverty to avoid paying domestics adequate wages, earned the wrath of employees: "The housewifes goes out playing cards in the afternoon while the girl or woman is slaving 12 to 14 hours per day."[48] Writers criticized women who did not care for or discipline their children properly, according to workers' standards for motherly comportment. A Chicagoan claimed, "Most all of the women are going out every night instead of being companions to their children. (Where they belong.)"[49]

In addition to enunciating expectations about employers' utilization of time, money, and energy, writers enumerated endless examples of emotional abuse and employers' selfishness, arrogance, and hypocrisy. Haughty attitudes, incessant demands, condescending treatment, and housewife-employers' self-absorption incensed domestic workers. No other job created such intimacy or presented the employee private so much knowledge about the employer. Other than condemning sexual harassment, household employees only mentioned men to note their occupations as evidence that their wives could pay higher wages.

Verbal viciousness and complete "disregard of personal rights" angered women.[50] Marie Adams of Wichita, Kansas, wrote Reverse word order: "private employee."

The employing women are simply taking advantage of the fact that so many people need work. They gloat over it to the girls' faces. . . . To crown it all when the girls are so weary that they can hardly serve a meal, or talk, they are nagged for not saying 'yes ma'am,' one hundred times a day. This would show more respect and politeness they are told. Just what use has a dog-tired girl for surface politeness? Would it not be much more appropriate to have a little bit of social justice?[51]

Employers were "wringing every ounce of physical and mental endurance or energy from the domestic servant," who was "brocken in health."[52] Anna Filak replaced three employees in the fourteen-room home of a Cleveland lawyer, noting that they "demand[ed] so much ruining girls health, shattering her nerves and breaking hope in humanity. You will find them among the welthy often."[53] Marie Adams wrote, "The girls are not allowed to rest all day and evening until they go to bed exhausted at night. They are in addition nagged and driven to speed up all those long hours of unending toil."[54] A young Pennsylvanian claimed, "Those ladies who hire us . . . take advantage and even abuse us and we become nerves wreck and once health is gone we suffer."[55]

"Fault-findings are worse than they ever were," a Newport, Kentucky, "trained, experienced cook" alleged. Edna Bradford wrote on behalf of hundreds of women she met working in a Cincinnati employment office. "We all of us girls have suffered in silence many years knowing the full bitter meaning of being trampled on of being pushed back laughed at scorned by their Employer they laughed and said we will get even with them we will lower wages we will see that they don't wear silk stockings or silk underwear we will bring them down, we will force them to be glad to work for little wages."[56] B. Faust of Flushing, New York, believed "smoking fiend women . . . [could] learn to do [a lot of things] without hurting their painted finger nails." She added, "What contemptable women some of these so called ladies are. . . . I know them all from social registre down, swines to me, they think nothing of working a women 18 hrs a day."[57]

Domestic workers criticized employed women who paid houseworkers poorly when dual-income couples could afford higher wages. An Ironwood, Michigan, "white slave" wrote, "There are many and many young married women working whose husbands have nice salaries and this deprives us young girls from earning our bread and butter."[58] A Los Angeles woman inquired of Frances Perkins, "Why is it that Clubwomen who work so hard for the forward movement of women ignore the needs of the fine class of women who work in their homes. . . . Is it that they don't want this class of women to move forward with the rest of the world?" This self-described "intelligent woman worker" concluded, "Wealthy women who want to be of use in this world, do not need to go into business and take some one else's bread away from them. There is plenty of work to be done to help us all forward."[59] She was a rare domestic worker who conceived of cross-class female unity.

Household workers objected not to work, but to overwork for low or no wages. "A poor housekeeper with nothing" was expected to fire the furnace, carry out ashes, scrub steps, make banana pie, wash clothes on a scrubbing board, purchase groceries, and shovel snow. She was "naged all the time I got supper said I had no pep was too slo."[60] Two Brooklyn sisters had "the responsibility of doing the work of a team of horses such as washing walls and ceilings and even want you to keep the furnace going and keep the employers car cleaned," and "when we rebuke against such work we are called lazy or such remarks are passed, what are you getting paid for. what were you hired for and if you don't like it get out and when you do quit and try to get another job our reputation isn't considered worth referring to."[61]

Live-in jobs made possible exploitation that was not experienced by day workers. Time off duty occasioned acrimonious exchanges. A married former secretary in Jersey City wrote, "When they give you a 'night off' they will constantly 'harp' on the fact that you went out and complain that no one can do their work the next day when they go out the night before; in other words begrudging even an evening for a little recreation."[62] A "young girl" from Queens wrote, "Once in a while we ask for evening off, our boss thinks and acts as though it was something criminal. Out of the seven days we get one evening off, that is Sunday. Monday he thinks he done a big favor and is very irritable and almost impossible to bear. This place happens to be a Roman Catholic Rectory, a priests home."[63] According to one Hollywood worker, "Some even do not offer any time off, but expect a person's whole life to be spent in their home giving service for them."[64]

Employers expected to control a live-in worker. Gladys Miller supported her mother, who worked part-time, and her twenty-four-year-old twin brother, a "cripple," working seven days a week for five years for a couple both employed at good jobs in Huntington, West Virginia: "My day starts at seven in the morning and ends around nine thirty at night, except three nights in the week, Monday, Wednesday, and Friday. I lacked one and one half years of finishing high school. Last September I started taking a business course at night. . . . If you will permit the use of slang, it is just 'burning the wife and husband up' because I am going to school, but I made up my mind that I was going to school and I am."[65] Lack of personal freedom was the most hated job aspect for live-in workers.

Some housewife-employers expected women to work for room and board alone. As a woman in Atlantic City, New Jersey, wrote, "I know girls, when they asked for more wages, were told they could go, saying they could get all the help they wanted for board and lodging."[66] A woman in California, wrote, "A very wealthy woman here in Pasadena said to her cook 'The working girls should be thankful to work for board and room only.'"[67] A Portland, Oregon, woman who "had the misfortune of my husband loosing his mind . . . leaving me four children to help support" reported, "If we complain of to much work it is throwed in our faces that we are lucky to have a place to stay."[68]

In prolific descriptions of harsh working conditions and disrespectful employers, domestic workers revealed sharp class wrath about their exploitation. Letters illustrate the breadth and depth of working-class women's intellects as they uncompromisingly asserted their dignity and class pride.

Race Consciousness, White Supremacy, and Slavery: "Help Us Poor Toil Worn White Women Slaves"

Numerous white domestic workers made a forceful argument for inclusion in NRA protections by labeling themselves slaves and recalling emancipation. According to a Rhinelander, Wisconsin, woman, "The slaves in Lincoln's time were treated better than most of these girls. And then you read in history that Lincoln freed the slaves, but I'm afraid a few were forgotten."[69] A Los Angelino who became a citizen in 1930 appealed to Eleanor Roosevelt to "help us out of this slavery."[70] In Bridgeport, Connecticut, May Donath cleaned a ten-room house, cooked for a family of five, and accomplished numerous tasks, fourteen hours daily. She wrote, "Abraham Lincoln freed the Negro slaves. But today we white women who work in private homes are far greater slaves than ever were in Lincoln's day." Her eight-page letter bristled with class anger about unfair and demeaning treatment: "There are thousands of the same cases as this every where in the United States." She insisted on her willingness to work and concluded with a plea to Frances Perkins: "Help us poor toil worn white women slaves."[71] Kate Drumm of Birmingham, Michigan, wrote, "Their are all forced to worrk 16 hours a day their thousands of them in mich and their nothing being done about it—it warse than slavery and growing worse every day."[72] A Flushing, New York, woman argued, "She felt she was within the law to get what she could for her money even if it did kill the girl, what of it? Slaves are cheap."[73]

What meanings did white women conjure with the metaphor of slavery and pleas to remember Lincoln? Emancipation persisted as a central narrative of U.S. history. Virtually every northern town named a school, a street, or public memorial for Lincoln. School-day history, citizenship classes, and popular culture, including annual commemorations of Lincoln's birth and Civil War deaths, reminded women of a presumably shared abhorrence for an abusive institution long abolished. Slavery symbolized exploitation and oppression that Americans had agreed was incompatible with democracy.

Historical logic undergirded white women's use of a racial metaphor to describe odious working conditions. Race and class exploitation, inseparable in enslavement, remained inextricably intertwined. White workers historically and consistently relied on that metaphor.[74] The pantheon of U.S. history offered no widely known and shared references to defeat of class oppression, but it celebrated abolition of racial bondage and venerated Lincoln. These were the tools most readily available and most likely to convince. The institution of slavery had justified harsh labor with contempt for African Americans. Exploited labor was the bedrock of domestic workers' parables, but they embellished class arguments with a racial metaphor. Arguing that they should not be treated like people of degraded status while affirming their willingness to work hard, white women relied on white privilege. This was not necessarily a conscious argument. White women, including immigrants, learned an assumption of racial superiority and the right to remain oblivious about it.

What does it mean that white women removed gender from the equation when they utilized the metaphor of slavery? Enslaved women, expected to do the same field labor as men, had been degendered. (They were also expected to reproduce the labor force and undertake the care that kept the enslaved alive and well.)[75] White domestics compared themselves to the genderless enslaved, while they worked at an explicitly female job. In fact, they argued for their rights as white and female.

Linking racialized slavery with inferiority was not far from white minds. Overt deprecation of African Americans permeated popular culture and media. "Ethnic notions," as the collector Janette Faulkner labeled them, materialized in greeting cards, calendars, knick-knacks, children's books, quilt patterns, and endless objects and images.[76] Corporatization of groceries and proliferation of advertising exposed more women to branded products such as Aunt Jemima pancake mix. Misrepresentations of African Americans entertained white people. *Amos 'n' Andy*, a comedy about a small Black taxicab company, acted and mispronounced by white men in Black voice, was the most popular and first nationally syndicated radio program.[77] Seventy percent of Americans attended movies weekly, where Black actors played stereotyped roles.[78]

Local as well as national representations conveyed misinformation. Minstrel shows and blackface predated the Depression and continued long afterward. A Studebaker social event in 1923 featured a minstrel show, as did a UAW event in 1937.[79] At Wilson's 1933 Stunt Night, "Miss Bertha Buckner gave a Negro shuffle" and a group including a male blackface performer called themselves "Minstrels."[80] When Wilson's Girls' Club sponsored a concert by the Eureka Jubilee Singers (1934), *Sew and Sew* described singers wearing "traditional picturesque 'cotton pickin' clothes'" and "numbers 'acted' as only colored people with their inimitable gift for pantomime, can do and act."[81] The cartoonist for South Bend's Polish-language newspaper, *Goniec Polski*, created negative Black characters, and the electric company regularly ran Polish-language ads featuring a caricatured, uniformed Black messenger.[82]

We can also read white domestics' analogy with slavery as a mechanism by which they distanced themselves from Black women. Noting that harsh working conditions were widespread, none explicitly mentioned Black houseworkers. Unaware and/or unconcerned that Black women's employment situation was worse than their own, they failed to recognize that their jobs sometimes came at the expense of Black women. Their class consciousness did not extend beyond their lack of race consciousness. Implicitly they justified better treatment on grounds of whiteness.

Most white people were unable to conceptualize shared interests and experiences with African Americans. They identified with their native-born status and/

or their ethnicity, with their religion, and as workers at particular corporations. When immigrants worked alongside immigrants from other cultures, the workplace played a role in assimilation into whiteness; CIO campaigns built interethnic, white, class consciousness.

African American letter writers and interviewees also detailed lengthy hours, miserly wages, demanding expectations, and harsh conditions in domestic work. They did not mention slavery. Often they called for change on behalf of all domestic workers. Recall Mrs. Katherine Rutherford, who eloquently described domestic work (see chapter 2): "Is there any way that you could help the poor woman, both white and colored who have to work in these private families for a living. These private families work the poor woman to death."[83]

Black writers made race-conscious arguments—most often that the cost of living was the same for Black people as white. They recounted being pushed to extreme exhaustion: "The prices to us on everything is the same as to them. The grocer or the dry goods salesman make no reductions to us, and when we get home from these places of employment we are so tired we can't get out for enjoyment and if we wasn't tired we wouldn't be able to take in a nickel show." Eleanor Daigre concluded, "They try work us to death." She implored Roosevelt, "I pray god that you will have a write up in the New Orleans newspapers reminding the housewifes of the salaries and have them to remember we are humans from god."[84] Martha Gilchrist, formerly a shirtwaist worker in Philadelphia, asked, "Why is it that a colored male or female can do the same work as a white male or female, but get less wages? But if Bond bread is twelve cents a loaf, the clerk doesn't say, you are colored, and make a smaller salary, it is cheap to you."[85] Mrs. Rutherford noted, "They are harder on the colored woman, they seem to think that a colored woman have no feeling of tiredness. . . . They have to work every inch of their life to get it done."[86]

How can we understand Black women's appeals? Women who could call upon the memory of slavery and compare their work with subjugation their ancestors had endured did not do so. They named street-corner hiring "slave markets," but did not utilize the slavery metaphor in letters. Their racially specific arguments addressed the high cost of living, the racial differential in wages, and work-induced exhaustion. *Fairness* was their password. The Black press, distributed widely beyond the urban areas where it originated, was one source for the cost-of-living argument, which also appeared in Depression-era letters penned by Black men.

This contrast between white women's belief in their entitlement to decent treatment and Black women's solidarity, calling for better treatment for all domestic workers, is instructive. Black working-class women knew more about the lives of white working-class women than white women did about them, even though both resided far outside the dominant power structure. White women asserted class consciousness and argued for inclusion in government protection, as did Black women, who encompassed white women in their appeals and named classed and racialized experiences. They knew that legal change was unlikely to happen unless it included white workers.

Historians have debated how working-class men of varied European ancestry, ethnicity, nationality, language, and religion came to regard themselves as white. The virtual end to immigration, mandated by the Immigration and National Origins Act of 1924, created the legal and demographic context. Americanizers attempted to create a more homogeneous population. For greenhorns of the early twentieth century, white privilege was neither invisible nor automatic. Veterans of the Great War thought of themselves as Americans. As James Barrett and David Roediger have noted, Americanization was always about race and nation: "Immigrants were never so white as when they wore blackface before audiences and cameras."[87] For children born or raised in the United States, white advantage came more easily. Unaccented English opened up a world of whiteness that came less fully to immigrants. Letter writers claimed themselves to be "good American citizens."

With notable exceptions (some CIO unions and the Communist Party), many white women became more entrenched in and attached to whiteness, which requires further consideration. Although they were unaware of this fact, I suggest that the Depression assisted in-between women, the "foreign element," to become generically white; it consolidated white identities. In the early 1940s white women went on hate strikes in defense industries, objecting to sharing bathrooms with Black women. Later, white women led protests against school desegregation in northern and southern cities. New generations of white working-class women continue to express racial contempt.

Lessons and Questions

It can hardly be surprising that African Americans suffered worse unemployment than white people throughout the 1930s. It is noteworthy that Black women and men shared similar depths of joblessness, while white women, as a group, experienced significantly less unemployment than white men, a structural feature of the gendered and racialized labor force.

The disproportionate number of Black women and men employed on New Deal projects in 1940 initiated a trend that has continued. African American women are far more likely than white women to be employed by federal, state, and local government. Stated differently, social and political movements have succeeded in opening more job opportunities to Black women in the public sector than in the private corporate sector.

In essential ways women's Depression strategies and actions did not differ across race. Paragons of practicality, women created the daily nourishment, rest, and rejuvenation—for themselves and for others—that was necessary to face a new day. Women whose self-esteem was wrapped up in their ability to work hard and long faced constant challenges during the Depression. Their endless flexibility and resourcefulness in managing the material world to provide care was not worthy of notice, nor did their intensified toil challenge the gender order. They struggled not only to survive but to maintain dignity and self-respect.

To ensure survival, white women adopted habits more common to Black women in employment, in their households, and outside families. In 1940, white wives more frequently held jobs; adolescent daughters more frequently remained in school; families doubled up; and unattached women shared housing not only with kin but with friends. In 1929, Black women had more commonly practiced all these strategies. During the Depression, white women took jobs that they might not have previously considered, especially in service occupations where Black women worked. White women were unaware that they increasingly practiced the same strategies as Black women. The big picture is often invisible to the individual.

The Depression consolidated whiteness. Whether European immigrants were members of "inferior races," "in-between," "provisionally white," "not quite white," "white by law," or even "white on arrival," they had to learn about race in America, including assuming a white identity. Long before millions of immigrants and tens of millions of their children died, they no longer received official notice, but simply became white. Becoming American meant learning to think of themselves as not Black. I am not arguing that white women understood their actions as confirming their whiteness. With the exception of some CIO unions and the Communist Party and its offshoots, few white working-class people thought about or took seriously interracial solidarity.

Women's and men's experiences of racial segregation were not parallel. Black and white women sometimes worked together in commercial service jobs. They jostled one another in lines and waiting rooms at relief agencies. Employers, policy makers, and bureaucrats took far more pains to segregate men than they did women. We need to understand why this was so and its implications. Racial integration of female service jobs continued to increase after 1940, with growth of the service sector and ongoing Black migration, but proliferation of clerical jobs also removed white women from the service sector.

Chicago, Cleveland, Philadelphia, and South Bend exemplify American industrialism undercut by capitalist crisis, after which it subsequently prospered, thanks to international war. A long-lasting combination of people, competition, conflict, and efforts at conciliation and community came into existence as metropolises established patterns of class and race power that persisted until the final third of the twentieth century. The closure of Studebaker in 1963 was an early death knell for American industry as Midwestern and northern cities' mid-century peak of industrial power devolved into the Rust Belt. The Civil Rights Movement and revision of immigration law in the 1960s transformed the country in ways that would have been unrecognizable in the 1930s.

During the years I have worked on this project, I have asked many questions about work, gender, race, and class, as well as patriarchy, white supremacy, and capitalism. As I conclude during the mass unemployment and disruptions of the COVID-19 pandemic, gendered, racialized, and classed unemployment and poverty persist and white supremacy flourishes. Examples of solidarity and impediments to class, race, and gender unity persist. They remind us how much work remains to be done to acquire "a little bit of social justice."

Acknowledgments

My mother raised me with Depression stories from a small anthracite town. Her unemployed, immigrant father ordered her, the oldest child, to quit school at age fifteen to support the family. For six years she did domestic work for a dentist's family for $4 weekly; she also got badly needed dental work. She picked apart old clothes to use as patterns to make garments for her five siblings. When I began to think systematically about women's work, Harriet Arnow, Alice Childress, Meridel LeSueur, Louise Meriwether, Tillie Olsen, Ann Petry, Jo Sinclair, and Sarah E. Wright appeared in person and/or in used book stores.

My gratitude overflows for the interest and support of colleagues, comrades, friends, and partners who sustained me: Maria Alaniz, Martha Dana, Susan Edwards, Donna Fenstermaker, Mikki Ferrill, Vera Ferris, Miriam Frank, Henry Gutierrez, Desma Holcomb, Joan Howarth, Marie Kochaver, David Lamont Landes, Daphne Muse, Nell Myhand, Anita Tijerina Revilla, Jennifer Rycenga, Denise Sullivan, Martha Watson, Ellie Waxman, and Alex Yamato. Mrs. Gladys Ferrill and Mrs. Eloise Ferris shared 1930s Chicago memories. The women and girls of The Dojo / Laurel Jujitsu; Lenzie Williams and Tai Chi Berkeley; Steven Baugh and Lohan School of Shaolin; Alex Feng, Sky Sandoval, and Zhi Dao Guan; and Sue Fox and the 12×12 quilters kept me going.

Archivists and others behind the scenes make historical research possible. Before the National Archives and Records Administration processed the materials of the Women's Bureau, Tom Gedosch and Joseph Howerton allowed me access to the stacks. I opened boxes in which brittle rubber bands held the essence of this book. After the WB archives had moved and been reorganized, Bill Creech and Thomas McAnear helped with citation puzzles. Keith Knauss and Michael Lawrence of Labor Studies, Indiana University, South Bend; Kathy Deka and Carol Pickerel of the Northern Indiana Historical Society; and Jeanne

Denham at the Studebaker Archives, shared local insights. I thank Adrienne Lash Jones, the biographer of Jane Edna Hunter (the founder of the Phillis Wheatley Association in Cleveland) for help in my search for records. Tommy Patty, former director of the PWA, offered suggestions, and Ella Becton, then director, unearthed other materials. John Grabowski at the Western Reserve Historical Society assisted in local research.

The Charles E. Culpepper Postdoctoral Fellowship at Oberlin College; a Rockefeller Humanist-in Residence Fellowship at Duke University and the University of North Carolina Center for Research on Women; and sabbaticals at San Jose State University (SJSU) and the University of Nevada, Las Vegas (UNLV) provided time for writing. Beatrice Bain Research Institute at University of California, Berkeley was a collegial home during sabbaticals. Small grants from Ohio State University, SJSU, and UNLV helped fund research trips.

Estelle Freedman's women's history dissertation group, especially Antonia Castaneda, Joanne Meyerowitz, and, of course, Estelle herself; Mary Jo Buhle, Bill Chafe, Miriam Frank, Jacqueline Dowd Hall, Nancy Hewitt, Desma Holcomb, Karla F.C. Holloway, Wendy Luttrell, Monica McDermott, Joanna Nunez, Susan Pomeroy, Jennifer Rycenga, Ula Taylor; reading groups long forgotten; and anonymous readers commented on chapters, drafts, or papers. Riff Raff Radical Writers Joan Annsfire, Giovanna Capone, Marjorie Larner, and Peg Rider posed useful nonacademic questions. Janet Zandy's commitment to working-class studies inspired me. Ron DiCenzo distinguished Hungarian and Polish names; a Polish graduate student translated *Goniec Polski*; Fatma Isikdag produced SPSS tables; Jennifer L. Carson performed Word Perfect to Microsoft Word wizardry; Malcolm Lowe consulted a series of computers. A career in women's studies empowered my interdisciplinary tendencies. Annual meetings of the Teaching Workshop in Women's History at the University of California, Los Angeles reminded me of why I am a historian. Students everywhere educated me.

In the final years of this journey, four friends, new and old, made a major difference. Desma Holcomb, organizer extraordinaire, economics researcher, and union educator made thoughtful editorial suggestions; her enthusiasm prodded and encouraged me. Impelled by the massacre of nine African Americans in Charleston, South Carolina in 2015, Rochelle Towers, a lifelong activist and organizer, and I led seven five-month anti-white-supremacy groups for white women, White Awake Oakland, from 2015 to 2018. We thrashed out strategies for ending white supremacy, a small historical task. John Hayakawa Torok, union activist, organizer, and theorist, appeared at the right moment. We discussed my manuscript chapter by chapter at our local political Palestinian restaurant, Reem's. Grey Osterud generously shared publishing advice and editorial insights; she pushed me to toot my own horn, a practice considered unbecoming in the next-door-to-Amish world in which I was raised.

At Rutgers University Press, Kimberly Guinta, Jasper Chang, and Vincent Nordhaus, as well as Kristen Bettcher at Westchester Publishing Services, brought this book into material reality. Miriam Frank, Desma Holcomb, and Marie Kochaver cheered me on. I regret that my mother, Helen Kuznaik Helmbold; my aunt, Rita Kuznaik Moores; and my dissertation adviser, Carl Degler, are not alive to hold this book in their hands.

Appendix A

• • • • • • • • • • • • • • • • • • • •

Interview Sources

I sampled voluminous interview records from six studies that the Women's Bureau (WB) of the U.S. Department of Labor conducted in the 1930s, selecting every *nth* woman who met my occupational criteria (employment in clerical, commercial service, or domestic jobs in the 1920s or 1930s).

During the summer and fall of 1930, investigators canvassed working-class neighborhoods in South Bend, Indiana, to interview employed women about changes in industry. They recorded detailed job histories and gathered data about policies, practices, wages, and hours at factories, laundries, and stores. Two years later, agents revisited many households, posed in-depth questions about the effects of the Depression, and cataloged a year (1931–1932) of men's workplace data. Sample women were overwhelmingly white, as was the city of South Bend. Half were immigrants and their daughters, primarily Hungarians and Poles. Half were single, more than one-third were married, and the remaining 15% formerly married. In 1930 the WB excluded women working intermittently, domestic workers, and the self-employed: proprietors of small family stores and women who took in sewing or laundry or cared for children. By 1932, women had become practitioners of all these strategies.[1]

Because the vast majority of Black women worked as domestics, agents interviewed only eighteen African Americans and reinterviewed eight, two of whom appeared in my sample.[2] Subsequently, I combed through every schedule and located a third household included in both studies and twelve 1930-only interviews.[3] I traced all fifteen women and their households through local sources.

To determine appropriate policy for jobless women "adrift," the WB interviewed clients at three social service agencies between the fall of 1932 and the spring of 1933. The Cleveland YWCA sample consisted of white, mostly young, single, Christian job seekers; the Y excluded Black and Jewish women. More than one-fourth of the 294 sample women had immigrated, and many more were daughters of immigrants. Seventy percent were under thirty, and one-fourth were married or formerly married. After concerted efforts to uncover comparable records at the Phillis Wheatley Association, I concluded that the PWA had destroyed them. In Chicago (236 women) and Philadelphia (317 women), applicants for "made work" and relief were 40% Black and one-tenth immigrants; two-thirds had been married; their average age was forty-five.[4] I oversampled clerical workers because service workers dominated applicants for relief.

Besides South Bend, the other richest source consisted of a representative group of 12,529 unattached Chicago women receiving direct relief in 1937. The Chicago Relief Administration, the University of Chicago School of Social Service Administration, and the WB collaborated to improve relief by careful analysis of clients. Researchers utilized rigorous standards of social investigation in lengthy home interviews, augmented caseworkers' notes, and wrote in-depth descriptions. Clients sixty-five and older (31%) were excluded because employability was the focus. In my sample (219), half were Black, 17% were immigrants, and one-third were native-born white. One-half were between the ages of fifty and sixty-four, the oldest sample; one-fifth never married.[5] I again oversampled clerical workers.

For South Bend, I identified European ethnicity by surnames, recognizing that a few women may have married men from different backgrounds. In other studies interviewers occasionally noted ethnicity. Women labeled "white" were not immigrants and usually not daughters of immigrants; I have not speculated about their backgrounds.

The samples represent demographic variation among white women more fully. None contain substantial numbers of married Black women, comparable to South Bend white wives, nor is there a group of young, single Black women, equivalent to job seekers at the YWCA. The broad range of Black women in the two Chicago samples and the Philadelphia sample mitigates this gap but does not erase it. I augmented interviews with dozens of autobiographies, biographies, fictionalized accounts, journalism, poetry, and social science research by and about Black working-class women in the 1930s.

Appendix B

• •

Social Scientists at the
Women's Bureau

Interviewees' comments cannot be fully understood outside the framework constructed by the Women's Bureau (WB) of the U.S. Department of Labor. Asking predetermined questions, using "the approach which best suited" each interviewer, agents communicated their assessments directly and indirectly. Investigators' evaluations corresponded to hierarchies of race, class, and Americanization. They accorded the most credibility and dignity to white women in South Bend, Indiana, and bestowed their harshest criticisms on relief applicants and clients. They regularly disparaged Black women. They blamed women for poverty, doubted their veracity, and denounced strategies with which they disagreed.[1]

Yet gender could connect women. An unemployed Bohemian immigrant, who had described her difficulties to a priest, confided, "I couldn't tell him I was hungry as I could tell a woman."[2] Despite power differences and social distances, the detail recorded—as many as ten pages of facts and anecdotes—demonstrates that researchers possessed considerable skills, acute powers of observation, sympathy, and even charm in eliciting information.

Interviewers frequently characterized Black women as lazy. Julia S, age forty-seven, had cleaned a furniture store and a barbershop and done daywork. Julia "depended on friends to tell her about work," the usual method by which Black women obtained domestic jobs, and "said she could not do hard work." When she applied to the Philadelphia County Relief Board in 1932, the agent described her as "husky" and "problematic" because she believed Julia had not searched for employment. She concluded, "Apparently lazy and indifferent."[3] Blanche C received tuberculosis treatments three times weekly; the interviewer wrote, "Apparently not especially desirous of working."[4] Variations on this theme appeared on records of Black women accustomed to physically demanding jobs.

Assessments that agents considered positive reflected racial assumptions. Ponder this portrayal:

> A rather poor house in demolition area, but apartment is clean and cheerful with curtains, pictures and a wash basket of clean clothes. All the earmarks of a religious, self-respecting household. Landlady and husband appear in harmony with this picture. Client claims they are old friends of hers—this seems probable from behavior. Client's own room is much dirtier and more untidy, perhaps because she cares for it herself and she is obviously unable to. Client is an Aunt Jemima type, dark broad face, dimples, etc. Manner is dignified, frank but not garrulous. She does not dwell on her troubles or physical handicap.

Eva D, sixty-three, widowed, cooked in schools and private homes, did daywork, and dressed hair. She walked with "great difficulty," had heart disease and hypertension, and received relief briefly, which contributed to her "very good impression." Stereotypes affected assessment of the poor, whether deemed worthy or unworthy.[5]

Investigators compared Black women with one another and contrasted their situations with presumed alternatives. A home was "rather dingy, but tidier than most colored homes worker has visited," and a woman "more intelligent than most of the Negroes I interviewed."[6] An agent described a bare room, newspapers for rugs, a coal stove for heat and cooking, and two oil lamps. "Client satisfied because no doubt more comfortable than she would be if living in the South." Winnie B never lived in the South, a fact recorded on the form on which the agent was writing.[7] Another interviewer depicted three large basement rooms as "really very spacious nice quarters. These colored people are quite well satisfied with stove heat and thus they can have larger quarters and for less rent." She characterized Hattie W as "lazy" and added, "Perhaps she would like to have a physical ailment so she would not have to work." Hattie farmed, cleaned offices, shelled nuts, worked in a laundry, and did daywork. Her answers did not always satisfy the agent, who concluded she was "mentally dull."[8] An investigator described a "dark, dirty hallway swarming with colored children."[9] Interviewers chastised women of both races for poor housekeeping. They neither contrasted white women with one another nor assumed their poverty was preferable to previous experience.

Compare two evaluations from 1933. An unemployed, widowed, Black clerical worker, age forty-eight, Philadelphia-born, turned to practical nursing but refused to accept work for room and board. The interviewer concluded that Mary M was employable, but "too 'choosey' of job. Does not want straight housework."

Seemed rather neurotic."[10] An unemployed and widowed white clerical worker, age fifty-eight, occasionally took daywork in desperation. Emma F was a "nice-looking woman, not used to scrubbing."[11] Rarely did researchers express concern about the effects of harsh labor on those accustomed to scrubbing—namely, Black and immigrant women. A fifty-two-year-old white woman, a spooler in a textile mill who turned to domestic work, was "employable where appearances didn't so much matter—disheveled and very wrinkled though spry with a good quick mind."[12] Portrayals of Black women rarely balanced denigration and affirmation.

Assessments of immigrants, less pejorative than those of Black women, were sometimes stereotyped. Consider the description of Rose W, age sixty-two, and her home: "Room quite light for a basement room; well ventilated; very cold; room was neat and clean but scantily furnished. Pipes ran through so that it was not possible to make the place look cozy, although [she] probably had the ability. She was very neat and clean; was rather stout; appeared to be a typical peasant Austrian woman; has been a very hard worker; now is very unhappy. Cannot speak plainly. She had a big fat featherbed."[13] Rose's housekeeping, featherbed, size, lifelong history of employment, and origin in Austria, rather than a Slavic culture, contributed to the appraisal that a "typical peasant" was a capable hard worker. In a publication the WB described South Bend neighborhoods as "conspicuously foreign."[14]

Investigators indulged in anti-Semitism; in stories of unethical employers and landlords, they only identified Jews. Gertrude B's eviction tale (see chapter 6) noted that the landlady was Jewish and one of her sons had a law office in the Chicago Loop.[15] Another recorded that Marion G, a white, middle-aged clerical worker, took a job at $10 weekly for a Jewish clothing company and spent five weeks "getting their books straightened out." The company went bankrupt. "She didn't get a cent in cash, but had to take whole amount in merchandise which was practically unsalable."[16] Notes on Jewish interviewees, however, were not stereotyped.

An account of a "perfect relief client" illuminates judgments of "nonperfect" clients. Mattie W, age thirty-six and divorced, was "light skinned, with non-Negroid features, long straight hair, neatly arranged. Dress was presentable. . . . Her speech was intelligent, vigorous, and apparently sincere." The agent differentiated Mattie from other African Americans with every common physical stereotype. Mattie had completed two years of high school and a year of normal school at Tuskegee Institute. A maid for fifteen years in apartment hotels, she strained her back lifting Murphy beds, quit in the fall of 1936, and lived on savings while searching for work. She applied to the Chicago Relief Administration (CRA) for relief and assistance in finding a job. Mattie wanted lighter work, a clerical position (a job in which she had experience) or sewing. She obtained Works Progress Administration certification and attempted repeatedly to get hired on a sewing project. As the interviewer noted, "She talks and acts like the relief agency's ideal of a perfect client–energetic, resourceful, anxious to take care of herself and appreciative of help, but with self-respect and without self-pity."[17]

In contrast, investigators disparaged the appearance, health, personality, housekeeping, and attitudes of relief applicants and clients whom they judged self-pitying, ungrateful, lazy, lacking motivation, or immoral. "Passive," "dependent," and "unappreciative" were common epithets. Agents found fault with perceived ingratitude, and they articulated expectations of appropriate behavior, including deference. Flora W, a fifty-eight-year-old Black woman, suffered from asthma, myocarditis, acute chronic bronchitis, and bladder problems and had been hospitalized for three weeks. The interviewer sketched and described Flora's "grossly deformed" foot and concluded, "Complains continually of her physical and economic condition."[18]

Investigators sometimes mistrusted relief clients' reports of poor health and doubted their willingness to work or difficulties in securing employment. Cardiorenal vascular disease, high blood pressure, and three gallstone operations prompted Antoinette L, fifty, a Lithuanian immigrant, to quit a restaurant kitchen job after thirteen years. The CRA judged her employable and "[suspected] that she may be faking the seriousness of her illness." The interviewer added that she "probably over-exaggerates her ills." Neither substantiated their judgments nor commented on her resourcefulness. Antoinette lived rent free with a friend and received only a grocery allowance.[19] Winnie B, whose room was considered preferable to living in the South, an experienced maid and laundry worker, refused jobs she considered too difficult. The public employment service rejected her because she was too old (sixty-one): "Client may be saying this to protect herself because she doesn't want to work."[20]

Presumed lawbreaking and immorality elicited censure. A "'slick-looking' person who looked to agent like either a gangster-politician or a prosperous bootlegger" visited a Hungarian American South Bend household where the husband was in jail. He brought "several bottles of what appeared to be home-made wine, but did not appear to be making a gift. . . . Agent thinks one or more of the men in the family is in the bootleg business, and that therefore there is probably other income and, possibly, savings."[21]

Interviewers especially disparaged nonmarital and interracial sexual relationships and labeled women prostitutes. Grace B, age forty-eight, white, was divorced from her first husband, a "theatrical man"; her second husband, a "full-blooded Hawaiian" circus worker, had been killed in a circus riot. The researcher judged her "very careless morally."[22] An agent suspected that Edith C, the white waitress thrown out of Thompson's cafeteria because she was too old (see chapter 2), "may have prostituted herself for [her husband]," an African American "in theatrical business." She noted that Edith had latent syphilis and a fibroid tumor. She "may be very ill or may be good deceiver."[23] Men's clothing, male visitors, or landladies' reports about tenants' sexual relationships were interpreted as prostitution, and thus immorality and unreported income.

Possession of the accoutrements of sexual attraction was noteworthy. "Quite an array of nail polish and cosmetics" covered the dresser of Clara C, a white woman age forty-eight. "Indications that Mrs. C carries on illicit relations with male tenant of rooming house" remained unspecified.[24] Johanna B, age forty-six, the daughter of a New York rabbi, "has bleached or dyed blonde hair, a lovely skin, and eyebrows arched. Her dress was sloppy. . . . The bed was unmade. Nails a bright color." The CRA listed reasons for her relief application: "ill health, unemployment, inability of friends to continue help, exhausted resources." The WB interviewer added, "And lack of desire perhaps because of physical and mental decay." Johanna had been married and had lived with a common-law husband. The WB agent added, "I had a feeling that she was covering up her real work (prostitute?)."[25]

Researchers disdainfully indulged stereotypes about Black women's sexuality and veracity. One dismissed a woman's previous husband and common-law husband as "biological incidents."[26] A seemingly sensitive investigator noted, "There was no place for privacy for interview" with Bessie E, thirty-four, who lived in a condemned building (see chapter 6). Bessie's record indicated syphilis, but "[she] tried to cover up. . . . One would say she realized worker knew her condition from record and tried to answer in such a way as to give her information without letting friends understand." Plausibly Bessie shielded her privacy from a prying white investigator rather than deceived her friends.[27] When Ophelia L, age forty-one and a widow, remarked that she was "too old to get another husband," the agent suggested "she was just Wally Simpson's age." Ophelia apparently did not respond to an assumption of her commonality with a wealthy white socialite for whom a king abdicated his throne.[28]

Some evaluations cannot be teased apart. Records of CRA clients document appraisals by at least two professional women, whose racial, ethnic, and class assumptions and judgments are identifiable—for example, "Has had temper tantrums and screamed a few times in the relief office. . . . Usually cooperative. Her language is often obscene and profane but she adjusts fairly well unless placed near a more depraved type when she is easily led to troublemaking." Were "temper tantrums" Anna P's frustrations and attempts to advocate for herself? Was a "more depraved type" a left-wing activist? I cannot answer these questions. Anna had been sterilized because she had a child out of wedlock (see chapter 5); her family history was extremely violent.[29]

The investigator's job required patience and prudence. Likely a few interviewees were mentally ill or alcoholics. Predictable mistrust of relief clients, phrased in the supposedly objective, professional style of the era, also reflects researchers' responses to constant contact with depression and poverty. To acknowledge their own emotions would have been unprofessional.

In publications, the WB documented unemployment, poverty, and insecurity through dry recitals of statistics, absent negative appraisals. It criticized Chicago's 1937 maximum relief payment as "meager" and noted "$9.25 for food allowance precluded the buying of nourishing food for over so long a period as a month."[30] When relief clients made this assessment, agents derided them as "dependent" or "complaining." Reiterating its own preexisting goals, shared by the University of Chicago School of Social Service Administration, the WB recommended establishing public health insurance and adding domestic workers to unemployment compensation.[31] The second goal would have disproportionately benefited Black women, the group judged most harshly.

The WB conducted research to provide evidence for policy goals. An interviewer wrote to Harriet Byrne, principal investigator and coauthor of the publication, "Your conclusions make a sympathetic attitude to the unattached woman natural on the basis of findings, and help blast the superficial popular judgment that their situation is due to laziness, immorality, or other personal fault."[32] The WB's commitment to reforms benefiting working-class women governed its public presentations. In internal files and correspondence, staff openly manifested their own superficial popular judgments.

In the 1930s rare white social scientists proved capable of removing racial blinders. Hortense Powdermaker, an anthropologist who studied Indianola, Mississippi, observed the transformation of a Black educator doing business with the white superintendent of schools: "She looked and acted like a different person from the strong, vibrant personality whom I had seen in her home, at meetings, in church, and alone with me. . . . She was the essence of meekness: eyes downcast, accepting with a smile being called 'Annie' by white people . . . waiting patiently. . . . She was a strong self-respecting person, chuckling as she deliberately fooled the whites, and she did it supremely well."[33]

Appendix C

•••••••••••••••••••••

The U.S. Census

Because the Bureau of the Census changed methodology, categories, and definitions between 1930 and 1940, I outline my solutions to comparing employment across the decade. Historically, the census contained the best—and often the only—measurements of labor force participation, occupational structure, and demography.[1] I have used the most equivalent figures.

Census data blur the distinction between employment and labor force participation. The *Fifteenth Census* (1930) actually measured the "gainfully employed" in 1929 because it included persons recently laid off. The *Sixteenth Census* (1940) tallied four groups: the employed; public emergency workers; those "seeking work, experienced;" and those "seeking work, new workers." To calculate employment in 1940, I added "employed" and "public emergency workers" and excluded job seekers. Scholars who compare "gainfully employed" women (1930) with those "in the labor force" (1940), including 1,249,569 women seeking work, conclude that there was a significant growth of the female labor force despite a decade of deep unemployment. The percentage of women employed decreased slightly. Comparison of dissimilar categories especially misrepresents Black women, since a disproportionate share were looking for work in 1940.

Changing enumerations of race/ethnicity/nativity, age, and marital status each presented difficulties. My solution was to forgo the use of a single set of numbers. The *Sixteenth Census* ceased reporting ethnicity, nativity, or language of European immigrants and their children and ceased counting Mexicans. Consequently, only Black/white comparisons are possible. I have contrasted the population of those over age fifteen in 1930 with the population of those over age fourteen in 1940. The 1940 census did not disaggregate employment by race and age or race and marital status simultaneously, further limiting comparisons.[2] Tables 5, 6, and 8 illustrate changes in each characteristic separately.

The census also redefined job categories. I constructed three broad female sectors; I added clerical and trade plus telegraph and telephone operators (classified in transportation and communication) in 1930 to compose a group similar to clerical, sales, and kindred workers in 1940. I compared domestic and personal service in 1930 with domestic service and service workers in 1940, except domestic and protective workers, plus laundry operatives. I subtracted laundry workers from operatives and kindred (manufacturing) workers in 1940.

The large majority of working-class men worked in three sectors in 1930: manufacturing and mechanical, transportation and communication, and domestic and personal service. From the *Sixteenth Census*, I added three groups (craftsmen, foremen, and kindred workers; operatives and kindred workers; and laborers) to create a category comparable to manufacturing and mechanical. I combined service and domestic service to create a group parallel to service in 1930. Transportation and communication workers were dispersed into other sectors in 1940. These substantial changes made me less confident about comparisons of male employment than comparisons of female employment across the decade.

Census data cannot fully gauge class experiences, and the precision of calculations should be ingested with grains of salt. I have made quantitative arguments only when there were substantial differences or changes. It is also worth noting that "foreign-born white," an imprecise description, includes immigrants who arrived as adults and as infants.

Appendix D

•••••••••••••••••••••

Tables

Table 1
Women's Labor Force Participation by Marital Status, Race, and Age, 1930

Group	National	Chicago	Cleveland	Philadelphia	South Bend
All single girls and women	50.5%	67.2%	63.5%	68.1%	63.2%
Native-born white	48.7%	65.9%	62.9%	66.9%	62.6%
Foreign-born white	73.3%	78.6%	72.8%	76.4%	75.6%
Black	52.1%	59.0%	53.6%	69.6%	53.2%
Other races*	31.4%	43.0%	—	—	—
Ages 15–19	28.5%	43.7%	39.1%	49.5%	40.7%
Native-born white	27.0%	43.4%	39.5%	49.3%	40.4%
Foreign-born white	52.6%	58.9%	51.3%	62.2%	55.2%
Black	35.6%	29.0%	26.6%	44.3%	33.0%
Ages 20–24	70.5%	86.1%	86.3%	85.9%	84.6%
Native-born white	69.8%	86.0%	86.8%	85.6%	84.5%
Foreign-born white	87.4%	90.8%	87.3%	89.6%	91.5%
Black	67.1%	75.8%	75.0%	83.5%	70.2%
Ages 25–44	75.4%	86.4%	85.9%	84.4%	86.2%
Native-born white	73.9%	85.8%	86.3%	83.4%	85.9%
Foreign-born white	87.2%	90.2%	87.4%	87.5%	89.2%
Black	77.2%	83.5%	77.3%	87.4%	84.8%
Ages 45 and over	47.5%	65.1%	64.5%	55.6%	64.9%
Native-born white	44.9%	65.3%	62.1%	53.6%	65.4%
Foreign-born white	58.6%	64.0%	58.9%	59.7%	62.2%
Black	61.7%	73.1%	63.4%	76.5%	50.0%

(continued)

Table 1 (continued)

Group	National	Chicago	Cleveland	Philadelphia	South Bend
All married women	11.7%	14.6%	14.1%	13.6%	15.1%
Native-born white	9.8%	14.5%	13.7%	11.3%	15.4%
Foreign-born white	8.5%	9.7%	10.6%	7.1%	11.2%
Black	33.2%	38.9%	32.3%	40.0%	28.2%
Other races*	9.4%	9.2%	7.2%	16.8%	—
Ages 15–19	12.9%	22.4%	16.7%	22.7%	21.1%
Native-born white	10.2%	22.5%	17.2%	20.4%	21.0%
Foreign-born white	13.3%	16.0%	12.2%	13.3%	27.8%
Black	25.1%	26.8%	16.8%	32.4%	19.4%
Ages 20–24	16.3%	24.3%	20.3%	22.8%	21.3%
Native-born white	14.0%	23.5%	20.0%	19.6%	23.2%
Foreign-born white	15.1%	17.9%	15.6%	14.3%	19.2%
Black	31.5%	38.5%	28.4%	40.5%	31.0%
Ages 25–34	14.0%	20.8%	17.2%	17.3%	18.4%
Native-born white	11.5%	18.0%	15.8%	13.7%	17.9%
Foreign-born white	11.6%	13.2%	13.9%	9.5%	17.8%
Black	35.9%	42.8%	34.4%	42.0%	29.7%
Ages 35–44		12.3%		13.3%	14.3%
Native-born white	9.8%	12.3%	12.7%	13.6%	10.4%
Foreign-born white	10.0%	11.6%	12.7%	8.0%	13.5%
Black	35.8%	40.0%	36.0%	40.9%	32.8%
Ages 45 and over	7.8%	7.5%	7.4%	7.1%	8.1%
Native-born white	6.6%	8.1%	7.4%	5.7%	6.9%
Foreign-born white	5.4%	5.3%	5.7%	4.4%	5.4%
Black	29.4%	29.8%	27.6%	34.9%	18.4%
All widowed and divorced	34.4%	36.7%	36.4%	33.1%	33.1%
Ages 15–19	47.8%				
Ages 20–24	64.4%				
Ages 25–44	68.2%				
Ages 45 and over	23.9%				
Native-born white	31.9%	43.6%	42.3%	32.1%	38.0%
Foreign-born white	21.1%	21.5%	23.0%	21.2%	17.8%
Black	65.0%	62.4%	62.3%	64.5%	51.0%
Other races*	32.2%	24.9%	—	—	—

SOURCES: BC, *Fifteenth Census: Population*, vol. 2, *General Report Statistics by Subjects*, 954, 955, 965, 1005; BC, *Fifteenth Census: Population*, vol. 4, *Occupations, by States*, 454, 510, 1300, 1301, 1425; BC, *Fifteenth Census: Population*, vol. 5, *General Report on Occupations*, 274.
NOTES: *"Other races" includes Asian Americans, Mexicans, and Native Americans. A dash (—) indicates fewer than one hundred women in that category. Ages of employed widowed and divorced women are available only for the national total.

Table 2

Occupation and Race of Employed Girls and Women, 1929 (ages ten and older)

Occupation	All Women	Native-born white	Foreign-born White	Black	Other Races*
Agriculture	909,939	367,228	26,413	495,284	21,014
	8.5%	4.8%	2.3%	26.9%	22.4%
Manufacturing	1,886,307	1,451,256	313,630	101,070	20,351
	17.5%	18.9%	27.1%	5.5%	21.7%
Transportation &	281,204	266,328	12,208	2,208	460
communication	2.6%	3.5%	1.1%	0.1%	0.5%
Trade	962,680	830,940	109,563	14,568	7,609
	9.0%	10.8%	9.5%	0.8%	8.1%
Professional	1,526,234	1,356,390	103,348	63,027	3,469
	14.2%	17.7%	8.9%	3.4%	3.7%
Domestic &	3,180,251	1,514,041	475,439	1,152,560	38,211
personal service	29.6%	19.8%	41.1%	62.6%	40.7%
Clerical	1,986,830	1,858,914	114,387	10,862	2,667
	18.5%	24.3%	9.9%	0.6%	2.8%
Total	10,752,116	7,661,508	1,156,056	1,840,642	93,910
	100%	100%	100%	100%	100%

SOURCE: BC, *Fifteenth Census: Population*, vol. 5, *General Report on Occupations*, 74.

NOTES: *"Other races" includes Asian Americans, Mexicans, and Native Americans. I excluded forestry and fishing, extraction of minerals, and service, not elsewhere classified; combined, they accounted for less than 0.2% of the female labor force in 1930.

Table 3

Occupation and Race of Employed Working-Class Girls and Women: Chicago, Cleveland, Philadelphia, and South Bend, 1929 (ages ten and older)

Occupation and Ethnicity	Chicago	Cleveland	Philadelphia	South Bend
Native-born white	285,044	68,741	169,280	9,431
	100%	100%	100%	100%
Manufacturing	46,896	14,322	50,015	2,701
	16.5%	20.8%	29.5%	28.6%
Trade	32,369	8,373	18,170	1,013
	11.4%	12.2%	10.7%	10.7%
Service (public and domestic)	37,825	11,029	20,613	1,736
	13.3%	16.4%	12.2%	18.4%
Clerical	116,253	21,865	52,052	2,656
	40.8%	31.8%	30.7%	28.2%
Foreign-born white	76,535	19,231	34,033	1,126
	100%	100%	100%	100%
Manufacturing	19,717	5,902	1,216	417
	25.8%	30.7%	35.7%	37.0%
Trade	9,313	2,327	4,064	114
	12.2%	12.1%	11.9%	10.1%
Service (public and domestic)	30,853	7,402	12,074	424
	40.3%	38.5%	35.5%	37.7%
Clerical	10,375	2,063	3,308	84
	13.6%	10.7%	9.7%	7.5%
Black	44,421	10,967	42,729	418
	100%	100%	100%	100%
Manufacturing	7,172	803	4,348	12
	16.1%	7.3%	10.2%	2.9%
Trade	1,156	214	364	5
	2.6%	2.0%	0.9%	1.2%
Service (public and domestic)	32,958	9,438	36,349	382
	74.2%	86.1%	85.1%	91.4%
Clerical	1,353	169	476	5
	3.0%	1.5%	1.1%	1.2%
Other races	750	29	9	3
Total employment	406,750	98,968	246,316	10,978
	100%	100%	100%	100%
Manufacturing	74,068	21,036	66,534	3,130
	18.2%	21.3%	27.0%	28.5%

Table 3 (continued)

Occupation and Ethnicity	Chicago	Cleveland	Philadelphia	South Bend
Trade	42,888	10,918	22,602	1,132
	10.5%	11.0%	9.2%	10.3%
Service (public and domestic)	101,934	27,879	69,070	2,545
	25.1%	28.2%	28.1%	23.2%
Clerical	128,028	24,099	55,840	2,745
	31.5%	24.4%	22.7%	25.0%

SOURCES: BC, *Fifteenth Census: Population*, vol. 4, *Occupations, by States*, 449–450 (Chicago); 1287–1288 (Cleveland); 1415 (Philadelphia); 508–509 (South Bend).

NOTE: Occupations employing middle-class women, such as professional jobs, are included in total employment but not enumerated in this table.

Table 4
Wages of Working-Class Women by Occupation, ca. 1930

Occupation	Weekly Wage	Location	Year
Clerical	$22.40	Ohio	1929[i]
Clerical	$22.80	Philadelphia	1930[ii]
Clerical	$23.00	Chicago	1930[iii]
Clerks, five-and-ten-cent stores	$12.00	Eighteen states	1928[iv]
Clerks, department stores	$17.00	New Jersey, cities	1931[v]
Factory operatives	$16.73	Ohio	1929[vi]
Factory operatives	$17.49	Illinois	1929[vi]
Factory operatives	$18.75	New York State	1929[vi]
Hotel service employees	$11.40	Chicago	1934[vii]
Restaurant workers	$9.80	Chicago	1934[vii]
Laundry workers, white	$15.25	Cleveland	1928[viii]
Laundry workers, Black	$10.85	Cleveland	1925[viii]
Laundry workers; white	$16.65	Chicago	1928[viii]
Laundry workers, Black	$12.45	Chicago	1928[viii]
Domestic work, live-out	$13.15	Philadelphia	1928[ix]
Domestic work, daywork	$3.00/day	Philadelphia	1928[ix]

SOURCES: [i] *WBB* 95, *Bookkeepers, Stenographers, and Office Clerks in Ohio, 1914–1929* (Washington, DC: GPO, 1932), 13; [ii] *WBB* 96, *Women Office Workers in Philadelphia* (Washington, DC, GPO, 1932), 12 (calculated from monthly wages, with 4.3 percent weeks per month.); [iii] *WBB* 120, *The Employment. of Women in Offices* (Washington, DC: GPO, 1934), 3; [iv] *WBB* 76, *Women in 5-and-10 Cent Stores and Limited-Price Chain Department Stores* (Washington, DC: GPO, 1930), 32–53; [v] *WBB* 125, *Employment Conditions in Department Stores in 1932–1933* (Washington, DC: GPO, 1936), 19; [vi] *WBB* 155, *Women in the Economy of the USA: A Summary Report* (Washington, DC: GPO, 1937), 126; [vii] *WBB* 123, *Employment in Hotels and Restaurants* (Washington, DC: GPO, 1936), 8, 13; [viii] *WBB* 78, *A Survey of Laundries and their Women Workers in Twenty-Three Cities* (Washington, DC: GPO, 1930), 63; [ix] *WBB* 93, *Household Employment in Philadelphia* (Washington, DC: GPO, 1932), 40.

Table 5

Changes in Rates of Female Employment by Race, 1929–1940

Group	Chicago	Cleveland	Philadelphia	South Bend	National
All girls and women					
1929, ages 15 and older	1,262,223	325,688	741,188	37,429	42,837,149
1929, employed	406,482	98,910	245,481	10,972	10,632,227
% employed	32.2%	30.4%	33.1%	29.3%	24.8%
1940, ages 14 and older	1,410,069	360,020	804,697	41,019	50,549,176
1940, employed	421,569	96,455	225,605	11,431	11,595,690
% employed	29.9%	26.8%	28.0%	27.9%	22.9%
White					
1929, ages 15 and older	1,164,277	298,915	656,911	36,217	38,220,229
1929, employed	361,338	87,925	202,695	10,551	8,764,506
% employed	31.0%	29.4%	30.9%	29.1%	22.9%
1940, ages 15 and older	1,291,191	326,044	701,979	39,689	45,605,134
1940, employed	388,955	87,749	191,462	11,117	9,959,272
% employed	29.6%	26.9%	27.2%	28.0%	21.8%
Black					
1929, ages 15 and older	93,384	26,600	83,992	1,204	4,099,552
1929, employed	44,397	10,957	42,692	418	1,776,922
% employed	47.5%	41.2%	50.8%	34.7%	43.3%
1940, ages 14 and older	118,333	33,919	102,462	1,325	4,785,233
1940, employed	32,477	8,696	34,102	311	1,602,441
% employed	27.4%	25.6%	33.3%	23.5%	33.5%
Rate of change, 1929–1940					
All women	−7.1%	−11.8%	−15.4%	−4.8%	−7.7%
White women	−4.5%	−8.5%	−12.0%	−3.8%	−4.8%
Black women	−42.3%	−37.9%	−34.5%	−32.3%	−22.6%

SOURCES: Chicago: BC, *Fifteenth Census: Population*, vol. 6, *Families*, 454, and BC, *Sixteenth Census: Population*, vol. 2, *Characteristics of the Population*, pt. 2, *Florida–Iowa*, 643; Cleveland: BC, *Fifteenth Census: Population*, vol. 4, *Occupations, by States*, 1300, and BC, *Sixteenth Census: Population*, vol. 2, *Characteristics of the Population*, pt. 5, *New York–Oregon*, 713; Philadelphia: BC, *Fifteenth Census: Population*, vol. 4, 1425, and BC, *Sixteenth Census: Population*, vol. 2, *Characteristics of the Population*, pt. 6, *Pennsylvania–Texas*, 214; South Bend: BC, *Fifteenth Census: Population*, vol. 4, 510, and BC, *Sixteenth Census: Population*, vol. 2, *Characteristics of the Population*, pt. 2: *Florida–Iowa*, 824; National: BC, *Fifteenth Census: Population*, vol. 4: 274, and BC, *Sixteenth Census: Population*, vol. 3, *The Labor Force*, pt. 1, *United States Summary*, 18.

Table 6
Changes in Women's Employment in the Service Sector by Race, 1929–1940

Group	Chicago	Cleveland	Philadelphia	South Bend
All girls and women, 1929 (ages 10 and older)	101,934 100%	27,879 100%	69,070 100%	2,545 100%
All girls and women, 1940 (ages 14 and older)	92,741 100%	25,307 100%	56,744 100%	2,664 100%
# of change	−9,193	−2,572	−12,326	119
Rate of change	−9.0%	−9.2%	−17.8%	4.7%
White women, 1929 % of sector	68,678 67.4%	18,431 66.1%	32,687 47.3%	2,160 84.9%
White women, 1940 % of sector	72,706 78.4%	19,508 77.1%	24,710 56.4%	2,419 90.8%
# of change	4,028	1,077	−7,977	259
Rate of change	16.3%	16.6%	19.2%	6.9%
Black women, 1929 % of sector	32,958 32.3%	9,438 33.9%	36,349 52.6%	382 15.0%
Black women, 1940 % of sector	20,975 22.6%	5,795 22.9%	24,710 43.5%	245 9.2%
# of change	−11,983	−3,643	−11,639	−137
Rate of change	−30.0%	−32.4%	−32.01%	−38.7%

SOURCES: BC, *Fifteenth Census: Population*, vol. 4, *Occupations, by States*, 450 (Chicago), 1288 (Cleveland), 1415 (Philadelphia), 509 (South Bend); BC, *Sixteenth Census: Population*, vol. 3, *The Labor Force*, pt. 2, *Alabama–Indiana*, 878 (Chicago); BC, *Sixteenth Census: Population*, vol. 3, *The Labor Force*, pt. 4, *Nebraska–Oregon*, 699 (Cleveland); BC, *Sixteenth Census: 1940, Population*, vol. 3, *The Labor Force*, pt. 5, *Pennsylvania–Wyoming*, 52 (Philadelphia); BC, *Sixteenth Census: Population*, vol. 3, pt. 2: 994 (South Bend).

Table 7
Changes in Rates of Women's Employment by Marital Status, 1929–1940

Group	1929	1940	Rate of Change
Female population, 15 and older (14 and older in 1940)	42,837,149	50,549,176	
Employed	10,632,227	11,595,690	−7.7%
% Employed	24.8%	22.9%	
Single, 15 and older (14 and older in 1940)	11,359,038	12,751,772	
Employed	5,734,825	5,547,047	−13.9%
% Employed	50.5%	43.5%	−11.3%
Proportion of female labor force	53.9%	47.8%	
Married, 15 and older (14 and older in 1940)	26,170,756	30,087,135	
Employed	3,071,302	4,290,754	22.2%

(continued)

Table 7 (continued)

Group	1929	1940	Rate of Change
% Employed	11.7%	14.3%	28.0%
Proportion of female labor force	28.9%	37.0%	
Widowed and divorced, 15 and older (14 and older in 1940)	5,307,355	6,522,655	
Employed	1,826,100	1,757,889	−21.5%
% Employed	34.4%	27.0%	−11.6%
Proportion of female labor force	17.2%	15.2%	

SOURCES: BC, *Fifteenth Census: Population*, vol. 5, *General Report on Occupations*, 274; BC, *Sixteenth Census: Population*, vol. 3, *The Labor Force*, pt. 1, *United States Summary*, 22; BC, *Sixteenth Census: Population*, vol. 4, *Characteristics by Age*, pt. 1, *United States Summary*, 1, 9, 17.

Table 8
Changes in Rates of Female Employment by Age, 1929–1940

Group	1929	1940	Rate of Change
Female population, 14 and older	44,013,048	50,549,176	
Employed	10,679,048	11,595,690	−5.8%
% Employed	24.3%	22.9%	
Ages 14–19	6,970,189	7,340,984	
Employed	1,590,100	1,019,820	−39.0%
% Employed	22.8%	13.9%	−43.6%
Proportion of female labor force	14.9%	8.8%	
Ages 20–24	5,533,563	5,895,443	
Employed	2,347,548	2,344,676	−6.1%
% Employed	42.4%	39.8%	−8.2%
Proportion of female labor force	22.0%	20.2%	
Ages 25–34	9,532,063	10,818,052	
Employed	2,654,338	3,315,639	10.1%
% Employed	27.8%	30.6%	14.9%
Proportion of female labor force	24.9%	28.6%	
Ages 35–44	8,382,521	9,168,426	
Employed	1,892,338	2,309,905	11.5%
% Employed	22.6%	25.2%	12.4%
Proportion of female labor force	17.7%	19.9%	
Ages 45–54	6,214,514	7,550,052	
Employed	1,266,026	1,557,449	1.0%
% Employed	20.4%	20.6%	12.6%
Proportion of female labor force	11.9%	13.4%	
Ages 55 and older	7,337,992	9,776,819	
Employed	915,296	1,048,201	−14.4%
% Employed	12.5%	10.7%	4.7%
Proportion of female labor force	8.6%	9.0%	

SOURCES: BC, *Fifteenth Census: Population*, vol. 5, *General Report on Occupations*, 115; BC, *Sixteenth Census: Population*, vol. 3, *The Labor Force*, pt. 1, *United States Summary*, 19.

Citation Conventions

In the interests of brevity, I outline the conventions I have used for citations from the Women's Bureau (WB) of the U. S. Department of Labor. Citations include published studies (Women's Bureau *Bulletins*, hereafter *WBB*) and archival materials from these studies, especially the interviews on which they were based. Letters written by domestic workers were archived by the WB and the National Recovery Administration (NRA). All records are located at the National Archives and Records Administration, College Park, Maryland (NACP).

Interviews

Interviews are distinguished by city (and by date in Chicago and South Bend).

Name, SB30, *WBB* 92, Boxes 127–137, WB, RG 86, NACP.

Name, number, SB32, *WBB* 108, Household Schedules Matched with 1930 Schedules, Boxes 157–186, WB, RG 86, NACP.

Name, number, city (Chicago33, Cleveland, and Philadelphia), *WBB* 139, Boxes 244–266, WB, RG 86, NACP.

Name, numbers, neighborhood, Chicago37, *WBB* 158, Boxes 359–365, WB, RG 86, NACP.

Women's Bureau Bulletins

WBB 92, Wage-Earning Women and the Industrial Conditions of 1930: A Survey of South Bend (Washington, DC: Government Printing Office, 1932) (hereafter, GPO).

Archival materials from WBB 92: interviews, correspondence, and other internal materials, Boxes 127–137, WBB 92, WB, RG 86, NACP.

WBB 108, The Effects of the Depression on Wage Earners' Families: A Second Survey of South Bend (Washington, DC: GPO, 1936).

Archival materials from WBB 108: interviews, correspondence and other internal materials, Boxes 157–186, WBB 108, WB, RG 86, NACP.

WBB 139, Women Unemployed Seeking Relief in 1933 (Washington, DC: GPO, 1936).

Archival materials from WBB 139, Chicago (Ch33), Cleveland, and Philadelphia: interviews, correspondence, and other internal materials, WBB 139, Boxes 244-266, WB, RG 86, NACP.

WBB 158, Unattached Women on Relief in Chicago, 1937 (Washington, DC: GPO, 1938).

Archival materials from WBB 158: interviews, correspondence and other internal materials, WBB 158, Boxes 359–365, WB, RG 86, NACP.

Letters from Domestic Workers

Author, recipient, date, place, Unpublished Studies and Research Material, Domestic Workers (Household Employment), 1919–1956, WB, RG 86, NACP.

Author, recipient, date, place, Domestic Workers Correspondence, NRA, RG9, NACP.

U.S. Census Materials

U.S. Bureau of the Census (hereafter BC) *Fifteenth Census of the United States, 1930* (Washington, DC: GPO, 1931–1933), and BC, *Sixteenth Census of the United States, 1940* (Washington, DC: GPO, 1941–1943) each contain dozens of volumes. I have supplied titles, volumes, and pages which are the sources of my statistics.

Notes

Introduction

1 Leona C, 1110, SB32.

2 Agnes V, 0614, SB32.

3 Betty A, Anna M, Mary K, and Cecilia A, 0175, SB32.

4 Anonymous quote, poster (Vancouver, BC: Press Gang, 1978).

5 I subsequently added thirteen Black women from South Bend; interview households also included women outside the labor force, bringing the total to about fourteen hundred women.

6 Ira Katznelson, *Fear Itself: The New Deal and the Origin of our Time* (New York: Liveright, 2013), 227–252.

7 Anna Feldner, Orange, CA, to "Our dear Mother of this country!" August 24, 1933, RG 86.

8 Phyllis Palmer, *Domesticity and Dirt: Housewives and Domestic Servants in the United States, 1920–1945* (Philadelphia: Temple University Press, 1989), 71–72, 177n15, 184n23, has suggested that day workers did not write because they might have gained greater control over work. Interviews convinced me that day workers lacked that control. We both sampled letters in the WB archives; I also read hundreds of letters in the National Recovery Administration (NRA) archives. Guidelines for sorting mail in federal offices determined letters' destinations and consequently whether they were archived in WB or NRA files. I found no difference in content.

9 Joe William Trotter Jr., *Workers on Arrival: Black Labor in the Making of America* (Oakland: University of California Press, 2019), especially esp. 185–210.

10 Bureau of the Census (hereafter BC), *Fifteenth Census, Population*, vol. 2, *General Report Statistics by Subjects*, 67–73, 202–203; Evelyn Nakano Glenn, *Unequal Freedom: How Race and Gender Shaped American Citizenship and Labor* (Cambridge, MA: Harvard University Press, 2004). Between one-tenth and one-fourth of the populations of West Coast cities were immigrants. Only Denver, Los Angeles, and Oakland had Black populations larger than five thousand in 1930; in Los Angeles and in San Antonio, Texas, Black, Mexican, and white communities constituted a tripartite racial/ethnic system.

11 *15th Census, Population, 1930*, vol. 2: 35, 67, 118, 120, 127, 129; *Fifteenth Census, Population*, vol. 5, *General Report on Occupations*, 246, 332; Louise Año Nuevo Kerr, "Chicanas in the Great Depression," in *Between Borders: Essays on Mexicana/ Chicana History*, ed. Adelaida R. Del Castillo (Encino, CA: Floricanto, 1990), 257–268; Gabriela F. Arredondo, *Mexican Chicago: Race, Identity, and Nation, 1916–1939* (Urbana: University of Illinois Press, 2008), 217nn142–143. Asian Americans and Mexicans combined accounted for less than 1% of Chicago's population.

12 Gerda Lerner, *Black Women in America: A Documentary History* (New York: Vintage, 1972). Black feminists theorized their particularities and challenged white feminist universalization. Frances Beal developed the concept of double jeopardy; see Frances Beal, *Black Women's Manifesto; Double Jeopardy: To Be Black and Female*, 1969, http://www.hartford-hwp.com/archives/45a/196.html The Third World Women's Alliance published the *Triple Jeopardy* newspaper; see Michelle Moravec, "Triple Jeopardy," *History in the City* (blog), March 4, 2015, http:// historyinthecity.blogspot.com/2015/03/triple-jeopardy.html. The Combahee River Collective declared "interlocking oppression"; see Combahee River Collective, *Combahee River Collective Statement*, 1977, Black Past, https://www.blackpast.org /african-american-history/combahee-river-collective-statement-1977/. See also Angela Davis, *Women, Race, and Class* (New York: Penguin, 1981); Akasha Gloria Hull, Patricia Bell-Scott, and Barbara Smith, eds., *All the Women Are White, All the Blacks Are Men, but Some of Us Are Brave* (Old Westbury, NY: Feminist Press, 1982). For Marxist feminism, see Women's Work Study, "Loom, Broom, and Womb: Producers, Maintainers, and Reproducers," *Frontiers: A Journal of Women's Studies* 1, no. 1 (1975): 1–41.

13 For critical race theory, see Derrick Bell, *Faces at the Bottom of the Well: The Permanence of American Racism* (New York: Basic Books, 1993); Richard Delgado, ed., *Critical Race Theory: The Cutting Edge* (Philadelphia: Temple University Press, 1995); Ian F. Haney Lopez, *White by Law: The Legal Construction of Race* (New York: New York University Press, 1996); and Richard Delgado and Jean Stefancic, eds., *Critical White Studies: Looking behind the Mirror* (Philadelphia: Temple University Press, 1997).

Building on W.E.B. DuBois's insight that white male workers received literal and psychological wages from whiteness, and on Cheryl Harris's analysis of whiteness as property, historians have argued that men had a "possessive investment" in white identity; that European immigrants were in between, not yet white, conditionally white, learning to be white, or "white on arrival." See W.E.B. DuBois, *Black Reconstruction in America, 1860–1880* (New York: Atheneum, 1972); Cheryl I. Harris, "Whiteness as Property," *Harvard Law Review* 106, no. 8 (1993): 1707–1791; David R. Roediger, *The Wages of Whiteness: Race and the Making of the American Working Class* (London: Verso, 1991); James Barrett and David Roediger, "Inbetween Peoples: Race, Nationality, and the 'New Immigrant' Working Class," *Journal of American Ethnic History* 16, no. 3 (1997): 3–44; George Lipsitz, *The Possessive Investment in Whiteness: How White People Profit from Identity Politics* (Philadelphia: Temple University Press, 1998); Matthew Frye Jacobson, *Whiteness of a Different Color: European Immigrants and the Alchemy of Race* (Cambridge, MA: Harvard University Press, 1998); Karen Brodkin, *How Jews Became White Folks and What That Says about Race in America* (New Brunswick, NJ: Rutgers University Press, 1999); Thomas Guglielmo, *White on Arrival: Italians, Race, Color, and Power in Chicago, 1890–1945* (Oxford: Oxford University Press, 2003); and Jennifer

Guglielmo and Salvatore Salerno, eds., *Are Italians White? How Race Is Made in America* (New York: Routledge, 2003).

Black feminist analysis predates—but has not been addressed by—(mostly male) whiteness theorists, who usually disregard women and family. David Roediger, *Working toward Whiteness: How America's Immigrants Became White* (New York: Basic Books, 2005), 157–198, includes women and daily life but does not analyze gender. In a rare feminist critique of whiteness historians, Dana Frank, "White Working-Class Women and the Race Question," *International Labor and Working-Class History*, no. 54 (1998): 80–102, describes women of color holding up the platform on which white women stand, capturing enduring hierarchies. Kimberlé Crenshaw coined the term "intersectionality;" see Kimberlé Crenshaw, "Demarginalizing the Intersection of Race and Sex: A Black Feminist Critique of Antidiscrimination Doctrine, Feminist Theory and Antiracist Politics," *University of Chicago Legal Forum* (1989): 139–167.

14 Patricia Hill Collins has made major contributions. Patricia Hill Collins, *Black Feminist Thought: Knowledge, Consciousness, and the Politics of Empowerment* (New York: Routledge, 1991), 43–66; *Fighting Words: Black Women and the Search for Justice* (Minneapolis: University of Minnesota Press, 1998), 201–228; *From Black Power to Hip Hop: Racism, Nationalism, and Feminism* (Philadelphia: Temple University Press, 2006), 123–160; and Patricia Hill Collins and Sirma Bilge, *Intersectionality* (Cambridge: Polity, 2016).

15 Judith Sealander, *As Minority Becomes Majority: Federal Reaction to the Phenomenon of Women in the Work Force, 1920–1963* (Westport, CT: Greenwood, 1983), 165, 167–180, 75–82; Mary Anderson, *Woman at Work: The Autobiography of Mary Anderson as Told to Mary N. Winslow* (Minneapolis: University of Minnesota Press, 1951), 159–172.

16 Anderson, *Woman at Work*, 3–87, 110–111, 151; Sealander, *Minority*, 40–46, 158; Mary Anderson to Edith Abbott, April 27, 1937, Correspondence, *WBB* 158, RG 86. Civil service salaries for WB economic analysts were $2,000, $2,600, and $3,200 in 1937.

17 This portrait of professional civil servants is drawn from Sealander, *As Minority Becomes Majority*, and my research in the WB archives.

18 Agnes Peterson to Mary Anderson, memorandum, n.d. [December 1932], Correspondence, *WBB* 139, RG 86; Sealander, *As Minority Becomes Majority*, 106, 239–242. The WB conferred with the Bureau of Jewish Social Research, the Laboratory Division of the YWCA, the National Committee on the Care of the Transient and Homeless, the New York Welfare Council, the Philadelphia Community Council, the Russell Sage Foundation, and Travelers' Aid. In the late 1930s Black women's organizations, including the National Council of Negro Women, began lobbying the WB to hire a Black professional staff member.

19 Karen W. Tice, *Tales of Wayward Girls and Immoral Women: Case Records and the Professionalization of Social Work* (Urbana: University of Illinois Press, 1998), 190, 13.

20 "Woman One-Person Families on Relief in Chicago, Instructions," Chicago37, Survey Materials, 3–5, *WBB* 158, RG 86.

21 "Women One-Person Families."

22 In 1933 the WB interviewed all Chicago women; in Cleveland and Philadelphia, agents questioned a subset, and caseworkers' notes constituted the records of others. *WBB* 139, *Women Unemployed*, 3, 9, 16; Joint Committee on Research of the Community Council of Philadelphia and the Pennsylvania School of Social Work, *Women without Work: A Study of 1654 Unemployed Destitute Women Living Alone*

in Philadelphia (Philadelphia: Joint Committee on Research of the Community Council of Philadelphia and the Pennsylvania School of Social Work, 1934), 5–6; Correspondence, *WBB* 139, RG86.

23 Margaret M, 905, Philadelphia.

24 Madeline M, 579, Chicago33.

25 Ula Taylor, "Women in the Documents: Thoughts on Uncovering the Personal, Political, and Professional," *Journal of Women's History* 20, no. 1 (2008): 187–196.

26 Chapter 6, analyzing women outside family economies, underscores the critical importance of community in the form of friendships.

27 The 1930 Census queried about race, ethnicity, parents' and grandparents' nativity, and mother tongue. The 1940 Census classified persons as "white, Negro, other" or sometimes as "white, non-white."

28 Annie G, 52, B16, Bridgeport, Chicago37.

29 Johanna B, 342, I6, Northern, Chicago37.

30 Sallie J, 538, L35, Washington Park, Chicago37.

31 Catherine K, 364, I28, Northern, Chicago37.

32 Mary B, B, 80, C6, Canal, Chicago37.

33 Elizabeth M, 528, L25, Washington Park, Chicago37.

34 Josephine W, 848, Chicago33.

35 Mary M, 787, SB32.

36 Louise Meriwether, *Daddy Was a Number Runner* (New York: Pyramid Books, 1970); Melvin Patrick Ely, *The Adventures of Amos 'n' Andy: A Social History of an American Phenomenon* (New York: Free Press, 1991).

37 Meridel LeSueur, *Women on the Breadlines* (Minneapolis: West End, 1984).

38 Lionel C. Bascom, ed., *A Renaissance in Harlem: Lost Essays of the WPA, by Ralph Ellison, Dorothy West, and Other Voices of a Generation* (New York: Harper Collins, 1999); Stephanie J. Shaw, "Using the WPA Ex-Slave Narratives to Study the Impact of the Great Depression, *Journal of Southern History*, 69, no. 3 (2003): 623–658. Historians have debated representations and veracity of interviews with former slaves. Unlike Federal Writers Project narratives, WB interviews were private, collected as evidence to sponsor policy; covered a broad age range; were located in northern cities; and conducted by white women. Former slaves "proved to be highly skilled in the tactics of evasion as well as diplomacy." Likewise, WB interviewees revealed information they chose, in a manner they selected. Catherine A. Stewart, *Long Past Slavery: Representing Race in the Federal Writers' Project* (Chapel Hill: University of North Carolina Press, 2016).

Chapter 1 Urban Working-Class Daily Lives and Work in the 1920s

1 Bonita C, 1105, SB32.

2 Sadie Tanner Mossell, "The Standard of Living among One Hundred Negro Migrant Families in Philadelphia," *Annals of the American Academy of Social and Political Science*, 98, no. 187 (1921): 169–218, is the only detailed standard of living study of African Americans in a northern city. Leila Houghteling, *The Income and Standard of Living of Unskilled Laborers in Chicago* (Chicago: University of Chicago Press, 1927), inconsistently illustrates racial differentials.

3 Frank Stricker, "Affluence for Whom?—Another Look at Prosperity and the Working Classes in the 1920s," *Labor History*, no. 24 (1983): 5–33.

4 Houghteling, *The Income and Standard of Living*, 25, 85.

5 Ewa Morawska, *For Bread with Butter: The Life-Worlds of East Central Europeans in Johnstown, Pennsylvania, 1890–1940* (Cambridge: Cambridge University Press, 1985), 84, 182–221.

6 Bureau of Labor Statistics (hereafter BLS), "Standard of Living of Employees of Ford Motor Co. in Detroit," *Monthly Labor Review*, no. 30 (1930): 1209–1252. The BLS investigated one hundred white families of male autoworkers earning Ford's minimum wage of $7 a day. Only normative families (husband, wife, two or three children younger than sixteen, maintained by a single male wage earner) qualified. See Stricker, "Affluence for Whom?," 26.

7 Stricker, "Affluence for Whom?," 22.

8 Houghteling, *Income and Standard of Living*, 129.

9 Stricker, "Affluence for Whom?," 23.

10 Joanne J. Meyerowitz, *Women Adrift: Independent Wage Earners in Chicago, 1880–1930* (Chicago: University of Chicago Press, 1988), 35–36.

11 BC, *Fifteenth Census: Population*, vol. 6, *Families* (Washington, DC: GPO, 1933), 11–13.

12 John Bodnar, Roger Simon, and Michael P. Weber, *Lives of Their Own: Blacks, Italians, and Poles in Pittsburgh, 1900–1960* (Urbana: University of Illinois Press, 1982), 153–154; Thaddeus C. Radzilowski, "Family, Women, and Gender: The Polish Experience," in *Polish Americans and Their History: Community, Culture, and Politics*, ed. John J. Bukowczyk (Pittsburgh: University of Pittsburgh Press, 1996), 59–60.

13 *Fifteenth Census: Population*, 6: 57, 354, 365, 396, 411, 1012, 1033, 1120, 1135.

14 Morawska, *For Bread with Butter*; BLS, "Standard of Living."

15 *Fifteenth Census: Population*, 6: 354, 396, 1012, 1120.

16 *WBB* 92, 58–60; Ronald Tobey, Charles Wetherell, and Jay Brigham, "Moving Out and Settling In: Residential Mobility, Home Owning, and the Public Enframing of Citizenship, 1921–1950," *American Historical Review* 95, no. 5 (1990): 1414. See also President's Research Committee on Social Trends, *Recent Social Trends in the United States: Report of the President's Research Committee on Social Trends*, 2 vols. (New York: McGraw-Hill, 1933).

17 Figures are calculated from BLS, "Standard of Living," 1236–1237.

18 Houghteling, *Income and Standard of Living*, 111–115.

19 *Fifteenth Census: Population*, vol. 6: 354; Edith Abbott, *The Tenements of Chicago, 1908–1935* (Chicago: University of Chicago Press, 1936); St. Clair Drake and Horace Cayton, *Black Metropolis: A Study of Negro Life in a Northern City*, 2 vols., rev. and enlarged ed. (New York: Harcourt, Brace, and World, 1970); James Grossman, *Land of Hope: Chicago, Black Southerners, and the Great Migration* (Chicago: University of Chicago Press, 1989); Houghteling, *The Income and Standard of Living*.

20 BLS, "Standard of Living," 1236–1239; Clair Brown, "Consumption Norms, Work Roles, and Economic Growth, 1918–1980," in *Gender in the Workplace*, ed. Clair Brown and Joseph A. Pechman (Washington, DC: Brookings Institution Press, 1987), 24; Susan Strasser, *Never Done: A History of American Housework* (New York: Pantheon Books, 1982), 265–267.

21 Mossell, "The Standard of Living," 197–198. Abbott, *The Tenements of Chicago*, 120–121, 178, 205, 222.

22 Maurice Leven, Harold G. Moulton, and Clark Warburton, *America's Capacity to Consume* (Washington, DC: Brookings Institution, 1934), 68, 246–247; Robert S. Lynd with Alice C. Hanson, "The People as Consumers," in President's Research

Committee, *Recent Social Trends*, 2:892. Clair Brown, "Consumption Norms," 24–25; Stricker, "Affluence for Whom?" 24–29. Figures are calculated from BLS, "Standard of Living," 1212–1217.

23 Lynd and Hanson, "The People as Consumers," 2:902.

24 Brown, "Consumption Norms," 36–37.

25 Stricker, "Affluence for Whom?," 29.

26 National Industrial Conference Board, Inc., *Cost of Living in Twelve Industrial Cities* (New York: National Industrial Conference Board, Inc., 1928), 168–69.

27 Nonfarm working-class families spent 6.8–18% of income on clothing. Leven, Moulton, and Warburton, *America's Capacity*, 246–247; Brown, "Consumption Norms," 24. BLS, "Standard of Living," 1212.

28 BLS, "Standard of Living," 1248–1252.

29 Mossell, "The Standard of Living," 199, 201. The wartime shipping embargo prevented them from sending possessions north.

30 Hazel Kyrk, *Economic Problems of the Family* (New York: Harper & Brothers, 1933), 260–266; Mossell, "The Standard of Living," 200; BLS, "Standard of Living," 1212, 1241; *WBB* 108, 10.

31 Faith M. Williams and Alice C. Hanson, *BLSB 638, Money Disbursements of Wage Earners and Clerical Workers, 1934–1936: Summary Volume* (Washington, DC: GPO, 1941), 37.

32 Ruth Schwartz Cowan, *More Work for Mother: The Ironies of Household Technology from the Open Hearth to the Microwave* (New York: Basic Books, 1983), 105–107; Strasser, *Never Done*, 113–124.

33 BLS, "Standard of Living," 1246–1252.

34 Christine Frederick, *Selling Mrs. Consumer* (New York: Business Bourse, 1929); Roland Marchand, *Advertising the American Dream: Making Way for Modernity, 1920–1940* (Berkeley: University of California Press, 1985), 66.

35 Strasser, *Never Done*, 242–262; Susan Strasser, *Satisfaction Guaranteed: The Making of the American Mass Market* (New York: Pantheon Books, 1989), 222–230, 248–249; Joann Vanek, "Time Spent in Housework," *Scientific American* 231, no. 5 (1974): 116–120.

36 Strasser, *Satisfaction Guaranteed*, 222–225.

37 Lizabeth Cohen, *Making a New Deal: Industrial Workers in Chicago, 1919–1939* (Cambridge: Cambridge University Press, 1990), 106–120. South Bend, IN, *City Directory* (Indianapolis: R. L. Polk and Company, 1929), 941–943.

38 Dom Robotnika [worker's house], HM; Eighth Grade Class, Stanley Clark School, *From Warsaw to the West Side: An Oral History of a Random Sample of Polish People in the South Bend Community* (South Bend: Stanley Clark School, 1994); *Fifteenth Census: Population*, vol. 6: 410.

39 Report for one week made monthly to National Industrial Conference Board, Studebaker, survey materials, *WBB* 92, RG8.

40 Jack J. Detzler, *South Bend, 1900–1910: The Awakening of a Small Town* (South Bend, IN: Northern Indiana Historical Society, 1959), 28–29; Dean R. Esslinger, *Immigrants and the City: Ethnicity and Mobility in a Nineteenth-Century Midwestern Community* (Port Washington, NY: National University Publications, 1975), 11, 21, 69–70, 75; "Wilson Brothers Shirt Factory," Studebaker National Museum (hereafter SNM), South Bend, Indiana. Empty brick buildings and overgrown lots testify to history; Oliver, Singer, Studebaker, and Wilson have long since folded or left town.

41 C. E. Young, ed., *South Bend World Famed* (South Bend, IN: Handelsman and Young, 1922), 14.

42 Figures are calculated from *Fifteenth Census Population*, vol. 3, *Reports by the States, Showing the Composition and Characteristics of the Population for Counties, Cities, and Townships or Other Minor Civil Divisions*, pt. 1, *Alabama–Missouri* (Washington, DC: GPO, 1932), 717.

43 Ron Kronewitter, "Press History Reflects South Bend's Rich Ethnic Mix," *South Bend Tribune*, February 16, 1986; Henry A. Verslype, *The Belgians of Indiana* (Nappanee, IN: Evangel, 1987), 291; Vendel Hajdu, "During the First Half Century," *A south bendi magyarok 50 eves letelepedesenek jubileumi Emlekkonye, 1882 -1932 [Golden Jubilee Album of Magyar People in South Bend]* (n.p. [South Bend, IN]: n.p., 1932), trans. Ernest Szasz, ed. Darlene Scherer, typescript, LFHS, SJCPL 2; Esslinger, *Immigrants and the City*, 34, 136–137.

44 Verslype, *The Belgians of Indiana*, 9, 54–56, 169–173.

45 Figures are calculated from *Fifteenth Census: Population*, vol. 2, *General Report Statistics by Subjects* (Washington, DC: GPO, 1933), 78, 248–249, 333; see also 558–560.

46 *15th Census: Population*, vol. 3, pt. 1: 61, 717.

47 Figures are calculated from *Fifteenth Census: Population*, vol. 4, *Occupations, by States* (Washington, DC: GPO, 1933), 506–508.

48 "Singer in SB," Ephemera File, Business Files, History Museum (hereafter HM); "Survey Materials: Wages, Earnings, and Hours," *WBB* 92, RG 86.

49 *Studebaker Co-operator*, 5, no. 5 (1924); *Studebaker Co-operator*, 6, no. 7 (1925), 7. Only Black men played on the foundry baseball team. Figures are calculated from *Fifteenth Census: Population*, vol. 4: 507.

50 *WBB* 92, *Wage Earning Women*, 9–10; Survey Materials: Wages, Earnings, and Hours, *WBB* 92, RG 86.

51 *Fifteenth Census: Population*, vol. 4:508–509.

52 Janusz Mucha, *Everyday Life and Festivity in a Local Ethnic Community: Polish-Americans in South Bend, Indiana* (Boulder, CO: East European Monographs, 1996).

53 *Golden Jubilee Album*, n.p.; *Ksiega Pamiatkowa Obchodu Srebrnego Jubilerszu Towarzystwa Gimnastycznego Z. Ballickiego No. 1* [The Commemorative book of the silver jubilee celebrations of the Z. Ballicki Gymnastic Society No. 1] (South Bend, IN: Z. B. Falcons Nest 80, 1922); *Rok Srebrengo Jubileuszu Program i Pamietnik* [Program and diary of the silver jubilee year] (South Bend, IN: Polish Falcon Nests 4, 80, 185, 200, 1939); figures are calculated from *Fifteenth Census: Population*, vol. 4: 506–508.

54 Johnny Vann, Black Americans of the South Bend–Mishawaka Area (South Bend, IN: Ethnic Heritage Studies Program, Indiana University–South Bend, 1975), 21–25; *Fifteenth Census: Population*, vol. 4: 506–509; Rev. B. F. Gordon, *The Negro in South Bend* (South Bend, IN: n.p., 1922) 95–96; program, Indiana-Michigan Youth Conference, 1936, Hering House Scrapbook, HM; program, Mid West Youth Conference, 1937, Hering House Scrapbook, HM; Darlene Clark Hine, *The Black Women in the Middle West Project: A Comprehensive Resource Guide, Illinois and Indiana* (Indianapolis: Indiana Historical Bureau, 1986); *When the Truth Is Told: A History of Black Women's Culture and Community in Indiana, 1875–1950* (Indianapolis: National Council of Negro Women, 1981).

55 Figures are calculated from *Fifteenth Census: Population*, vol. 4: 506–509.

56 Today the Oliver mansion, Copshaholm, houses The History Museum; the Studebaker mansion, Tippecanoe, is an upscale restaurant.

57 Esslinger, *Immigrants and the City*, 39, 113; Rev. Thomas T. McAvoy, *History of the Catholic Church in the South Bend Area* (South Bend, IN: Aquinas Library and Book Shop, 1953), n.p.; Donald Stabrowski, *Holy Cross and the South Bend Polonia* (Notre Dame, IN: Indiana Province Archives Center, 1991); Andrew Petrass, "Hungarian Builders of the American Nation," in *Golden Jubilee Album*, n.p.; Rev. John Szabo, "Our Lady of Hungary Parish," *Golden Jubilee Album*, n.p.; Hajdu, "During the First Half Century."

58 South Bend, IN, *City Directory* (1932), 667–668; Dunbar Community Center, *Annual Report and Tenth Anniversary Program*, 1935, Hering House Scrapbook, HM.

59 Szabo, "Our Lady of Hungary Parish," n.p.

60 Charles E. Dempsey and Alberta E. Dempsey, comps., "Through the Years, 1907–1978: A History of First AME Zion Church, South Bend, Indiana," scrapbook, HM.

61 By chance, I happened to be there as the wrecking ball demolished St. Stephen's in 2003; Black, Hungarian, Mexican, and Polish neighbors mourned and gawked at the spectacle.

62 VerSlype, *The Belgians of Indiana*, 154. Hajdu, "During the First Half Century," 25.

63 Vann, "Black Americans," 16; South Bend *City Directory*, 1929, 18 *Annual Report*, 1926, Hering House Scrapbook, HM.

64 *Fifteenth Census: Population*, vol. 3, pt. 1: 69, 717.

65 Kronewitter, "Press History." *Varosi Elet* ceased publication in 1953, followed by *Goniec Polski* in 1964.

66 Petrass, "Hungarian Builders of the American Nation," *Golden Jubilee Album of the Magyar People*, n.p.; Frank Renkiewicz, "An American Journey: The Poles in South Bend," *Old Courthouse News* 2, no. 2 (1968): n.p.; *Fifty Golden Years in Christ's Vineyard: Rev. Boleslaus J. Sztuczko, CSC, 1910–1960* (n.p.[South Bend, IN, St. Hedwig Catholic Church], 1960).

67 Keith Knauss and Michael Lawrence, interview with the author, Department of Labor Studies, Indiana University–South Bend, May 31, 1991.

68 *Fifteenth Census: Population*, vol. 2: 1388. Eighth Grade Class, Stanley Clark School, "From Warsaw to the West Side," 7–12.

69 The German-language newspaper ceased publishing in 1918; Kronewitter, "Press History." The Deutsches Fortbildungs Verein celebrated its twenty-fifth anniversary in 1939; *Twenty-Fifth Anniversary, Deutsches Fortbildungs Verein*, HM.

70 The two cities included 1,648 first- and second-generation Swedes, 1,626 Italians, 583 Yiddish-speaking immigrants, and an uncounted number of Ashkenazi Jewish children. With the exception of the census and city directories, fifty-one Chinese men and fourteen Mexicans enumerated in 1930 were invisible in South Bend local sources; *Fifteenth Census: Population*, vol. 2: 248–250, 333, 385, 392–393; *Fifteenth Census: Population*, vol. 3, pt. 1: 720–721, 723; South Bend *City Directory*, 1929, 953; and South Bend *City Directory*, 1932, 667–668.

71 *Fifteenth Census: Population*, vol. 6: 431; Vann, "Black Americans," 20–21.

72 *Studebaker Accelerator* 5, no. 11 (August 18, 1932), SNM.

73 Edna M, 161, SB32.

74 *Fifteenth Census: Manufactures, 1929*, vol. 3, *Reports by States, Statistics for Industrial Areas, Counties, and Cities*, 174; J. D. "Red" Hill, *A Brief History of the Labor Movement of Studebaker Local 5, U.A.W.-C.I.O.* (SB: Studebaker Local 5, Education and Publicity Committee, 1953), 9; Studebaker report to National Industrial Conference Board for week ending September 14, 1929, research materials, *WBB* 92,

RG 86; Studebaker Corporation, *Studebaker Centennial Report* (SB, IN: Studebaker Corporation, 1952), 17.

75 *Studebaker Co-operator* 1, no. 7 (1920): 3–6, 34, SNM.

76 Elisabeth Klaus, "A Family of Families: When Family Relations Are Work Relations" (PhD diss., University of Notre Dame, 1986), 298–299.

77 Jack J. Detzler, *South Bend, 1910–1920: A Decade Dedicated to Reform* (South Bend, IN: Northern Indiana Historical Society, 1960), 96. Jack J. Detzler, *South Bend, 1920–1930: The Emergence of a City* (South Bend, IN: Northern Indiana Historical Society, 1960), 64, 66. Klaus, "A Family of Families," 93, 118. The Studebaker *Accelerator*, *Co-operator*, and *Spotlight* (all at SNM) are written and photographic records of corporate welfare capitalism.

78 *Fifteenth Census: Population*, vol. 3, pt. 1: 68; Detzler, *South Bend, 1920–1930*, 46–47.

79 *South Bend Tribune*, February 14, 1919, quoted in Detzler, *South Bend, 1910–1920*, 96; 8A Class, 1921, comp., "The Melting Pot," (South Bend, In: Washington School); Detzler, *South Bend, 1920–1930*, 76–77.

80 *Fifteenth Census: Population*, vol. 2: 463–464, 480.

81 Petrass, "Hungarian Builders of the American Nation," *Golden Jubilee Album*, n.p.

82 Dempsey and Dempsey, "Through the Years."

83 "Rain and City Officials Halt Outbreak Peril," *South Bend News-Times*, May 18, 1924; Detzler, *South Bend, 1920–1930*, 83–85; Knauss and Lawrence interview; Kathleen M. Blee, "Women in the 1920s Ku Klux Klan Movement," *Feminist Studies* 17, no. 1 (1991): 57–77.

84 *Studebaker Co-operator* 4, no. 12 (1923), SNM.

85 *Sew and Sew*, 1, no. 3 (1933): 4; *Sew and Sew* 2, no. 1 (1934): 9.

86 *Studebaker Accelerator*, August 18, 1932; *Studebaker Accelerator*, September 21, 1932, SNM.

87 *Fifteenth Census: Manufactures, 1929*, vol. 1, *General Report: Statistics by Subjects*, 249. New York and Detroit completed the top five.

88 *Fifteenth Census: Population*, vol. 2: 67, 71, 72, 74, 77.

89 Writers Program of the WPA, *Pennsylvania: A Guide to the Keystone State* (New York: Oxford University Press, 1940), 256–267.

90 Gary Gerstle, *American Crucible: Race and Nation in the Twentieth Century* (Princeton, NJ: Princeton University Press, 2001).

91 *Fifteenth Census: Population*, vol. 2: 74, 77, 78, 316, 329, 333.

92 *Fifteenth Census: Manufactures*, vol. 3: 158–159.

93 *Fifteenth Census: Manufactures*, vol. 3: 422–423; "Industry," *The Encyclopedia of Cleveland History*, ed. David D. Van Tassel and John J. Grabowski (Bloomington: Indiana University Press, 1987), 549.

94 *Fifteenth Census: Manufactures*, vol. 3: 466–467; Walter Licht, *Getting Work: Philadelphia, 1840–1950* (Cambridge, MA: Harvard University Press, 1992), 1–16.

95 James R. Barrett and David Roediger, "Inbetween Peoples: Race, Nationality, and the 'New Immigrant' Working Class," *Journal of American Ethnic History* 16, no. 3 (1997): 3–44.

96 Dana Frank, "White Working-Class Women and the Race Question," *International Labor and Working-Class History*, no. 54 (1998): 80–102.

97 Jo Sinclair's *The Changelings*, a story of friendship between a daughter of Jewish immigrants and a daughter of Black migrants that was first drafted in 1930, captures Cleveland's ethnic and racial tensions; see Elisabeth Sandberg, "On Racism and Ethnocentrism," *The Changelings* (Old Westbury, NY: Feminist Press, 1983), 350.

98 *WBB* 92, *Wage-Earning Women*, 3.

99 *Fifteenth Census: Population*, vol. 2: 67–73, 202.
100 Carole Marks, *Farewell—We're Good and Gone: The Great Black Migration* (Bloomington: Indiana University Press, 1989); Grossman, *Land of Hope*; Joe William Trotter, ed., *The Great Migration in Historical Perspective: New Dimensions of Race, Class, and Gender* (Bloomington: Indiana University Press, 1991); Kimberly Phillips, *AlabamaNorth: African-American Migrants, Community, and Working-Class Activism in Cleveland, 1915–1945* (Urbana: University of Illinois Press, 1999); Farah Jasmine Griffin, *"Who Set You Flowin'?" The African-American Migration Narrative* (New York: Oxford University Press, 1995).
101 *Fifteenth Census: Population*, vol. 2: 67.
102 E. Digby Baltzell, "Introduction to the 1967 Edition," W.E.B. DuBois, *The Philadelphia Negro: A Social Study* (1899, repr. New York: Schocken Books, 1967), xxxiv.
103 Kenneth L. Kusmer, *A Ghetto Takes Shape: Black Cleveland, 1870–1930* (Urbana: University of Illinois Press, 1976), 165, 210–214; Phillips, *AlabamaNorth*. Somewhat exceptionally, well into the 1930s African Americans and immigrants lived in some of the same Cleveland neighborhoods.
104 Kusmer, *A Ghetto Takes Shape*, 178–184.
105 Drake and Cayton, *Black Metropolis*, 1: 104–107.
106 V. P. Franklin, "The Philadelphia Race Riot of 1918," *African Americans in Pennsylvania: Shifting Historical Perspectives*, ed. Joe William Trotter Jr. and Eric Ledell Smith (University Park: Pennsylvania State University Press / Pennsylvania Historical and Museum Commission, 1997), 316–329.
107 Van Tassel and Grabowski, *Encyclopedia of Cleveland*, 711.
108 Drake and Cayton, *Black Metropolis*, 2:716–754.
109 Drake and Cayton, *Black Metropolis*, 1:57; David R. Roediger, *Working toward Whiteness: How America's Immigrants Became White: The Strange Journey from Ellis Island to the Suburbs* (New York: Basic Books, 2005), 103–104.
110 Janette Faulkner's pioneering exhibits of her collections brought these objects to attention. Janette Faulkner, *Ethnic Notions: Black Images in the White Mind*, updated and rev. ed. (Berkeley: Berkeley Art Center, 2000); Marlon Riggs, dir., *Ethnic Notions* (San Francisco: California Newsreel, 1986); Patricia A. Turner, *Ceramic Uncles and Celluloid Mammies: Black Images and Their Influence on Culture* (New York: Anchor Books, 1994); Kenneth W. Goings, *Mammy and Uncle Mose: Black Collectibles and American Stereotyping* (Bloomington: Indiana University Press, 1994); M. M. Manring, *Slave in a Box: The Strange Career of Aunt Jemima* (Charlottesville: University of Virginia Press, 1998).
111 Cohen, *Making a New Deal*, 129–143.
112 *Fifteenth Census: Population*, vol. 6: 70.
113 Patrick Ely, *The Adventures of Amos 'n' Andy: A Social History of an American Phenomenon* (New York: Free Press, 1991).
114 Edward R. Kantowicz, "Polish Chicago: Survival through Solidarity," *The Ethnic Frontier: Essays in the History of Group Survival in Chicago and the Midwest*, ed. Melvin G. Holli and Peter d'A. Jones (Grand Rapids, MI: William B. Eerdmans, 1977), 183, 187, 196.
115 *Fifteenth Census: Population*, vol. 3, pt. 1: 61; Christopher Robert Reed, *The Rise of Chicago's Black Metropolis, 1920–1929* (Urbana: University of Illinois Press, 2011); Grossman, *Land of Hope*; Drake and Cayton, *Black Metropolis*, is a classic account of Black Chicago.
116 Drake and Cayton, *Black Metropolis*, 2:379–494, 716–754.

117 Pauline H, 261, Cleveland.

118 *Fifteenth Census: Population*, vol. 2: 1091, 1143, 1146, 1155; *Fifteenth Census: Population*, vol. 3, pt. 1: 114.

119 *Fifteenth Census: Population*, vol. 4: 440, 489, 1267, 1402.

120 Elizabeth Ewen, *Immigrant Women in the Land of Dollars: Life and Culture on the Lower East Side, 1890–1925* (New York: Monthly Review Press, 1985), 104.

121 Leslie Woodcock Tentler, *Wage-Earning Women: Industrial Work and Family Life in the United States 1800–1930* (New York: Oxford University Press, 1979), 93; Kathy Peiss, *Cheap Amusements: Working Women and Leisure in Turn-of-the-Century New York* (Philadelphia: Temple University Press, 1986), 67–72.

122 Rachel G, 790, SB32; Susan A. Glenn, *Daughters of the Shtetl: Life and Labor in the Immigrant Generation* (Ithaca, NY: Cornell University Press, 1990), 79–89.

123 Elizabeth Clark-Lewis, "'This Work Had a End': African-American Domestic Workers in Washington, DC, 1910–1940," in *"To Toil the Livelong Day": America's Women at Work, 1780–1980*, ed. Carol Groneman and Mary Beth Norton (Ithaca, NY: Cornell University Press, 1987), 196–212; Elizabeth Clark-Lewis, *Living in, Living out: African American Domestics and the Great Migration* (New York: Kodansha, 1996).

124 Marie S, 422, J37, Oakwood, Chicago37.

125 Jacqueline Jones, *Labor of Love, Labor of Sorrow: Black Women, Work, and the Family from Slavery to the Present* (New York: Basic Books, 1985, 158–159.

126 Marcia Chatelain, *South Side Girls Growing Up in the Great Migration* (Durham, NC: Duke University Press, 2015); James Borchert, *Alley Life in Washington: Family, Community, Religion, and Folklife in the City, 1850–1970* (Urbana: University of Illinois Press, 1980), 143–149.

127 Bodnar, Simon, and Weber, *Lives of Their Own*, 89–93, 108.

128 David M. Katzman, *Seven Days a Week: Women and Domestic Service in Industrializing America* (New York: Oxford University Press, 1978), 216–218; Judith Rollins, *Between Women: Domestics and Their Employers* (Philadelphia: Temple University Press, 1985), 150–151; Jones, *Labor of Love*, 149–150, 157.

129 *Fifteenth Census: Population*, vol. 2: 1143.

130 Sylvia Woods, "You Have to Fight for Freedom," *Rank and File: Personal Histories by Working-Class Organizers*, ed. Alice Lynd and Staughton Lynd (Boston: Beacon, 1973), 113–119.

131 Meyerowitz, *Women Adrift*, 1–20, 36–37, 149–50n29; Darlene Clark Hine, "Rape and the Inner Lives of Black Women in the Middle West: Preliminary Thoughts on the Culture of Dissemblance," *Signs* 14, no. 4 (1989): 912–920.

132 Jones, *Labor of Love*, 162.

133 Figures are calculated from *Fifteenth Census: Population*, vol. 2: 954, 955, 965, 1005; *Fifteenth Census: Population*, vol. 4: 454, 510, 1301, 1425; *Fifteenth Census: Population*, vol. 5: *General Report on Occupations* (Washington, DC: GPO, 1933), 274.

134 Phyllis A. Wallace, *Black Women in the Labor Force* (Cambridge, MA: MIT Press, 1980); Margaret C. Simms and Julianne M. Malveaux, eds., *Slipping through the Cracks: The Status of Black Women* (New Brunswick, NJ: Transaction Books, 1986); Teresa Amott and Julie Matthaei, *Race, Gender, and Work: A Multi-cultural Economic History of Women in the United States*, rev. ed. (Boston: South End, 1996); Jones, *Labor of Love*.

135 Vera M, 225, SB32.

136 *Fifteenth Census: Population*, vol. 5: 330, 329, 331.

137 Mabel W, 903, SB32.

138 Queen Victoria C, 136, Ch33.

139 Mary T, 243, SB32.

140 Mabel H, E30, 140, E30, Halsted, Chicago37.

141 Mrs. Harry K, 77, SB32.

142 Lynn Weiner, *From Working Girl to Working Mother: The Female Labor Force in the United States, 1820–1980* (Chapel Hill: University of North Carolina Press, 1985), 85, 92–93.

143 Rose Z, 380, SB32.

144 Eva A, 12, Chicago33.

145 Mary A, 185, SB32.

146 Della H, 68, B32, Bridgeport, Chicago37.

147 Anna U, 824, Chicago33.

148 *Fifteenth Census: Population*, vol. 4: 454, 510, 1300, 1425; *Fifteenth Census: Population*, vol. 5: 274. The census lumped together women older than forty-five, obscuring analysis. Drake and Cayton, *Black Metropolis*, 2:584, note that older Black women without visible husbands identified as widows.

149 Sarah D, 30, A30, Archer, Chicago37.

150 *Fifteenth Census: Population*, vol. 5: 117.

151 Labor force participation in the 1930 census measures 1929 employment. In April 1930, when the census was taken, labor force participants included numerous recently unemployed workers. *Fifteenth Census: Population*, vol. 5: 274.

152 *Fifteenth Census: Population*, vol. 5: 74, 117.

153 Figures are calculated from *Fifteenth Census: Population*, vol. 5: 274. Half or more of several demographic groups worked for wages: single women, widowed and divorced Black women, and widows and divorcées younger than forty-five.

154 Figures are calculated from *Fifteenth Census: Population*, vol. 5: 274.

155 *Fifteenth Census: Population*, vol. 5: 74, 117.

156 *Fifteenth Census: Population*, vol. 5: 74.

157 August Meier and Elliott Rudwick, *Black Detroit and the Rise of the UAW* (New York: Oxford University Press, 1979), 5–9.

158 David R. Roediger, *The Wages of Whiteness: Race and the Making of the American Working Class* (London: Verso, 1991), discusses how immigrant men attempted to avoid "n——r jobs."

159 *Fifteenth Census: Population*, vol. 5: 74–75.

160 Dana Frank, "White Working-Class Women," 80–102.

161 Amott and Matthaei, *Race, Gender, and Work*.

162 Mary, Bessie, and Emma T, 937, SB32.

163 *WBB* 218, *Women's Occupations through Seven Decades* (Washington, DC: GPO, 1947), 34, 75; *Fifteenth Census: Population*, vol. 5: 74–75; Margery W. Davies, *Woman's Place Is at the Typewriter: Office Work and Office Workers, 1870–1930* (Philadelphia: Temple University Press, 1982); Elyce Rotella, *From Home to Office: U.S. Women at Work, 1870–1930* (Ann Arbor, MI: UMI Research Press, 1981); Sharon Hartman Strom, "'We're No Kitty Foyles': Organizing Office Workers for the Congress of Industrial Organizations, 1937–1950," in *Women, Work, and Protest: A Century of U.S. Women's Labor History*, ed. Ruth Milkman (Boston: Routledge and Kegan Paul, 1985), 206–234; Lisa M. Fine, *The Souls of the Sky-scraper: Female Clerical Workers in Chicago, 1870–1930* (Philadelphia: Temple University Press, 1990); Sharon Hartman Strom, *Beyond the Typewriter: Gender, Class, and the Origins of Modern American Office Work, 1900–1930* (Urbana: University of Illinois Press, 1992); Angel Kwolek-Folland, *Engendering Business:*

Men and Women in the Corporate Office, 1870–1930 (Baltimore: Johns Hopkins University Press, 1994).

164 Figures are calculated from *Fifteenth Census: Population*, vol. 5: 136.

165 Figures are calculated from *Fifteenth Census: Population*, vol. 5: 136–137, 280, 290.

166 *WBB* 120, *Employment of Women in Offices* (Washington, DC: GPO, 1934), 12–13, 92; *WBB* 188-2, *Office Work in Los Angeles* (1942), Survey Materials, RG 86; *WBB* 188-3, *Office Work in Kansas City* (1942), Survey Materials, RG 86; *WBB* 188-5, *Office Work in Philadelphia* (1942), Survey Materials, RG 86; *Fifteenth Census: Population*, vol. 5: 85; *Fifteenth Census: Population*, vol. 4: 450; Drake and Cayton, *Black Metropolis*, 2:430–469.

167 Grace S, 725, SB32.

168 *WBB* 218, *Women's Occupations*, 84; Frances R. Donovan, *The Saleslady* (Chicago: University of Chicago Press, 1929); Susan Porter Benson, *Counter Cultures: Saleswomen, Managers, and Customers in American Department Stores, 1890–1940* (Urbana: University of Illinois Press, 1986), 178.

169 *WBB* 76, *Women in 5-and-10-Cent Stores and Limited-Price Chain Department Stores* (Washington, DC: GPO, 1930), 6; Robert Heide and John Gilman, *Dime-Store Dream Parade: Popular Culture, 1925–1955* (New York: E. P. Dutton, 1979).

170 *WBB* 125, *Employment Conditions in Department Stores in 1932–1933* (Washington, DC: GPO, 1936), 21–22; Benson, *Counter Cultures*, 200–209.

171 Figures are calculated from *Fifteenth Census: Population*, vol. 5: 130–131, 278.

172 Figures are calculated from *Fifteenth Census: Population*, vol. 5: 276, 118–119.

173 Figures are calculated from *Fifteenth Census: Population*, vol. 5: 76–80.

174 Jones, *Labor of Love*, 208–213.

175 Figures are calculated from *Fifteenth Census: Population*, vol. 5: 76–80.

176 Sterling D. Spero and Abram L. Harris, *The Black Worker: The Negro and the Labor Movement* (1931, repr. New York: Atheneum, 1972), 337–351; Jones, *Labor of Love*, 209–210.

177 Beatrice B, 556, L53, Washington Park, Chicago37.

178 Margaret M, 671, SB32.

179 Rose S, 367, SB32.

180 Luvara D, 180, Chicago33.

181 Rose M, 588, SB32.

182 Betty H, 433, SB32.

183 Sophia P, 176, SB32.

184 Lena J, A20, Archer, 20, Chicago37.

185 *Fifteenth Census: Population*, vol. 5: 85, 136–137, 280, 290.

186 Dorothy Sue Cobble, *Dishing It Out: Waitresses and Their Unions in the Twentieth Century* (Urbana: University of Illinois Press, 1991), 32.

187 Onda H, 1049, SB32.

188 *WBB* 151, *Injuries to Women in Personal Service Occupations in Ohio* (Washington, DC.: GPO, 1937), 3–10.

189 Lorraine G, 260, Chicago33.

190 Irene T, 993, SB32.

191 Kathy Peiss, *Hope in a Jar: The Making of America's Beauty Culture* (New York: Henry Holt, 1998); Lois W. Banner, *American Beauty: A Social History, through Two Centuries of the American Idea, Ideal, and Image of the Beautiful Woman* (New York: Alfred A. Knopf, 1983), 202–225, 271–291; Lynd and Hanson, "The People as Consumers," *Recent Social Trends*, 2:905; Marchand, *Advertising the American Dream*, 175–179.

192 Figures are calculated from *Fifteenth Census: Population*, vol. 5: 280.

193 *WBB* 133, *Employment Conditions in Beauty Shops: A Study of Four Cities* (Washington, DC: GPO, 1935), 5–10, 39–40; Tiffany M. Gill, *Beauty Shop Politics: African American Women's Activism in the Beauty Industry* (Urbana: University of Illinois Press, 2010).

194 *Fifteenth Census: Population*, vol. 5: 134–135, 280.

195 Figures are calculated from *Fifteenth Census: Population*, vol. 4: 450, 454, 1288, 1300, 1415, 1425.

196 Paule Marshall, *Brown Girl, Brownstones* (New York: Avon Books, 1959), 27–28.

197 *Fifteenth Census: Manufactures, 1929*, vol. 2, *Reports by Industries* (Washington, DC: GPO, 1933), 1396.

198 *WBB* 78, *A Survey of Laundries and Their Women Workers in 23 Cities* (Washington, DC: GPO, 1930), 5–6, 124–127.

199 South Bend, IN, *City Directories* (1930–1940).

200 *Fifteenth Census: Population*, vol. 4: 457, 1306, 1429; *Fifteenth Census: Population*, vol. 5: 85, 134–135, 280.

201 *WBB* 78, *Survey of Laundries*, 124–126; *Fifteenth Census: Population*, vol. 4: 450, 509, 1288, 1415.

202 *WBB* 78, *Survey of Laundries*, 17–36, 97–99.

203 Florence B, 506, L3, Washington Park, Chicago37.

204 Woods, "You Have to Fight," 119–121. Woods appeared in the films *Union Maids* (1976) and *Seeing Red* (1983).

205 *Fifteenth Census: Population*, vol. 5: 84–85; *Fifteenth Census: Population*, vol. 4: 450, 1288, 1415.

206 Beatrice W, 892, Chicago33.

207 Mrs. I, 437, SB32.

208 Figures are calculated from *Fifteenth Census: Population*, vol. 5: 85.

209 Ellabell L, SB30, Workplace Interviews: Domestic Miscellaneous, *WBB* 92; Anna F, 1075, SB32.

210 Rose M. Bradley, New Bedford, MA, to NRA, August 30, 1933, RG 9.

211 Figures are calculated from *Fifteenth Census: Population*, vol. 5: 85.

212 Elizabeth Clark-Lewis, "'This Work Had a' End': The Transition from Live-In to Day Work" (Working Paper no. 2, Center for Research on Women, Memphis State University, 1985), 16; Clark-Lewis, *Living in, Living out*; Rollins, *Between Women*, 155–173, 180. Phyllis Palmer, *Domesticity and Dirt: Housewives and Domestic Servants in the United States, 1920–1945* (Philadelphia: Temple University Press, 1989).

213 David M. Katzman, *Seven Days a Week: Women and Domestic Service in Industrializing America* (Oxford: Oxford University Press, 1978), 2–43.

214 Evelyn Nakano Glenn, *Issei, Nisei, War Bride: Three Generations of Japanese American Women in Domestic Service* (Philadelphia: Temple University Press, 1986); Vicki L. Ruiz, "By the Day or Week: Mexicana Domestic Workers in El Paso," in Groneman and Norton, *"To Toil the Livelong Day,"* 269–283; Mary Romero, *Maid in the U.S.A.* (New York: Routledge, 1992); Katzman, *Seven Days a Week*; Evelyn Nakano Glenn, *Unequal Freedom: How Race and Gender Shaped American Citizenship and Labor* (Cambridge, MA: Harvard University Press, 2004); Vanessa May, *Unprotected Labor: Household Workers, Politics, and Middle-Class Reform in New York, 1870–1940* (Chapel Hill: University of North Carolina Press, 2011).

215 Figures are calculated from *Fifteenth Census: Population*, vol. 4: 1415.

216 Figures are calculated from *Fifteenth Census: Population*, vol. 5: 74, 84–85.

217 Katzman, *Seven Days a Week*, 87–94.
218 Tera W. Hunter, *To 'Joy My Freedom: Southern Black Women's Lives and Labors after the Civil War* (Cambridge, MA: Harvard University Press, 1998), 51–53.
219 Figures are calculated from *Fifteenth Census: Population*, vol. 5: 74.
220 Mary W, 387, SB32.
221 Rose H, 477, SB32.
222 Mary K, 822, Philadelphia.
223 Figures are calculated from *Fifteenth Census: Population*, vol. 4: 508–509.
224 Figures are calculated from *Fifteenth Census: Population*, vol. 5: 76, 85. I added laundresses, cooks, and other servants to calculate domestic workers.

Chapter 2   Job Deterioration and Unemployment

1 Ruth Milkman, "Women's Work and Economic Crisis: Some Lessons of the Great Depression," *Review of Radical Political Economics*, 8, no. 1 (1976): 79–80. BC, *Fifteenth Census: Population*, vol. 2, *General Report Statistics by Subjects*, 125–129, 131–133, 197–200, 219. Unemployment stayed below 5% in the 1920s, then jumped to 8.7% in 1930, almost doubled to 15.9% in 1931, and peaked at 24.9% in 1933; BC, *Historical Statistics of the United States, Colonial Times to 1970*, Bicentennial ed. (Washington, DC: GPO, 1975), series D, 85–86.
2 Alice Kessler-Harris, *Out to Work: A History of Wage-Earning Women in the United States* (New York: Oxford University Press, 1982), 250–272.
3 Edna M, 161, SB32.
4 Clementine S, 176, SB32.
5 Figures are calculated from *Fifteenth Census: Population*, vol. 2: 219.
6 *WBB* 92, *Wage-Earning Women and the Industrial Conditions of 1930*, 52.
7 Studebaker figures calculated from payrolls, *WBB* 92, RG 86.
8 "Report for One Week Made Monthly to National Industrial Conference Board–South Bend—Studebaker," 1930 Correspondence, *WBB* 92, RG 86.
9 Betty K, 245, SB32.
10 Ball Band, Singer, and Wilson figures calculated from Wages, Earnings, and Hours, *WBB* 92, RG 86.
11 Catherine S, Helen S, 710, SB32.
12 Bertha W, 58, SB32; Gizella M, 495, SB32.
13 Mary K, 1093, SB32.
14 Helen S, Martha C, Nettie S, 802, SB32.
15 Theresa B, 279, SB32.
16 Cecyle J, 528, SB32.
17 Helen S, 802, SB32.
18 Betty H, 433, SB32.
19 Elisabeth Klaus, "A Family of Families: When Family Relations are Work Relations" (PhD diss., Notre Dame University, 1986), 221; J. D. "Red" Hill, *A Brief History of the Labor Movement of Studebaker Local No. 5, U.A.W.-C.I.O.* (South Bend, IN: Studebaker Local No. 5, Education and Publicity Committee, 1953), 10.
20 Irene S, 23, SB32. Bench workers operated machines that created springs for car seats.
21 Studebaker Corporation, *Studebaker Centennial Report* (South Bend, IN: Studebaker Corporation, 1952), 25.
22 "Survey of South Bend and Mishawaka, Indiana, Field Report," July 24, 1937, Records Relating to the City Survey File, 1935–1940, Federal Home Loan Bank Board, Home Owners Loan Corporation, RG 195.

23 Betty K, 245, SB32.

24 Julia B, 282, SB32.

25 Ruth H, 538, SB32.

26 Leah C, 610, SB32.

27 Leona C, 1110, SB32; South Bend, IN *City Directories* (Indianapolis: R. L. Polk and Company, 1930–1940) listed Leona as a maid at Oliver Hotel every year through 1940.

28 Mary K, 777, SB32.

29 South Bend IN *City Directories* (1929–1940).

30 Julia K, 593, SB32.

31 Onda H, 1049, SB32.

32 *WBB* 92, *Wage-Earning Women*, 6, 40.

33 Mrs. G (Della G), Individual Interviews, *WBB*92, RG 86; South Bend, IN, *City Directories* (1930–1940).

34 Loretta V, 468, SB32; South Bend, IN *City Directories* (1930–1940) listed Loretta as an elevator operator every year through 1940. She apparently kept her job throughout the Depression.

35 Loretta V, 468, SB32; South Bend, IN *City Directories* (1930–1934).

36 Velzora H, SB30. South Bend, IN *City Directories* (1930–1940).

37 Two of three Studebaker employees died and the third departed. City directory listings were sometimes incomplete, confusing, or contradicted interview data; South Bend, IN *City Directories*.

38 *WBB* 108, *Effects of the Depression*, 13–31.

39 Wages, Earnings, and Hours, employer files, *WBB* 92, RG 86.

40 *WBB* 108, *Effects of the Depression*, 20. Even though 25.9% of unemployed wives named personal reasons for joblessness, married women still suffered worse unemployment than single women. Calculated from *WBB* 108, *Effects of the Depression*, 23

41 Julia K, 593, SB32.

42 Survey Materials: Wages, Hours, and Earnings, *WBB* 92, RG 86.

43 Mary A, 185, SB32.

44 "Survey of South Bend and Mishawaka, Field Report, July 24, 1937, FHLBB, HOLC City Surveys, RG 195.

45 Figures are calculated from *Fifteenth Census: Population*, vol. 4, *Occupations, by States* (Washington, DC: GPO, 1933), 471; and, *Sixteenth Census: 1940, Population*, vol. 3, *The Labor Force*, pt. 2, *Alabama–Indiana* (Washington, DC: GPO, 1943), 952. See Appendix C.

46 Figures are calculated from *Fifteenth Census: Population*, vol. 4: 506–509; *Sixteenth Census of the United States: 1940, Population*, vol. 3, *The Labor Force*, pt. 1, *United States Summary* (Washington, DC: GPO, 1943): 63–64; *Sixteenth Census: Population*, vol. 3, pt. 2: 990–991, 994.

47 Figures are calculated from *Fifteenth Census of the United States: 1930, Unemployment*, vol. 2, *General Report* (Washington, DC: GPO, 1932), 472–474, 476–478, 479–481.

48 Minutes of the Board of Trustees of the Phillis Wheatley Association, June 9, 1931, series 1, Board of Trustees and Committees, PWA, Western Reserve Historical Society.

49 Evelyn D, 428, J43, Oakwood, Chicago37.

50 Grace K, 428, Chicago33.

51 *Fifteenth Census: Population*, vol. 4: 450, 1288, 1415; *Fifteenth Census: Special Census of Unemployment*, 2: 481, 478, 474.

52 Arleathie B, 390, J5, Oakwood, Chicago37.
53 Elizabeth H, 630, Philadelphia.
54 Calculated from *15th Census, Special Census of Unemployment*, 2: 481.
55 Sarah P, 944, Chicago33.
56 Corrine H, 304, Chicago33.
57 Robert E. Weems Jr., *Black Business in the Black Metropolis: The Chicago Metropolitan Assurance Company, 1925–1985* (Bloomington: Indiana University Press, 1996), 18.
58 Figures are calculated from *Fifteenth Census: Unemployment*, vol. 2: 481.
59 Amanda D, 191, Chicago33.
60 Madeline M, 579, Chicago33.
61 Lucille P, 192, D45, Chase Park, Chicago37.
62 Dorothy Sue Cobble, "'Practical Women': Waitress Unionists and the Controversies over Gender Roles in the Food Service Industry, 1900–1980," *Labor History* 29, no. 1 (1988): 11–18.
63 Arleathie B, 390, J5, Oakwood, Chicago37.
64 Figures are calculated from *Fifteenth Census: Unemployment*, vol. 2: 479–481.
65 Rosie C, 128, Chicago33.
66 Grace B, 84, Chicago33. The employment agency charged $.15 or $.25.
67 Matilde B, 40, Chicago33.
68 Lida E. Bissell, Glendale, CA, to FDR, August 31, 1933, RG 9.
69 Marie K. Adams, Wichita, Kansas, to Frances Perkins, July 5, 1934, RG 86.
70 Frances K, 362, Cleveland.
71 Margaret Domayer, President, Amicitia Club, YWCA, Des Moines, Iowa, to General Hugh Johnson, September 9, 1933, RG 9.
72 Misses Helen and Betty Davis, Brooklyn, NY, to General Johnson, August 27, 1933, RG 9.
73 Jean Gynther et al., New York City, to Hugh S. Johnson, January 8, 1934, RG 9.
74 Helen F, 174, Cleveland.
75 Mrs. Hattie Dudley, Kittanning, PA, to FDR, n.d. [received September 30, 1933], RG 86.
76 Mrs. Katherine Rutherford, Baltimore, to FDR, July 12, 1933, RG 86.
77 Anna F, 184, Cleveland.
78 Mrs. Ann Brown, Cleveland, to Mrs. Franklin Roosevelt, n.d., RG 9.
79 Sarah H, 270, Cleveland.
80 Brenda Clegg, *"Black Female Domestics during the Great Depression in New York City"* (PhD diss., University of Michigan, 1983), 95–97.
81 Miss Mary M. Switzer, Mansfield, OH, to FDR, August 18, 1933, RG 86.
82 Mrs. M. G. Plunkett, Boston, to Eleanor Roosevelt, June 11, 1934, RG 9.
83 Mrs. L. F. Blanford, Chicago, to Frances Perkins, November 26, 1933, RG 86.
84 A Slave, Bristol, PA, to Frances Perkins, n.d. [1934 or 1935], RG 86.
85 Mrs. F. M. Chase, Whittier, CA, to Frances Perkins, January 18, 1934, RG 86.
86 Mrs. Clara Green, Peoria, IL, to FDR, October 25, 1933, RG 9.
87 Elizabeth S, 651, Cleveland. Many writers enclosed want ads in letters to New Dealers.
88 Olga U, 681, Cleveland.
89 Miss J. MacCulloch, Birmingham, MI, to FDR, September 19, 1933, RG 86.
90 Mary S, 1370, Philadelphia.
91 Caroline Vikartofsky, Ironwood, MI, to Frances Perkins, January 3, 1934, RG 86.

92 Catherine B, 282, H6, Lower North, Chicago37.

93 Viola C, 124, Chicago33.

94 Lois Scharf, *To Work and to Wed: Female Employment, Feminism, and the Great Depression* (Westport, CT.: Greenwood, 1980).

95 Laura G, 162, D15, Chase Park, Chicago37.

96 Millie M, 354, I18, Northern, Chicago37.

97 Mary P, 178, D31, Chase Park, Chicago37.

98 Survey Materials, Wages, Hours, and Earnings, *WBB* 92, RG 86.

99 Mary P, 938, SB32. Mary's son, Albert, reported that Singer limited the number employed from any family.

100 Edith C, 402, J17, Oakwood, Chicago37.

101 Tillie H, 352, Chicago33; Tillie H, 242, F33, Irving Park, Chicago37. Tillie appeared in both Chicago samples.

102 Louise Booth, New Rochelle, NY, to FDR, August 4, 1933, RG 9.

103 Kate Drumm to Miss Perckes, Birmingham, MI, August 19, 1933, RG 86.

104 Miss Leone Boulanger, Rhinelander, WI, to Hugh Johnson, July 21, 1934, RG 9.

105 Myrtle Whitaker, Grand Rapids, MI, to Frances Perkins, August 13, 1933, RG 86.

106 Julia B, 112, E2, Halsted, Chicago37.

107 Rebecca C, 168, Chicago33.

108 Scharf, *To Work and to Wed.*

109 *Fifteenth Census: Population*, vol. 5, *General Report on Occupations* (Washington, DC: GPO, 1933), 276–280, 314.

110 Scharf, *To Work and to Wed*; *WBB* 120, *Employment of Women in Offices* (1932) 12–13, 29–30, 46–47, 62–64, 84–85, 103, 105, 122–123; Survey Materials, RG 86.

111 Cecilia A, 175, SB32; Mrs. I R, 256, SB32.

112 Alice Kessler-Harris, *A Woman's Wage: Historical Meanings and Social Consequences* (Lexington: University Press of Kentucky, 1990).

113 Survey Materials, *WBB* 188–2, *Office Work in Los Angeles* (1942), RG 86; Survey Materials, *WBB* 188–3, *Office Work in Kansas City* (1942), RG 86; Survey Materials, *WBB* 188–5, *Office Work in Philadelphia* (1942), RG 86.

114 Margery W. Davies, *Woman's Place Is at the Typewriter: Office Work and Office Workers, 1870–1930* (Philadelphia: Temple University Press, 1982), 152–154.

115 Cobble, *Dishing It Out*, 38.

116 Josephine S, 564, Cleveland.

117 Robert Heide and John Gilman, *Dime-Store Dream Parade: Popular Culture, 1925–1955* (New York: E. P. Dutton, 1979), 28–30; *WBB* 133, *Employment Conditions in Beauty Shops: A Study of Four Cities* (Washington, DC: GPO, 1935), 7–9; Lois W. Banner, *American Beauty: A Social History, through Two Centuries of the American Idea, Ideal, and Image of the Beautiful Woman* (New York: Alfred A. Knopf, 1983), 202–225, 271–283; Stella Blum, ed., *Everyday Fashions of the Thirties as Pictured in Sears Catalogs* (New York: Dover, 1986).

118 For deafness, see Elgie M, 409, Cleveland; for pimples, see Mary C, 93, Cleveland.

119 Bertha B, 37, Cleveland.

120 Working-class lesbian history of the 1930s has paid scant attention to workplace issues. See Elizabeth Lapovsky Kennedy and Madeline D. Davis, *Boots of Leather, Slippers of Gold: The History of a Lesbian Community* (New York: Routledge, 1993), 32–38; Lillian Faderman, *Odd Girls and Twilight Lovers: A History of Lesbian Life in Twentieth-Century America* (New York: Columbia University Press, 1991), 79–81, 93–117.

121 Mary, Bessie, Emma T, 937, SB32.

122 Anna A M, 175, SB32; South Bend, IN *City Directories* (1930–1940).

123 "Our Voice with the Smile," *Studebaker Spotlight* 1, no. 4 (1937): 3.

124 Catherine S, 1120, SB32.

125 Figures calculated from BC, *Fifteenth Census, Unemployment*, vol. 2: 481.

126 St. Clair Drake and Horace Cayton, *Black Metropolis: A Study of Negro Life in a Northern City*, 2 vols., rev. and enlarged ed. (New York: Harcourt, Brace, and World, 1970), 2:450–451, 460–462. *WBB* 133, *Employment Conditions in Beauty Shops*, 11–21, 40–42.

127 Some women utilized neither business and laundries also had commercial clients.

128 Kathy Peiss, *Hope in a Jar: The Making of America's Beauty Culture* (New York: Henry Holt, 1998); Philip Scranton, ed., *Beauty and Business: Commerce, Gender, and Culture in Modern America* (New York: Routledge, 2001); Tiffany M. Gill, *Beauty Shop Politics: African American Women's Activism in the Beauty Industry* (Urbana: University of Illinois Press, 2010).

129 Gertrude B, 392, J7, Oakwood, Chicago37.

130 Cecyle J, Mary J, 528, SB32.

131 Lucille D, 141, Cleveland.

132 Blanche L, 662, SB32.

133 Roxy L, 0472, Chicago33.

134 Retta K, 0311, Cleveland.

135 Almeda R, 930, SB32.

136 Sanford M. Jacoby, *Employing Bureaucracy: Managers, Unions, and the Transformation of Work in American Industry, 1900–1945* (New York: Columbia University Press, 1985), 167–239; Sharon Hartman Strom, *Beyond the Typewriter: Gender, Class, and the Origins of Modern American Office Work, 1900–1930* (Urbana: University of Illinois Press, 1992), 109–171.

137 Caroline Manning to Mary Anderson, September 4, 1930, Correspondence File, *WBB* 92, RG 86.

138 Hill, *A Brief History*, 9.

139 John Bodnar, "Power and Memory in Oral History: Workers and Managers at Studebaker," *Journal of American History* 75, no. 4 (1989): 1207; Hill, *A Brief History*, 9–10.

140 Hill, *A Brief History*, 11.

141 Agnes V, 614, SB32.

142 Klaus, "A Family of Families," 221.

143 Esther B, Helen B, Martha B, 587, SB32.

144 Alice Childress, *Like One of the Family: Conversations from a Domestic's Life* (Boston: Beacon, 1986, originally published Brooklyn: Independence Publishers, 1956); Trudier Harris, *From Mammies to Militants: Domestics in Black American Literature* (Philadelphia: Temple University Press, 1982); Judith Rollins, *Between Women: Domestics and Their Employers* (Philadelphia: Temple University Press, 1985); Mary Romero, *Maid in the USA* (New York: Routledge, 1992); Bonnie Thornton Dill, "'Making Your Job Good Yourself': Domestic Service and the Construction of Personal Dignity," in *Women and the Politics of Empowerment*, ed. Ann Bookman and Sandra Morgen (Philadelphia: Temple University Press, 1988), 33–52; BarbaraNeely's Blanche White novels afford hilarious examples of these strategies.

145 *WBB* 125, *Employment Conditions in Department Stores in 1932–1933: A Study in Selected Cities of Five States* (Washington, DC: GPO, 1936), 10; Susan Porter

Benson, *Counter Cultures: Saleswomen, Managers, and Customers in American Department Stores, 1890–1940* (Urbana: University of Illinois Press, 1986).
146 Vera V, 470, SB32.
147 Dorothy M, 537, Chicago33.
148 Vera N, 596, SB32.
149 Betty B, 78, C4, Canal, Chicago37.
150 Figures are calculated from *Fifteenth Census: Unemployment*, vol. 2: 472–474, 476–478, 479–481.

Chapter 3   Employment Strategies and Their Consequences

1 Sophia H, 695, Philadelphia.
2 Margaret M, 905, Philadelphia.
3 Helen B, 201, Philadelphia.
4 Mary P, 938, SB32.
5 Elizabeth H, 630, Philadelphia.
6 Helen S, Martha C, Nettie S, Elfreda S, 802, SB32. For informal recruitment among kin and ethnic networks, see John Bodnar, Roger Simon, and Michael P. Weber, *Lives of Their Own: Blacks, Italians, and Poles in Pittsburgh, 1900–1960* (Urbana: University of Illinois Press, 1982), Bodnar, Simon, and Weber, *Lives of Their Own*, 55–68; and Gerald Zahavi, "Negotiated Loyalty: Welfare Capitalism and the Shoeworkers of Endicott Johnson, 1920–1940," *Journal of American History* 71, no. 3 (1983): 602–620.
7 Laura G, 162, D15, Chase Park, Chicago37.
8 Anne S, 1285, Philadelphia; Mary S, 1370, Philadelphia.
9 Mrs. M. H. Jones, Oakland, CA, to Frances Perkins, February 2, 1934, RG 86.
10 Mrs. Helen Mahone, Dayton, OH, to Mary Anderson, November 18, 1933, RG 86.
11 Miss Colette J. Kelly, President, Household Workers Welfare Association, Cleveland, to Department of Labor, October 29, 1934, RG 86.
12 Memo to agents from ALP [Agnes L. Peterson], 3-25-33, "Instructions for Guidance in Interpreting and Recording the Information on the Record Cards of the Friendly Service Bureau," YWCA Cleveland schedule of the WB, Survey Materials, *WBB* 139, RG 86.
13 Helen H, 243, Cleveland.
14 Martha E, 152, Cleveland.
15 Mae M, 441, Cleveland.
16 Mary S, 609, Cleveland.
17 Mary C, 93, Cleveland.
18 Ann W, 702, Cleveland.
19 Jane Edna Hunter, *A Nickel and a Prayer* (Cleveland: Elli Kani, 1940), 154–155.
20 Minutes of the Home Economics and Employment Committees, 1925–1939, Series 1, Board of Trustees and Committees, Phillis Wheatley Association (hereafter PWA), Western Reserve Historical Society (hereafter WRHS); Service Report to Welfare Federation, 1920–1931, Series 1, Board of Trustees and Committees, PWA, WRHS.
21 Kenneth L. Kusmer, *A Ghetto Takes Shape: Black Cleveland, 1870–1930* (Urbana: University of Illinois Press, 1976), 151; Minutes of Employment Committee, February 1, 1926, and March 1, 1926, Series 1, Board of Trustees and Committees, PWA, WRHS.

22 Minutes of the Board of Trustees, 1914–1942, Home Economics and Employment Committees, 1925–1939, PWA, WRHS; Service Report to Welfare Federation, Series 1, Board of Trustees and Committees, PWA, WRHS; Hunter, *A Nickel and a Prayer*; Adrienne Lash Jones, *Jane Edna Hunter: a Case Study of Black Leadership, 1910–1950* (Brooklyn, NY: Carlson, 1990).

23 Miss Lucy Shirrell, San Francisco, to Frances Perkins, July 30, 1933, RG 86.

24 Helen B, 48, Chicago33.

25 Ellen McD, 426, Cleveland.

26 Walter Licht, *Getting Work: Philadelphia, 1840–1950* (Cambridge, MA: Harvard University Press, 1992), 125.

27 Pettie W, 1525, Philadelphia.

28 Betty B, 74, Chicago33.

29 Velma T, 773, Chicago33.

30 Madeline M, 579, Chicago33.

31 Clara G, 1564, Philadelphia; Katherine M, 1650, Philadelphia.

32 Minnie M, 1040, Philadelphia.

33 Mary S, 747, Chicago33.

34 Ethel Erickson, Philadelphia, to Agnes Peterson, April 1, 1933, Correspondence, WBB 139, RG 86. As a teenager in Philadelphia, Pearl Bailey "used to go out to 'Jew Town' around Thirtieth and Diamond. . . . On Fridays I would go to scrub and clean to make spending change." Pearl Bailey, *The Raw Pearl* (New York: Harcourt, Brace, and World, 1968), 11.

35 Mary D, 432, J47, Oakwood, Chicago37; St. Clair Drake and Horace Cayton, *Black Metropolis: A Study of Negro Life in a Northern City*, 2 vols., rev. and enlarged ed. (New York: Harcourt, Brace, and World, 1970), 1:246.

36 Brenda Clegg, "Black Female Domestics during the Great Depression in New York City" (PhD diss., University of Michigan, 1983), 60–66, 49.

37 Anonymous, "And Mine: A True Story by a Negro Worker of the North," *Writing Red: An Anthology of American Women Writers, 1930–1940*, ed. Charlotte Nekola and Paula Rabinowitz (New York: Feminist Press, 1987), 272 (originally published in *Working Woman*, October, 1934).

38 Ella Baker and Marvel Cooke, "The Bronx Slave Market," *Crisis*, no. 42 (1935): 330–331, 340; Clegg, "Black Female Domestics," 60–83; Cheryl Greenburg, *Troubling the Waters: Black-Jewish Relations in the American Century* (Princeton, NJ: Princeton University Press, 2010); Hasia Diner, *In the Almost Promised Land: American Jews and Blacks, 1915–1935* (Baltimore: Johns Hopkins University Press, 1995).

39 Gertrude D, 138, Cleveland.

40 Velma T, 773, Chicago33.

41 Dora M, 372, I36, Northern, Chicago37.

42 Stella Blum, ed., *Everyday Fashions of the Twenties as Pictured in Sears and Other Catalogues* (New York: Dover, 1981), 128; Stella Blum, ed., *Everyday Fashions of the Thirties as Pictured in Sears Catalogues* (New York: Dover, 1986).

43 Lucille P, 192, D45, Chase Park, Chicago37.

44 Helen F, 174, Cleveland.

45 Dora M, 372, I36, Northern, Chicago37.

46 A few women revealed these practices to interviewers. Cheryl I. Harris, "Whiteness as Property," *Harvard Law Review* 106, no. 8 (1993): 1710–1713.

47 Olive T, 463, Cleveland; WBB 120, *The Employment of Women in Offices* (Washington, DC: GPO, 1934), 29.

48 Mary B, 466, K18, Union Park, Chicago37.
49 Mary S, 1370, Philadelphia. This forty-year-old Lithuanian immigrant reported that she "goes to Jewtown," the single reference to white women participating in slave markets.
50 Betty B, 74, Chicago33.
51 Lucille P, 192, D45, Chase Park, Chicago37.
52 Ruth D, 10, A10, Archer, Chicago37.
53 Eva A, 12, Chicago33.
54 Amanda D, 191, Chicago33.
55 Eileen Boris, *Home to Work: Motherhood and the Politics of Industrial Homework in the United States* (New York: Cambridge University Press, 1994).
56 Annabelle S, 731, Chicago33.
57 Susan Porter Benson, *Counter Cultures: Saleswomen, Managers, and Customers in American Department Stores, 1890–1940* (Urbana: University of Illinois Press, 1986), 186.
58 Marie K. Adams, Wichita, KS, to Frances Perkins, July 5, 1934, RG 86.
59 Bertha B, 37, Cleveland.
60 Anna T, 812, Chicago33. The interviewer noted, "I would say applicant was colored, but am not *sure* and did not ask her."
61 *WBB* 139, *Women Unemployed*, 11.
62 Nydia K, 327, Cleveland.
63 Edith Abbott, *The Tenements of Chicago, 1908–1935* (Chicago: University of Chicago Press, 1936), 341–361. Drake and Cayton, *Black Metropolis*, 2:576–581.
64 Louise C, 44, B8, Bridgeport, Chicago37.
65 Joanne J. Meyerowitz, *Women Adrift: Independent Wage Earners in Chicago, 1880–1930* (Chicago: University of Chicago Press, 1988), 69–91; *Fifteenth Census: Population*, vol. 6, *Families*, 67, 406. In the four cities, white immigrant and native-born households showed little difference in rates of keeping lodgers. In other destinations of the Great Migration even more Black households included roomers. In southern cities like Atlanta, Birmingham, and Richmond, Virginia, the rate was lower, 15–20%. James Borchert, *Alley Life in Washington: Family, Community, Religion, and Folklife in the City, 1850–1970* (Urbana: University of Illinois Press, 1980), 80–81.
66 Figures are calculated from *Sixteenth Census: Population*, vol. 4, *Characteristics by Age*, pt. 2, *Alabama–Louisiana*, 627. The Fifteenth Census enumerated households containing lodgers; the Sixteenth Census counted lodgers and relatives.
67 Lottie G, 410, J25, Oakwood, Chicago37.
68 Cora J, K34, 482, Union Park, Chicago37.
69 Frances B, 956, Chicago33.
70 Hazel Z, 524, SB32; South Bend, IN, *City Directory* (1940).
71 Theresa M, 129, SB32.
72 Anna T, 736, Chicago33.
73 Bertha W, 58, SB32. The woman who made housedresses was mentioned by her neighbor, Blanche U, 875, SB32.
74 Eva A, 12, Chicago33.
75 Millie M, 354, I18, Northern, Chicago37.
76 Carrie C, 256, G10, Lawndale, Chicago37; *WBB* 133, *Employment Conditions in Beauty Shops: A Study of Four Cities* (Washington, DC: GPO, 1935), 39.
77 Catherine R, 557, Cleveland.

78 Annabelle S, 731, Chicago33.
79 Kate N, 466, Cleveland.
80 Jean S, 561, Cleveland.
81 Ida E, 212, Chicago33.
82 Gladys C, 158, Chicago33.
83 Madeline M, 579, Chicago33.
84 Lulu L, 489, Chicago33.
85 Rose B, 594, SB32.
86 LaShawn Harris, *Sex Workers, Psychics, and Numbers Runners: Black Women in New York City's Underground Economy* (Urbana: University of Illinois Press, 2016); Shane White, Stephen Garton, Stephen Robertson, and Graham White, *Playing the Numbers: Gambling in Harlem between the Wars* (Cambridge, MA: Harvard University Press, 2010); Sharon Harley, "'Working for Nothing but a Living': Black Women in the Underground Economy," *Sister Circle: Black Women and Work*, ed. Sharon Harley and the Black Women and Work Collective (New Brunswick, NJ: Rutgers University Press, 2002), 48–66; Victoria Wolcott, *Remaking Respectability: African American Women in Interwar Detroit* (Chapel Hill: University of North Carolina Press, 2001).
87 Drake and Cayton, *Black Metropolis*, 2:470–494. Christopher Robert Reed, *The Rise of Chicago's Black Metropolis, 1920–1929* (Urbana: University of Illinois Press, 2011), 69–70, 139.
88 Drake and Cayton, *Black Metropolis*, 2:494.
89 Eva A, 12, Chicago33.
90 Meridel LeSueur, *Women on the Breadlines* (Minneapolis: West End, 1984), 140.
91 Drake and Cayton, *Black Metropolis*, 2:597.
92 Johanna B, I6, 342, Northern, Chicago37.
93 Edith C, J17, 402, Oakwood, Chicago37.
94 Drake and Cayton, *Black Metropolis*, 2: 596–597.
95 Bessie C, K36, 484, Union Park, Chicago37.
96 Drake and Cayton, *Black Metropolis*, 2: 597.
97 *Sixteenth Census: Internal Migration, 1935 to 1940: Color and Sex of Migrants*, 26. This census understated migration because it measured only the second half of the decade.
98 Josephine S, SB30, Individual Interviews, *WBB* 92, RG 86.
99 Leona C, 110, SB32; *South Bend Times*, July 11 and 12, 1938.
100 See Appendix A regarding South Bend Black women surveyed by the WB. *WBB* 92, *Wage-Earning Women*, 6; *WBB* 108, *Effects of the Depression*, 4.
101 South Bend *City Directories* (1930–1940).
102 *Sixteenth Census: Housing*, vol. 4, *General Characteristics*, pt. 2, *Iowa–Montana*, 907.
103 BC, *Historical Statistics of the United States, Colonial Times to 1970*, Bicentennial ed. (Washington, DC: GPO, 1975), series D, 85–86. Figures are calculated from *Sixteenth Census: Population*, vol. 3, *The Labor Force*, pt. 1, *United States Summary*, 62, 64.
104 Census categories changed over the decade. A net gain of 251,540 female clerical and sales positions included 114,248 women employed as clerical and sales workers on public emergency work. *Fifteenth Census: Population*, vol. 5, *General Report on Occupations*, 81–83, 85; *Sixteenth Census: Population*, vol. 3, pt. 1: 76, 87.
105 Figures are calculated from *Fifteenth Census: Population*, vol. 5: 82; and *Sixteenth Census: Population*, vol. 3, pt. 1: 76.

106 Figures are calculated from, *Fifteenth Census: Population*, vol. 5: 74, 76–80; and *Sixteenth Census: Population*, 3, pt. 1: 90.

107 *Fifteenth Census, Population*, vol. 4, *Occupations, by States* 450, 1288, 1415; *Sixteenth Census Population*, vol. 3, *The Labor Force*, pt. 2, *Alabama–Indiana*, 878; *Sixteenth Census Population*, vol. 3, *The Labor Force*, pt. 4, *Nebraska–Oregon*, 699; *Sixteenth Census, Population*, vol. 3, *The Labor Force*, pt. 5, *Pennsylvania–Wyoming*, 52.

108 Figures are calculated from *Fifteenth Census: Population*, vol. 5: 85; and, *Sixteenth Census: Population*, vol. 3, pt. 1: 90.

109 Figures are calculated from *Fifteenth Census: Population*, 5: 74, 76–80; and, *Sixteenth Census: Population*, vol. 3, pt. 1: 90.

110 Figures are calculated from *Fifteenth Census: Population*, vol. 4: 450; *Fifteenth Census: Population*, vol. 5: 85; *Sixteenth Census: Population*, 3, pt. 1: 90; and *Sixteenth Census: Population*, vol. 3, pt. 2: 878. Nationally, Black women lost far fewer elevator jobs.

111 *Fifteenth Census: Population*, vol. 5: 84, 134–135, 280; *Sixteenth Census: Population*, vol. 3, pt. 1: 90, 100, 111.

112 I have no explanation for this decline in service occupations.

113 "A domestic worker," Denver, to Frances Perkins, August 7, 1933, RG 86.

114 Margaret Domayer, President, Amicitia Club, YWCA, Des Moines, IA, to General Hugh Johnson, September 9, 1933, RG 9.

115 The Sixteenth Census did not disaggregate employment data by race and age and marital status simultaneously, limiting possible comparisons.

116 *Fifteenth Census: Population*, vol. 5: 76, 81–82, 84–85, 118–119, 128–137; *Sixteenth Census: Population*, vol. 3, pt. 1: 90, 1000, 111; Lynn Y. Weiner, *From Working Girl to Working Mother: The Female Labor Force in the United States, 1920–1980* (Chapel Hill: University of North Carolina Press, 1985).

117 *Fifteenth Census: Population*, vol. 5: 81–82, 85, 128–137, 278, 280. *Sixteenth Census: Population*, vol. 3, pt. 1: 90, 100, 111.

118 *Fifteenth Census: Population*, vol. 5: 76, 118–119, 276; *Sixteenth Census: Population*, vol. 3, pt. 1: 90, 100, 111.

119 Julia Kirk Blackwelder, "Women in the Work Force: Atlanta, New Orleans, and San Antonio, 1930 to 1940," *Journal of Urban History* 4, no. 3 (1978): 331–358; Julia Kirk Blackwelder, *Women of the Depression: Caste and Culture in San Antonio, 1929–1939* (College Station: Texas A&M University Press, 1984), 84–85.

120 I could not apply my method to San Antonio; the Sixteenth Census categorized Mexicans as white.

121 *Fifteenth Census: Population*, vol. 4: 394; *Sixteenth Census: Population*, vol. 2, *Characteristics of the Population*, pt. 2, *Florida–Iowa*, 378.

122 The Census ceased enumerating ethnicity and nativity in 1940, limiting my analysis.

123 Dana Frank, "White Working-Class Women and the Race Question," *International Labor and Working-Class History*, no. 54 (1998): 80–102.

124 Derrick Bell, *Faces at the Bottom of the Well: The Permanence of Racism* (New York: Basic Books, 1993), also utilizes the well metaphor.

125 *Fifteenth Census: Population*, vol. 5: 74; *Sixteenth Census: Population*, vol. 3, pt. 1: 76–80. For changes in men's occupations, see appendix C.

126 Figures are calculated from *Fifteenth Census: Population*, vol. 4: 506–508; *Sixteenth Census: Population*, vol. 3, pt. 1: 61, 63; and *Sixteenth Census: Population*, vol. 3, pt. 2: 990–991. More than one-fourth (26.8%) of the Black male labor force, but only 3.9% of the white male labor force, held public emergency jobs in South Bend.

127 Langston Hughes, "Let America Be America Again," in *The Collected Poems of Langston Hughes*, ed. Arnold Rampersad (New York: Vintage Classics, 1994), 190.

128 Figures are calculated from *Sixteenth Census: Population*, vol. 3, pt. 1: 62, 64.

129 Teresa Amott and Julie Matthaei, *Race, Gender, and Work: A Multi-cultural Economic History of Women in the United States*, rev. ed. (Boston: South End, 1996), 179.

130 Lynn C. Burbridge, "The Reliance of African-American Women on Government and Third Sector Employment," *American Economic Review* 84, no. 2 (1994): 103–107.

Chapter 4 The Family Economy

1 Calina V, 0970, SB32.

2 Loretta V, 468, SB32. In 1933 Stewart was listed as a barber in the *City Directory*, and then he apparently left town; South Bend, IN, *City Directories* (Indianapolis: R. K. Polk, 1933–1934).

3 *WBB* 92, *Wage-Earning Women and the Industrial Conditions of 1930: A Survey of South Bend* 46–47, 49, 52. Of more than six thousand wage earners, less than one-third worked steadily, almost half worked irregularly, and one-fifth were unemployed.

4 *WBB* 108, *Effects of the Depression: The Effects of the Depression on Wage Earners' Families: A Second Survey of South Bend*, 26.

5 Edith Abbott, *The Tenements of Chicago, 1908–1935* (Chicago: University of Chicago Press, 1936).

6 Roxie H, 0646, SB32.

7 Mrs. Frank W. (Marie), 0190, SB32.

8 The sources unanimously attribute housework to women. Boys more often crossed gender boundaries than men. In later twentieth century popular media, men occasionally related nostalgic stories about learning domestic skills, including quilting, as boys in the 1930s.

9 Studebaker made land available for gardens, and Oliver Farm Implements donated land to the Committee of 100 for community gardens. *Studebaker Accelerator* 4, no. 14 (July 29, 1931); *Studebaker Accelerator* 5, no. 7 (April 13, 1932); *Studebaker Accelerator* 5, no. 13 (October 26, 1932), SNM; *South Bend Tribune*, April 25, 1932.

10 Mary B, 657, SB32.

11 Josephine B, 850, SB32.

12 Jessie H, 846, SB32.

13 Robert S. Lynd with Alice C. Hanson, "The People as Consumers," in President's Research Committee on Social Trends, *Recent Social Trends in the United States: Report of the President's Research Committee on Social Trends*, 2 vols. (New York: McGraw-Hill, 1933), 2:907.

14 Treva F, 648, SB32.

15 Hazel L, 1020, SB32.

16 *BLSB* 635, *Retail Prices of Food, 1923–1936* (Washington: GPO, 1938), 78–79. Calculated from Bureau of Labor Statistics (hereafter BLS), "Standard of Living of Employees of Ford Motor Co. in Detroit," *Monthly Labor Review*, no. 30 (1930): 1213–1218.

17 *WBB* 92, *Wage-Earning Women*, 56.

18 *WBB* 92, *Wage-Earning Women*, 55. Black Chicagoans preferred to purchase packaged, standard brand goods and shop in chain stores, insuring protection

against unscrupulous storekeepers. Lizabeth Cohen, *Making a New Deal: Industrial Workers in Chicago, 1919–1939* (Cambridge: Cambridge University Press, 1990), 151–152.

19 Anna K, 196, SB32.

20 Mary E, Hattie E, Loretta E, 47, SB32.

21 SB *City Directory* (1929), 941–943; SB *City Directory* (1932), 207, 680–682; SB *City Directory* (1935), 727–729; Cohen, *Making a New Deal*, 234–238.

22 Helen C, 877, SB32.

23 Mary S, 638, SB32; Mary W, 268, SB32.

24 Nellie G, 60, SB32.

25 Irene T, 993, SB32.

26 Marvin V. Arnett, *Pieces from Life's Crazy Quilt* (Lincoln: University of Nebraska Press, 2000), 97–98.

27 National Industrial Conference Board, *The Cost of Living in Twelve Industrial Cities* (New York: National Industrial Conference Board, 1928), 63. Ford families in Detroit bought an average of 5.1 tons of bituminous coal, for $43.20 total in 1929; BLS, "Standard of Living," 1238.

28 Flora R, 534, SB32.

29 Helen S, Martha C, Nettie S, Elfreda S, 802, SB32.

30 Chloe H, 647, SB32.

31 Hazel L, 1020, SB32.

32 In 1899 caring for an up-to-date coal stove—sifting and emptying ashes, laying fires, tending fires, carrying coal, and blackening the stove top—took almost an hour daily and required heavy lifting. In six days the stove burned 292 pounds of coal and fourteen pounds of kindling; twenty-seven pounds of burnable coal were sifted from ashes. Susan Strasser, *Never Done: A History of American Housework* (New York: Pantheon Books, 1982), 40–41, 54–56; Ruth Schwartz Cowan, *More Work for Mother: The Ironies of Household Technology from the Open Hearth to the Microwave* (New York: Basic Books, 1983), 98, 163–164.

33 Mary G, 314, SB32.

34 Jessie H, 846, SB32.

35 BLS, "Standard of Living," 1239.

36 BLS, "Standard of Living," 1246–1247. Twenty-two percent of Detroit Ford families reported laundry expenses.

37 Mary T, 243, SB32.

38 Cowan, *More Work*, 185; BLS, "Standard of Living," 1241, 1250–1252; Strasser, *Never Done*, 105.

39 Loretta E, Hattie E, Mary E, 47, SB32.

40 Hazel L, 1020, SB32.

41 Fannie H, 1096, SB32.

42 *BLSB* 637, *Money Disbursements of Wage Earners and Clerical Workers in the North Atlantic Region, 1934–36*, vol. 2, *Eleven Cities* (Washington, DC: GPO, 1939), 95, 109.

43 Figures are calculated from *BLSB* 636, *Money Disbursements of Wage Earners and Clerical Workers in Eight Cities in the East North Central Region, 1934–1936* (Washington, DC: GPO, 1940), 97–98.

44 *BLSB* 637, vol. 2: 95, 109. Criteria for inclusion in BLS studies would have excluded most South Bend working-class families: household income of at least $500; no receipt of relief; at least one earner employed for thirty-six weeks, earning at least $300; and no earners with monthly incomes above $200. The BLS studied a more privileged group than the WB interviewed. *BLSB* 636, 82. These averages exclude households without income in 1932.

45 *WBB* 108, *Effects of the Depression,* 10.

46 The four-week period ranged from July through November 1932. Working-class jobs paid wages weekly, and a year contained thirteen four-week periods. The average income in the four-week period was slightly higher: $62.90.

47 Researchers noted wages of all household members for four weeks preceding interviews in 1932. In 1930 they recorded only women's wages. Estimates of pre-Depression household income rely on typical wages at specific factories. Average annual income for households with earnings in 1932, projected from four-week income, was just over $800.

48 *BLSB* 638, *Money Disbursements of Wage Earners and Clerical Workers, 1934–36: Summary Volume* (Washington, DC: GPO, 1941), 188.

49 Incomes of sample households were higher than 1,029 South Bend households surveyed that year (whose median four-week income was approximately $39, and almost five-sixths of whom earned less than one hundred dollars), likely because more sample households included multiple earners.

50 Florence C, 610, SB32; Necrology File, Local Family and History Services, St. Joseph County Public Library.

51 Leona C, 1110, SB32; South Bend *City Directories* (1930–1940); *South Bend Tribune,* August 11, 1938; *South Bend Tribune,* August 12, 1938. Fannie's other four children lived in Chicago; after William's death she divided her time between the two cities. She died in Chicago and was buried in South Bend in 1938. In 1940 Leona remained in the family home, still a maid at the Oliver Hotel.

52 Figures are calculated from *WBB* 108, *Effects of the Depression,* 10; Records Relating to the City Survey File, 1935–1940, South Bend and Mishawaka, Indiana File, Federal Home Loan Bank Board (hereafter FHLBB), Home Owners Loan Corporation (HOLC), RG 195, NACP.

53 Hazel L, 1020, SB32.

54 Elizabeth M, 1007, SB32. Utilizing BLS estimates for food consumption, the M household consisted of 6.4 "equivalent adult males." BLS, "Standard of Living," 1213.

55 Ethel I, 437, SB32.

56 Social workers debated requiring forfeiture of life insurance to establish eligibility for relief. Flora Slocum, "Lost Resources in Life Insurance: A Study of Dependent Families in St. Louis," *Social Service Review* 7, no. 4 (1933): 619–639; Flora Slocum, "A Study of Life Insurance Adjustments in 275 Relief Families," *Social Service Review* 8, no. 2 (1934): 302–325.

57 Crystal H, 526, SB32.

58 Bonita C, 1105, SB32.

59 Germaine R, 558, SB32.

60 Betty A, Anna M, Mary K, Cecilia A, 175, SB32.

61 Lizabeth Cohen, *A Consumer's Republic: The Politics of Mass Consumption in Postwar America* (New York: Alfred A. Knopf, 2003); Susan Porter Benson, *Household Accounts: Working-Class Family Economies in the Interwar United States* (Ithaca, NY: Cornell University Press, 2007).

62 *BLSB* 638, *Money Disbursements of Wage Earners and Clerical Workers, 1934–1936, Summary Volume* (Washington, D.C.: GPO, 1941), 1, 8; *BLSB* 637, *Money Disbursements of Wage Earners and Clerical Workers in the North Atlantic Region, 1934–36,* vol. 1 (Washington, DC: GPO, 1939), 71; *BLSB* 637, vol. 2: 93.

63 Catherine S, 105, SB32.

64 Theresa B, 737, SB32; South Bend *City Directories* (1930–1932). The directories contain many errors and sometimes contradict interviews.

65 Anna H, 1027, SB32.

66 *Sixteenth Census: Housing*, vol. 2, *General Characteristics*, pt. 2, *Iowa–Montana*, 907, 926, 929–930. South Bend homeownership fell from 59.6% to 53.1% over the decade. The low rate of foreclosure in St. Joseph County was affected by the use of land contracts. "Summary, Survey of South Bend and Mishawaka, Indiana, Field Report," July 24, 1937, 2–3, Records Relating to the City Survey File, 1935–1940, FHLBB, HOLC, RG 195.

67 Roland S. Vaile and Helen G. Canoyer, *Income and Consumption* (New York: Henry Holt, 1938), 213. Economists did not employ the language of class, but prescribed expenditures at "subsistence" and "minimum comfort" standards of living.

68 Less than one-fourth (22.3%) of households spent an "appropriate" amount for housing; the remainder (28%) owned their homes outright.

69 Hazel L, 1020, SB32; South Bend *City Directories* (1930–1935).

70 Retta K, 311, SB32.

71 James N. Gregory, *The Southern Diaspora: How the Great Migrations of Black and White Southerners Transformed America* (Chapel Hill: University of North Carolina Press, 2005).

72 *WBB* 108, *Effects of the Depression*, 1–2; "No Schedules Taken," table, Survey Materials, *WBB* 108, RG 86. In 1932 diligent agents made multiple visits, queried neighbors, and consulted city directories to track down women whom they had interviewed two years earlier. Among 785 households with whom they were unable to obtain second interviews, they ascertained that 628 had moved, and they acquired some information for almost four hundred.

73 South Bend and Mishawaka, Indiana, Area Descriptions, Records Relating to the City Survey File, 1935–1940, FHLBB, HOLC, RG 195; Cohen, *Making a New Deal*, 276.

74 Ronald Tobey, Charles Wetherell, and Jay Brigham, "Moving Out and Settling In: Residential Mobility, Home Owning, and the Public Enframing of Citizenship, 1921–1950," *American Historical Review* 95, no. 5 (1990): 1413–1417; Richard Sterner, *The Negro's Share: A Study of Income, Consumption, Housing and Public Assistance* (New York: Harper and Brothers, 1943), 310–323; Richard Rothstein, *The Color of Law: A Forgotten History of How Our Government Segregated America* (New York: Liveright, 2017), 64.

75 Louise A. Tilly and Joan W. Scott, *Women, Work, and Family* (New York: Holt, Rinehart, and Winston, 1978).

76 One of the Hundreds, Cleveland, to Frances Perkins, July 28, 1935, RG 86.

77 Amy C, 403, SB32.

78 Katherine W, 566, SB32.

79 Anna F, 1075, SB32.

80 Leane Zugsmith, "Room in the World," in *Writing Red: An Anthology of American Women Writers, 1930–1940*, ed. Charlotte Nekola and Paula Rabinowitz (New York: Feminist Press, 1987), 46.

81 Louise Meriwether, *Daddy Was a Number Runner* (New York: Pyramid Books, 1970), 60–61.

82 Elizabeth Faue, *Community of Suffering and Struggle: Women, Men, and the Labor Movement in Minneapolis, 1915–1945* (Chapel Hill: University of North Carolina Press, 1991), 44, 67, 191.

83 Karen Brodkin Sacks, "Euro-Ethnic Working-Class Women's Community Culture." *Frontiers: A Journal of Women Studies* 14, no. 1 (1993): 1–23.

Chapter 5   Interrupted Expectations

1 Susan Porter Benson, *Household Accounts: Working-Class Family Economies in the Interwar United States* (Ithaca, NY: Cornell University Press, 2007), argues that men took a greater role in household labor than I have found to be the case.

2 Interviews contain less evidence from two-parent Black families than white. I read dozens of autobiographies, biographies, and fictionalized accounts that confirm similar breadth of experiences within Black and white family economies.

3 Helen M, 435, Cleveland.

4 *WBB* 139, *Women Unemployed*, 10.

5 Rose H, 477, SB32.

6 Constance Baker Motley, *Equal Justice under Law: An Autobiography* (New York: Farrar, Straus and Giroux, 1998), 30.

7 Evelyn D, 428, J43, Oakwood, Chicago37.

8 Anna A, 175, SB32; South Bend, IN, *City Directories* (Indianapolis: R. L. Polk and Co., 1930–1940).

9 Genevieve L, 1087, SB32.

10 Edna H, 538, SB32; South Bend *City Directories* (1930–1936). Robert began work in 1936.

11 Emma D, 665, SB32.

12 Anna G, 369, SB32.

13 Sophie E, 320, SB32. Sophie may have been asleep; the WB agent interviewed Walter.

14 Gary Gerstle, *American Crucible: Race and Nation in the Twentieth Century* (Princeton, NJ: Princeton University Press, 2001), 177–178.

15 *WBB* 92, *Wage-Earning Women*, 54–57.

16 Doris L, 399, Cleveland.

17 Benson, *Household Accounts*.

18 In 1940, 15.2% of married women were in the labor force, an increase of 29.9% over the decade.

19 The Sixteenth Census (1940) census did not link marital status, race, and age of employed women, limiting full comparisons across the decade.

20 Winifred Wandersee Bolin, "The Economics of Middle-Income Family Life: Working Women during the Great Depression," *Journal of American History* 65, no. 1 (1978): 60–74; Winifred D. Wandersee, *Women's Work and Family Values, 1920–1940* (Cambridge, MA: Harvard University Press, 1981).

21 *WBB* 108, *Effects of the Depression*, 4, 16–31.

22 Julia K, 330, Cleveland.

23 Ruth K, 351, Cleveland.

24 *Sixteenth Census: Population*, vol. 2, *Characteristics of the Population*, pt. 2, *Florida–Iowa*, 641, 822; *Sixteenth Census: Population*, vol. 2, *Characteristics of the Population*, pt. 5, *New York–Oregon*, 711; *Sixteenth Census: Population*, vol. 2, *Characteristics of the Population*, pt. 6, *Pennsylvania–Texas*, 212.

25 Samuel A. Stouffer and Lyle M. Spencer, "Marriage and Divorce in Recent Years," *Annals of the American Academy of Political and Social Science*, no. 188 (1936): 56–59, 63; BC, *Historical Statistics of the United States, Colonial Times to 1970*, Bicentennial ed. (Washington, DC: GPO, 1975), pt. 1, 64. Rural marriage rates remained higher, so national figures underestimate decline in urban marriages.

26 Sophia P, Clementine S, 176, SB32.

27 Calculated from *Historical Statistics*, pt. 1, 49.

28 George W. Kosmak, "Pathological Aspects of Reproduction," *Annals of the American Academy of Political and Social Science*, no. 188 (1936): 81.

29 Norman E. Himes, *Medical History of Contraception* (Baltimore: Williams and Wilkins, 1936), 336–345, 386; Linda Gordon, *Woman's Body, Woman's Right: A Social History of Birth Control in America* (New York: Penguin Books, 1977), 312, 317; Jessie M. Rodrique, "The Black Community and the Birth-Control Movement," in *Unequal Sisters: A Multicultural Reader in U.S. Women's History*, ed. Ellen Carol DuBois and Vicki L. Ruiz (New York: Routledge, 1990), 333–344.

30 Himes, *Medical History*, 374; Kosmak, "Pathological Aspects," 80.

31 Lorena Hickok, *One Third of a Nation: Lorena Hickok Reports on the Great Depression*, ed. Richard Lowitt and Maurine Beasley (Urbana: University of Illinois Press, 1981), xii, 324–325.

32 Anna P, 476, K28, Union Park, Chicago37. Anna's case histories at Cook County Hospital, the CRA, and the SBW were part of her relief record. Unmarried mothers were often castigated as "feebleminded." Linda Gordon, *Pitied but Not Entitled: Single Mothers and the History of Welfare* (New York: Free Press, 1994), 28, 323n61.

33 South Bend Association of Commerce, "Six Years in South Bend," in "Summary, Survey of South Bend and Mishawaka, Indiana, Field Report," July 24, 1937, Records Relating to the City Survey File, 1935–1940, Records of the Federal Home Loan Bank Board, Home Owners Loan Corporation, RG 195.

34 In informal conversations about the 1930s, elders made such comments as, "Everyone could tell you where there was someone who would perform an abortion."

35 Dorothy C, 931, SB32.

36 Maya Angelou, *I Know Why the Caged Bird Sings* (New York: Random House, 1970), 4.

37 Matilda C, 96, Cleveland.

38 Christine B, 32, Chicago33.

39 Beatrice T, 661, Cleveland.

40 Doris K, 309, Cleveland; Retta K, 311, Cleveland.

41 Beatrice B, 556, L53, Washington Park, Chicago37.

42 Odelia V, 508, SB32.

43 Among seventy to seventy-four-year-olds, 23.5% of Black women, but 7.1% of native-born white and 5.6% of immigrant white women, held jobs in 1929. *Fifteenth Census: Population*, vol. 5, *General Report on Occupations*, 117. The Sixteenth Census did not specify age groups beyond fifty-five.

44 Gertrude K, 1087, SB32; South Bend *City Directories* (1930–1940).

45 In the South Bend sample, twenty-six daughters' families and eleven sons' families lived with parents.

46 Mary H, Virginia M, 327, SB32.

47 Ruth H, 538, SB32.

48 Betty A, Anna M, Mary K, Cecilia A, 175, SB32; South Bend *City Directories* (1930–1940).

49 Charity D, 406, J21, Oakwood, Chicago37.

50 Marie S, 422, J37, Oakwood, Chicago37.

51 Karen Brodkin Sacks, "Euro-Ethnic Working-Class Women's Community Culture." *Frontiers: A Journal of Women Studies* 14, no. 1 (1993): 1–23; Benson, *Household Accounts*. Benson also utilized WB interviews, primarily from the 1920s. We have reached some of the same conclusions, but our differences reflect our foci. Her interest in cooperative working-class heterosexual marriages led her to particular interviews. My interest in comparisons across differences of race, age, and

marital and familial status likewise led to my selection of sources. Her book, completed as her health failed and after her death, does not mention how she selected or sampled interviews.

52 Josephine B, Irene B, 850, SB32; South Bend *City Directory* (1932).

53 Eleanor K, 313, Cleveland.

54 Irene N, 459, Cleveland.

55 Grace K, 42, Chicago33.

56 One of the Hundreds, Cleveland, to Frances Perkins, July 28, 1935, RG 86.

57 Margaret T, 663, Cleveland.

58 Nellie, 0446, Philadelphia.

59 Helen B, 0201, Philadelphia.

60 "Louise Meriwether," *Black Women in America: A Historical Encyclopedia*, ed. Darlene Clark Hine, 2 vols. (Brooklyn, NY: Carlson, 1993), 2:783–784.

61 Louise Meriwether, *Daddy Was a Number Runner* (New York: Pyramid Books, 1970), 29–30.

62 Meriwether, *Daddy*, 46–47.

63 Stouffer and Spencer, "Marriage and Divorce," 58; *Historical Statistics*, 64.

64 Mollie S, 374, I38, Northern, Chicago37.

65 Elizabeth H, 56, B20, Bridgeport, Chicago37.

66 Mary B, 430, J45, Oakwood, Chicago37.

67 Gertrude W, 474, K26, Union Park, Chicago37.

68 Betty B, 78, C4, Canal, Chicago37.

69 Susie T, 520, L17, Washington Park, Chicago37.

70 Alberta C, 46, B10, Bridgeport, Chicago37.

71 Emma F, 236, Chicago33.

72 Irene G, 417, SB32.

73 Vera N, 596, SB32.

74 Leona C, 1110, SB32; Necrology File, Local Family and History Services, St. Joseph County Public Library.

75 Betty G, 943, SB32.

76 Esther B, 612, SB32.

77 Helen D, 1043, SB32.

78 Mary T, 243, SB32.

79 Richard Wright, *American Hunger* (New York: Harper and Row, 1977), 64.

Chapter 6   Outside the Family Economy

1 Figures are calculated from BC, *Sixteenth Census: Population*, vol. 4, *Characteristics by Age*, pt. 1, *United States Summary*, 26, 169–170, 177. In Chicago and Philadelphia, 10% of the female population headed households (including women living alone). Nationwide in urban areas, 15% of women of color were household heads. The proportion of female household heads was actually significantly higher because a tiny number of girls lived outside families. Joanne J. Meyerowitz, *Women Adrift: Independent Wage Earners in Chicago, 1880–1930* (Chicago: University of Chicago Press, 1988).

2 Figures are calculated from *WBB* 158, *Unattached Women on Relief in Chicago, 1937*, 4, 6, 20. The 1937 Chicago sample provides much of the evidence in this chapter. Government assistance imposed obligations but did not define women. These women represent the broad spectrum of working-class women living on their own.

3 The quote in this section's title comes from the interview with Mildred D, 158, D11, Chase Park, Chicago37.

4 Lucille P, 192, D45, Chase Park, Chicago37.

5 Catherine T, 378, I42, Northern, Chicago37.

6 Mary P, 98, C24, Canal, Chicago37.

7 Daniel Patrick Moynihan, *The Negro Family: A Case for National Action* (Washington, DC: Office of Policy Planning and Research, U.S. Department of Labor, 1965).

8 Darlene Clark Hine, "Rape and the Inner Lives of Black Women in the Middle West: Preliminary Thoughts on the Culture of Dissemblance," *Signs* 14, no. 4 (1989): 912–920.

9 Emma S, 134, E24, Halsted, Chicago37.

10 Carrie D, 148, Cleveland.

11 St. Clair Drake and Horace Cayton, *Black Metropolis: A Study of Negro Life in a Northern City*, 2 vols., rev. and enlarged ed. (New York: Harcourt, Brace, and World, 1970), 2:576.

12 Figures are calculated from Joint Committee on Research of the Community Council of Philadelphia and the Pennsylvania School of Social Work, *Women without Work: A Study of 1654 Unemployed Destitute Women Living Alone in Philadelphia* (Philadelphia: Joint Committee on Research of the Community Council of Philadelphia and the Pennsylvania School of Social Work, 1934) 26.

13 Drake and Cayton, *Black Metropolis*, 2:576.

14 Gertrude B, 392, J7, Oakwood, Chicago37.

15 Dora M, 372, I36, Northern, Chicago37.

16 Maud J, 0365, Chicago33.

17 Pearl M, 144, E34, Halsted, Chicago37.

18 Nan Cinnater, "Women Hoboes of the Great Depression: Survival in Hard Times," paper presented at the Sixth Berkshire Conference on the History of Women, Smith College, June 1984; Thomas Minehan, *Boy and Girl Tramps of America* (New York: Grosset and Dunlap, 1934).

19 Christine K, 244, F35, Irving Park, Chicago37; Margaret B, 218, F 9, Irving Park, Chicago37.

20 Mollie B, 154, D7, Chase Park, Chicago37.

21 Mamie G, 568, M11, Woodlawn, Chicago37.

22 Tillie H, 242, F33, Irving Park, Chicago37.

23 Lena J, 512, L9, Washington Park, Chicago37.

24 Alvina K, 166, D19, Chase Park, Chicago37.

25 Bessie E, 18, A12, Archer, Chicago37.

26 Julia L, 264, G18, Lawndale, Chicago37.

27 Meridel LeSueur, *Women on the Breadlines* (Minneapolis: West End, 1984). Meridel LeSueur, *The Girl* (Cambridge, MA: West End, 1978), 137–140, describes an abandoned warehouse in St. Paul where dozens of women lived.

28 Dora M, 372, I36, Northern, Chicago37.

29 Almost half the Chicago population lived in multiunit dwellings. Homeownership was far less common there than in South Bend. *Fifteenth Census: Population*, vol. 6, *Families*, 354, 365.

30 Celia B, 152, D5, Chase Park, Chicago37.

31 Amanda T, 426, J41, Oakwood, Chicago37.

32 Cecile Hillyer, Chicago, to Harriet Byrne, September 4, 1937, Correspondence Files, *WBB* 158, RG 86.

33 *WBB* 158, *Unattached Women*, 9. A few women received extra cash for special diets prescribed by doctors. Some received fuel or utilities allowances, but no rent money, or less than $12 for rent.

34 Laura G, 162, D15, Chase Park, Chicago37.

35 *WBB* 158, *Unattached Women*, 13.

36 Gertrude B, 392, J7, Oakwood, Chicago37.

37 Catherine T, 378, I42, Northern, Chicago37.

38 *WBB* 158, *Unattached Women*, 82.

39 Dora M, 372, I36, Northern, Chicago37.

40 *WBB* 158, *Unattached Women*, 72, 74.

41 Nellie B, 114, E4, Halsted, Chicago37.

42 *WBB* 158, *Unattached Women*, 4, 6, 8, 20, 51–56, 67–68.

43 Figures calculated from *WBB* 158, *Unattached Women*, 22.

44 Annabelle S, 731, Chicago33.

45 In the Philadelphia sample, almost as many women (39.4%) lived with friends, landladies, or roomers as lived alone (41.3%). Only 12.3% lived with relatives. One-third received help from friends and neighbors and one-fifth from kin. In the 1933 Chicago sample, three times as many women mentioned friends' and land-ladies' help as family members.

46 *Fifteenth Census: Population*, vol. 6: 67; *Sixteenth Census: Population*, vol. 4, *Characteristics by Age*, pt. 2, *Alabama–Louisiana*: 624.

47 Anna M, 564, Chicago33.

48 Cecile Hillyer to Harriet Byrne, September 29, 1937, Correspondence, *WBB* 158, RG 86.

49 Grace S, 617, Cleveland; Margaret T, 663, Cleveland.

50 Helen B, 201, Philadelphia.

51 Mandolyn B, 296, J11, Oakwood, Chicago37.

52 Anna R, 492, K44, Union Park, Chicago37; Victoria S, 582, M25, Woodlawn, Chicago37.

53 Histories of working-class lesbians pay little attention to jobs, living arrangements, or familial relations. Lillian Faderman, *Odd Girls and Twilight Lovers: A History of Lesbian Life in 20th-Century America* (New York: Penguin, 1992), 79–81, 93–117; Elizabeth Lapovsky Kennedy and Madeline D. Davis, *Boots of Leather, Slippers of Gold: The History of a Lesbian Community* (New York: Routledge, 1993) 32–38; Box-Car Bertha [Thomson] with Ben L. Reitman, *Sister of the Road: The Autobiography of Box-Car Bertha*, as told to Dr. Ben L. Reitman (New York: Harper and Row, 1937, reprinted 1975); Meyerowitz, *Women Adrift*, 95–96, 113–114; Drake and Cayton, *Black Metropolis*, 2:573; George Chauncey, *Gay New York: Gender, Urban Culture, and the Making of the Gay Male World, 1890–1940* (New York: Basic Books, 1994); Susan K. Cahn, *Coming on Strong: Gender and Sexuality in Women's Sport* (Cambridge, MA: Harvard University Press, 1995).

54 Evelyn D, 428, J43, Oakwood, Chicago37.

55 Lottie G, 86, C12, Canal, Chicago37.

56 Marie M, 940, Chicago33.

57 Gertrude A, 148, D1, Chase Park, Chicago37. The agent commented that Gertrude had taken in the Mexican family "to avoid having to become a lonely rooming-house specimen." Gertrude noted that the couple were "very nice" to her and called a doctor when an injection for varicose veins infected her leg.

58 Bessie W, 260, G14, Lawndale, Chicago37.

59 Mary C, 206, D59, Chase Park, Chicago37.

60 Sarah G, J27, Oakwood, 412, Chicago37.
61 Darlene Clark Hine, "Rape and the Inner Lives of Black Women in the Middle West: Preliminary Thoughts on the Culture of Dissemblance," *Signs: Journal of Women in Culture and Society* 14, no. 4 (1989): 912–920; Kali N. Gross, *Colored Amazons: Crime, Violence, and Black Women in the City of Brotherly Love, 1880–1910* (Durham, NC: Duke University Press, 2006), 76; Sarah Haley, *No Mercy Here: Gender, Punishment, and the Making of Jim Crow Modernity* (Chapel Hill: University of North Carolina Press, 2016).
62 Kimberly Phillips, *AlabamaNorth: African-American Migrants, Community, and Working-Class Activism in Cleveland, 1915–1945* (Urbana: University of Illinois Press, 1999).

Chapter 7 Relief

1 Josephine Chapin Brown, *Public Relief, 1929–1939* (New York: Henry Holt, 1940), 21 (and see 3–59); Howard W. Odum, "Public Welfare Activities," in President's Research Committee on Social Trends, *Recent Social Trends in the United States: Report of the President's Research Committee on Social Trends*, 2 vols. (New York: McGraw-Hill, 1933), 2:1265; Carroll H. Woody, "The Growth of Governmental Functions," *Recent Social Trends*, 1283–1284, 1306, 1326.
2 Sydnor H. Walker, "Privately Supported Social Work," in President's Research Committee, *Recent Social Trends*, 2:1188; Karen W. Tice, *Tales of Wayward Girls and Immoral Women: Case Records and the Professionalization of Social Work* (Urbana: University of Illinois Press, 1998).
3 Leyton E. Carter, ed., *The Cleveland Year Book, 1930* (Cleveland: Cleveland Foundation, 1931), 147–174; Lucia Johnson Bing, *Social Work in Greater Cleveland* (Cleveland: Welfare Federation of Cleveland, 1938), 249–250.
4 Jack J. Detzler, *South Bend, 1920–1930: The Emergence of a City* (South Bend, IN: Northern Indiana Historical Society, 1960), 51–53; Clippings Files: Charities, Local Family and History Services (hereafter LFHS), St. Joseph County Public Library (hereafter SJCPL).
5 Mimi Abramovitz, *Regulating the Lives of Women: Social Welfare Policy from Colonial Times to the Present* (Boston: South End, 1988); Linda Gordon, ed., *Women, the State, and Welfare* (Madison: University of Wisconsin Press, 1990); Linda Gordon, *Pitied but Not Entitled: Single Mothers and the History of Welfare* (New York: Free Press, 1994). Not all social workers fit these stereotypes, and there was a radical social work movement during the 1930s. See Judith Ann Trolander, *Settlement Houses and the Great Depression* (Detroit: Wayne State University Press, 1975); Elizabeth Lasch-Quinn, *Black Neighbors: Race and the Limits of Reform in the American Settlement House Movement, 1890–1945* (Chapel Hill: University of North Carolina Press, 1993); and Tice, *Tales of Wayward Girls*, 1–16, 222n9.
6 Winifred Bell, *Aid to Dependent Children* (New York: Columbia University Press, 1965), 16.
7 Abramovitz, *Regulating the Lives of Women*, 190–206; Grace Abbott, *The Child and the State*, 2 vols. (Chicago: University of Chicago Press, 1938), 2:239; *Children's Bureau Publication* (hereafter *CBP*) 220, *Mothers' Aid, 1931* (Washington, DC: GPO, 1933), 18, 28–29; Gordon, *Pitied but Not Entitled*.
8 Barbara Nelson, "The Origins of the Two-Channel Welfare State: Workmen's Compensation and Mothers' Aid," 123–151, in Gordon, Linda, ed. *Women, the State, and Welfare* (Madison: University of Wisconsin Press, 1990), 123–151.

9 Tice, *Tales of Wayward Girls*, 23.

10 *CBP* 237, *Trends in Different Types of Public and Private Relief in Urban Areas, 1929–35* (Washington, DC: GPO, 1937), 104–106.

11 *CBP* 184, *Administration of Mothers' Aid in Ten Localities with Special Reference to Health, Housing, Education, and Recreation* (Washington, DC: GPO, 1928), 70–75.

12 *Fifteenth Census: Manufactures, 1929*, vol. 2, *Reports by Industries; 15th Census, Population*, vol. 2:1005; *Fifteenth Census: Population*, vol. 4, *Occupations, by States*, 510; *Fifteenth Census: Population*, vol. 6, *Families*, 5–6, 9, 408.

13 Linda Gordon, *Heroes of their Own Lives: The Politics and History of Family Violence* (New York: Viking, 1988), 280; Beverly Stadum, *Poor Women and Their Families: Hard Working Charity Cases, 1900–1930* (Albany: State University of New York Press, 1992).

14 Anne Meis Knupfer, *The Chicago Black Renaissance and Women's Activism* (Urbana: University of Illinois Press, 2006), 93–97; Marcia Chatelaine, *South Side Girls: Growing Up in the Great Migration* (Durham, NC: Duke University Press, 2015).

15 James Grossman, *Land of Hope: Chicago, Black Southerners, and the Great Migration* (Chicago: University of Chicago Press, 1989), 140–143, 170–174; Joanne L. Goodwin, *Gender and the Politics of Welfare Reform: Mothers' Pensions in Chicago, 1911–1929* (Chicago: University of Chicago Press, 1997), 67–68, 222n25; Trolander, *Settlement Houses*, 134–147; Lasch-Quinn, *Black Neighbors*.

16 *Goniec Polski*, January 9, 1932; *Goniec Polski*, February 10, 1932; *Goniec Polski*, March 22, 1933.

17 Donald Stabrowski, *Holy Cross and the South Bend Polonia* (Notre Dame, IN: Indiana Province Archives Center, 1991), 44–60; Frank Anthony Renkiewicz, "The Polish Settlement of St. Joseph County, Indiana: 1855–1935" (PhD diss., University of Notre Dame, 1967).

18 *Goniec Polski*, March 16, 1932; *Goniec Polski*, March 11, 1933.

19 First and Ninth Annual Reports, Hering House Scrapbook, History Museum (hereafter HM); *South Bend News-Times*, December 3, 1931.

20 Christopher G. Wye, "The New Deal and the Negro Community: Toward a Broader Conceptualization," *Journal of American History* 59, no. 3 (1972): 631–633; Bing, *Social Work in Greater Cleveland*, 134, 163, 169.

21 Knupfer, *Chicago Black Renaissance*, 97–101.

22 St. Clair Drake and Horace Cayton, *Black Metropolis: A Study of Negro Life in a Northern City*, 2 vols., rev. and enlarged ed. (New York: Harcourt, Brace, and World, 1970), 2:418–421.

23 Lottie G, C12, Canal, 86, Chicago37.

24 *South Bend Tribune*, August 31, 1931.

25 *South Bend News-Times*, June 30, 1933. Figures are calculated from *Fifteenth Census: Population*, vol. 6:56.

26 Rose B, 594, SB32.

27 Mary P, 1018, SB32.

28 Mary A, 185, SB32.

29 *South Bend Tribune*, April 23, 1931; *South Bend News-Times*, April 22, 1932; Theresa M, 129, SB32.

30 Carter, *The Cleveland Year Book, 1930*, 147–174; Raymond F. Clapp, "A Decade of Social Work in Cleveland," *Social Service Review* 9, no. 1 (1935): 58–67; Joanna C. Colcord, with William C. Koplovitz and Russell H. Kurtz, *Emergency Work Relief as Carried Out in Twenty-Six American Communities, 1930–1931, with Suggestions for Setting Up a Program* (New York: Russell Sage Foundation, 1932), 80–84.

31 Carter, *The Cleveland Year Book, 1930*, 30, 147–174; Clapp, "A Decade of Social Work"; Colcord, Koplovitz, and Kurtz, *Emergency Work Relief*, 80–84.

32 Carter, *The Cleveland Year Book, 1930*, 159.

33 *Fifteenth Census: Population*, vol. 6:1012.

34 Howard Whipple Green, *Nine Years of Relief: Greater Cleveland, 1928–1937* (Cleveland: Cleveland Health Council, 1938); Howard Whipple Green, *Two Hundred Millions for Relief in Cleveland, 1928–1938* (Cleveland: Cleveland Health Council, 1938).

35 Figures are calculated from Green, *Two Hundred Millions*, 2.

36 *South Bend Tribune*, September 14, 1932.

37 Dorothy C, 931, SB32.

38 Mrs. L. P, 642, SB32.

39 *South Bend News-Times*, September 5, 1931; *South Bend News-Times*, September 8, 1931; *South Bend News-Times*, October 29, 1931; *South Bend Tribune*, November 2, 1931.

40 *South Bend News-Times*, December 31, 1931, *South Bend News-Times*, January 8, 1932; *South Bend Tribune*, February 6, 1932.

41 Clippings Files, Charities: City Rescue Mission, Committee of 100, Federation for Social Service, Relief, Social Service Exchange, LFHS, SJCPL.

42 *Studebaker Accelerator* 4, no. 14 (July 29, 1931); *Studebaker Accelerator* 5, no. 7 (April 13, 1932); *Studebaker Accelerator* 5, no. 13 (October 26, 1932); *South Bend Tribune*, 25 April 1932.

43 Helen S, 802, SB32.

44 *CBP* 237, *Trends in Different Types*, 104, 97, 114. Figures are calculated from *Fifteenth Census: Population*, vol. 6: 56.

45 *CBP* 237, *Trends in Different Types*, 74, 80, 82.

46 WB social scientists and University of Pennsylvania School of Social Work faculty did recognize their existence. See *WBB* 139, *Women Unemployed*. Chicago, which had the most social services for unattached women, was, not incidentally, home of a renowned school of social work led by unmarried women. Not necessarily unattached, some had lesbian partnerships.

47 *WBB* 139, 13; "Lodging, Food, and Cash Grants Extended through the Friendly Service Bureau of the YWCA, Cleveland, Ohio," Survey Materials, *WBB* 139, RG 86; Kay R, 534, Cleveland; Fame S, 594, Cleveland.

48 Minutes of the Board of Trustees, Phillis Wheatley Association, June 14, 1932 and December 13, 1932; Service Reports to the Welfare Federation, Series 1, Western Reserve Historical Society; Jane Edna Hunter, *A Nickel and a Prayer* (Cleveland: Elli Kani, 1940), 154–165.

49 Mrs. Ann Brown, Cleveland, to Mrs. Franklin D. Roosevelt, n.d. [1933], RG 9.

50 *WBB* 139, *Women Unemployed*, 3; Joint Committee on Research, *Women without Work*, 5; Roger D. Simon, "Great Depression," in *The Encyclopedia of Greater Philadelphia*, n.d., http://philadelphiaencyclopedia.org/archive/great-depression/.

51 "Memorandum for Miss Peterson, Chicago, January 6, 1934," Correspondence, *WBB* 139, RG 86.

52 Shelters housed transient and homeless men, who were not judged incompetent.

53 "Memorandum: A Summary of the Number of Unattached Women Applying for Relief and the Method and Facilities Available for Their Assistance at the SBW in Chicago," Survey Materials, *WBB* 139, RG 86.

54 *WBB* 139, *Women Unemployed*, 9.

55 Box-Car Bertha [Thompson] as told to Dr. Ben L. Reitman, *Sister of the Road: The Autobiography of Box-Car Bertha* (1935; reprinted New York: Harper and Row, 1975), 243.

56 "General Statement, Governing Amount of Relief," and "Memorandum: A Summary of the Number," Survey Materials, *WBB* 139, RG 86; *WBB* 139, *Women Unemployed*, 9.

57 Anna K, 196, SB32. Among two dozen female-headed families with school-age children in the South Bend sample, only Anna K received a mother's pension.

58 Anna E, 150, Cleveland.

59 *CBP* 237, *Trends in Different Types*, 104–106.

60 *CBP* 237, *Trends in Different Types*, 74–85. Private expenditures peaked in 1931 or 1932.

61 Linda Gordon, "Social Insurance and Public Assistance: The Influence of Gender in Welfare Thought in the United States, 1890–1935," *American Historical Review* 97, no. 1 (1992): 19–54.

62 Nancy E. Rose, *Workfare or Fair Work: Women, Welfare, and Government Work Programs* (New Brunswick, NJ: Rutgers University Press, 1995).

63 "Just a bunch of ambitious jobless girls," New Jersey, to Frances Perkins, November 16, 1933, RG 86.

64 Donald S. Howard, *The WPA and Federal Relief Policy* (New York: Russell Sage Foundation, 1943), 278–285; Susan Ware, *Holding Their Own: American Women in the 1930s* (Boston: Twayne, 1982), 39–41; Lois Scharf, *To Work and to Wed: Female Employment, Feminism, and the Great Depression* (Westport, CT.: Greenwood, 1980), 122; Susan Ware, *Beyond Suffrage: Women in the New Deal* (Cambridge, MA: Harvard University Press, 1981), 111–114.

65 Howard, *The WPA and Federal Relief Policy*, 278–285; Ware, *Holding Their Own*, 39–41; Nancy E. Rose, *Put to Work: Relief Programs in the Great Depression* (New York: Monthly Review Press, 1994). A peak of 405,700 women was on WPA payrolls in 1938.

66 Ware, *Beyond Suffrage*, 109.

67 Howard, *The WPA and Federal Relief Policy*, 128, 241; Ware, *Holding Their Own*, 40.

68 Alberta C, 46, B10, Bridgeport, Chicago37.

69 Frances B, 562, M5, Woodlawn, Chicago37.

70 Howard, *The WPA and Federal Relief Policy*, 280–285.

71 Federal Works Agency, *Final Report on the WPA Program, 1935–1943* (Washington, D.C.: GPO, 1946), 44–45, cited in Abramovitz, *Regulating the Lives of Women*, 283.

72 Howard, *The WPA and Federal Relief Policy*, 278–296, 341.

73 Drake and Cayton, *Black Metropolis*, 2:386.

74 *WBB* 158, *Unattached Women*, 72; Cecile Hillyer, Chicago, to Harriet Byrne, September 29, 1937, Correspondence, *WBB* 158, RG 86.

75 *WBB* 158, *Unattached Women*, 3.

76 Single men received less money for rent and clothing and more for food. CRA "Monthly Budget Allowances," Survey Materials, *WBB* 158, RG 86.

77 Cecile Hillyer, Chicago, to Harriet Byrne, September 26, 1937, Correspondence, *WBB* 158, RG 86.

78 *WBB* 158, *Unattached Women*, 2. Figures are calculated from *Fifteenth Census: Population*, vol. 3, *Reports by the States*, pt. 1, *Alabama–Missouri*, 64.

79 *WBB* 158, *Unattached Women*, 66; figures are calculated from *WBB* 158, *Unattached Women*, 22.

80 Old Age Assistance and Aid to the Blind, other provisions of the Social Security Act, granted higher benefits and a higher rate of federal reimbursement.

81 Federal Security Agency, *Fourth Annual Report of the Social Security Board, 1939* (Washington, DC: GPO, 1940), 95–99; Abramovitz, *Regulating the Lives of Women*, 313–319.

82 Mary Poole, *The Segregated Origins of Social Security: African Americans and the Welfare State* (Chapel Hill: University of North Carolina Press, 2006).

83 Abramovitz, *Regulating the Lives of Women*, 241–271.

84 Hering House, Twelfth, Thirteenth, and Fourteenth Annual Reports and Anniversary Programs, Hering House Scrapbook, HM.

85 Welfare recipients and feminist scholars have noted parallels between satisfying the demands of one man and "the man." Rochelle Lefkowitz and Ann Withorn, eds., *For Crying Out Loud: Women and Poverty in the United States* (New York: Pilgrim, 1986).

86 Elizabeth K, 433, Chicago33; "Municipal Departments of Public Welfare," *Social Service Review* 6, no. 3 (1932): 510–511; Frank C. Glick, "The Illinois Emergency Relief Commission," *Social Service Review* 7, no. 1 (1933): 23.

87 Sarah H, 356, Chicago33.

88 Emma S, 760, Chicago33.

89 Alice M, 990, Philadelphia.

90 Carter, *The Cleveland Year Book 1930*, 172–173.

91 Margaret Z, 1555, Philadelphia.

92 Amelia B, 72, Chicago33.

93 Colcord, Koplovitz, and Kurtz, *Emergency Work Relief*, 168.

94 Catherine B, 282, H6, Lower North, Chicago37.

95 Helen R. Jeter, "Salaries and Professional Education of Social Workers in Family Welfare and Relief Agencies in Chicago," *Social Service Review* 7, no. 2 (1933): 225–253.

96 Mattie A, 386, J1, Oakwood, Chicago37.

97 Marjorie O. Johnson, Chicago, to Miss Byrne, July 28, 1938, Correspondence, *WBB* 158, RG 86. Johnson, a graduate student, worked on the 1937 survey.

98 "Memorandum for Miss Peterson, from Mrs. Koletta's remarks," January 6, 1934, Chicago33 Correspondence, *WBB* 139, R86.

99 "Memorandum: A Summary of the Number of Unattached Women," 14, Survey Materials, *WBB* 139, RG86.

100 Rotman was affiliated with Hobo College, a self-organized workers' school in Chicago.

101 Joint Committee on Research, *Women without Work*, 40.

102 Marion N, 596, M39, Woodlawn, Chicago37.

103 Mattie N, 60, B24, Bridgeport, Chicago37.

104 Annie G, 52, B16, Bridgeport, Chicago37.

105 Edith C, 402, J17, Oakwood, Chicago37.

106 Mary C, 206, D59, Chase Park, Chicago37.

107 Stadum, *Poor Women*, 131.

108 Justine K, 346, Cleveland.

109 Marie W, 190, SB32.

110 Mary K, 1011, SB32.

111 Bessie W, 876, Chicago33.

112 Julia T, 675, Cleveland

113 Florence McLane, Flushing, NY, to Frances Perkins, May 17, 1934, RG 86.

114 Anna C, 114, Cleveland.

115 Anna D, 350, Philadelphia.

116 Jennie D, 411, Philadelphia; Virginia B, 90, Philadelphia; Nellie E, 446, Philadelphia; Mae W, 888, Chicago33.

117 Mary M, 592, Chicago33.

118 Lillian C, 116, Chicago33.

119 Clara R, 668, Chicago33.

120 Despairing 14, Chicago, to Frances Perkins, n.d. [received January 27, 1934], RG 86.

121 Sarah B, 92, Chicago33.

122 Lorraine G, 260, Chicago33.

123 Box-Car Bertha, *Sister of the Road*, 134–135.

124 Millie M, 354, I18, Northern, Chicago37.

125 Mary B, K18, 466, Union Park, Chicago37.

126 Madge R, D55, 202, Chase Park, Chicago37.

127 Linda Gordon, "Family Violence, Feminism, and Social Control," in Gordon, ed., *Women, the State, and Welfare*, 189.

128 *WBB* 139, *Women Unemployed*, 4, 17; Joint Committee on Research, *Women without Work*, 15, 22.

129 *WBB* 158, *Unattached Women*, 2, 9.

Conclusion

1 Arleathie B, 390, J5, Oakwood, Chicago37.

2 Paul Dixon and Thomas B. Allen, *The Bonus Army: An American Epic* (New York: Walker, 2004); Annelise Orleck, "'We Are That Mythical Thing Called the Public': Militant Housewives during the Great Depression," *Feminist Studies* 19, no. 1 (1993): 147–172; Darlene Clark Hine and Kathleen Thompson, *A Shining Thread of Hope: The History of Black Women in America* (New York: Broadway Books, 1998), 245–247; Vicki L. Ruiz, *Cannery Women, Cannery Lives: Mexican Women, Unionization, and the California Food Processing Industry, 1930–1950* (Albuquerque: University of New Mexico Press, 1987); Sharon Hartman Strom, "'We're No Kitty Foyles': Organizing Office Workers for the Congress of Industrial Organizations, 1937–1950," in *Women, Work, and Protest: A Century of U.S. Women's Labor History*, ed. Ruth Milkman (Boston: Routledge and Kegan Paul, 1985), 206–234; Nancy F. Gabin, *Feminism in the Labor Movement: Women and the United Auto Workers, 1935–1975* (Ithaca, NY: Cornell University Press, 1990); Roy Rosenzweig, "Organizing the Unemployed: The Early Years of the Great Depression, 1929–1933," *Radical America*, no. 10 (1976): 170–171. Randi Storch, *Red Chicago: American Communism at Its Grassroots, 1928–35* (Urbana: University of Illinois Press, 2007), includes multiple activist concerns.

3 Rose L, 598, SB32.

4 Alice K, 1100, SB32.

5 Lizabeth Cohen, *Making a New Deal: Industrial Workers in Chicago, 1919–1939* (Cambridge: Cambridge University Press, 1990).

6 Bessie B, 690, SB32.

7 Julia K, 593, SB32.

8 Helen S, 802, SB32.

9 Leah C, 610, SB32.

10 *Studebaker Accelerator,* 5, no. 8 (May 25, 1932).

11 Elizabeth M, 1007, SB32.

12 *South Bend Tribune,* January 23, 1933.

13 *South Bend News-Times,* February 7, 1933; *South Bend News-Times,* February 8, 1933; *South Bend Tribune,* February 7, 1933; *South Bend Tribune,* February 8, 1933; *South Bend Tribune,* June 12, 1933; Mary Frederickson, "Citizens for Democracy: The Industrial Programs of the YWCA," in *Sisterhood and Solidarity: Workers'*

Education for Women, 1914–1984, ed. Joyce L. Kornbluh and Mary Frederickson (Philadelphia: Temple University Press, 1984), 75–106; Marion W. Roydhouse, "Partners in Progress: The Affiliated Schools for Women Workers, 1928–1939," in Kornbluh and Frederickson, *Sisterhood and Solidarity*, 187–221.

14 Mary T, 243, SB32; *Studebaker Accelerator*, 4, no. 18 (September 23, 1931). Someone at the WB erased two paragraphs from their interview record, following notes on the Unemployed Council. I have used their full names because they were publicly visible.

15 *South Bend News-Times*, April 7, 1933; "Reasons Why You Should Vote Communist: Election Platform of the Communist Party, SB, Indiana," Clippings file: Political Parties, Communist Party, Local Family and History Services (hereafter LFHS), St. Joseph County Public Library (hereafter SJCPL).

16 "Mass Protest Meeting," flyer, courtesy of Keith Knauss, Division of Labor Studies, Indiana University–South Bend (hereafter IUSB).

17 "Reasons Why You Should Vote Communist."

18 South Bend, IN, *City Directories* (Indianapolis, IN: R.L. Polk and Company, 1930–1940).

19 Miles W. Coiner, "Sit-Down '36" Indiana Labor History Project, IUSB, 1980; oral histories, Michiana Oral Labor History Project, Division of Labor Studies, IUSB.

20 J. D. "Red" Hill, *A Brief History of the Labor Movement of Studebaker Local No. 5, U.A.W.-C.I.O.* (South Bend, IN: Studebaker Local No. 5, Education and Publicity Committee, 1953); Michael Beatty, Patrick Furlong, and Loren Pennington, *Studebaker: Less Than They Promised* (South Bend: and books, 1984), 15–20. Stephen Longstreet, *A Century on Wheels, the Story of Studebaker; a History, 1852–1952* (New York: Henry Holt & Co., 1952), 102–103. Bodnar, "Power and Memory in Oral History," 1201–1221. Neither Polish nor Hungarian names appear among officers of UAW Locals 5 or 9 or their women's auxiliaries in the 1930s. UAW Archives, Reuther Library Manuscripts, Wayne State University.

21 *Sew and Sew*, v. 1, # 3 (December, 1933), HM.

22 *Sew and Sew*, v. 1–2, HM; "Local Labor 1930–1945," courtesy of Keith Knauss, Division of Labor Studies, IUSB.

23 Michael J. Lawrence, *The History of Teamsters Local 364, 1933 through 1989, South Bend, Indiana* (South Bend, IN: Chauffeurs, Teamsters and Helpers Local Union no. 364, 1990), 5.

24 Hering House, renamed the Dunbar Community Center, affiliated with the Community Fund in 1934.

25 Eric S. Gellman, *Death Blow to Jim Crow: The National Negro Congress and the Rise of Militant Civil Rights* (Chapel Hill: University of North Carolina Press, 2012).

26 *South Bend News-Times*, June 14, 1937; Hering House Scrapbook, HM. Surviving records are inadequate to trace connections, if any, between Black male activists who participated in 1933 demonstrations and who ran for local office in 1934 and the youth activists of 1937.

27 Evelyn Louise Crawford and MaryLouise Patterson, eds., *Letters from Langston: From the Harlem Renaissance to the Red Scare and Beyond* (Oakland: University of California Press, 2016), 139.

28 *South Bend Tribune* May 7, 1938, Clippings File: Communist Party, LFHS, SJCPL.

29 Robin D. G. Kelley, *Hammer and Hoe: Alabama Communists during the Great Depression* (Chapel Hill: University of North Carolina Press, 1990).

30 *South Bend News-Times*, April 7, 1933.

31 Gary Gerstle, *American Crucible: Race and Nation in the Twentieth Century* (Princeton, NJ: Princeton University Press, 2001).

32 Harriet G, 452, K4, Union Park, Chicago37.

33 Harriet B, 026, Chicago33; Harriet B, 346, I10, Northern, Chicago37. Harriet appeared in both Chicago samples. A declassed woman, she received $30.12, far more than the maximum relief allotment, and lived in a four-room apartment with a cat and dog. Her daughter, who helped her financially but would not live with her, played in the Chicago Women's Symphony.

34 Mary B, 466, K18, Union Park, Chicago37; Alan Brinkley, *Voices of Protest: Huey Long, Father Coughlin, and the Great Depression* (New York: Random House, 1982).

35 Vera F, 179, Cleveland.

36 Mrs. Mary Royle, Jersey City, NJ, to FDR, February 9, 1933, RG 86.

37 Miss Lucy Shirrell to Frances Perkins, San Francisco, California, July 30, 1933, RG 86.

38 Mrs. Irene Pollard, Los Angeles, to Eleanor Roosevelt, September 1, 1933, RG 9.

39 Eva Grogan, Portland, OR, to FDR, n.d. [received November 7, 1933], RG 9.

40 Melvina Messer, San Francisco, to Women's Department of Labor, n.d. [received August 25, 1933], RG 86.

41 Josephine A. Morales, Secretary, Domestic Workers Association, El Paso, TX, to General Hugh S. Johnson, August 31, 1933, RG 9; Vicki L. Ruiz, "By the Day or Week: Mexicana Domestic Workers in El Paso," in *"To Toil the Livelong Day": America's Women at Work, 1780-1980*, ed. Carol Groneman and Mary Beth Norton (Ithaca, NY: Cornell University Press, 1987), 269–283.

42 Caroline M, 552, Chicago33.

43 Bridget M, 536, Chicago33.

44 Mrs. Lulu Lawson, Chicago, to Eleanor Roosevelt, August 1, 1933, RG 86.

45 Mrs. Susan Bartlett, Brockton, MA, to Eleanor Roosevelt, May 19, 1934, RG 9.

46 Mrs. Helen Mahon, Dayton, OH, to Miss Anderson, November 26, 1933, RG 86.

47 Anna Cox, Brooklyn, NY, to Frances Perkins, August 21, 1933, RG 86.

48 Miss Lucy Shirrell, San Francisco, to Frances Perkins, July 30, 1933, RG 86.

49 Mrs. L. F. Blanford, Chicago, to WB, November 19, 1933, RG 86.

50 Z. Elizabeth Moman, President, National Association for Domestic Workers, Jackson, MS, to friend, n.d. [1932–1936], RG 86.

51 Marie K. Adams, Wichita, KS, to Frances Perkins, July 5, 1934, RG 86.

52 Thoma Vass, North Plainfield, NJ, to Frances Perkins, August 5, 1933, RG 86; Magdalene Kammerer, Atlantic City, NJ, to Frances Perkins, October 8, 1933, RG 86.

53 Anna Filak, Cleveland, to Frances Perkins, February 17, 1934, RG 86.

54 Marie K. Adams, Wichita, KS, to Frances Perkins, July 5, 1934, RG 86.

55 Catherine Lake, Jeanette, PA, to Eleanor Roosevelt, April 24, 1935, RG 86.

56 Edna E. Bradford, Newport, KY, to Frances Perkins, June 23, 1933, RG 86.

57 B. Faust, Flushing, NY, to National Recovery Administration, December 26, 1933, RG 9.

58 Caroline Vikartofsky, Ironwood, MI, to Frances Perkins, January 3, 1934, RG 86.

59 "An intelligent woman worker," Los Angeles, to Frances Perkins, August 13, 1933, RG 86.

60 "A poor house keeper with nothing," n.p., to Marie Correl, n.d. [1933], RG 86.

61 Misses Helen and Betty Davis, Brooklyn, NY, to General Johnson, August 27, 1933, RG 9.

62 Mrs. O. Wihlborg, Jersey City, NJ, to Department of Labor, March 12, 1934, Jersey City, New Jersey, RG 86.

63 Florence McLane, Flushing, NY, to Frances Perkins, May 17, 1934, RG 86.

64 Frances M. Lidman, Hollywood, CA, to FDR, July 26, 1935, RG 86.
65 Miss Gladys Miller, Huntington, WV, to Frances Perkins, January 31, 1935.
66 Magdalene Kammerer, Atlantic City, NJ, to Frances Perkins, October 8, 1933, RG 86.
67 Catherine M. Bontje, Pasadena, CA, to His Honour President FDR, n.d. [received November 6, 1933], RG 9.
68 Eva Grogan, Portland, OR, to FDR, n.d. [received November 7, 1933], RG 9.
69 Leona Boulanger to Mr. Johnson, Rhinelander, Wisconsin, July 21, 1934, RG 9.
70 Anna Feldner, Orange, CA, to "Our dear Mother of this country!" August 24, 1933, RG 86.
71 May Donath, Bridgeport, CT, to Miss Perkins, February 17, 1934, RG 86.
72 Kate Drumm, Birmingham, MI, to Miss Perckes, received August 22, 1933, RG 86.
73 B. Faust, Flushing, NY, to FDR, December 26, 1933, RG 9.
74 David R. Roediger, *The Wages of Whiteness: Race and the Making of the American Working Class* (London: Verso, 1991), 65–92.
75 Owners also valued enslaved women for their reproductive potential. Jennifer L. Morgan, *Laboring Women: Gender and Reproduction in the Making of New World Slavery* (Philadelphia: University of Pennsylvania Press, 2004).
76 Janette Faulkner et al., *Ethnic Notions: Black Images in the White Mind*, updated and rev. ed. (Berkeley: Berkeley Art Center, 2000); Cuesta Benberry, "White Perceptions of Blacks in Quilts and Related Media," *Uncoverings*, no. 4 (Mill Valley, CA: American Quilt Study Group, 1983), 59–74.
77 Patrick Ely, *The Adventures of Amos 'n' Andy: A Social History of an American Phenomenon* (New York: Free Press, 1991); Elizabeth McLeod, *The Original Amos 'n' Andy: Freeman Gosden, Charles Correll and the 1928–1943 Radio Serial* (Jefferson, NC: McFarland, 2005).
78 Donald Bogle, *Bright Boulevards, Bold Dreams: The Story of Black Hollywood* (New York: One World Books, 2005).
79 *Studebaker Co-operator*, 4, no. 12 (1923): 4–7; UAW Local 5 Records, Walter P. Reuther Library, Wayne State University.
80 *Sew and Sew*, v. 1, no. 3 (1933): p. 4, HM.
81 *Sew and Sew*, v. 2, no. 1 (1934): p. 9, HM.
82 *Goniec Polski*, March 12, 1932, p. 5; *Goniec Polski*, February 11, 1933.
83 Mrs. Katherine Rutherford, Baltimore, to FDR, July 12, 1933, RG 86.
84 Eleanor M. Daigre, New Orleans, to FDR, April 4, 1934, RG 9.
85 Martha Gilchrist, Philadelphia, to FDR, March 24, 1934, RG 86.
86 Mrs. Katherine Rutherford, Baltimore, to FDR, July 12, 1933, RG 86.
87 James Barrett and David Roediger, "Inbetween Peoples: Race, Nationality, and the 'New Immigrant' Working Class," *Journal of American Ethnic History* 16, no. 3 (1997): 15.

Appendix A   Interview Sources

1 Women's Bureau Bulletin (hereafter *WBB*) 108, *The Effects of the Depression*, pp. 1–2.
2 *WBB* 92, *Wage-Earning Women*, 6; *WBB* 108, *Effects of the Depression*, 4.
3 Apparently, schedules for five Black women interviewed twice have been misfiled, and published totals are inaccurate. The additional thirteen households are absent from statistical analyses.
4 *WBB* 139, *Women Unemployed*; Survey Materials *WBB* 139, RG 86.
5 *WBB* 158, *Unattached Women*; Survey Materials *WBB* 158, RG 86.

Appendix B   Social Scientists at the Women's Bureau

1 I discerned no patterns among dozens of interviewers: WB investigators, caseworkers, and social work faculty and graduate students.
2 Mary S, 747, Chicago33.
3 Julia S, 1320, Philadelphia.
4 Blanche C, 215, Philadelphia.
5 Eva D, 110, C36, Canal, Chicago37.
6 Elizabeth W, 472, K24, Union Park, Chicago37; Alice G, 546, L43, Washington Park, Chicago37.
7 Winnie B, 398, J13, Oakwood, Chicago37.
8 Hattie W, 304, H28, Lower North, Chicago37.
9 Lena J, 020, A20, Archer, Chicago37.
10 Mary M, 1572, Philadelphia.
11 Emma F, 236, Chicago33.
12 Mary J, 0765, Philadelphia.
13 Rose W, 216, F7, Irving Park, Chicago37.
14 *WBB* 92, *Wage-Earning Women,* 3.
15 Gertrude B, 392, J7, Oakwood, Chicago37.
16 Marion G, 284, Chicago33.
17 Mattie A, 386, J1, Oakwood, Chicago37.
18 Flora W, 18, A18, Archer, Chicago37.
19 Antoinette L, 108, C34, Canal, Chicago37.
20 Winnie B, 398, J13, Oakwood, Chicago37.
21 Anna V, 1035, SB32.
22 Grace B, 322, H46, Lower North, Chicago37.
23 Edith C, 402, J17, Oakwood, Chicago37.
24 Clara C, 8, A8, Archer, Chicago37.
25 Johanna B, 342, I6, Northern, Chicago37.
26 Sarah J, 58, B22, Bridgeport, Chicago37.
27 Bessie E, 12, A12, Archer, Chicago37.
28 Ophelia L, 416, J31, Oakwood, Chicago37.
29 Anna P, K28, 476, Union Park, Chicago37.
30 *WBB* 158, *Unattached Women,* 12–13.
31 *WBB* 158, *Unattached Women,* 6, 8, 12–21, 51–56, 67–68; E. E. Ferebee, Chief Statistician, CRA, Chicago, to Harriet Byrne, July 21, 1937, December 20, 1937, 1937 Correspondence File, *WBB* 158; E. E. Ferebee, Chicago, to Mary Anderson, December 20, 1937, 1937 Correspondence File, *WBB* 158.
32 Marjorie O. Johnson, Chicago, to Harriet Byrne, July 28, 1938, 1938 Correspondence File, *WBB* 158.
33 Hortense Powdermaker, *Stranger and Friend: The Way of an Anthropologist* (New York: W. W. Norton, 1966), 149, 167.

Appendix C   The U.S. Census

1 Paul Schor, *Counting Americans: How the US Census Classified the Nation*, trans. Lys Ann Weiss (New York: Oxford University Press, 2017).
2 Some comparisons between 1929 and 1940 exclude 73,068 girls, ages ten through thirteen, who were employed in 1929.

Index

About the Author

LOIS RITA HELMBOLD chaired women's studies at the University of Nevada, Las Vegas and at San Jose State University. As a Fulbright Senior Lecturer she taught U.S. history in Japan and Turkey. She is now an antiracism social activist, quilter, and martial artist in Oakland, California.